The Japanese Party System

SECOND EDITION

The Japanese Party System

Ronald J. Hrebenar

UNIVERSITY OF UTAH

with contributions by
Peter Berton, Akira Nakamura,
J.A.A. Stockwin, and Nobuo Tomita

Foreword by Haruhiro Fukui

Westview Press

BOULDER • SAN FRANCISCO • OXFORD

Published in 1992 in the United States of America by Westview Press, Inc., 5500 Central Avenue, Boulder, Colorado 80301-2847, and in the United Kingdom by Westview Press, 36 Lonsdale Road, Summertown, Oxford OX2 7EW

Library of Congress Cataloging-in-Publication Data
Hrebenar, Ronald J., 1945–
The Japanese party system / Ronald J. Hrebenar with contributions by Peter Berton . . . [et al.]. — 2nd ed.
p. cm.
Includes bibliographical references and index.
ISBN 0-8133-8033-2 (HC). — ISBN 0-8133-8034-0 (paper)
1. Jiyū Minshutō. 2. Political parties—Japan. I. Berton, Peter, 1922– . II. Title.
JQ1698.A1H74 1992
324.252—dc20 91-28379
CIP

Printed and bound in the United States of America

The paper used in this publication meets the requirements of the American National Standard for Permanence of Paper for Printed Library Materials Z39.48-1984.

10 9 8 7 6 5 4 3 2 1

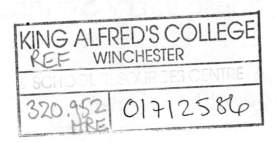

Contents

Tables and Figures

Tables

Figures

Foreword

Much time has passed and many events have occurred, as Dr. Ronald Hrebenar pointed out in his preface to the first edition of this book, since *Parties and Politics in Contemporary Japan* by Robert Scalapino and Junnosuke Masumi was first published in 1962. That was a time when popular and scholarly interest in Japanese politics and society in the West in general, and in the United States in particular, was probably considerably higher than normal, thanks to the 1960 Security Treaty crisis that had shaken the then ten-year-old U.S.-Japanese alliance to its foundations as nothing had ever shaken it. Yet that was also a time when few articles about anything to do with Japan were to be found in the Western media and when the general level of public awareness and knowledge of Japan's culture, history, politics, or economy in this country, or anywhere else for that matter, was abysmally low.

Before the publication of the Scalapino and Masumi book, few detailed studies of contemporary Japanese politics were available in any language other than Japanese. The mainstay of English-language textbooks for upper-division and graduate students of Japanese politics at U.S. colleges consisted of such works as *The New Japan: Government and Politics* (1956), by Harold Quigley and John Turner; *Japanese People and Politics* (1956), by Chitoshi Yanaga; *Japanese Politics: An Introductory Survey* (1957), by Nobutaka Ike; *Village Japan* (1960), by Richard K. Beardsley, John W. Hall, and Robert E. Ward; and *Government in Japan* (1961), by Ardath W. Burks. When it was published, the Scalapino and Masumi book was clearly a valuable addition to the literature.

During the last quarter-century, the situation has dramatically changed. The Western and, particularly, U.S. media now frequently and routinely carry articles about contemporary Japanese politics and economy as well as about the country's history, culture, and arts. The list of scholarly English-language books and articles on Japanese politics is incomparably longer today than it was in the early 1960s. Furthermore, the analysis and the data available in recent titles represent an unmistakable advance over the pioneering studies of the 1950s and 1960s. This is evident even from a partial list of the most recent titles on contemporary Japanese politics, such as *Law and*

Social Change in Postwar Japan (1987), by Frank K. Upham; *The Japanese Way of Politics* (1988), by Gerald L. Curtis; *Dynamic and Immobilist Politics in Japan* (1988), edited by J.A.A. Stockwin; *Democracy in Japan* (1989), edited by Takeshi Ishida and Ellis S. Krauss; *Japan's Administrative Elite* (1989), by B. C. Koh; and *Losing Face: Status Politics in Japan* (1990), by Susan J. Pharr. Likewise, many notable books on the contemporary Japanese political economy also have been published in the last few years, including, inter alia, *Crisis and Compensation: Public Policy and Political Stability in Japan, 1949–1986* (1988), by Kent Calder; *The Misunderstood Miracle: Industrial Development and Political Change in Japan* (1988), by David Friedman; *Financial Politics in Contemporary Japan* (1989), by Frances McCall Rosenbluth; *Between MITI and the Market: Industrial Policy for High Technology* (1989), by Daniel I. Okimoto; and *Japan's Economic Structure: Should It Change?* (1990), edited by Kōzō Yamamura. Today we thus have ready access to far more numerous, diverse, and dependable sources of information and insights on most aspects of Japanese politics, economy, and society than we have ever had.

In many respects, however, the abundance of information about contemporary Japan in general and Japanese politics in particular is more apparent than real. In fact, despite the unquestionably great contributions made by such recent works as those listed earlier, surprisingly little accurate and detailed information is available in English on some of the country's basic political institutions, including its political parties and interest groups. Dr. Hrebenar was quite right to point out in his preface to the first edition of this book that little had been written so far on any of the new parties that emerged during the previous quarter-century. The situation has not changed in this respect since 1986. There are thus some obvious and important gaps in the scholarly literature on contemporary Japanese politics.

As its title suggests, this revised edition of the five-year-old book by Hrebenar and four coauthors aims to fill one such gap—specifically, the gap on contemporary Japanese parties and the party system. It seeks to achieve two goals in particular: first, to present an up-to-date and comprehensive set of data on each existing Japanese party; and, second, to encourage and facilitate cross-national comparative studies of party systems. A careful reading of the original edition in its manuscript form led me to conclude that the authors had admirably succeeded in achieving both stated goals; they do so in the new edition as well.

The book begins with three introductory chapters, all contributed by the main author, Ronald Hrebenar. All three chapters, but the second and third chapters in particular, are extremely well conceived and useful. Chapter 1 provides a concise overview of the postwar Japanese party system and the major patterns of its change over time. Chapter 2 offers one of the very few systematic and detailed analyses available in English of the impact of electoral laws—the Public Offices Election Law and the Political Funds Control Law—on Japanese parties and the party system. Particularly interesting and useful in this connection is the discussion of the malapportionment issue and the relevant court decisions. Chapter 3 presents a rare and detailed discussion of the role of money in Japanese politics.

The individual contemporary Japanese parties are then discussed one by one in the next six chapters. Chapter 4 is an updated and expanded version of the earlier work on the Japan Socialist party (JSP) by one of the very few serious students of that party, J.A.A. Stockwin. Chapter 5, by Peter Berton, similarly summarizes and updates the author's earlier work on the Japan Communist party (JCP). Both are thoroughly professional pieces by old and experienced hands.

The three chapters by Hrebenar that follow (Chapters 6, 7, and 8) deal with the several newer centrist parties—the Kōmeitō, or Clean Government party, the Democratic Socialist party, the New Liberal Club (now disbanded), the Social Democratic Federation, and other "mini-parties"—that have seldom been examined in any detail in standard English-language textbooks. For purely informational purposes, these are particularly useful chapters, filling out what has been a nearly total void in the English-language literature on contemporary Japanese parties.

By comparison, Chapter 9 on the Liberal Democratic party, by two Japanese authors, Nobuo Tomita and Akira Nakamura, in addition to Hrebenar, covers a somewhat more familiar terrain, if only because more has been written in English on Japan's ruling party than on any other. Nonetheless, the chapter contains a good deal of new information and insights on aspects of the party and its behavior not found elsewhere. Like the chapters on the JSP and JCP, this is a solid chapter characterized by much expertise and sophistication.

The last and concluding chapter by Hrebenar discusses the prospects for the future of the LDP-centered coalition government. Although it does not present any projection or scenario that is novel or surprising, the discussion is entirely sensible and persuasive. It is a most appropriate conclusion to a textbook that is characterized throughout by a consistently low-key, no-nonsense, and level-headed approach.

This is an updated version of a nuts-and-bolts textbook in the best sense of the term. With its numerous informative tables and figures, it is and will remain a most welcome text both to teachers and students of contemporary Japanese politics. As one of the book's primary beneficiaries on this score, I am very grateful to its authors, especially Dr. Hrebenar, for producing such a useful and readable source of vital information on one of the central institutions of contemporary Japanese government politics.

Haruhiro Fukui
January 1991

Preface

Almost thirty years have passed since Robert Scalapino and Junnosuke Masumi published their important work on postwar Japanese parties and elections, *Parties and Politics in Contemporary Japan*.[1] Much has happened to the Japanese party system since 1962. A multiparty system had begun to take form, just as Scalapino and Masumi were finishing their writing in the early 1960s, with the split of the Democratic Socialists from the Japan Socialist party. Four years later, the Kōmeitō, or Clean Government party, was created by the Sōka Gakkai religious organization. Then, during the 1970s, a flood of splinter and new minor parties appeared on the national political scene—the most notable being the two splinter parties, the New Liberal Club from the Liberal Democratic party and the Social Democratic Federation from the Socialist party. Thus, what had been a solid two-party system during the period ending the decade of the 1960s had suddenly proliferated into a seven-party system characterized by a near parity in Diet seats between the conservatives and the opposition parties. This latter pattern culminated in the LDP-NLC coalition government that was formed in the second Nakasone cabinet following the elections of December 1983.

This book is designed for two specific audiences. First, to those interested in Japanese party politics it offers an enormous amount of information and interpretation by some of the most knowledgeable experts in the world. Little has been written in English about the important new parties that have emerged since 1960. The Democratic Socialist party (DSP), for example, is almost completely unknown in the West despite its increasingly likely role as a major coalition partner of the LDP during the latter half of the 1980s. When I started researching the DSP in Tokyo in 1977, I was amazed that the DSP headquarters officials could not remember the last Western scholar who had visited their offices (although they did recall the whirlwind tours taken of all the party offices). Some articles have appeared in major political science journals on the other parties in the system, but many of these have been aimed at specific policy orientations or at a particular party event. This book seeks to present as comprehensively as possible a set of data on each of the parties currently operating within the Japanese party system.

Consistent with that objective, an appendix is included with a wealth of data concerning the Japanese general elections through 1990 and current patterns of party support in Japan. As Roger Benjamin and Kan Ori wrote in 1981,

> A second problem concerns *the lack of descriptive knowledge about the Japanese party system. . . . We remain in the dark about many aspects of the Japanese party system.* The post–World War II party system has been in place less than 35 years. During that period, there has been substantial, even bewildering fluctuation in party vote support; there have been many mergers between parties and many policy stands taken and reversed. There have been repeated efforts to examine factions, but few data have been accumulated.[2] (emphasis added)

Accordingly, the present book attempts both to diminish this information gap and to fill the void that has developed since the Scalapino and Masumi book became out of date.

The second major audience this book hopes to address comprises those scholars interested in either comparative political parties or comparative politics in general. In the ten chapters of this book, such scholars will discover a wealth of data and discussion relating to Japan's place within the broader framework of world political parties and elections. A major theme of the introductory chapter—a theme that threads its way throughout the book—is the fact that Japan shares many political patterns with its highly developed sister democracies around the world. Of course, Japan is also different, just as each nation is unique in many respects, but it can and does compare well with other similar systems. In fact, it is the descriptive material throughout the book that my coauthors and I feel is our most significant contribution to comparative politics. In the absence of such basic data, which have long been largely unavailable to most comparative scholars, any meaningful comparative analysis is seriously handicapped.

This book originated with my study of the New Liberal Club shortly after the party emerged in the summer of 1976. I then went on to conduct research on the Democratic Socialist and Kōmeitō parties in subsequent research trips to Japan in 1977, 1979, and 1982–1983. Meanwhile, the idea to expand the book beyond the so-called moderate or center parties to encompass the entire party system prompted me to seek out the cooperation of some of the most knowledgeable scholars in the world of Japanese political parties. Peter Berton, of the University of Southern California, has contributed his enormous understanding of and impressive data base on the Japan Communist party. And J.A.A. Stockwin, despite the difficult transition involved in shifting his base of operations from Australia to Oxford University as the initial director of the Nissan Institute for Japanese Studies, kept his promise to conduct a new survey of the conditions of the Japanese Socialist party for this volume. Last, but certainly not least, Professors Nobuo Tomita and Akira Nakamura of Meiji University in Tokyo, two well-known and extremely knowledgeable experts on Japanese politics, agreed to share with me their understanding of the structure and role of the LDP in Japanese politics. To these scholars, who collectively ensured the authoritative and professional coverage of Japanese politics that appears in this book, I extend my sincere appreciation. Indeed, without their significant contributions, this book would never have been completed.

I also wish to thank the many others who made important contributions to the research and writing of this book. Many will have to remain unnamed because of the official positions they hold within their respective parties. Several officials of the center parties, for instance, went far out of their way to answer my questions and to set up interviews with key leaders in their parties. I am especially grateful to Kōno Yōhei and Ishikawa Tatsuo of the now defunct New Liberal Club, who gave me a great deal of support. Again, without mentioning specific names, I also wish to thank the staffs of the DSP, the Dōmei, and the Kōmeitō for their constant willingness to look up "one more answer" for me. To all the various academics in both the United States and Japan who read and reread some of my chapters, I acknowledge that any errors remaining are entirely my responsibility. Equally important, I thank them for their sincere efforts on my behalf.

I once again thank those who helped to produce the first edition of this book: Westview acquisitions editors Holly Arrow, Miriam Gilbert, and Deborah Lynes; Westview copy editor Chris Arden; and the University of Utah typists Marge Coulan, Barbara Hill, Tammy Sapp, and Cindy Simpson. I am also grateful to those who worked on the second edition: Westview acquisitions editor Susan McEachern, production editors Beverly LeSuer and Michelle Starika, copy editor Ida May Norton, and University of Utah typist Debbie Frye, who typed all the tables and figures.

My special appreciation goes to Otake Hideo for his helpful observations while I was a visiting professor at Tohuku University Law School in 1982–1983. My appreciation is also extended to the *Japan Interpreter* and *Asian Survey* for their permission to use data from the articles I had previously published in those journals. Finally, I wish to thank the Fulbright Commission, Dr. and Mrs. Yamachika Katsumi, and Dr. Sugita Teruji and Mrs. Sugita Reiko for providing me the support necessary for the seven very long research trips to Japan that culminated in the data base for this book.

Ronald J. Hrebenar
January 1991

NOTES

1. Robert A. Scalapino and Junnosuke Masumi, *Parties and Politics in Contemporary Japan* (Berkeley, Calif.: University of California Press, 1962).
2. Roger Benjamin and Kan Ori, *Tradition and Change in Postindustrial Japan: The Role of the Political Parties* (New York: Praeger Publishers, 1981), p. 9.

Note on Personal Names

As is the common practice in Japan, all Japanese names are written with the family name first and the given name last. If the Japanese scholar is living in the United States or is publishing in English, I have presented his or her name in the U.S. style—for example, Haruhiro Fukui, Nobuo Tomita, and Akira Nakamura. Among the abbreviations used throughout the book, the following are the most common: Liberal Democratic party (LDP), Japan Socialist party (JSP), Kōmeitō (CGP), Democratic Socialist party (DSP), Japan Communist party (JCP), New Liberal Club (NLC), and Social Democratic Federation (SDF).

R.J.H.

PART ONE

Introduction to the Japanese Party System

1

The Changing Postwar Party System

RONALD J. HREBENAR

The Japanese political system is democratic, has several parties, legislates through a parliament (the Diet), and has a well-educated, supportive, but basically uninvolved electorate. It is also defined by the continuous rule for three decades of the conservative Liberal Democratic party (LDP), which held a majority of seats in the Diet between its formation in 1955 until it lost its majority in the House of Councillors in 1989. In this introductory chapter these basic characteristics of the Japanese party system will be explored in order to provide the reader with a foundation for the subsequent detailed examination of the six parties in the current party system. The chapter is based on a variety of types of data, especially public opinion polls of the Japanese electorate.

FROM A ONE-AND-A-HALF PARTY SYSTEM TO A MULTIPARTY SYSTEM

When Japan returned to a democratic, parliamentary system in 1946, a period of great confusion in party politics preceded the first postwar elections, which were held in April 1946. The Diet members of the great prewar parties had mostly been purged by the U.S. Occupation authorities. Of the incumbent Diet members of the Progressive party, 260 out of 274 were purged; in addition, 30 of the 43 Liberal party Diet members, 21 of 23 Cooperative Diet members and even 10 of the 17 Socialist Diet members were prevented from running for public office. Thus, the first postwar election introduced a nearly new set of candidates to the voters. Not only the candidates but also the parties were new. A total of 267 "parties" participated in these elections. Many of these parties were just the personal organization or label of a given politician; others operated only in a very limited geographical area; still others were the reconstituted organizations of some of the famous pre-1940 parties. Among the successful candidates to the lower house (the House of Representatives, or HR) at this election, only 19 percent had served in that body previously. However, over the next decade these parties gradually disappeared until, in 1955, a merger of conservative parties on the one hand and Socialist parties on the other produced a de facto two-party system on the national level. In the first House election (1958) held after the two mergers, the Liberal Democratic party and the Japan Socialist party (JSP) captured 453 of the 455 House seats won by political parties. One seat was won by the Japan Communist party (JCP), a second seat was won by a minor party, and 12 seats were held by independents.

This two-party system lasted only two years. In January 1960 the JSP split into two parts, with 40 of its moderate Diet members departing to create the Democratic Socialist party (DSP). A reorganized JCP went from a single seat in the 1958 elections to 3 seats in 1960, to 14 in 1969, and to 38 in 1972. Meanwhile, the lay organization, Sōka Gakkai, of the Nichiren Shōshū Buddhist sect, had formed its own political party in 1964—namely, the Kōmeitō, or Clean Government party (CGP)—and it captured 25 seats in 1967 and 47 seats in 1969. Thus, by the 1960s, what seemed to be a "two-party system" (in the words of many Japanese political commentators) consisting of the LDP and JSP or, as some called it, a "one-and-one-half party system" (the LDP plus a splintered and seemingly permanent opposition JSP and a very small DSP), quickly moved to true multiparty status as the DSP demonstrated its staying power and the JCP and CGP proved they could regularly win 20 to 50 House seats. By the mid-1970s, these five parties seemed to be permanent parts of the Japanese national political system. In the 1972 House elections, the percentage of seats won by the LDP and JSP had dropped to 81.5 percent from the 99.5 percent they had held in 1958.

There was defection in the ranks of the LDP in the summer of 1976. Though minor in terms of numbers, the defection was significant in its impact on the proliferation of new parties. Kōno Yōhei, a young LDP Diet member, led five other Diet members out of the LDP, set up a new Diet-level party, and named it the New Liberal Club (NLC). From this humble start of only a few seats, the NLC exploded to 18 in the December 1976 election and touched off a Kōno and NLC boom in the Japanese media. The NLC boom subsequently encouraged the establishment of other new parties in the 1977, 1979, 1980, 1983, and 1986 general elections. The 1983 elections to the upper house (the House of Councillors, or HC) had on the ballot twelve new small parties (mini-*seitō*), which collectively captured over 15 percent of the vote and won 5 seats (10 percent). Japan now has a seemingly established multiparty system operating on the national level of politics.

COMPARING THE PREWAR AND POSTWAR PARTY SYSTEMS

A comparison of the post–World War II party system with the system that existed in prewar Japan is useful. Considerable scholarly effort has produced a very good perspective on the problems of the prewar Japanese party system. The work, for example, of G. Berger, Peter Duus, Robert A. Scalapino, T. J. Pempel, and others is well done and well known to scholars of Japanese politics.[1]

As all political institutions are products of their history, it is necessary to present some generalizations about the prewar party system. Pempel has noted that the prewar party system was inflexible in its retention of ties to rural agricultural and urban commercial bases despite the rise of new social groups. Consequently, the parties of the 1930s were "largely irrelevant, either as the vehicles or the reflections of social changes."[2] Pempel suggests that contemporary Japanese parties have the same problem of being "locked into past constituencies."[3] Those "past constituencies" would have been the rural sectors for the LDP and the industrial labor unions for the socialists.

In actuality, then, parties did not have a long history of significant influence in Japanese politics. Following a long emergence period beginning in the decade after the Meiji Restoration of the 1860s, it was not until the post–World War I period that cabinets were formed on the basis of electoral results. Yet by the 1930s, parties were effectively excluded from real political power. Sustained party control of Japanese government can be perceived as having begun only in the years since the end of World War II.

Another parallel between the pre- and postwar party systems is the dependence of the conservatives on "big business." Just as the Jiyuto and Seiyukai were the "financial children" of the *zaibatsu* (Mitsui, Mitsubishi, Sumitomo, and others), the postwar LDP, NLC, and DSP are the dependents of the Keidanren and other business organizations of modern Japan.

In the prewar system, the incumbent parties always won; in the postwar system the LDP has lost only one election, the largely symbolic 1989 House of Councillors elections. Moreover, in both party systems, the incumbent parties never lost power as a result of electoral defeat. As Pempel notes, government changed, but it did so usually *prior* to the elections.[4] In addition, the conservative parties in both systems were infiltrated by the bureaucracy. Such support forced the parties to deal with the elite on a day-to-day basis rather than encouraging the development of mass followings or support groups to confront it.

Having observed the similarities between the two party systems, we can now look at their differences. For example, the prewar party system was characterized by the lack of a dominant party. Only 18 percent of the prewar elections produced a majority party, whereas in the post-1955 period, every election (after independents were sorted out) produced an LDP lower house majority. Moreover, during the prewar period, only 18 percent of the governments were actually party cabinets; since the war, all governments have been put together by party leaders.[5]

When compared with the prewar party system, the postwar system is significantly broader in its ideological range. Despite the existence of leftist parties, the prewar party system was overwhelmingly conservative. Leftist parties were seldom allowed to participate fairly in elections. Whereas the prewar system was in essence a mechanism to legitimize the ruling clique, the postwar system, despite certain significant distortions such as malapportionment, is a much fairer representation of the political attitudes of Japan's electorate.

The postwar Japanese party system is a difficult one to portray on a liberal-conservative continuum. Although most might agree with the placement of the LDP on the conservative end and the JSP and JCP on the leftist end of the continuum, the so-called center parties might be much more difficult to position correctly. Do the DSP, CGP, and SDF (Social Democratic Federation) collectively represent the center, the left-center, or the right-center? Or do they really belong in the center at all? Some argue that the DSP and CGP are essentially conservative parties despite their socialist rhetoric. Others ask whether the party farthest to the left in Japan is the JCP or the JSP.

A ONE-PARTY-PREDOMINANT SYSTEM

The Japanese party system has been described in a variety of ways—that is, as a one-party, a one-and-one-half party, a two-party, and a multiparty system. Actually, part of the explanation for this variety of labels lies more in their "snapshot" nature (i.e., their descriptive function at a particular moment in time) than in the fundamentally different interpretations of the nature of the system. When Robert Scalapino and Junnosuke Masumi surveyed the Japanese political scene in 1960, they observed the two-party system of the ruling LDP, a strong opposition in the JSP, and two very small parties (i.e., the JCP and the newly formed DSP). Thus they described the political scene as a "one-and-one-half" party system in its actual operation because the "one" party is always in power and the "half" party is permanently out of power.[6] Nobutaka Ike correctly perceived that, by the early 1970s, the Japanese party system had fundamentally changed. It was now a system with five parties receiving significant portions of the vote, but Ike did not choose to call it a multiparty system because the opposition parties never shared political power with the LDP. He thus decided to label it a "one-party-dominant system." Such a system, Ike observed, was not unique to Japan but could also be found in Mexico and India.[7]

Perhaps the best work done in the area of party system classifications is credited to Giovanni Sartori, whose *Parties and Party Systems: A Framework for Analysis* classifies party systems by numbers of parties and the significance of the parties within the system.[8] Let us focus on the category into which Sartori places Japan—the predominant-party system. Sartori argues that a predominant-party system differs significantly from the dominant-party system described by Maurice Duverger and Gabriel Almond.[9] Using their broader definitions, Sartori classifies twenty-one systems (ranging from France [1968] to Uruguay [1966]) into the latter category. The dominant-party system is generally conceived as being one in which a single party is significantly stronger than the others. Sartori, however, suggests that *pre*dominant-party systems include both (1) party pluralism (in which other parties are legal and legitimate) and (2) one-party domination (in which the same party manages to win, over time, an absolute majority of seats in Parliament). Japan fits this predominant-party-system class very effectively, given that its six-party system has been coupled with unbroken LDP lower house majorities since the founding of this system in 1955. In fact, it can be argued that Japan is the "ultimate predominant-party system" given that of all the industrialized democracies only Japan has had uninterrupted one-party rule on the national level since the 1950s. If one had to come up with a single concept that best characterized the nature of the Japanese party system, it would probably be this one-party rule of the LDP since 1955. Hence the crucial question to be asked if one is to understand the Japanese postwar party system: Why have the opposition parties been unable to replace the LDP as the rulers on the national level of Japanese politics?

THE PERMANENT OPPOSITION

One problem for the opposition has been the difficulty of forming the various opposition parties into a coalition capable of taking power away from the LDP. The nature of the alternative coalition government able to replace the single-party rule of the LDP was a major topic of conversation in Japanese political circles throughout the late 1970s and the 1980s. And discussion of just how such a coalition could be constructed has frustrated opposition politicians as they tried somehow to piece together enough seats to displace the LDP. Because such a displacement seems to be virtually impossible, discussion turned in the early 1980s to the question of which opposition parties could join with the LDP and assist the conservatives in ruling Japan.

The Japanese public, as well, has been involved in these coalition-making efforts, through both their electoral voting decisions and expression of their opinions on possible coalition patterns through the newspaper polls. In the spring of 1980, just prior to the "double elections" of June of that year, a "coalition boom" occurred in the media and among opposition party leaders. One major poll found that half of the public wanted an end to the continuation of single-party rule by the LDP; 30 percent wanted it to continue; and 20 percent had no opinion or refused to answer the question. Less clear were the public's feelings about the nature of the coalition that would replace the LDP in power. A small plurality supported a coalition of conservative and so-called middle-of-the-road parties—that is, the LDP, NLC, DSP, and CGP (18 percent). The second choice was a "grand coalition" of all parties except the JCP (15 percent). The third preference (15 percent) was for a conservative coalition of the LDP and NLC. A leftist coalition centered on the JSP in combination with Kōmeitō received 8 percent support, and the extreme leftist coalition of the JSP and JCP was the choice of 5 percent. Finally, a minority government of the LDP alone was the choice of almost 11 percent of the people polled.

Nearly three years later, a coalition between the LDP and the NLC was constructed on a limited basis. When the LDP joined with the NLC in December 1983 to form a coalition government, it opened a new era of

Japanese politics that many people had been anticipating since the 1976 election. In this instance, the coalition was one of convenience rather than necessity, given that although the LDP won only 250 seats out of 511 total—a shortfall of 6 seats from a pure majority—it came to control 259 seats when nine conservative independents joined the party immediately following the election. Soon after, the LDP accepted the NLC into the government in an attempt to give the party the additional votes it needed in the House to effectively manage the Diet.

Prior to 1983, the most realistic hope held by the opposition parties for entering a national government as a coalition partner was that a split in the LDP would occur and that a new government would be formed by several departing LDP factions in combination with the numerous perennial opposition parties. Each time the LDP has suffered an electoral setback (as in 1979 and 1983) or endured another scandal (recent LDP prime ministers who have been severely hurt by scandals include Tanaka Kakuei, Takeshita Noburu, and Uno Sōsuke), the media has carried rumors that the factions were about to leave and join with the DSP, CGP, or other parties to change the landscape of Japanese politics; yet, each time, the advantages of staying have also apparently outweighed those of bolting and joining with the long-time opposition.

Clearly, the Japanese public does not demand a one-party LDP government during the 1990s. A *Sankei Shimbun* poll taken just before the February 1990 lower house elections indicated 19 percent supported an LDP one-party government, while 54 percent wished to see some form of LDP–opposition parties coalition.[10] After the elections, the *Mainichi* poll showed the governmental combinations the Japanese public was supporting for organizing Japanese national government: one-party LDP government, 12 percent; one-party JSP government, 2 percent; LDP + CGP + DSP coalition, 17 percent; LDP + JSP coalition, 29 percent; part of the LDP + middle-of-the-road parties + part of the JSP, 15 percent; JSP + DSP + CGP coalition, 9 percent; and JSP + JCP coalition, 2 percent.[11]

The best description of the reasons behind the continued rule of the LDP is that stemming from the classic military and political recommendation to "divide and conquer." And as Michael Taylor and V. M. Herman have noted, "The more divided the opposition, the easier it is to rule."[12] In other words, a fragmented opposition tends to be less moderate and thus will probably increase the prospects for systemic instability, but it is also less efficient in its ability to replace the ruling party and thereby contributes to the stability of the ruling party.

Perhaps the most difficult concept to implant into a polity is the concept of opposition. Yet, ironically, this idea was apparently so firmly adopted by Japan that it became a permanent characteristic for at least the JSP and JCP, the original opposition parties of the 1955 system. A central aspect of opposition is that it must always be ready to take over the seat of government on a periodic basis. As already noted, however, Japan is unique among developed democracies in that it has not experienced such an alteration in power in nearly four decades. Moreover, as the late Raymond Aron observed in a lecture at the London School of Economics and Political Science on October 27, 1981:

> For the last thirty years, the same party has been in power in Japan; opposition parties, which sometimes win in local elections, do exist; newspapers, which freely criticize those in power, also exist. Because of this continuity, Japan has risen to be one of the foremost nations; it is Japan which has best withstood the shocks of the oil crisis; it is Japan which has been most successful in achieving a close cooperation between the Ministry of Industry and private enterprises; it is Japan which most successfully combines medium (even long-term) planning and the free play of the market. None of this would have been possible if, from one day to the next, the plans of the government and its priorities and values were in danger of being upset by the results of the elections. In our countries, proud of alternation in government, the changes in public opinion and in the electorate every two, four, or seven years, add to the hazards of the world economic climate.
>
> On reflection, I abandoned this somewhat facile argument. Does Japanese prosperity owe a great deal to the lack of alternation, or is it the other way round? The same party wins the elections because the majority of the electors approve of its policy and admit that it is successful. Do not the alternations in Europe and America express the dissatisfaction of the governed? And is not peaceful alternation better than violent revolt?
>
> . . . A second consideration dissuades me from drawing conclusions from the Japanese experience. Japan, as we well know, cannot be imitated. It retains the cult of unanimity, symbolised in the sacred person of the emperor, a cult which democratic practices conceal but do not destroy. No other people seems to be so homogeneous; nowhere is social control so effective, omnipresent, gently peremptory. Some observers may remark that the continuity of the party in power is grounded in a disciplined base, on a life-style which Western men would consider incompatible with their individualistic philosophy. Democratized Japan has not become individualistic. Let us therefore leave Japan aside, and merely note that there is one country—and perhaps only one—which demonstrates, against the tide of fashionable opinion, that a political party can withstand the wear and tear of government and that a democratic regime without alternation does not always degenerate.[13]

In the category of nations in which parties do not alternate in power, the situation is usually a result of governmental violence against its opponents—a violence that prevents them from communicating to voters, running their slates of candidates, or even having a legal party organization. But this pattern of governmental oppression does not apply to Japan. Elections in Japan are open, and the opposition parties are legal and have many open channels of communication with the Japanese electorate. Several European nations (Sweden, for example) have experienced patterns of one-party domination somewhat similar to that in Japan. Of course, there were many reasons for the continuation in power of the Social Democratic party of

Sweden, but a significant parallel to the Japanese experience is the fact that the opposition parties in Sweden were badly fragmented. These parties lacked the necessary resources to challenge the ruling party and had no alternatives that would identify the opposition with a distinctive character of its own. The opposition was also hindered by weak organizations. As Swedish Prime Minister Tage Erlander said in 1951, "[this is] an opposition that represents almost half of the citizens, but which never has an opportunity of trying its strength as the government and which never has practice in assuming the responsibilities which this involves."[14]

Erlander's description could easily fit the Japanese party system as well. Why have the Japanese voters continued to maintain the LDP in power election after election for nearly four decades? This question can be looked at in a variety of ways, but let us begin with the responses to a 1982 *Yomiuri Shimbun* poll question concerning the reasons why a person would support the cabinet of LDP Prime Minister Suzuki Zenkō. The most common response was "because it was an LDP cabinet" (44 percent). Other responses pertained to the cabinet's "sense of stability" (16 percent), to trust in the prime minister (9 percent), and to appreciation for the cabinet's actions, both domestic and foreign (15 percent).[15] Following the 1990 lower house victory for the LDP, the *Tokyo Shimbun* poll asked the Japanese public why the opposition parties failed to win the elections. Thirty-four percent answered "because the opposition parties' policies were not attractive," and 33 percent replied "because the people feared political instability."[16]

The LDP has clearly established itself as the party in Japan responsible both for the great prosperity the country has experienced and for the set of diplomatic and security policies under which Japan has regained a measure of worldwide respect since the dark days after the Pacific War. By contrast, the five opposition parties have not been able to establish their image as a responsible alternative to the rule of the LDP. When the *Yomiuri Shimbun* asked its respondents in September 1985 why the LDP had remained in office for so long, the three most frequent responses were as follows: "There is no other political party" (48.4 percent); "They agree with its policies" (38.2 percent); and "The other parties cannot cooperate against the LDP" (34.2 percent).[17]

In one of his 1982 speeches, former LDP Prime Minister Miki Takeo spoke of the problem of failed opposition in Japan: "Party politics with no change of administration is a divergence from the norm. And if one party holds on to power too long, it becomes corrupt. I would therefore like to propose to the members of the opposition that they form a new party capable of taking upon itself the government of Japan. What Japan needs today is the formation and healthy growth of a new party which will not throw the nation into confusion or cause anxiety to the people."[18]

To some it may seem strange that an LDP factional leader and former LDP prime minister is encouraging the opposition to reform in order to defeat his party. However, Miki had always been a nonmainstream leader in the LDP; moreover, his tenure in the prime ministership had been characterized by the systematic attack upon him and his policies by most of the other factional leaders—especially those of the Tanaka Kakuei and Fukuda Takeo factions. Realistically speaking, there are perhaps only two ways out of the present stalemate of Japanese politics: (1) as Miki suggested, through the construction of a new alternative party and the destruction of the current fragmented opposition; or (2) through the destruction of the LDP, the withdrawal of one or more of the major factions, and the joining of the moderate elements of the existing opposition.

Another of the critical problems faced by the Japanese opposition revolves around the concept of "excluded" or "nonlegitimate" parties.[19] For example, despite the fact that the Communist party of Italy is the second largest party in the nation in election after election, it is never included in the inevitable coalition cabinet. The Japan Communist party (JCP) has a somewhat similar problem. It is specifically excluded from all coalition proposals discussed by the LDP, Kōmeitō, DSP, and SDF. Only the JSP stands by it as a potential coalition partner. As no non-LDP coalition government could be formed without the JCP's 30 or so seats, the only possible coalitions must be LDP directed. The JSP is also an "excluded party," but it is excluded in a sense slightly different from that of the Italian model. In the famous Katayama government of 1947, the JSP did take the lead in establishing the only leftist government in Japanese history. But it also fell apart quickly and was by nearly every account a failure. The socialists were so discredited by this fiasco, by their subsequent splits, and by their ideological wrangling over the next three decades that the JSP has become a "delegitimized party" (delegitimized in that few see the JSP as a possible participant in a future national-level government of Japan). The socialists have become the "gang that couldn't shoot straight," and few have much confidence in their ability to lead Japan's national government in these difficult times. Granted, they are capable of leading the prefectural government on occasion, but given Japan's unitary system, there is little danger in permitting such a minor check on nearly uncontrolled LDP hegemony in Japan.

One can see indications of the "illegitimacy" of the JSP in its lack of support among even the critics of the continued role of the conservatives. In July 1981, an *Asahi Shimbun* editorial on the Tokyo Metropolitan Assembly elections called for the total overhaul of the JSP—"even if this means dissolving the party."[20] In the paper's popular column "Vox Populi, Vox Dei," the writer noted:

> As the number one opposition party, we should be able to find many of its members qualified to hold important posts, such as that of finance minister or director-general of the Environment Agency, but actually, we cannot name a single one. . . . the JSP is not a political party. . . . the JSP is a party of government-employed. . . . The public opinion poll carried out by the *Asahi Shimbun* showed that people checked the word "undependable" more than any other when asked to describe the image of the JSP. As long as the leading opposition party cannot be trusted by the general public, the LDP is safe.[21]

Results from the 1989 upper house and the 1990 lower house elections actually help us understand Japanese voters' lack of confidence in the JSP. In the House of Councillors elections, voters could cast a "safe protest vote" against the LDP without worrying about an LDP loss endangering the performance of their national government because the upper house has little real political power. However, when the significant elections for the all-powerful lower house came up about six months later, many voters thought it was too dangerous to cast such a protest vote, and the LDP went on to a clear victory.

One of the severe problems of the JSP is that this party of the working class is poorly supported by that class. Only 28 percent of the labor union members in the Kansai area supported the JSP, according to a 1977 poll by the Labor Research Institute. Even if we examine just the party support of the members of Sōhyō (the labor confederation supporter of the JSP), we find that only 44 percent were willing to identify themselves as JSP supporters.[22] Thus, when the Labor Ministry reported in December 1983 that the union members had declined in number to 29 percent of the labor force—the lowest point for organized labor in Japan since 1948, when the yearly statistics were initiated—the plight of the JSP became quite clear. In short, this is a party that represents a declining sector of society—and that sector is not supporting the JSP very enthusiastically in the first place. Although 1 million new workers were added to the labor force in 1983, the membership of Sōhyō fell .9 percent to 4.5 million.[23] Hence, assuming that less than a third of the labor vote goes to the JSP regularly, one can view the JSP as a party supported by less than a third of a third of the unionized working force.

Even the JSP's own polling efforts have detected the magnitude of the burden under which this party is operating. In a JSP-sponsored poll conducted in late 1982, the support rate for the party was only 9.8 percent compared to a support rate for the LDP of 36.7 percent. For a series of questions pertaining to images of the parties, the negative responses were greater than the positive ones in every case for the JSP: For the "reliable" category, negative responses exceeded the positive by 18.1 percent; "familiar," by 17.6 percent; "youthful," by 20.4 percent; "future oriented," by 24.4 percent; "clean," by 0.9 percent; and "aggressive," by 15.6 percent. Responses to the same set of images for the LDP were all strongly positive, except in the categories of "cleanliness" and "youthfulness."[24]

Many Japanese think of the opposition parties as being largely incompetent. In a government-sponsored poll conducted in late 1980, the respondents felt that the main reason the LDP has remained in power for so long was that the opposition parties lacked competence to take over the government (27 percent) and that the opposition parties could not conceivably improve government (21 percent). Then, when asked in a *Yomiuri Shimbun* poll in September 1985 as to why the JSP continues to decline in political power, 38 percent responded that the JSP cannot lead even the opposition; 36 percent indicated that the JSP's policies were not realistic; and 33 percent said that the JSP was always fighting within itself. The study by Tomita, Baerwald, Hoshino, and Nakamura of the 1977 upper house elections also concluded that the image of the JSP was basically a negative one.[25] In an *Asahi Shimbun* poll, 9 percent of those polled viewed the JSP as being primarily the representative of labor and the general public, 6 percent felt the party was necessary, and 5 percent appreciated its activities. In contrast to these relatively positive responses, which totaled 20 percent, 39 percent of the respondents held negative images: 13 percent believed the JSP was undependable; 10 percent disliked it because it was too radical; 9 percent considered the party inactive, even though it criticizes the LDP; 3 percent viewed it as being dominated by labor unions; and 4 percent found it to be faction ridden.[26]

In describing the outcome of the 1980 "double elections," Satō Seizaburō concluded that it was evident the voters felt that the "government could not be trusted to the opposition parties."[27] Upon surveying Tokyoites on their evaluations of the various parties (with respect, specifically, to the question of which parties had the best policies), he found that 45 percent of the respondents indicated the LDP, 11 percent indicated the Kōmeitō, and another 11 percent indicated the JSP. As to the party with the "most talent," 75 percent identified the LDP.[28] This latter response is not all that surprising given that the LDP, alone, has held cabinet positions since 1955 (with the few exceptions, in 1983–1986, of the several nonparty persons who held the Education Ministry position in addition to the NLC's Tagawa Seiichi, Yamaguchi Toshio, and Kōno Yōhei). Talent, in this case, seems to be somewhat related to visibility in positions of responsibility.

The parity (*hakuchu*) between the LDP and the opposition during part of the last decade has brought some prestigious opportunities to the opposition parties. Following the 1979 elections, for example, opposition party Diet members chaired 4 of the 16 regular committees and 7 of the 9 special committees in the House of Representatives, as well as 7 of the 16 standing and 4 of the 7 special committees in the House of Councillors. In 1990 opposition party members chaired 8 of the 16 regular committees in the House of Councillors as well as half of the 8 special committees. In addition, since the 1970s, the vice-speaker of the lower house and the vice-president of the upper house have been members of the JSP. It still remains to be seen if these high-prestige Diet positions contribute to a change of attitude among the public regarding the fitness of the JSP and other opposition parties to rule Japan. The behavior patterns of the opposition, which found their extreme as recently as in the early 1970s, have become more moderate. Slowdown demonstrations (also known as "cow walking") ended in the late 1970s, as have votes of no-confidence against the entire cabinet. Moreover, as Ellis Krauss noted with regard to the 1975–1977 period, the percentage of cabinet-sponsored legislation passed without opposition from a single party rose from 43 percent to 68 percent. The DSP supported 70 percent of the LDP bills; the opposition (except for the JCP) voted for over 70 percent of the cabinet-sponsored legislation; and even the JCP voted for approximately two-thirds of the LDP bills. Krauss calls this pattern one of "concurrent majority."[29] It is only when the LDP loses its large majority that it has to take the demands of the opposition into account. During the post–1979 election Diet sessions, the LDP was forced to revise its budgets when the opposition refused to cooperate and support the LDP proposals. After the LDP lost its upper house majority, the LDP was forced by JSP and JCP opposition to abandon its plan to send Japanese troops to support the Middle East operations against Iraq in 1990.

What can the opposition parties do to reverse the long-term pattern of LDP domination? Robert Dahl has noted six strategies that might be pursued by an opposition: (1) strict electoral competition, (2) coalition seeking, (3) bargaining with the government, (4) multiple-site conflict and bargaining, (5) organizational survival, and (6) revolution. Each nation has its unique pattern of opposition, and, as Dahl further notes, there is no standard pattern among Western democracies.[30] However, with respect to Japan in particular, opposition may originally have pursued a pattern of electoral competition; recently, moreover, it embarked on a strategy of co-opted coalition seeking with the LDP, primarily because it realized that it cannot replace the LDP without destroying the conservative party. The acceptance of the NLC into the cabinet for the first time in 1983, as well as the LDP's 1984-1985 negotiations with the DSP for possible inclusion into future cabinets, would seem to indicate that Japan may be about to enter into a "coalitional era" similar, perhaps, to that of Italy.

Other points can be made to explain continued LDP dominance.[31] Krauss and Pierre suggest the LDP adopted a series of parliamentary strategies that successfully dealt with the challenges of the opposition parties during the 1970s and 1980s.[32] But more importantly, as Muramatsu and Krauss have noted, the LDP was flexible enough to change with the times. The LDP adopted as its own the popular demands for increased social expenditures and environmental protection. With these and other policies, the LDP was able to broaden its supporting coalition during the 1980s and remain the world's last dominant one-party rule in a true democratic political system.[33]

CONSERVATIVE RULE AND THE NATURE OF THE JAPANESE ELECTORATE

The main characteristics of electoral behavior in Japan have been an interesting case of high levels of voter turnout in elections combined with a disinterest or perhaps even hostility toward politicians and political parties and, except in the actual act of voting, a very passive, noninvolved citizenry.

Japan is an important case for the comparative study of political participation. It is a highly developed industrialized nation with less than five decades of real experience with mass participatory democracy. Japan is also probably the world's most "social" society—a society literally composed of many groups—and such groups can be very important for the structuring of political activities. As Y. Kuroda has observed, for many Japanese, voting is not so much a political activity as it is a part of general social behavior.[34] Citizens are encouraged to vote as a function of their responsibility to the social unit to which they belong, whether occupational, geographical, or self-chosen. Indeed, throughout the postwar period, rural communities have competed among themselves for the honor of having the highest voter-turnout rate in an administrative district. In Hokkaidō during the 1979 elections, cash awards were given communities with the highest turnout. When one town could muster only 86 percent of its voters in the 1975 elections, town leaders declared, "We must not repeat that dishonorable record." Many communities in Ibaraki prefecture planned to distribute televisions and other prizes to encourage citizens to vote. And other towns have distributed sports equipment to subcommunities recording good turnout levels.[35] Bradley Richardson has noted that the Japanese feelings of civic obligation are very important motivations for voting in Japan. The idea of the citizen having distinct obligations and duties is, of course, a long-term theme in Japanese political culture, dating at least back to the Tokugawa period.[36]

In recent years, Japan, like the United States, has experienced a decline in voter turnout that has worried many Japanese. In 1983 elections were held on the prefectural levels for governors and assemblies and on the national level for both chambers of the Diet. In each of these four contests, new postwar low points in voting turnout were registered: the prefectural governorship turnout was 63 percent, the prefectural assembly turnout, 69 percent; the House of Councillors turnout, 57 percent; and the House of Representatives turnout, 68 percent. The 1985 Tokyo Metropolitan Assembly elections also revealed a record low voter turnout.

It is interesting to note that the Japanese pattern of turnout is similar to that found in the United States—the more rural the district, the higher the turnout rate. In the 1990 U.S. off-year general elections for Congress and state-level offices, the highest turnout rates were registered in Maine and Montana. By comparison, the highest turnouts in Japan in the 1990 House of Representatives elections were in rural Shimane (86.45 percent), Tottori (84.0 percent), Ōita (82.18 percent), Fukui (83.79 percent), and Yamagata (83.26 percent), whereas the lowest turnouts were in the metropolitan prefectures of Ōsaka (65.06 percent) and Tokyo (65.55 percent). See Table 1.1 for the turnout rates by constituency types in Japan.

One reason for the reduced levels of voter turnout in recent elections is the decline in competition for many of the contests in Japan. On the gubernatorial level, a recent trend has been the running of a candidate as a joint candidate of the LDP and three or four other parties. For instance, Suzuki Shunichi, the winner of the Tokyo governorship in 1983, was the joint nominee of the LDP, CGP, DSP, and NLC. He was opposed by Matsuoka Hideo, the candidate of the JSP and JCP. Suzuki won by a margin of 870,000 votes. In Ōsaka, also in 1983, the winning governor won by 920,000 votes and was a joint candidate of all parties except for the JCP. The pattern continues into the 1990s. Governor Saitō of Shizuoka, recommended by all

TABLE 1.1
Turnout rates in House of Representatives elections: 1976-1983 (by constituency type in percent)

	Elections			
Constituency Type	*1983*	*1980*	*1979*	*1976*
Big cities	59.3	67.6	56.2	65.1
Cities	69.1	75.3	69.8	75.5
Small cities	72.0	77.8	73.8	76.3
Semirural	77.0	80.6	76.8	79.6
Rural	73.3	79.5	76.2	79.8
National	67.9	74.5	68.0	73.4
Semirural/big city differential	17.7	13.0	20.6	14.5

Source: Compiled by author.

the parties except the JCP, was reelected in October 1990 by a vote of 942,000 to 128,000 over the JCP candidate. As of 1990, 34 of the 46 prefectural governors were such coalitional candidates.

In this situation, one that seems to have become increasingly common in recent years, the outcome is clear far before the actual election day. Why should voters make a special effort to participate in such an election? A discussion of the declining rates of competition for Diet elections is presented in Chapter 2.

As the Japanese are often described as group oriented, it should not be surprising that organizations advocate that their memberships vote together for certain parties or candidates. Patterns of social-based voting can be detected in the support patterns of many Japanese organizations. Major labor confederations, for instance, have been strongly supportive of the various Socialist parties. And Japan's various religious associations are quite active in urging their members to support candidates of favored political parties beyond the expected Sōka Gakkai–Kōmeitō relationship. One of the largest of these organizations is the Rissho Kōseikai, a neo-Buddhist group numbering 5 million members and strongly supportive of many LDP candidates. Rissho Kōseikai leaders have estimated that between 2 million and 3 million votes from members were cast for the endorsed conservative candidates in the 1980 double elections.[37] Among other major "new religions" (those formed since 1945), the Seichō-no le supported the LDP in 1980, while others such as Sekai Kyūsei Kyō, Reiyu, Perfect Liberty, and Bussho Gonen-kai made great efforts to elect conservative candidates usually selected from their own membership ranks.[38]

More specifically directed toward the Japanese phenomenon is A. D. Shupe's study of political participation in Japan, which revealed that three measures—voting, political distrust, and political cynicism—stand apart from the other modes of participation. The lack of relationship between the act of voting and participation in politically oriented Japanese organizations is a major difference between the Japanese political system and the expectations of Western political theory. Shupe concluded that voting in Japan is such a passive act that it fits with the traditional Japanese pattern of avoiding overt political actions if at all possible.[39]

Bradley Richardson and Scott Flanagan suggest that the best model for understanding Japanese voting behavior is one based on social networks. The social network model appears to work for Japan given the persistence of personal ties, the significance of the group in an individual's life, and the ability of the group to enforce conformity among its members.[40] Flanagan argues that Japanese voting behavior can be understood in terms of such traditional attitudes as the recommendation system (*subsensei*), feelings of obligation (*giri*), local district consciousness (*jimoto*), and supporters' organizations (*kōenkai*).[41] Regarding *subsensei*, rural Japan is largely organized and given political direction by its deference to community leaders, who traditionally control or influence the votes of many of their fellow citizens. Often entire groups will follow the recommendations of a particular leader. In the urban areas, such a pattern can often follow the wishes of a particular group (union, professionial, or religious) leader. *Giri* refers to a sense of obligation based on personal relationships, which constitute a very significant aspect of Japanese society. One often sees a rather strange geographical pattern in a given candidate's voter support. Regarding *jimoto* not only does the "home town" turn out for the local candidate (and the candidate provides constituent services for the home town or district), but the personal ties involved even more firmly cement the voting relationship. Finally, almost all LDP and many other party candidates have their own *kōenkai,* which function to seal the personal relationship between candidate and voter. A *kōenkai* will cost the politician great amounts of money to maintain, but it translates into votes come election day.

These patterns, described by Flanagan in 1968, are still part of Japanese political life in the 1990s—but they are so to a lesser degree, largely because the Japanese society has become more urbanized. As J. Watanuki suggested in 1967, "cultural politics" still exists in the rural sector of Japan.[42] In this style of politics, "political participation [is] based on the culturally prescribed personal relationships of indebtedness" established between persons and their social superiors, kin, or peers. However, Shupe has correctly noted a breaking down of this pattern inasmuch as traditional relationships have been frequently replaced by more functional or occupational bonds—especially for those who have moved from rural to urban areas.[43] In addition, Curtis has identified a rise in the number of candidate-controlled supporters' organizations, which for the conservatives and many JSP members have "bypassed the rural bosses."[44]

The passive form of citizen participation in Japan is effectively illustrated by the surveys taken by the NHK Public Opinion Research Institute in 1973 and 1978, which focused on the value orientations of Japanese citizens. Among the various interesting questions dealing with preferred life-styles, roles in marriage, and moral and religious values were questions pertaining to political values. In the 1973 survey, specifically, the question "What is the most desirable form of political behavior for the general public?" yielded the following responses: (a) We should select an excellent politician by election and entrust political affairs to him (63 percent); (b) When a problem occurs, we should make sure that the politician we support reflects our opinions in politics (12 percent); and (c) We should help the growth of the political party or body that we usually support, so that we can realize our views (17 percent). K. Kojima and D. Kazama designated response (a) as the disassociative orientation toward politics, (b) as the intermediate orientation, and (c) as the association orientation. Because 63 percent of the sample supported the disassociative orientation, the NHK researchers concluded that the Japanese people's "concept of participation in politics is largely limited to voting."[45]

A lack of trust for politicians seems to be widespread throughout Japanese society. Among the working class, there is little public support even for reformist politicians. A July 1979 poll of 5,000 members of six unions in the Tokyo-Yokohama area produced the following results: Of those surveyed, 1 percent trusted conservative politicians; 1 percent trusted fortune tellers; and 1.8 percent trusted progressive politicians. Negative responses regarding conservative and progressive politicians ("I don't trust them" or "I don't trust them very much") were 79.1 percent and 70.5 percent, respectively. Yet, when asked what profession they considered the most important in Japanese society, these workers gave first place to politicians, followed by production workers, judges, and doctors.[46]

Another indication of the lack of trust in Japanese politicians came from the results of a poll quoted in a *Mainichi Shimbun* editorial in 1980. Respondents were asked to what degree they could trust the following, and these were their responses: weather forecasts (84 percent); newspapers (81 percent), doctors (77 percent), fortune tellers (21 percent), and politicians (3 percent).[47] This response fits well with the pattern found in U.S. cities operating under what Daniel Elazar calls an individualistic political culture—certainly a strange term to use as a parallel for the Japanese political culture, which is most decidedly nonindividualistic.[48] The city of Chicago, for instance, is full of professional politicians who prosper in their professions and have relatively little interchange with average citizens except in their role as "brokers." These politicians are perhaps looked down upon by the residents of the city, but they are also recognized as very important to the survival of the democracy. As previously noted, the Japanese workers, when asked to name the profession they considered to be most important, gave first place to politicians.[49]

The NHK surveys apparently discovered no correlation between the sense of political efficacy and the level of political knowledge. However, when the two dimensions were analyzed together, the NHK researchers discovered that almost half (i.e., 47 percent) of the Japanese population sampled exhibited both low political knowledge and a low sense of political efficacy. At the other end of the scale, only 10 percent of the sample fell into the category of high political knowledge and a high sense of efficacy. These figures were quite stable through the 1970s, but small changes were recorded at the upper and lower ends of the age-group spectrum; that is, better educated, older respondents revealed high rates in both knowledge and efficacy, whereas even the best-educated youth were found in the low knowledge–low efficacy grouping.[50]

We can see one remnant of the persistence of traditional political values if we look at which level of politics is of the greatest interest to Japanese voters. In sharp contrast with the United States, where local elections often draw less than 20 percent of the eligible electorate, a sizable proportion of Japanese voters (37 percent) in a Prime Minister's Office poll conducted in 1982 cited the election of city, ward, town, and village assembly members as the most important election for them. Approximately 20 percent selected House of Representatives elections, and about 17 percent chose the election of the heads of their local governments. Only 4 percent indicated prefectural gubernatorial elections; 3 percent, prefectural assembly elections; and 1 percent, House of Councillors elections. The location of the citizen's home is quite important in shaping how he or she viewed elections. People living in smaller towns and villages placed great importance on their local city elections, but Tokyo residents thought the national-level House elections were most significant.[51]

In general, however, most Japanese seem to have little interest in Japanese politics. The average citizen does not spend much of his or her time talking about politics. Nearly half the Japanese public (46 percent) indicated in a 1982 Prime Minister's Office poll that they "seldom talked about" social and political topics, while 40 percent said they "sometimes talked about" such topics. Those who seldom discussed politics increased by 5 percent over a 1980 poll, and those who sometimes discussed politics declined by 3 percent—a result some felt supported the theory that the trend toward political apathy actually accelerated in the 1980s.[52]

An important characteristic of any party system is the intensity with which voters identify with the component parties. In the Japanese political system, a major characteristic is weak identification with the political parties in the system. S. Verba found that only 16 percent of the Japanese expressed a strong degree of identity with their political parties—the lowest such figure among the nations studied by this author. Conversely, 53 percent exhibited weak identifications—the highest such total in the Verba study. In addition, nearly 30 percent identified themselves as independents. Only India had more independents than Japan at the time of this survey. Finally, it has been estimated that only 4 to 7 percent of Japanese formally belong to political parties, a percentage range that is equivalent to the levels in India and the United States.[53] After studying a number of democracies, Richardson concluded in 1975 that Japanese party attachment levels (70 percent) were comparable to those of Norway, India, and Germany and far behind the populations of the United States (90 percent) and Great Britain (90 percent).[54] Of greater interest, still, are the comparatively low intensities of party support found in Japan as compared to the two major Western democracies. The Japanese pattern of *low overall support levels* and *low intensities* of support was distinctive among the nations studied. In the United States, the percentage of nonparty supporters (independents) declines as they get older, but in Japan these nonsupporters are found in relatively similar proportions across the various age cohorts. Little difference is found among male re-

TABLE 1.2
Partisan divisions at the local level of politics in Japan, 1990
(66,957 city, ward, and village assembly members)

Party	*Seats*	*Change*
Independents	52,012	(-843)
LDP	3,117	(-418)
JCP	3,800	(+295)
CGP	3,359	(+167)
JSP	2,885	(-207)
DSP	808	(-78)
Minor parties	72	(-96)
SDF	16	(-11)

Note: ( ) = change from 1984 totals.

Source: Data from Home Affairs Ministry (December 4, 1990).

spondents by age groups, but women in general tend to be weaker "party identifiers" and older women are the most apolitical category of all.[55] Richardson also found party loyalties among young Japanese to be less developed than those among U.S. youth.[56]

Richardson has also concluded that the party is often not a very salient institution for many Japanese living within an electoral environment. Often on the national level, but most commonly on the local level, many candidates run and are elected as independents. Table 1.2 indicates the number of nonpartisan office holders at the local assembly level in 1990; Table 1.3 reveals the partisan divisions at the prefectural assembly level in the same year. Note that although the local levels were largely nonpartisan, the prefectural level was decidedly party oriented—a pattern similar to that in the United States, with its nonpartisan city elections and very partisan county- and state-level contests. One should also keep in mind that even in the Japanese House of Representatives' constituencies, the real battle is often among various factions of the LDP rather than between the LDP and the opposition parties. The 1990 lower house elections in Aomori First District illustrated well this type of intraparty competition. Six candidates contested four seats with one being the "symbolic" JCP candidate and another being the JSP and top vote-winning candidate in the district. Four LDP candidates backed by the Abe Shintarō, Miyazawa Kiichi, Kōmoto Toshio, and Takeshita Noboru factions battled among themselves for the three remaining seats. The lack of presence of the parties and party symbols especially at the local levels of politics, Richardson has concluded, makes Japanese electoral politics different from those of many other comparable nations.[57] Yet, when the politics of the United States is compared to that of Japan, the pattern seems to be very similar with respect to partisan activities by governmental levels.

As most Japanese are not emotionally tied to a specific party, it seems reasonable that Japanese would know more about the individual parliamentary candidates than citizens in other democracies.[58] In survey after survey, Japanese voters emphasize the "candidate" over either "party." A *Nihon Keizai Shimbun* poll in March 1990 asked Japanese voters what standard had

TABLE 1.3
Prefectural assembly members, by party, 1990

Party	*Seats*	*Change*
LDP	1,440	(-166)
JSP	469	(+71)
Independents (Mostly conservative)	426	(+53)
CGP	217	(+2)
JCP	141	(+36)
DSP	101	(-4)
Minor parties	45	(-30)
SDF	5	(-1)

Note: ( ) = change from 1984 totals.

Source: Data from Home Affairs Ministry (December 4, 1990).

guided their vote for candidates in the 1990 lower house elections. Half responded that they considered the policies of the candidate and the party; 36 percent mentioned the candidate's personality; 15 percent needed a sense of affinity with the candidate; 11 percent relied on the degree that they were familiar with the name of the candidate; and 12 percent followed the recommendations of other persons or mass media coverage of the campaign.[59] As Richardson has indicated, only in House of Councillors elections do the voters emphasize party more than candidate in making their voting decisions. Whereas rural voters tend to see Diet members as their envoys to the capital, urban voters place more emphasis on party labels and issue orientations.[60]

By and large, most Japanese do not strongly dislike the two major political parties. In an *Asahi Shimbun* poll in 1979, only a total of 12 percent most disliked either of the two big parties (8 percent disliked the LDP most, and 4 percent disliked the JSP). One to 3 percent most disliked the NLC, SDF, and DSP, but the two most disliked parties were the JCP (38 percent) and the Kōmeitō (12 percent).[61] Some effort has been made to place the major parties on various continua based on the public's perceptions and images of the parties. Note, for example, the following poll responses from 1977:

Conservative	LDP DSP NLC CGP JSP JCP	*Progressive*
Dependable	LDP NLC JSP CGP DSP JCP	*Undependable*
Like	NLC LDP JSP DSP CGP JCP	*Dislike*
Danger	JCP CGP JSP DSP NLC LDP	*Safe*
Bright	NLC JSP CGP DSP LDP JCP	*Grim*

It is interesting to observe that the DSP was considered the second most conservative party in Japan, but also a relatively undependable one.

Just because most Japanese do not strongly identify with their political parties does not mean that the Japanese voters do not think parties are important. Most Japanese appear to think the political parties and financial circles (*zaikai*) are the powers that move Japan. Five percent of the respondents to a 1979 poll believed election results to be most significant; 9 percent indicated the bureaucracy; 2 percent, mass movements, 4 percent, interest groups; 6 percent, other nations; 9 percent, the idea of public opinion; 28 percent, financial circles; and 27 percent, political parties.[62]

One reason the LDP has remained in power for so many years is that the Japanese electorate is essentially conservative and resistant to change. It is conservative not in a true ideological sense, but in the sense that it resists fundamental changes. Moreover, as Murakami Yasusuke has suggested, the LDP is largely based on consummatory values, in that it emphasizes stability and order but not a return to traditional values.[63] Responses to public opinion polls in Japan tend to support the existence of a conservative Japanese public. Seventy-three percent of the respondents to a *Mainichi Shimbun* poll conducted in December 1980 answered affirmatively the question, "Are you satisfied with your present life?" Only 18 percent answered negatively, while 8 percent gave other answers or no answer.[64] In a Ministry of Health and Welfare poll in October 1979, the respondents to the question, "Do you think your way of thinking and acting is rather conservative or rather reformist?" replied with conservative answers. Seventy-three percent described themselves as conservative while 22 percent answered "reformist." The pattern varied little among the various age cohorts.[65] That most Japanese tend to think of themselves as conservative rather than progressive or liberal can also be seen in the results of an LDP Public Relations poll released in September 1979. Of the nationwide sample, 47 percent identified themselves as conservatives while 31 percent viewed themselves as progressive. Similar polling in the United States has shown a strong conservative plurality among its citizens.[66]

Although the LDP has traditionally based its voting strength on a foundation of rural interests and small-business people, in recent years it has moved to add the urban middle class to its coalition. The conventional wisdom had been to assume that this latter group was more likely to support opposition party candidates, but, as Gerald Curtis has argued, the "LDP has been transformed from a party dependent on farmer and small businessmen support to one whose main base of support lies in the new urban middle class."[67] Polls have shown strong support for the LDP among young urban voters. In the 1980 elections, support for the LDP among the group far exceeded that for any of the other parties. Curtis sees this new urban middle class as essentially conservative in the sense of favoring stability and being reluctant to endorse radical changes in existing governmental policies.

The poll data and election results indicate that the LDP is not only the leading party of rural Japan but the most powerful party in urban Japan as well. Table 1.4 indicates the LDP and JSP power bases for House of Representatives elections between 1976 and 1983. Note that of the five types of constituencies, the LDP has won its largest number of seats in each election in the rural constituencies. The LDP won 61.4 percent of the vote in rural constituencies compared with 29.6 percent in the metropolitan constituencies. It is interesting to see that whereas the LDP wins about 5 million votes in each constituency type and 25 percent of the seats in the metropolitan

TABLE 1.4
LDP and JSP seat totals by constituency type (1976-1983)

	LDP Seats Won				1983 Election		
	'83	'80	'79	'76	Seats	Votes	% of Votes
Metropolitan	35	41	32	37	(123)	4,753,773	29.6
Cities	42	50	45	43	(95)	5,477,837	43.9
Towns	53	63	55	54	(102)	5,678,544	51.2
Semirural	52	55	51	52	(88)	4,563,530	56.1
Rural	68	75	65	63	(103)	5,509,094	61.4
Totals	250	284	248	249	(511)	25,982,782	45.8
	JSP Seats Won				1983 Election		
	'83	'80	'79	'76	Seats	Votes	% of Votes
Metropolitan	23	21	22	23	(123)	2,643,443	16.4
Cities	25	20	21	27	(95)	2,670,196	21.4
Towns	21	19	19	23	(102)	2,077,286	18.7
Semirural	22	25	22	27	(88)	1,812,715	22.3
Rural	21	22	23	23	(103)	1,862,079	20.8
Totals	112	107	107	123	(511)	11,065,050	19.5

Source: Compiled by author.

TABLE 1.5
Party vote percentages by constituency types, 1986 and 1990 HR elections

	1986 Elections							
	LDP	NLC	JSP	CGP	JCP	DSP	SDF	Did not vote
Metropolitian	23.2	2.3	10.5	10.9	8.9	5.0	1.1	38.1
Cities	38.2	1.9	12.8	7.0	6.2	4.7	- -	29.2
Semirural	50.1	- -	14.3	2.5	3.7	4.8	.4	24.2
Rural	54.4	- -	13.0	2.8	4.3	2.5	.8	22.2
	1990 Elections							
	LDP	NLC	JSP	CGP	JCP	DSP	SDF	Did not vote
Metropolitian	24.7	.8	17.0	9.6	8.0	3.5	1.2	35.2
Cities	40.2	- -	19.7	5.2	5.5	4.1	- -	25.3
Semirural	48.1	- -	18.4	3.0	3.9	3.6	.4	22.6
Rural	56.1	- -	19.3	- -	2.2	1.1	1.4	20.0

Source: Asahi Shimbun (July 8, 1986, and February 20, 1990).

districts, the JSP pattern is more mixed. The latter received its highest vote percentages in the semirural constituencies and twice obtained its highest seat totals in the city districts, twice in the semirural districts, and once in the rural districts.

The pattern of voting noted in Table 1.4 continued in the 1986 and 1990 lower house elections. As the data in Table 1.5 indicate, the LDP still wins its highest percentage of votes in the rural and semirural districts, but it is also the strongest urban and metropolitan party as well. In fact, its vote-drawing power in the cities continues to grow.

In many democracies young voters are often the force behind liberal or leftist parties. Japanese youth, however, appear to be uncommonly conservative in their political orientation. A December 1978 survey of 60,000 male students in their third year in universities and colleges throughout Japan revealed that 54 percent supported no political party, and another 7 percent responded to the question with "don't know." Of the 40 percent who named a party they supported, the LDP was the party with the greatest support: LDP, 17.3 percent; JSP, 6.5 percent; NLC, 6.3 percent; JCP, 2.5 percent; SDF, 2.3 percent; DSP, 2 percent; and the Kōmeitō, 1.1 percent. Thus the combined conservative support level of 23 percent (LDP and NLC) overwhelmed the combined leftist percentage (JSP and JCP) of 9 percent. A poll of 2,470 incoming freshmen at the elite Tokyo University produced a very similar conservative pattern of party support. Tokyo University freshmen were largely nonpolitical, with 60 percent not supporting any political party; but of the 40 percent who did, 62 percent supported the two conservative parties. It is interesting to note that support for the JCP, which had been running at a 20 percent rate among those students supporting parties, fell to only 3 percent in the late 1970s.[68]

Japanese youths appear to be dissatisfied with their society and yet quite reluctant to engage in serious reforms. When the NRC survey asked its sample of college junior males if they were satisfied with the nature of government in Japan, only 1.3 percent replied that they were satisfied and 18.8 percent were "more or less satisfied." On the other hand, 33.8 percent were "dissatisfied" and 45.8 percent were "more or less dissatisfied." Yet this majority of dissatisfied students were not eager to change the governmental system. Forty-six percent felt "insecure about a major change in society," and only 22 percent wanted "basically to alter the political and economic system."[69] Many of these dissatisfied but conservative students will eventually end up as the businessmen of Japan. In a poll conducted by the Japan Junior Chamber of Commerce of business executives under 40 years of age in 1980, 62 percent supported the Japan-U.S. Security Treaty; 54 percent supported a nuclear-armed Japan "some day in the future," and 71.3 percent supported the LDP.[70] In their study of the 1980 "double elections," Ōyama Shigeo and Michisada Hirose, using *Asahi Shimbun* poll data from a sample of more than 100,000 people, concluded that although young Japanese (ages 20 to 24 years) were the most nonpartisan (47 percent), their support rate for the LDP (28 percent) was greater than their combined support for all six of the opposition parties (25 percent). In addition, since the 1979 House of Representatives elections, the young voters have evidenced increasing support for the LDP. Among those voters in the 20-to-24-year-old age group, support for the LDP increased from 39 percent in 1976 to 49 percent in 1980.[71] Similarly, among the voters in their late 20s, LDP support rose by 9 percent between 1976 and 1980. The large jumps in LDP support among these younger voters occurred in and around the major regional cities and contributed to the fine showing of the party in the 1980 elections.

With respect to the age cohorts in Japan, interest in politics and voting turnout has been observed to be lowest among those in their 20s—especially the youngest group aged 20 to 24. This group makes up a disproportional percentage of the nonparty supporters in Japan (the so-called floating vote).

Of this uncommitted vote, which makes up roughly 40 percent of the electorate, only 16 percent of the voters are over 70; but the category also includes 45.6 percent of those in their 20s. In their analysis of the 1979 House elections, Okamoto Hiroshi and Ōyama Shigeo discovered that 44.7 percent of the nonpartisans voted for the LDP compared to 20.8 percent for the JSP. Consequently, of the total LDP vote in 1979, 69 percent was derived from its own partisans, 21 percent from nonpartisans, and the remaining 10 percent from partisans of other parties.[72]

The floating vote, which totaled 44.5 percent of a sample of Japanese voters in 1979, is usually categorized into three major types of citizens: (1) those concerned about society and politics but irritated by contemporary politics and parties, (2) those whose life activities are centered on the home and who show little interest in politics, and (3) those whose lives are centered on pastimes and who have little political interest. Most of the people in this floating-vote category are 20 to 40 years old. The *Asahi Shimbun* poll just prior to the 1979 general election reported that 53 percent of the public had "an interest in politics in normal times," while 42 percent did not and 5 percent refused to answer the questions.[73]

Given the restrictive nature of Japanese electoral law (see Chapter 2) and the resultant passive nature of many Japanese voters, it should not be surprising that some Japanese journalists refer to the Japanese system as a "spectator democracy."[74] Tominomori Eiji has suggested that this term refers to the Japanese pattern of high interest in and high dissatisfaction with government and politics, but he has also noted the great separation between the citizen and the Japanese party system.[75] In an *Asahi Shimbun* poll only 18 percent of the respondents felt they could consult party members or political parties. Only 16 percent either had personal ties with parties or had participated in the activities of parties. A majority (57 percent), on the other hand, responded that they did not support a party, did not trust parties, had no interest in parties, or felt that parties had no connection with their daily life.[76] Flanagan and Richardson perceived two different groups of spectators in contemporary Japan: the older, less-educated, rural, deferential, and politically disinterested (i.e., traditional) group, and the newer group of younger, better-educated, urban, issue-oriented, and cynical citizens.[77] The election campaign laws deliberately seek to keep citizens from participating in the election process; thus it is not surprising that the vast majority of Japanese appear to be mere spectators.

One of Japan's most interesting characteristics is the lack of traditional cleavages common in European societies. In terms of party support, Japan exhibits no significant religious, racial, or ethnic splits. Yet this is not surprising, given that Japan is perhaps one of the most homogeneous nations (with respect to population characteristics) and also one of the least religious. As Richardson and Flanagan have argued, Japanese electoral cleavages tend to be based on political issues such as support for the 1947 constitution and the Japan-U.S. Security Treaty, relations with the Communist bloc, and the continuing debate over capitalism and socialism as principles for societal organization.[78]

The data presented in the preceding pages make clear the reason for long-term LDP rule—at least in terms of voting behavior patterns. Not only is the LDP rural stronghold still intact and, thanks to the continuing malapportionment of the Diet, still powerful, but the conservatives have expanded their support in the cities as well and continue to be a powerful national party—the only party fielding sufficient candidates to run the national government by itself.

THE STRUCTURE OF JAPANESE PARTIES

One of the major methods of comparative analysis of party systems involves careful examination of the structural aspects of the component parties. The Japanese political parties described in the remaining chapters of this book are usually portrayed as being elite cadre parties. As modern Japanese parties began on the parliamentary level and only later extended their organizations to the subnational levels, it is not surprising that they today retain almost all of their organizational strength on the national level.[79] The inability of the national parties to construct effective grass-roots operations is at least partly a function of the important tendency of the Japanese electorate to view politics as a necessary but distasteful activity—one that should be avoided as much as possible by the average citizen. Moreover, Japanese electoral law tries to keep the citizens and the parties as separate as possible. On various occasions, the party leaders have attempted to build grass-roots organizations, but each time they failed. That is, the JSP (in its drive for 100,000 members), the LDP (in its expansion to 2.4 million members for LDP presidential primaries, discovered for the most part to be paper members only), and the NLC (in its offer of "political participation for the price of a cup of coffee," although an insufficient number of supporters responded to finance the party) have all failed in recent years. The parties relied either on their Diet members' fundraising efforts (as in the SDF) or on the nearly total support of their supporting organizations: Sōka Gakkai in the case of CGP, Dōmei in the case of DSP, Sōhyō in the case of JSP, and corporate Japan in the case of LDP and NLC. Of the six major Japanese parties, only the JCP has a reasonable mass-party organization as well as its own independent fundraising and campaign support activities.

Thus, Japanese parties tend to be highly centralized, exclusive in their membership patterns, and often lacking in even the essential organizational strengths necessary to perform the traditional functions of political parties.[80] Because it is often difficult to compare data on party organizations, the Japanese model cannot easily be placed among its counterparts abroad. Certainly the Japanese Socialist parties (the JSP, DSP, and SDF) lack the mass membership base of the Socialist parties of Western Europe. Moreover, although the conservative parties of Japan, Western Europe, and the United States share a common reliance on corporate support, the Japanese parties appear to have, by far, the weakest organizational ties to the average citizen.

With respect to informal organization, however, Japanese parties have factional patterns similar to those of the parties of Italy. The Socialist party of Italy (PSI) and the JSP of Japan each have 4 or 5 major factions and a pattern of secession of several splinter parties (the Socialist Proletarians and the Social Democrats in Italy and the DSP and SDF in Japan). Like the Japanese factions, those in Italy tend to be well organized and cohesive: According to Raphael Zariski, "Factions have their own newspapers or journals, their own parliamentary subgroups, their own sources of income, and their own share of party patronage."[81] Factionalism also plays a key role in the nomination of party officials and parliamentary candidates in Italy.

Part of the reason behind the existence of factions can be traced to individual political ambitions and the creation of organizations to further these ambitions. Factions may also be based on ideological orientation. It would be an accurate generalization to note that the LDP and the Italian Christian Democratic Party (CDP) share a pattern of factions largely based on personal ties, ambition, patronage, and fundraising, whereas the JSP and PSI tend to have more ideologically based factions. In both the LDP and CDP, cabinet and subcabinet positions are awarded largely on the basis of factional shares and legislator seniority.

Thus, one of the most distinctive features of the Japanese party system—factions—mirrors the pattern exhibited by a number of Western European parties. As noted, the foreign party system most similar to the Japanese system seems to be the Italian system. In both Japan and Italy, the informal organizations (factions) are as important, if not more important, than the formal party structure. Italy, by Sartori's count, has five to seven "relevant parties" (as does Japan) and as many as twenty-five "sub-party currents" in the ruling Christian-Democratic and Socialist parties.[82] Although the Japanese LDP featured five or six major factions in the 1970s, the CDP of Italy displayed eight or nine "currents" of significance during that period. Both the LDP and CDP factions are largely "semi-sovereign" in that members owe their primary allegiance to the factions rather than to the parties.[83] As Sartori concluded, "With respect to factional politics the similarity between Italy and Japan seems impressive: It is a similarity verging on twinship."[84]

Among the dissimilarities is the Italian tendency to conduct electoral campaigns on the basis of parties, while the Japanese also use factions and personal campaign support organizations in LDP and JSP campaigns, but the CGP, JCP, and DSP run their campaigns largely by party. As Sartori has further noted, the Italian system requires coalition governments with factional alliances crossing party lines, whereas the Japanese system avoids coalitions (except for the very unusual case in 1983–1986 involving LDP-NLC coalitions) and has factions operating within their respective parties.[85] Finally, as Sartori has indicated, the Japanese factions came into being through the "fusions" of 1955, but the Italian factions were generated by "fissions" (i.e., by the gradual development of factions from an original party).[86] The important point to remember in this comparison of Japanese and Italian party factions is simply that the Japanese system is not unique (as many Japanese think it is)—it shares important characteristics with other parliamentary systems.

In summary, then, the Japanese political system is multiparty in nature, with a predominant party that has controlled national politics since 1955. The reason for the LDP's rule can be found in part in Japan's essentially conservative and passive electorate and in part in the ineptitude of the opposition parties (especially the JSP, the main opposition party). In the next two chapters, the rules of the electoral game will be presented in terms of their impact on the party system; then, in the remainder of the book, each of the major and minor parties will be separately analyzed.

NOTES

1. G. Berger, *Parties Out of Power in Japan, 1931–1941* (Princeton, N.J.: Princeton University Press, 1977); Robert A. Scalapino, *Democracy and the Party Movement in Pre-War Japan* (Berkeley: University of California Press, 1953); Peter Duus, *Party Rivalry and Political Change in Taisho Japan* (Cambridge, Mass.: Harvard University Press).
2. T. J. Pempel, "Political Parties and Social Change: The Japanese Experience," in L. Maisel and J. Cooper, eds., *Political Parties: Development and Decay* (Beverly Hills, Calif.: Sage, 1978), p. 312.
3. Ibid., pp. 311–312.
4. Ibid., p. 313.
5. Ibid., p. 319.
6. Robert A. Scalapino and Junnosuke Masumi, *Parties and Politics in Contemporary Japan* (Berkeley: University of California Press, 1962).
7. Nobutaka Ike, *Japanese Politics: Patron-Client Democracy* (New York: Knopf, 1972), p. 76.
8. G. Sartori, *Parties and Party Systems: A Framework for Analysis* (Cambridge: Cambridge University Press, 1976), chapter 5.
9. Maurice Duverger, "La Sociologie des Partis Politiques," in G. Gurvitch, ed., *Traite de Sociologie* (Paris: Presses Universitaires, 1960), p. 44; G. Almond, in G. Almond and J. Coleman, eds., *The Politics of the Developing Areas* (Princeton, N.J.: Princeton University Press, 1960), pp. 40–42.
10. *Sankei Shimbun* (February 10, 1990).
11. *Mainichi Shimbun* (April 13, 1990).
12. Michael Taylor and V. M. Herman, "Party Systems and Governmental Stability," *American Political Science Review* 65, no. 1 (March 1971), p. 32.
13. Raymond Aron, "Alternation in Government in the Industrialized Countries," speech given at the London School of Economics, October 27, 1981.
14. Quoted in Robert Dahl, ed., *Political Opposition in Western Democracies* (New Haven, Conn.: Yale University Press, 1966).
15. *Yomiuri Shimbun* (February 6, 1982).
16. *Tokyo Shimbun* (April 3, 1990).
17. *Yomiuri Shimbun* (September 21, 1985).
18. *Japan Times* (July 29, 1982).
19. See Ariel Levite and Sidney Tarrow, "The Legitimization of Excluded Parties in Dominant Party Systems: A Comparison of Israel and Italy," *Comparative Politics* 15, no. 3, pp. 295–324. See also Arion and Barnes, *Journal of Politics* 36 (August 1974), pp. 592–614.
20. *Asahi Shimbun* (July 8, 1981).
21. "Vox Populi Vox Dei," *Asahi Shimbun* (July 7, 1981).

22. *Sankei Shimbun* (June 26, 1977).
23. *Japan Times* (December 26, 1983).
24. *Mainichi Daily News* (December 12, 1982).
25. *Japan Times* (January 9, 1981).
26. See Nobuo Tomita, H. Baerwald, K. Hoshino, and Akira Nakamura, "Japanese Politics at a Crossroads: The 11th House of Councillors Election," *Bulletin of the Institute of Social Sciences* (Meiji University) 1, no. 3 (1978). See also *Yomiuri Shimbun* (September 21, 1985).
27. *Look Japan* (August 10, 1980).
28. Ibid.
29. Ellis Krauss, *Conflict in Japan* (Honolulu: University of Hawaii Press, 1984).
30. Dahl, *Political Opposition in Western Democracies*, p. 344.
31. T. J. Pempel, ed., *Uncommon Democracies: The One-Party Dominant Regimes* (Ithaca, N.Y.: Cornell University Press, 1990).
32. Ellis S. Krauss and Jon Pierre, "The Decline of Dominant Parties: Parliamentary Parties in Sweden and Japan in the 1970s," in Pempel, *Uncommon Democracies*, pp. 225–259.
33. Michio Muramatsu and Ellis S. Krauss, "The Dominant Party and Social Conditions in Japan," in Pempel, *Uncommon Democracies*, pp. 282–305.
34. Y. Kuroda, *Reed Town, Japan: A Study in Community Power Structure and Political Change* (Honolulu: University of Hawaii Press, 1974), p. 194.
35. *Mainichi Daily News* (April 8, 1979).
36. Bradley M. Richardson, *The Political Culture of Japan* (Berkeley, Calif.: University of California Press, 1974), pp. 85–90. Also see Bradley M. Richardson, "Japan's Habitual Voters: Partisanship on the Emotional Periphery," *Comparative Political Studies* 19, no. 3 (October 1986), pp. 356–384; and Bradley Richardson, "Constituency Candidates Versus Parties in Japanese Voting Behavior," *American Political Science Review* 82 (1988), pp. 695–718.
37. *Mainichi Daily News* (June 12, 1980).
38. *Mainichi Daily News* (June 2, 1980).
39. A. D. Shupe, "Social Participation and Voting Turnout: The Case of Japan," *Comparative Political Studies* 12, no. 2 (July 1979), p. 238.
40. Bradley M. Richardson and Scott C. Flanagan, *Politics in Japan* (Boston: Little, Brown, 1984).
41. See Scott C. Flanagan, "Voting Behavior in Japan," *Comparative Political Studies* 1, no. 3 (October 1968), pp. 396–411. See also James W. White, "Civic Attitudes, Political Participation, and System Stability in Japan," *Comparative Political Studies* 14, no. 3 (October 1981), p. 372; Flanagan and Richardson, "Political Disaffection and Political Stability," in R. T. Jannuzzi, ed., *Comparative Social Research* (Greenwich, Conn.: JAI Press, 1980), pp. 19–27; and Ofer Feldman and Kasohisa Kawakami, "Leaders and Leadership in Japanese Politics," *Comparative Political Studies* 22, no. 3 (1989), p. 280.
42. J. Watanuki, "Patterns of Politics in Present-Day Japan," in S. M. Lipset and S. Rokban, eds., *Party Systems and Voter Alignments* (New York: Free Press, 1967).
43. Shupe, "Social Participation and Voting Turnout," p. 232.
44. G. Curtis, *Election Campaigning: Japanese Style* (New York: Columbia University Press, 1971), p. 209.
45. See Daiji Kazama and Toyoko Akiyama, "Japanese Value Orientation: Persistence and Change," *Studies of Broadcasting*, no. 16 (1980). See also K. Kojima and D. Kazama, "Japanese Value Orientations," *Studies in Broadcasting*, no. 1 (1975); Scott C. Flanagan, "Changing Values in Advanced Industrial Societies," *Comparative Po-*

litical Studies 14, no. 4 (January 1982), pp. 403; Ronald Inglehart, "Changing Values in Japan and the West," *Comparative Political Studies* 14, no. 4 (January 1982), pp. 445–479; and M. Maruyama, "Patterns of Individualism and the Case of Japan: A Conceptual Scheme," in M. B. Jansen, ed., *Changing Japanese Attitudes Toward Modernization* (Princeton, N.J.: Princeton University Press, 1965); and Ikuo Kabashima and Jeffery Broadbent, "Referent Pluralism: Mass Media and Politics in Japan," *Journal of Japanese Studies* 12, no. 2 (1986), pp. 329–359.

46. Reported in *Asahi Evening News* (December 14, 1979).

47. *Mainichi Daily News* (January 3, 1980).

48. Daniel Elazar, *American Federalism: A View from the States* (New York: Harper & Row, 1972), chapters 2 and 3.

49. *Asahi Evening News* (December 14, 1979).

50. Kojima and Kazama, "Japanese Value Orientations."

51. *Japan Times* (April 13, 1982).

52. Ibid.

53. S. Verba and J. King, *Participation and Political Equality* (Cambridge: Cambridge University Press, 1978), p. 96.

54. Bradley M. Richardson, "Party Loyalties and Party Saliency in Japan," *Comparative Political Studies* 8, no. 1 (April 1975), p. 42.

55. Ibid.

56. Ibid., p. 43

57. Ibid., p. 47.

58. Richardson, "Party Loyalties," p. 49.

59. *Nihon Keizai Shimbun* (March 26, 1990).

60. Richardson, "Party Loyalties," p. 49.

61. *Asahi Shimbun* (September 10, 1979).

62. Ibid.

63. Yasusuke Murakami, "The Age of New Middle Mass Politics: The Case of Japan," *Journal of Japanese Studies* 8, no. 1 (Winter 1982), p. 171. The original work by Murakami on this subject appeared in *Chūō Kōron*, (December 1980).

64. *Mainichi Shimbun* poll (December 1980).

65. See the Ministry of Health and Welfare poll conducted in October 1979, reported in *Japan Times* (January 9, 1981).

66. *Liberal Star* (December 10, 1979).

67. *Look Japan* (August 10, 1980).

68. *Mainichi Daily News* (May 5, 1979).

69. *Asahi Evening News* (August 14, 1978, and July 18, 1978); *Japan Times* (June 15, 1979).

70. *Mainichi Daily News* (March 30, 1980).

71. Ōyama Shigeo and Michisada Hirose, "Nonpartisans and Youths Turn to the LDP," *Japan Echo* 7, no. 4 (1980), pp. 18–37.

72. Okamoto Hiroshi and Ōyama Shigeo, "Teiryu de henka shita senkyo no Yoso" [Electoral forecast faces unexpected turn of events], *Asahi Jānaru* (October 19, 1979).

73. *Asahi Shimbun* (September 10, 1979).

74. *Asahi Evening News* (April 5, 1976).

75. Ibid.

76. Ibid.

77. Richardson and Flanagan, *Politics in Japan*, p. 225.

78. Scott C. Flanagan and Bradley M. Richardson, *Japanese Electoral Behavior: Social Cleavages, Social Networks and Partisanship* (Beverly Hills, Calif.: Sage, 1973), p. 108.

79. Ibid., p. 88.

80. Ibid., p. 99.

81. Raphael Zariski, *Italy: The Politics of Uneven Development* (Hinsdale, Ill.: Dryden, 1972), p. 147.

82. Sartori, *Parties and Party Systems*, p. 88.

83. Alan S. Zuckerman, *The Politics of Faction: Christian Democratic Rule in Italy* (New Haven, Conn: Yale University Press, 1979).

84. Sartori, *Parties and Party Systems*, p. 20.

85. Ibid., p. 92.

86. Ibid.

2

Rules of the Game: The Impact of the Electoral System on Political Parties

RONALD J. HREBENAR

Unique in many respects among the electoral systems of democratic nations, Japan's electoral laws have had a significant impact on the nation's postwar political party system. Characterized by multimember parliamentary districts, chronic malapportionment, and straitjacket campaign activities restrictions, Japanese electoral laws have operated to keep Japan a one-party-dominant nation. The Liberal Democratic party (LDP) has ruled the nation uninterruptedly, without ever needing to resort to coalition, since its inception in 1955. Of the many political, economic, and social influences that have assisted the LDP during this period of dominance, one of the most significant has been the favorable impact of the electoral system on the LDP's parliamentary fortunes. The fragmentation of the Japanese political party system can be viewed only against the background of the election system that facilitates such developments. In the following sections the basic elements of the Japanese election system will be presented, and the political outcomes of these elements will be analyzed in terms of their effects on the party system.

Japan's six political parties, the LDP, the Socialist party (JSP), the Communist party (JCP), the Kōmeitō (CGP), the Democratic Socialist party, (DSP), and the Social Democratic Federation (SDF), operate in an environment that is legally regulated by the two fundamental electoral laws—the Public Offices Elections Law and the Political Funds Control Law. The latter, which was extensively revised in 1975, deals with the very significant problem of attempting to regulate the flow of *seiji kenkin* (political contributions) within the body politic of Japan. The nature of this reform battle will be analyzed in the next chapter. Meanwhile, we shall consider the more important law, the Public Offices Elections Law, which, with its very special mechanisms and provisions, establishes the rules of the game for election to the Diet and the wide variety of prefectural and local government legislative and executive offices. Its stated purpose as found in Article 1 is "to establish an electoral system . . . based on the spirit of the Japanese Constitution, to ensure that these elections are conducted fairly and properly according to the freely expressed will of the electors, and thus aim at the healthy growth of democratic politics."[1] This law establishes the unique Japanese multimember/single-vote election districts and the national proportional representation (PR) district for the House of Councillors. Other aspects of this law that vitally affect the Japanese party system are the omission of a workable reapportionment provision and the establishment of a comprehensive set of stringent campaign restrictions, both of which have operated to preserve LDP majorities in the Diet. These important aspects of Japanese electoral law will be analyzed within the context of their bias for or against the various parties and in terms of LDP responses to demands for meaningful reform.

THE IMPACT OF DISTRICT MAGNITUDE

Central to the operation of the Japanese electoral system is the manner in which the national-level legislators are distributed throughout the nation. This apportionment of legislators into constituencies can best be understood in terms of district magnitude—namely, the number of seats assigned by electoral law to any election district. Two major categories of district magnitudes are found throughout the world: the single-seat, or small-constituency, system; and the multimember constituency system, which can be subdivided into medium and large multimember districts. Single-seat districts are used in the United States for congressional elections, and in the Canadian, British, and Australian national lower-house elections. The political outcomes of the single-member, single-ballot system have been well researched, and the normal tendency to reward dominant parties with many seats in excess of their vote percentages is well known. However, the multimember districts of the largest magnitudes are usually found in electoral systems using some form of proportional representation; the more extreme form of this system is found in the Netherlands and in Israel, where the election district is the entire nation.

Japan's current system of medium-magnitude districts for national legislative elections is unique among democratic nations. Japanese House of Representatives (HR) district magnitudes range from 2 to 5 seats, except for one single-seat district and one 6-seat district. Following a revision of Japanese election HR districts prior to the 1986 elections, the 512 seats are now divided among 130 constituencies for a mean magnitude of 3.94 seats per district. Four of the districts are 2-seat constituencies; 42 are 3-seat constituencies; 39 districts have 4 seats each; and 43 districts elect 5 Diet members. The Anami Islands have the single-seat constituency, and Hokkaido's first district has 6 seats. What makes the Japanese system unique is the combination of multimember districts and a single nontransferable vote. This combination produces a de facto result without being a formal PR election system.

TABLE 2.1
Total party vote and seat percentages: Election system bias in the 1990 general election (House of Representatives)

Party	*Party Vote*	*Percentage of Total Vote*	*Seats*	*Percentage of Seats*	*1990 Bias*
LDP	30,315,417	46.1	275	53.7	+7.6
JSP	16,025,472	24.4	136	26.6	+2.2
CGP	5,242,675	8.0	45	8.8	+.8
JCP	5,226,987	8.0	16	3.1	-4.9
DSP	3,178,949	4.8	14	2.7	-2.1
SDF	566,957	.8	4	.8	-.1
Independent	5,147,854	7.9	22	4.3	-3.6
Totals	65,704,311	100.0	512	100.0	

Note: The one-seat district was captured by the LDP.

Source: Compiled by author.

The Japanese have experimented with each of the major types of constituencies over the past century. Before the current medium-sized constituency was introduced in 1925, the single-seat constituency was part of Japan's first election law of 1889 and was readopted in 1919 following the use of a large multimember system in the first two decades of this century. The 1946 election was held in association with a large multimember system, but all of the other postwar elections were held under the medium-sized multimember constituency system.

One explanation for the adoption of a medium-sized constituency system in 1925 is that it protected the three parties that were joined in governmental coalition at that time: Seiyukai, Kenseikai, and Kokumintō. The Seiyukai wanted a small district system, whereas the other parties wanted a large district system based on prefectures. The compromise decision was the adoption of the medium-sized district system.[2]

In actual operation the Japanese 2-to-6-seat constituency system produces a nonformal but de facto pattern of party seat divisions that is roughly proportional to the parties' percentage of the total national vote. The two major parties tend to win seats in approximately the same proportion in all three types of district magnitudes, but the middle-sized parties tend to win most of their seats in the larger districts. The seat-winning power of the LDP and JSP is impressive. Frequently, the LDP and JSP together have won all 3 seats in the smallest districts, and 3 out of 4 or 5 in the larger districts.[3]

The degree of proportionality between party votes and seat percentages for the 1990 House elections can be seen in Table 2.1. The major parties, the LDP and JSP, both cross the important barrier of 20 percent of the total vote and consequently receive additional seats above their vote proportions. The party that appears to suffer the greatest discrimination under the medium-sized constituency system is the JCP, which won only 3 percent of the seats but 8.0 percent of the total vote. In fact, in 1976 both the JCP and Kōmeitō won about 10 percent of the vote, but the Kōmeitō party won 38 more seats than its Communist rival. The explanation for this discrepancy can be found in the different strategies of the two parties in the selection of constituencies in which to run their candidates. The JCP generally tries to run a candidate in each of the nation's 130 districts, whereas the Kōmeitō runs candidates in selected constituencies and in 1990 endorsed only 58 candidates. Consequently, although the JCP collects votes from every part of Japan, the separate totals are frequently insufficient to elect Communist Diet members. The JCP is willing to accept this situation, given the educational nature of its campaigns in many districts.

The relationship between constituency magnitude and LDP success was clear in the 1990 HR elections. The fewer seats elected in a district, the better success rate the LDP achieved. The LDP won the seat in the single-seat district; 62.5 percent of the seats in the 2-seat districts; 57.9 percent in the 3-seat districts; 53.3 percent in the 4-seat districts; 52.6 percent in the 5-seat districts; and 33.3 percent in the 6-seat district.

The burden of calculating the correct number of candidates each party should endorse in specific districts is another important outcome of the medium-sized constituency system. If, for example, in a 5-member district a party miscalculates its electoral power and endorses two candidates, the party vote in that district divided among its candidates may place both out of the top five vote winners. This strategic element is a problem only for the LDP and JSP, which run multiple candidates in some districts.[4] In 1969, the JSP failed to calculate the relationship between its vote-drawing power and the number of party candidates, and thus suffered the consequences. The Socialists decided to increase sharply the number of party candidates; then, when the voters' support declined, the party's seat total declined by 50 seats. In 1972, given a more realistic endorsement policy in which the vote percentage was nearly identical to that in the previous election, 28 seats were added to the previous JSP total.

Although the JSP wasted only 4.6 percent of its total vote on unsuccessful candidates in the 1990 HR elections, it failed to offer the correct number of candidates in several key constituencies. The JSP ran only 149 candidates and ran more than one candidate in only 29 districts. Even if every JSP candidate had won, the party still would have been 108 seats short of a majority in the HR. In two urban constituencies, the JSP clearly should have run additional candidates. In Chiba 1, the JSP candidate came in first with 221,216 votes, while an LDP candidate won the last seat with just 106,202 votes. Likewise, in the third Ōsaka constituency, the first-place JSP candidates totaled over 223,000 votes, and the last-place DSP candidate won his seat with just 102,000 votes.

The concern of the smaller parties is more one of deciding whether they have a chance to win one seat in a district and, if that prospect is not likely, whether to join in a "joint struggle" coalition in that district. In recent joint struggles, JSP-JCP and DSP-Kōmeitō coalitions have been the most frequent.

An example of how the LDP can miscalculate the correct number of candidates can be found in the Ōsaka fifth constituency in the 1983 HR elections. In this 4-seat district, the winners were the Kōmeitō (143,532 votes),

TABLE 2.2
Number of party candidates in recent House of Representatives elections

Party	*1980*	*1983*	*1986*	*1990*
LDP	310	339	332	338
JSP	149	144	138	149
JCP	129	129	129	131
KOM	64	59	61	58
DSP	50	54	56	44
NLC	250	17	--	--
USF	5	4	5	6
Minor	42	18	15	71
Independent	61	84	100	156
Totals	835	848	836	953

Source: Adapted from data in the *Yomiuri Shimbun* (February 17, 1990).

the JCP (122,200), the DSP (109,497), and the JSP (100,734), whereas all four defeated candidates were from the LDP, representing three different factions with a combined total of over 197,000 votes.

Four additional points regarding the political effects of the medium-sized constituency system should be made. First, it tends to result in low levels of party competition because parties tend to run candidates only in those districts where there is a reasonable chance to win an HR seat (the JCP being the exception). The 1986 HR elections were the second least competitive of the postwar elections in terms of the number of candidates seeking Diet seats. Including minor parties and independents, only 838 candidates competed for 512 seats—a ratio of 1.64 candidates per seat.[5] The extreme case has been represented by a number of districts in which three Diet members were elected among only three serious candidates plus a symbolic JCP candidate. Usually 80 percent of the seats are considered safe, and meaningful competition often occurs only for the last seat in a district (see Table 2.2).

At least partially as a result of the effects of the medium-sized constituency system, competition rates in elections have plummeted to postwar levels. The number of candidates seeking seats in the upper house was also a postwar low. Even on the prefectural and local levels, competition is dying out as the parties reduce their candidate totals to contest only sure and possible seats. In the March 1979 prefectural elections, of the 2,645 seats up for election 18.3 percent were uncontested. Approximately 33 percent of the mayoral elections held in 1978 and 1979 were uncontested, and in towns and villages the number uncontested rose to over 50 percent.

Second, the multimember, single-vote districts result in serious intraparty conflict among the parties that run multiple candidates. The LDP, which nearly always runs two or more candidates in a district, has experienced serious intraparty conflict because each candidate seeks to build his or her share of the conservative vote and usually accomplishes this by subtracting votes from his party running mates. This intraparty conflict has been one of the supporting forces behind the LDP's factional system, inasmuch as the financial and political support to establish a separate candidate campaign organization has been provided by such LDP factional leaders as Takeshita Noboru, the late Abe Shintarō, and Watanabe Michio. Often the real opponent of an LDP candidate in his district will be the other LDP candidates sponsored by rival factional leaders eager to add one more follower to their Diet organizations. Moreover, although in the spring of 1977 the LDP's factions were formally dissolved in an effort to refurbish the tarnished image of the party, other LDP members (such as former party Policy Affairs Research Council Chairman Matsuno Raizo) argued correctly the previous summer that the party factions would never disappear as long as the present medium-sized constituency system is in operation.

Third, the medium-sized constituency system operating as a proportional representation system has encouraged the birth of new political parties that can compete with reasonable expectations of success with as little as 5 percent of the vote. Whereas it seemed in 1955 that the "two-party era" had arrived in Japanese politics, the success of subsequent spinoff parties such as the DSP, as well as the creation of the Kōmeitō, would never have been possible under a small seat system.

Finally, the proliferation of political parties under the medium-sized system has resulted in the fragmentation of the opposition into small parties seemingly incapable of forming an alternative government. Ever since the 1976 election raised the hopes of the opposition, a great deal of speculation has been generated regarding potential coalitions of opposition parties in the future. The primary speculation centers on the JSP's desire for an all-opposition party coalition (including the JCP) and on the rejection of that idea by the middle-of-the-road parties, especially the Kōmeitō and the DSP. Thus, the fragmentation of the opposition into relatively impotent, small organizations has facilitated the LDP's continuance in power.

Similar patterns of multimember districts with single, nontransferable votes have been observed in elections for the Diet's upper house, the House of Councillors (HC). The 252 members of the House of Councillors are elected from two types of constituencies: local (152) and national (100). The local districts are based on prefectural boundaries, and each prefecture elects one to four Councillors every three years. The LDP has monopolized the 26 single-seat districts, winning 96 percent of the seats in 1983 and 88 percent in 1986. However, in the "protest 1989 HC elections," the LDP managed to win only 3 of the contested 26 seats. Usually the fifteen 2-seat districts are dominated by the LDP and the JSP. In the 1986 HC elections, these two parties won 27 of the 30 seats, and even in 1989, the two powerful parties lost only 5 seats to other candidates. The smaller parties (CGP, JCP, DSP, SDF) won most of their local constituency seats in the 3- and 4-seat districts. In the two 4-seat districts, the minor parties held the LDP and JSP to 5 seats in 1986 and to only 3 seats in 1989. The LDP was able to win only slightly more than half the seats in the four 3-seat constituencies where the CGP managed to win 3 of the 12 seats in 1989. Overall, the LDP won 45 percent of the local constituency vote in 1986 while winning 66 percent of the seats, but its share fell in 1989—to 30.7 of the vote and to 28 percent of seats.

In the national constituency, the LDP has been at a serious disadvantage. Prior to 1983, 100 Councillors were elected in a nationwide constituency in which each voter cast only a single, nontransferable vote. Every three years, half of these seats are up for election. In 1989, the LDP captured only 30.0 percent of these seats. The reasons for the LDP weakness could be found in the party's lack of grass-roots organization and its inability to organize its supporters to vote in an efficient manner. The JCP, for example, divided the country among its disciplined local organizations and assigned each specific candidate to a certain region, thus concentrating the votes for individual candidates in certain parts of the nation. The Kōmeitō followed a similar strategy, as did the JSP in the 1977 elections. However, the LDP had to rely on its general vote-gathering power, with the result that a large number of votes were wasted for a handful of very popular candidates.[6] Each of the smaller parties won seat proportions in excess of their vote proportions in the 1974 upper house national constituency. In 1977, the success of the smaller parties in this favorable environment encouraged new political parties to field candidates in the national constituency. They included the NLC for the first time, the Socialist Citizens League (formed by the late former JSP Vice-Chairman Eda Saburō), the United Progressive Liberals, and the Japan Women's party. Hence the nature of Japan's multimember districts in both chambers of the national Diet and in almost every level of prefectural and local politics encouraged a proliferation of political parties in much the same manner as a formal proportional representation system would have done. The year 1977 finally confirmed the end of the "one-and-one-half" or "1955 party system"; certainly the conducive environment of the multimember districts is the most important structural support for Japan's multiparty era.

THE MALAPPORTIONMENT PROBLEM

On April 14, 1976, the Japanese Supreme Court issued a decision that initially appeared to have the potential to radically alter the postwar patterns of the nation's politics. The court's 8-to-7 decision ruled that the allocation of lower house seats was unconstitutional because of malapportionment, which denied equal rights to urban voters as guaranteed by the Japanese constitution. The case was brought to the courts by a group of voters from the Tokyo "bedroom" prefecture of Chiba and was the first challenge to the malapportionment problem, found in both houses of the Diet, to reach the Supreme Court. Normally the Japanese judicial system, especially the Supreme Court, has been extremely reluctant to become involved in any case affecting the political party system. However, the combination of powerful postwar migratory patterns from rural to urban sectors of the nation and the reluctance of the ruling LDP to adjust the resulting imbalances forced the court to consider such a case.[7]

Since World War II, the Japanese population has shifted from 25 million urban people and 50 million rural people to 82 million urban people and 38 million rural people, with nearly a third of the population jammed into a metropolitan band consisting, for the most part, of Tokyo, Ōsaka, and Nagoya.

TABLE 2.3
Reapportionment in the HR prior to the 1986 elections

Constituency		*No. Seats in 1983*	*No. Seats in 1986*	*Change*
Hokkaido	1	5	6	+1
Akita	2	4	3	(-1)
Yamagata	2	4	3	(-1)
Saitama	2	3	4	+1
Saitama	4	3	4	+1
Chiba	1	4	5	+1
Chiba	4	3	4	+1
Tokyo	11	4	5	+1
Kanagawa	3	3	4	+1
Niigata	2	4	3	(-1)
Niigata	4	3	2	(-1)
Ishikawa	2	3	2	(-1)
Ōsaka	3	4	5	+1
Hyōgo	5	3	2	(-1)
Kagoshima		3	2	(-1)
Totals		53	54	+1

Source: Compiled by author.

The Home Affairs Ministry reported that during the first nine years of the 1970s, the population increased in large and ordinary cities by 33 and 18 percent respectively, whereas the national population increased by 10.4 percent. During the same period, the population of Japanese towns and villages declined by 7.7 percent.

As stipulated in the Public Offices Election Law, the Diet must adjust the numbers of Diet members in each electoral district so that they are proportionate to the population size after each five-year census. But the law is not equipped with the mechanism to deal with such regular reapportionments; moreover, for reasons of political advantage, the conservatives have refused to reapportion the Diet completely. Instead, they have relied on partial adjustments, such as the addition of new seats to urban constituencies, when forced by occasional public and political pressures. Nineteen seats were added in 1964, and an additional 20 increased the total to 511 House of Representatives seats in the 1976 election. Most recently, prior to the 1986 HR elections, seats in 8 constituencies were increased and in 7 decreased, for a net gain of 1 seat and a new total of 512. Under these adjustments, the first 6-member HR district was created in Hokkaidō, and four 2-seat districts were newly established (see Table 2.3).

Despite this most recent change, however, a serious problem remains. The problem becomes obvious when a comparison is made of the results from the 1990 HR elections. Thirteen candidates failed to win a seat, although their vote totals exceeded 100,000, whereas a JCP candidate in Tokyo's eight district won a seat with only 44,154 votes. The surprise is that it was an urban district, not the usual rural district, that had the winner with the fewest votes.

TABLE 2.4
Malapportionment in the House of Representatives (registered voters per Diet seat)

	Ten Most Underrepresented Districts		
Ranking	*District*	*Number of Diet members*	*Voters per Diet members (A)*
1	Kanagawa 4	4	336,061
2	Chiba 4	4	325,408
3	Saitama 1	3	307,340
4	Saitama 5	3	304,400
5	Tokyo 7	4	300,995
6	Kanagawa 3	4	297,572
7	Hiroshima 1	3	296,213
8	Ōsaka 5	4	295,114
9	Tokyo 10	3	289,943
10	Fukuoka 1	5	289,106
Best Apportioned	Shizuoka 2	5	177,479

		Ten Most Overrepresented Districts		
	District	*Seats*	*Voters per Diet member (B)*	*Ratio A/B*
1	Miyazaki 2	3	105,682	3.18
2	Miyagi 2	4	105,855	3.07
3	Anami Islands	1	105,893	2.90
4	Nagano 3	4	106,589	2.86
5	Ōita 2	3	107,833	2.79
6	Mie 2	4	107,849	2.76
7	Kumamoto 2	5	109,517	2.70
8	Iwate 2	4	110,326	2.67
9	Fukushima 2	5	110,333	2.63
10	Wakayama 2	3	110,376	2.62

Note: National average is approximately 170,000 registered voters per Diet Member.

Source: Data adapted from *Political Handbook.* Figures as of February 18, 1990.

Despite the curious 1990 result, the metropolitan prefectures and their adjacent "bedroom" prefectures have been the primary victims of the failure of LDP politicians to carry out their legal responsibilities to reapportion the Diet fairly. Kawagawa prefecture, adjacent to Tokyo, has the dubious honor of containing the most underrepresented constituency in Japan. In 1990, its fourth district contained 336,061 persons per Diet member, whereas the most overrepresented district, Miyazaki's second, had only 105,682 persons per Diet member—a ratio of 3.18 to one (Table 2.4). When the present electoral system was established in 1947, the apportionment of Diet members to population was generally considered fair because it reflected the heavily rural nature of the Japanese population in the early postwar years. Of course, the urban population grew tremendously during the 1950s and 1960s, but the seat apportionment still largely reflects the bygone era.

It is also clear that the major losers of this lower house malapportionment are the citizens of urban and metropolitan areas as well as the smaller political parties that gather most of their support in the large cities. The *Asahi Shimbun*, in its analysis of lower house malapportionment, concluded in 1976 that a fair reapportionment would add 67 seats to urban constituencies and subtract an equal number from the rural areas.[8] Currently, urban voters are discriminated against as a result of the rural bias of the Diet. This bias can be seen in LDP public policies, which are geared to benefit the agricultural sectors in such basic areas as rice production subsidies and special arrangements to protect domestic beef producers—all at the expense of the urban consumer. The smaller opposition parties are disadvantaged by malapportionment in that they have fewer seats to compete for in urban areas, where most of their strength can be found. Kōmeitō, DSP, JCP, and JSP all score their highest percentages in the twenty-three metropolitan constituencies. Ironically, the JSP now appears to be a truly national party, winning about 20 percent of the total votes in urban constituencies but scoring slightly better than that 20 percent rate in the rural part of the nation. Meanwhile, in 1980 the LDP won a respectable 32.9 pecent of the metropolitan votes but obtained more than 70.4 percent of the votes in the rural constituencies.[9] In 1976 the LDP and JSP won 225 of the 275 rural House of Representatives seats but could win only 79 of the 139 urban seats. The *Asahi Shimbun* established that if the lower house was fairly apportioned, the LDP would suffer a new loss of 27 seats and the JSP a loss of 7 seats, whereas the Kōmeitō, JCP, and DSP would gain 12, 19, and 2, respectively. Thus the major political parties most victimized by malapportionment are the two urban-based ones, the JCP and the Kōmeitō.[10]

Tawara Kotarō, a former editorial writer for *Sankei Shimbun* and political commentator for Fuji Television, has argued that the "real cause of Japan's political problems is the odd system of medium-sized districts. Meaningful political reform won't be possible, nor will any broad-based coalition work out, if this system is left intact."[11] However, one reason significant reforms have not been implemented is the low levels of public support for such changes. A *Mainichi Shimbun* poll published in February 1990 indicated that 29 percent of the public was content with the current 3:1 imbalance in HR districts; about half (46 percent) wanted the imbalance reduced to 2:1; and only 15 percent wanted it reduced to 1:1.[12] The public is also uncertain about the proposed reforms in the size of election districts. Another *Mainichi Shimbun* poll published in February 1990 indicated that 40 percent thought the existing medium-sized constituencies were the best type; 10 percent wanted a system of all small constituencies; and 23 percent supported the proposed small districts plus PR system. The remaining 27 percent supported other ideas or had no opinion.[13]

Even more serious in terms of the degree of malapportionment is the problem of the imbalance of local constituency seats in the House of Councillors. Of the 252 Councillors, 152 are elected in local districts based on prefectural boundaries, which elect from 2 to 8 members per district; half that number stand for election every three years. When the election system was first implemented in 1947, the Councillors were apportioned among the prefectures in proportion to the population distribution recorded in the 1946 census. Since the initial allocations, only one change has been made—namely, the addition of a pair of seats for Okinawa prefecture in 1970, when Japan regained political control of the islands. As in the lower house, the

TABLE 2.5
Malapportionment in the House of Councillors (local constituencies, by number of registered voters per Councillor)

Most Underrepresented Constituencies			*Most Overrepresented Constituencies*		
Prefecture	*Voters per Councillor*	*Ratio*	*Prefecture*	*Voters per Councillor*	*Ratio*
1. Kanagawa	1,431,227	6.25	1. Tottori	229,034	1.00
2. Tokyo	1,123,882	4.91	2. Shimane	294,861	1.29
3. Saitama	1,103,109	4.82	3. Fukui	299,525	1.31
4. Ōsaka	1,050,617	4.59	4. Yamanashi	313,423	1.37
5. Chiba	976,334	4.26	5. Tokushima	313,853	1.37

Source: Adapted by author from data in *Political Handbook*, 1990.

massive shift of population to the cities has created a serious imbalance that greatly favors the rural prefectures (see Table 2.5). In the 1989 HC elections, an LDP candidate in Ōsaka failed to win a seat with 701,588 votes, whereas an independent backed by the JSP won a seat in Tottori prefecture with only 180,123 votes. As of July 1989, the ratio between the most underrepresented prefecture, Kanagawa, and the most overrepresented, Tottori, was 6.25 to 1. In Kanagawa, the heavily urbanized area to the south of Tokyo, each Councillor represented 1,431,227 voters, whereas in rural Tottori each Councillor represented over 229,034. Until the 1989 HC elections, the LDP almost completely dominated the rural prefectural constituencies, which elected only a single upper house member in each election. The chronic and serious malapportionment affecting both chambers helps perpetuate the LDP's continuing domination of the HR and until 1989 helped maintain the LDP's majority in the HC.

THE POLITICS OF REFORM

The reform of election laws involves issues that go far beyond the problem of adjusting seat allocation to fairly represent different groups or classes of voters. Such reforms involve the very survival of political parties as well as the preservation of political power and, therefore, are adopted with utmost care and consideration regarding their political consequences. Fortuitously for the LDP, it has been assisted in its desire to delay such reforms by the nature of the Supreme Court's malapportionment decision. In contrast to the U.S. malapportionment decisions of the 1960s, the Japanese court did not require the legislative branch to reapportion within a specific period of time; rather, it indicated that it was the responsibility of the Diet and the cabinet to produce a constitutional law.[14] As noted previously, a number of voter groups attempted on several occasions to force the Diet to reapportion before the December 1983 elections, but in each case their suits were rejected by the lower courts as inappropriate for consideration on the grounds that reapportionment was a legislative rather than a judicial task.

As a result of the LDP's unwillingness to reapportion either house of the Diet following the 1976 Supreme Court decision, several lawsuits were filed by citizen groups in efforts to force the courts to act more decisively.

Following the June 1980 double elections, seventeen new lawsuits were filed. Four suits filed after the 1976 elections produced high court decisions—two for each house. In September 1978, the Tokyo High Court delivered contradictory decisions in two lower house cases. The ninth bench ruled on a case brought by plaintiffs from Tokyo, Chiba, and Kanagawa and declared the malapportionment unconstitutional. The three-judge panel argued that since the overpopulated urban districts enjoyed cultural and economic advantages, the underpopulated rural districts should have a compensatory advantage in the form of overrepresentation in the Diet. Two days later, the fifteenth bench of the same court ruled in a different suit that the malapportionment was unconstitutional. Several suits were filed in an attempt to stop the 1979 and 1980 general elections, but the courts dismissed them. In December 1980, the Tokyo High Court again ruled that the 1980 general elections were unconstitutional, but it rejected a request to void the election results. Presiding Judge Yoshioka Jusumu ruled that a 2-to-1 ratio in population differences between the most overrepresented and the most underrepresented constituencies would be constitutional.[15] In a High Court decision in 1976, however, the upper house malapportionment ratio of 5.26 to 1 was declared constitutional. It is clear that the Supreme Court will have to sort out these conflicting rulings and decide if it wants to place its prestige on the line in a confrontation with the LDP.

On September 18, 1985, the Supreme Court ruling on cases from Tokyo, Ōsaka, Sapporo, and Hiroshima concluded that the December 1983 general elections were unlawful because the Diet seats were distributed so disproportionately as to contravene the constitutional guarantee of equality under the law. This decision went beyond the Court's initial ruling in this area in 1976 inasmuch as it labeled the table of Diet seats now effective as unconstitutional; moreover, although it did not declare the 1983 elections unconstitutional, it indicated that if the Diet did not correct the problem, it may declare as unconstitutional the next such elections.

There were several courses the LDP could have followed regarding the question of electoral system reforms. Initially, it decided to do nothing for a time and then to evaluate the new political situation following the 1977 House of Councillors elections. In October 1976 the Election Research Council of the LDP reported its electoral reform recommendations. It suggested that the LDP as a party should support the transformation of the House of Representatives electoral system from medium-sized constituencies to one of small-sized constituencies, with some seats being awarded by means of proportional representation. The council also recommended that the national constituency of the House of Councillors be changed to a system of proportional representation. In late May 1977, the LDP submitted to the Diet its plan for the reform of upper house elections—a plan that specifically called for reform of the PR national constituency and a shift of 4 seats total from Hokkaidō and Tochigi prefectures to Tokyo and Kanagawa prefectures in the local constituencies. This proposal countered the opposition parties' proposal for the addition of 18 seats to the urban prefectures.[16] Clearly, the

LDP response was not an acceptable solution to the opposition's demands for fair reapportionment; however, the LDP insisted on the simultaneous reform of both problems, and, as the *Asahi Shimbun* indicated, the LDP goal seemed to be the "mutual suicide of both proposals." Conservative arguments against reapportionment have included the point that Diet members should represent actual voters rather than population size. During the 1990 general elections, the voting rate of Shimane was 86.93 percent and that of Ōsaka's first District only 59.71 percent. Another argument has been the idea of "qualitative equality," whereby the disadvantaged rural areas would be compensated by electoral advantages. Finally, many have argued the practical point that space limitations preclude increasing the number of lower house seats beyond the existing 512 and that a shifting of seats would mean that Diet members in rural areas would have to give up their seats. But no Diet member would voluntarily vote to do so, and there are few opportunities for governmental appointments for these out-of-work politicians. On the other hand, it should be noted that every five years, the various local assemblies adjust their seats to fit population shifts. For example, the 1985 Tokyo Metropolitan Assembly elections were held under a new reapportionment plan in which seats were shifted from the overrepresented districts to the fastest growing parts of Tokyo. The LDP won a big victory in these elections, whereas the JSP continued its long-term decline in its seat totals in this most important prefectural assembly in Japan. The LDP success in Tokyo thus indicates that a shift in the Diet seats from the rural to the urban areas would not necessarily seriously injure the LDP. It is clearly the most powerful party in Tokyo and in such bedroom prefectures as Chiba.

The LDP's most recent response to the House of Representatives malapportionment problem was the submission in 1985 of the 8-7 Proposal, which provided for the deletion of seats from seven overrepresented districts (Hyōgo 5, Kagoshima 3, Ishikawa 2, Niigata 2 and 4, Akita 2, and Yamagata 2) and for the addition of seats to eight underrepresented districts (Chiba 4, Kanagawa 3, Saitama 2, Tokyo 11, Chiba 1, Hokkaidō 1, Ōsaka 3, and Saitama 4). However, when the new census reports were issued in the fall of 1985, it was clear that even the 8-7 Proposal was but a small step toward the solution of the lower house malapportionment problem.

On August 19, 1982, the LDP succeeded in passing a major electoral reform bill through the Diet—a bill that, in fact, could be considered the first major electoral reform under the 1947 postwar constitution. Beginning with the 1983 elections, the 100 national constituency seats of the House of Councillors were—and continue to be—elected under a proportional representation system. The PR system uses the d'Hondt method, which requires voters to cast their national constituency votes for a party, not for individual candidates as in previous elections. As all votes must be cast for parties, the independents in the upper house are forced to join together in party slates in order to have a place on the ballot. If a party is to earn a ballot spot, it must have one of the following: (1) five Diet members, (2) 4 percent or more of the total popular vote in the last national election, or (3) more than ten candidates (local and national constituencies) in an upper house election. The deposit for national constituency candidates has been raised to 4 million yen (i.e., double the amount for local constituency candidates). Each participating party will be required to form a list of candidates who will be elected to Councillor seats based on the percentage of the total vote cast for each party.[17] In a computer simulation of the 1980 results using the new system, it was estimated that the LDP (+1) and independents/minor parties (+5) would probably be the big winners under the new system, whereas the Kōmeitō (−3), JSP (−2), and DSP (−1) would likely be the big losers.[18]

The adoption of the PR system in the upper house was largely supported by the Japanese media as a means of reducing the skyrocketing costs of election campaigning in the national constituency.[19] The *Mainichi Shimbun* described the PR system as "epoch making" and suggested that it would have "a revolutionary effect on the traditional Japanese election system."[20] This reform was strongly supported by the LDP and JSP—both of which saw it as a golden opportunity to reduce campaign costs. The LDP has estimated that it spent 7 billion yen on its 1980 national constituency campaigns, whereas the JSP's main support organization, Sōhyō, has estimated that it spent 300 million yen per candidate in 1980. The PR reform was strongly opposed by the Kōmeitō and the JCP—the best-organized parties in such election campaigns.[21]

When the first PR national constituency elections were held in 1983, the newspaper predictions were only partially realized. The LDP captured only 35.33 percent of the vote and won 19 seats of the 50 contested. These totals represented declines of over 7 percent (2 seats) as compared to its 1980 non-PR results. In fact, the only big winners in the 1983 House of Councillors PR elections were the JCP (+2) and a number of new, single-issue mini-parties, which collectively won 4 seats plus the pair of seats won by the NLC and the SDF. The Kōmeitō and the JSP either held the same number of seats or slightly declined in seat totals despite significant increases in their party vote percentages. All in all, none of the major parties (except the JCP) were happy with the results.

In the 1986 PR races for 50 HC seats, the LDP won 22 seats on 38.5 percent of the vote; the JSP, 9; the CGP, 7; the JCP, 5; and the DSP, 3. Four seats were won by minor parties. When the LDP's PR vote in 1989 fell to 27.3 percent, its seats declined to 15; the JSP won 20 seats; the CGP, 6; the DSP, 2; and minor parties, 3. Perhaps the biggest surprise in the 1989 elections was the victory of a popular professional wrestler, Antonio Inoki, on the Sports Party ticket, which advocated "peace through sports."

The real battle to watch for in the future is the one over the reforms proposed for the House of Representatives elections. The LDP has no intention of responding to the Supreme Court's decision with a scheme of complete reapportionment of the lower house districts. At best, if agreement cannot be reached regarding more fundamental changes in the law, the LDP will suggest the addition of more seats for the urban areas (just as it has done twice in the past). The conservatives have found that they have an excellent chance to win 25 percent of any new seats assigned to the urban districts. In the 1976 election, for example, the LDP won 5 of the additional 20 seats and might have won several more but for the advent of the NLC.[22] The LDP, despite the strengths of the JCP and the Kōmeitō, is still the single most powerful party even in the metropolitan areas. In Tokyo in 1990, the LDP won 18 out of 44 seats; in Ōsaka, it captured 8 out of 27. Hence the LDP's best strategy is to continue its pattern of incremental additions to urban districts while ignoring demands to reduce the number of Diet members in their rural, overrepresented strongholds. Moreover, since a major portion of JSP Diet seats also comes from rural prefectures, both of the largest parties are favored by a policy of maintaining the current imbalance for as long as possible.

More likely to occur in the next decade is a complete change in the electoral devices for HR elections. The Japanese have tried all the major types of election systems at one time or another, with the exception of proportional representation. It has long been discussed in LDP closed meetings that the best way to preserve conservative control of government when the party's vote is no longer sufficient to produce absolute seat majorities is through adoption of a single-seat district system. This method was first proposed in the postwar era by the Hatoyama coalition cabinet, which introduced just such a small-constituency plan into the Diet in the 1950s; but the plan was tabled after significant opposition threatened to halt more important legislation in the Diet. Revived during the 1960s and again tabled, it was proposed by the Tanaka government in 1973 in a somewhat different form. The Tanaka scheme, which called for a combination of single-seat districts and PR seats, was similar to the proposals that had emerged from a series of governmental Electoral System Councils during the 1960s and early 1970s.

All of the opposition parties were strongly opposed to the single-seat constituency reform. The JSP and JCP party organs, in particular, called for the "complete crushing of the minor constituency system," terming it a threat to democracy and saying that the "LDP plan aimed at one-party despotism."[23] At that time a new political word referring to Tanaka Kakuei's reapportionment plan, *Kaku-mandering*, appeared in Japan. The conservatives have played an interesting game with regard to their support of major reform in the election system. When the opposition parties have demanded that the government reapportion the Diet seats fairly, the LDP has replied that it will also change to a single-seat system, which all understand will eliminate many members of the opposition.

In 1990 the LDP received the report of a special election reform study committee, which recommended a radical revision in the HR election system. The most significant reforms called for a change to the small-constituency system of 300 HR members elected from single-member districts, plus an additional 171 HR members elected from a PR system based on regions. Under the system, Japan is divided into 11 regions (e.g., Hokkaidō, Tōhoku, and Tokyo), with each region assigned a number of HR members based on population. In general, the LDP and JSP supported the change; the JCP and CGP strongly opposed the idea.

The *Yomiuri Shimbun*'s analysis of the impact of a similar plan to have 301 single-district seats and 200 PR seats based on the 1990 general election voting results suggested that the LDP would increase its seats from 275 to 390 (115 in PR and 275 in the single-member districts). The JSP would fall to 80 seats (54/26); the CGP to 13 (13/0); the JCP to 11 (11/0); the DSP to 6 (6/0); and all other political organizations to 1 seat. However, if the voting patterns of the 1989 HC elections are used with the PR/single-member district system, the JSP soars to 334 seats (88/246) and the LDP drops to only 123 seats (68/55). The LDP approved this draft plan in late November 1990 and planned to introduce these proposed election system changes into the Diet in January 1991.[24] Although Prime Minister Kaifu has pledged his support for them, one would have to hesitate before predicting these reforms will be implemented soon. The Election System Council has proposed more than a half dozen such major reform plans in the last thirty years, and not one has been fully implemented.

THE POLITICS OF CAMPAIGN REGULATION

Japanese election campaigns are conducted under a set of comprehensive laws deemed to be the most restrictive in the democratic world.[25] When the Home Ministry promulgated campaign rules in 1924, it acted under the assumption that the nation's voters were not sufficiently sophisticated to evaluate effectively the appeals of politicians and thus might be easy targets for the rising Socialist movement that so worried Japanese leaders in the early part of the century.[26] Almost every type of campaign activity that would involve the voter in any but the most superficial way was prohibited. In particular, door-to-door campaigning, signature drives, polling, providing food or drink, mass meetings, parades, unscheduled speeches, multiple campaign vehicles, and candidate-produced literature are illegal in contemporary Japanese campaigns. Instead, a candidate's contacts with his or her potential voters must, by law, be channeled through a limited number of government-produced postcards, posters placed on official signboards, a maximum of five government-paid newspaper ads of a specific size and content, several television and radio announcements, a number of joint speech meetings, and government-financed handbills and brochures.

Many of these restrictions are commonly flouted by the candidates, especially those restrictions regarding the official campaigning period and the provision of food and drink to potential voters.[27] For instance, the House of Councillors campaign period (officially only twenty-three days long) concluded in 1977 on July 10, but illegal posters had been put up by the middle of February—more than five months before the 1977 elections. Candidates have also been known to demonstrate tremendous ingenuity in evading the intent of the campaign restrictions. Some potential candidates have increased their contacts with voters by holding political study meetings with increasing frequency as an election draws near. Others have sent telegrams to constituents announcing the end of a Diet session, communicating winter or summer greetings, or expressing congratulations for almost any kind of event. Still others have simply ignored the restrictions, as in 1975, when the prohibitions of donations by campaigners prompted one LDP candidate to say, "We go on going just as before as common sense dictates."

Among the Western democracies, only Japan and South Korea have such a ban on canvassing. In 1950 the Hiroshima High Court ruled the POEL ban on door-to-door canvassing unconstitutional because it ostensibly violated Article 21, which guarantees freedom of expression. Such a ban has been declared unconstitutional by lower district courts on nine occasions since the mid-1960s. However, the Supreme Court declared the ban constitutional in a decision on a Tokyo case in June 1980. One poll conducted prior to the 1979 general elections indicated that 90 percent of the candidates supported the removal of the ban on canvassing.[28]

The campaign restrictions have done little to reduce the costs of election campaigning but have had other serious outcomes. The combined effect of the restricted nature of a typical campaign has been to prevent Japanese voters from becoming involved to any significant degree in a politician's campaign. The voters are expected to be passive and noninvolved—mere spectators watching the election as though it were a *Noh* play, without excitement. As survey after survey has produced evidence of such low voter involvement and interest in Japanese elections, there is general agreement among Japanese political scientists that the unreasonable campaign restrictions should be liberalized to facilitate greater participation.

The current system also operates to protect the incumbents from successful challenges. As most candidate-voter contacts must be channeled through official media routes, new names have little chance to gain the name recognition or issue familiarity necessary to defeat an incumbent. And since most Diet members are also members of the LDP and JSP, the restrictions obviously work to protect these two parties. Moreover, the laws have been adjusted to establish environments conducive to the success to the major parties. Changes enacted in 1975 focused on the question of distributing campaign literature or party newspaper "extra" editions primarily at train stations or department stores. An alliance developed between the LDP and JSP, which favored the restriction of these types of campaigning frequently used by the JCP and the Kōmeitō. The reasons behind this split of opinion were quite clear: Whereas the JCP and the Kōmeitō had sufficient staff to utilize this technique effectively, the LDP and JSP did not have the volunteers to compete with the Communists and the Buddhists. In another proposed reform, the LDP has indicated a desire to restrict or abolish the joint speech meetings requirements—one of the three pillars of Japanese-style election campaigns. (The other pillars are the official elections bulletins and the candidates' radio and television broadcasts.) In particular, the LDP members seem to object to the time required and to the catcalls and angry shouts that often invade such events. Both the JSP and JCP are opposed to any such limiting of joint speech meetings, however.

TABLE 2.6
Expansion of suffrage in Japan

Year	*Qualification* Tax Payment	Minimum Age	Sex	*Eligible Voters as Percentage of Population*	*Number of Eligible Voters*
1889	¥15	25	M	1.1%	450,000
1900	¥10	25	M	2.1%	980,000
1919	¥3	25	M	5.4%	3,060,000
1925	--	25	M	20.0%	12,400,000
1945	--	20	--	--	36,870,000
1983	--	20	--	--	84,252,608
1990	--	20	--	--	90,322,908

Source: Adapted from *Facts and Figures on Japan* (Tokyo: Foreign Press Center of Japan, 1980). Updated by author.

One consequence of the government's attempts to regulate campaign behavior has been the reduction of public respect for politicians, who are constantly observed to be breaking and evading the election laws. All in all, then, the campaign restrictions have not been effective. The costs of elections have not been reduced to reasonable levels, and the restriction of the use of media in campaigns has forced politicians to revert to even more expensive, and often illegal, means of communication.[29] Essentially, the experience of these laws has been such as to demonstrate the futility of attempting to prevent the necessary communication between candidates and voters.

THE EXPANSION OF THE JAPANESE ELECTORATE

When the first House of Representatives elections were held on July 1, 1890, suffrage was restricted to male citizens 25 years of age and older who had paid 15 yen or more in taxes for at least a year. With these restrictions, only about 450,000 males were qualified to vote—a mere 1.13 percent of the total population of 44.5 million. Among the electorate, 93.91 percent voted in that first election. An amendment in 1900 enfranchised all male citizens paying annual taxes of 10 yen or more and thus increased the electorate to 2.2 percent of the population. Following another small increase in 1919, a major change occurred in 1925 when the tax requirement was eliminated, thus enlarging the eligible electorate by 400 percent to a total of 20 percent of the population. Female suffrage came after World War II, and the current voter age of 20 years old was established in 1945 (see Table 2.6).

Because the Japanese government assumes the responsibility of ensuring that voters are properly registered, nearly all eligible citizens are registered to vote. As of February 1990, 90.3 million Japanese were on the voting rolls, out of a total population of about 121 million persons.[30] Voter turnout in national elections has usually been in the 65 to 80 percent range, but in prefectural and local elections it is considerably lower.

The second component of the election laws that attempts to control the nature of Japanese political parties and campaigns is the Political Funds Control Law. This law has been much discussed in Japan during the last decade as scandal after scandal has highlighted its inability to control the corruption that seems to pervade Japanese campaigns. In the next chapter, we will examine the major weaknesses of this law and its effects on the Japanese party system.

NOTES

1. See Law No. 100 of April 15, 1950, revised in 1975. For a summary of this law in English, see *Election System in Japan* (Tokyo: Ministry of Home Affairs, 1985). The author wishes to acknowledge the invaluable assistance given to him in this project by Japanese scholars in the field of electoral law. Both Professor Nishihira Sigeki of Sophia University and Professor Sakagami Nobuo of Tokyo shared with me their recent research findings and special insights into Japanese election laws and devices. The helpful assistance of Professor Kyōgoku Junichi of Tokyo University during my 1975 research trip was also much appreciated. The most useful Japanese language studies on this subject are Sakagami Nabuo's *Nihon Senkyo Seidoron* (Tokyo: Seiji Kōhō, 1972) and Nishihira Sigeki's *Nihon No Senkyo* (Tokyo: Shiseido, 1969). My research was supported by a grant from the Research Committee of the University of Utah.

2. Kiyoaki Murata, "An Election Reform," *Japan Times* (May 14, 1982).

3. In the years from 1963 to 1972, the LDP was remarkably consistent in capturing lower house seats in all three district magnitudes. The party captured 61 percent of the seats in three-member districts; 59 percent of the seats in four-member districts; and 56 percent of the seats in five-member districts. The main rival, the JSP, won about 26 percent of the seats in each type of district over that period. See Nishihira Shigeki, *Nihon No Senkyo.*

4. In the 1980 elections the LDP officially endorsed 310 candidates, whereas the JSP ran only 149. The JCP supported 129 candidates, Kōmeitō, DSP, NLC, and the SDF ran 64, 50, 25, and 5 candidates, respectively, in carefully selected districts. Thus the LDP is seen by the voters as the only party that offers a sufficient number of candidates that it can govern without resort to coalition. The DSP's case is interesting in that its total vote percentage decreased in 1976 but its seat total increased. The explanation is simply that the party cut back on the number of official candidates, thus reducing its national total vote but also concentrating its resources in fewer districts. It was also during the 1976 election that all six parties were represented in only 10 of the 130 districts and the "old five parties" were in competition in only 45 constituencies.

5. Changes in the Political Offices Control Law enacted in 1975 tripled the deposit money that a candidate must forfeit if he does not receive a certain percentage of the total votes cast in his district. The deposits are now 1 million yen (US$5,880) for House candidates and local district candidates for the upper house, whereas national constituency candidates must poll at least as many votes to equal one-fifth of the total obtained by dividing the total vote by the number of seats in the district. In 1980, 146 candidates lost their deposits, including 60 JCP candidates. This deposit system is another method designed to limit the degree of competition in the Japanese elections.

6. The difficulties faced by the LDP in the national constituency can be demonstrated by the case of Miyata Teru, who won a seat with 2.59 million votes in 1974, although 7 LDP candidates with over 500,000 votes apiece failed to secure seats. The LDP is unable to regionally apportion its votes (as the JCP has done so successfully), but the JSP and DSP can use their affiliated labor unions or religious organizations (e.g., Kōmeitō) to allocate their votes effectively.

7. For a study of the postwar small-district system and malapportionment in Japan, see Shimizu Keihachiro, *Sengo Nihon no Senkyo no Jittai* [The real picture of elections in postwar Japan] (Tokyo: Kokin Shoin, 1958).

8. *Asahi Shimbun* (December 8, 1976).

9. In 1980, the LDP won 33 percent of the vote in twenty-three metropolitan constituencies, followed by Kōmeitō's 19 percent. The LDP's vote percentage in city, semiurban, semirural, and rural constituencies increased to 61 percent, 50 percent, 66 percent, and 70 percent, respectively. See *Mainichi Shimbun* (June 24, 1980).

10. According to the *Asahi Shimbun*, if the results of the 1980 general elections of the House of Representatives had been reapportioned on the basis of a plan suggested by the Kanagawa citizens' group, the estimated seat totals would have been as follows: LDP, 265; JSP, 102; CGP, 41; DSP, 32; JCP, 36; NLC, 17; and SDF, 2. See *Asahi Shimbun* (January 16–18, 1981).

11. *Chūō Kōron* (April 1990), pp. 128–141.

12. *Mainichi Shimbun* (February 2, 1990).

13. *Mainichi Shimbun* (February 10, 1990).

14. This was only the third such unconstitutional declaration, and it overturned four previous decisions in this area. The court did not choose to define "equality of votes," but the meaning inferred by some was that a 2:1 ratio between the most overrepresented and underrepresented districts would be considered legal. The court also said that population-change reapportionment should be carried out "within a reasonable period of time" but failed to define what that phrase meant. "Jijo–Hanketsu" (conditional judgment) was the description given the 1976 Supreme Court decision by Professor Satō Isao from Jōchi University in an analysis of that landmark decision in *Asahi Journal* (April 30, 1976).

15. *Japan Times* (December 24, 1980).

16. See Sakagami Nobuo, "Direction of Revision of Election Law After the Supreme Court's Decision," *Seiji Kōhō*, no. 2 (1976), p. 59. There have been several such plans for upper house reapportionment, including one offered by four opposition parties for the addition of 26 new seats to the urban local districts. This plan reduces the ratio of malapportionment to a near acceptable 2.75:1, whereas the LDP plan of shifting four seats puts the ratio at 4.75:1.

17. *Yomiuri Shimbun* (August 19, 1982).

18. *Kohoku Shimbun* (August 19, 1982).

19. See the LDP's *Liberal Star* of September 10, 1980; the *Asahi Shimbun* editorial of July 31, 1980; and the *Daily Yomiuri* editorial of May 31, 1980.

20. See the *Mainichi Shimbun* editorial of July 4, 1982.

21. *Asahi Evening News* (July 15, 1982).

22. In fact when additional seats have been added to urban constituencies (indeed, 20 seats were added in the 1976 elections), the LDP has managed to secure a respectable proportion of these new seats. Of the new seats in 1976 the LDP won 5, and if we include the conservative NLC victors in the conservative camp, exactly half of the total were so grouped. Of the 20 seats available, the JSP won 7, the NLC, Kōmeitō, and DSP won 5, 3, and 3, respectively; and the JCP lost a net of 3 seats owing to the splitting of larger-magnitude districts into two new districts.

23. Kawamura Toshi, "Intrigue and Background of Tanaka Cabinet," Toriyama Sadao, "LDP Plan Aimed at One Party Despotism," and "Parliamentary Democracy and Small Constituency System," *Zenei* (June 1973); Itō Shigeru, "For the Complete Crushing of the Minor Constituency System," *Shakaitō* (July 1973).

24. *Yomiuri Shimbun* (April 27, 1990). Also see *Yomiuri Shimbun* (November 28, 1990).

25. The evolution of the campaign restrictions has been well reported by Gerald Curtis. The initial law after World War II allowed a party to engage in political activities during campaigns as long as those actions were not aimed at securing votes for the party's candidate. Revised in 1952 and 1954, the law prohibited all political party activities during the campaign period. Parties could legally participate in campaigns only as third parties, similar to voters. Another revision in 1962 made it possible for parties to participate in election campaigns to secure votes for candidates in general but not for a particular candidate. For example, a party could display posters announcing a speech by one of its candidates, but it could not mention the candidate on the poster. A more recent revision in 1975 significantly expanded the range of permissible party activities during the campaign period. If a party met certain minimum size requirements, it could display posters asking for support in an election. Restrictions on handbills were also liberalized. Party leaders may mention their candidates' names at speech meetings and endorse them. Parties can also advertise in newspapers and on TV and radio, but the names of specific candidates may not be mentioned. Gerald L. Curtis, *The Japanese Way of Politics* (New York: Columbia University Press, 1988), pp. 166–167.

The decisions as to which days will be election days and how the voters will indicate their candidate preferences are uniquely Japanese in nature. Election days fall on Sundays in Japan. Because Sunday is a holiday, primary and junior high schools can be used as voting sites; moreover, it is assumed that more citizens will be able to vote on a Sunday. But the choice of which Sunday is usually left up to the politicians. Frequently, the old Japanese lunar calendar will be consulted to ascertain which Sundays are "taian" (lucky) days. Ironically, of the four Sundays considered for the 1980 elections, the LDP leaders reportedly favored July 13 over the actual election day of June 22, but they were forced to change the date after the vote of no-confidence carried. See *Daily Yomiuri* (March 14, 1980).

According to the election law, vacancies in the HC are filled by a special election called within forty days after the prefectural Elections Administration Commission receives notice of a vacancy resulting from death or resignation. Vacancies in the HR are not filled by special elections, but are left vacant until the next HR general elections. Consequently, the HC by-elections are considered referenda on government performance and politics; for example, the Aichi prefecture HC special election in fall 1990 was considered a gauge of public opinion on the proposed sending of Japanese Self-Defense Forces to Saudi Arabia during the Kuwait crisis. When the LDP candidate failed to win a big victory over the JSP candidate who made the sending of troops her major issue, this outcome and other political signs forced the government to abandon its plans.

26. Elections during the early Meiji period were often violent. Especially noteworthy were the elections of March 1894, in which one person was killed, 252 persons were wounded, and 1,075 cases of bribery were reported. See *Japan Times* (February 28, 1898).

27. Curtis notes that many of the campaign restrictions, such as the prohibition on canvassing, are ignored by a growing number of campaigners. There is no strong constituency for reform—not among the parties or in the Home Ministry—because of the practice of widespread evasions. Gerald Curtis, *The Japanese Way of Politics*, p. 171.

28. See *Japan Times* (June 17, 1980) and *Asahi Evening News* (October 6, 1979).

29. Throughout the four years preceding the 1976 general elections, the police issued 24,400 warnings of illegal campaign activities. During the actual campaign period, 991 persons were arrested and 18 others were placed on a nationwide wanted

list for election law violations. The police questioned 4,511 persons on suspicion of vote buying (the average cost per vote being between 2,000 and 3,000 yen, thus reflecting the recession occurring at the time), 281 for house-to-house visits, and 256 for illegal distribution of campaign literature.

30. *Yomiuri Shimbun* (January 16, 1983).

3

The Money Base of Japanese Politics

RONALD J. HREBENAR

Ozaki Yukio, a Japanese writer in the early Shōwa era, once noted that "the leader of a party in our country must have five qualifications: one to four are money, and the fifth one is political ability."[1] Fifty years later, it appears that very little has changed in the nature of Japanese politics. Money is still the crucial ingredient in political success. A great portion of the political activities of the major leaders of the various parties and factions is devoted to the raising of political funds. This activity became a very controversial issue in Japan as a result of the Tanaka scandal, the 1974 House of Councillors' spending excesses, the various aircraft purchase scandals, and the Recruit Cosmos scandal, in which a large number of conservative politicians were implicated. In this chapter we will examine the nature of political money (*seiji kenkin*) in Japan within the context of the law that purports to regulate this crucial activity—namely, the Political Funds Control Law (PFCL). We will also look at various fund-raising techniques in some detail and focus on the last major overhaul of the PFCL in an effort to understand the problems of political financing facing the party system.

THE POLITICAL FUNDS CONTROL LAW

As noted, the law that requires the reporting of various political funding activities is the Political Funds Control Law. A revised version of this law went into effect on January 1, 1976, during what was an apparent effort to reform some of the major weaknesses of the old reporting law. The revisions, which constituted part of the larger election-reform package discussed previously, were passed by the Diet after a bitter political battle that raged throughout the summer of 1975. The requirements for disclosure of the sources of political money were tightened by the revisions, and some of the major loopholes present in the old law were at least narrowed, if not eliminated. Under the old law, for example, less than 20 percent of the funds collected by the five parties were identified by source in the 1975 midyear disclosures. Even this small percentage is misleading, for 78 percent of the LDP funds were obtained from a collection organization, Kokumin Seiji Kyōkai, which serves merely as a funnel for collecting money from corporations for the LDP.

Only .8 percent of the JCP funds, .3 percent of the JSP funds, and none of the Kōmeitō's funds were identified by sources.[2] And the failure of disclosure becomes even more obvious when the LDP factional funding is examined. The major LDP factions led by Ōhira Masayoshi, Miki Takeo, and Fukuda Takeo provided no reports on their sources of funds. In addition, whereas the old law allowed parties and factions to cover up sources of funds by listing them as party fees, subscriptions to party organs, or "on the street" contributions, the revised law requires that all income and expenditures over 10,000 yen be reported. However, in view of the common practice in which falsified data are reported, there seems to be little hope that these new rules will make the law any less the "bamboo sieve" than it has always been.

Each fall, the annual reports on the nature of political fund-raising is released to the nation's media. Although this is the *official* report of the PFCL, in many respects it bears little relationship to reality. At the same time as the major parties' incomes are reported, the official statements of political funding are released for over 3,000 other political organizations. These include the various LDP factional organizations as well as the large "funnel" organizations that collect funds for the LDP and DSP. Overall, the various organizations reported in excess of 334 billion yen ($1.3 billion) in political contributions in 1989. (These dollar equivalents of yen are calculated at the early 1991 exchange rate of $1 = 130 yen.) The huge amounts of money spent on Japanese politics must be put into perspective, however. Japanese business, for example, reported that it spent $32 billion for entertainment and gifts (*kosaihi*) for employees and customers.

DISCLOSURES OF THE PFCL POLITICAL FUNDS REPORTS

The Japan Communist party was first again (in terms of revenue), followed by the LDP and Kōmeitō. Table 3.1 also provides the totals for the major "funnel" (fund-collecting) organizations of the LDP and the DSP. The funds from these organizations, which were donated to the parent parties, are included in the party totals in the upper half of the table.

Although many political critics contend that political fund reports are inaccurate in many significant ways, they can be useful in discerning general trends or patterns. Each of the major parties, for example, has a characteristic fund-raising pattern that tells us something about the nature of that party. The JCP's leading totals for the last dozen years certainly do not accurately reflect its fund-raising capabilities vis-à-vis the LDP. The JCP's totals (and those of the CGP as well) reflect income derived from party businesses. As production costs are usually about 80 percent of declared income, one can estimate the JCP's real income at about 4 billion yen.[3] The LDP, whose reported income is just a headquarters income, vastly underreports its real income. In addition to 24.6 billion yen in party funds, the seven factions of the LDP reported funds collected at a total of 6.39 billion yen, and ten individual politicians reported combined donations received of well over 3 billion yen. Yet however large these sums may seem, most political observers believe the real total income of the LDP is 500 percent more than reported.

Japan's major opposition party, the JSP, reported receiving 5 billion yen. In constant financial trouble, the JSP is the one party that relies most heavily on membership dues and also derives much of its income from the sale of party publications (see Table 3.2).

Kōmeitō's income is for the most part (76 percent) derived from party publications; almost all the remainder is accounted for by party member dues. The moderate DSP was the second most favored recipient of corporate Japan's political donations. Forty percent of its 1989 income came in the form of corporate donations. Its two biggest corporate backers in 1989 were Toyota and Mitsubishi Heavy Industries. The poorest party is the SDF, which largely relies on government subsidies in the form of legislature research money (600,000 yen per Diet member per month) for 40 percent of its income.

Table 3.3 lists the LDP sources of revenue in 1989 by industries. Nearly one-third of the LDP's revenue comes from the banking industry; longtime financial supporters of LDP, construction and real estate, are in second place with 15 percent. It is interesting that labor unions, thought by many to be solidly behind the JSP and DSP, provide the same amount of money for the LDP as do the giant trading companies. Curtis notes that the pattern of corporate giving changed after 1975. Previous major supporters such as the steel industry declined as contributors, and new growth industries such as consumer electronics, securities and life insurance, and local banks grew in importance as fund sources.[4]

Fund-raising totals reported by the LDP factions must be viewed with some care. In the early 1980s, both the Fukuda Takeo and Nakasone Yasuhiro factions were reporting billion-yen incomes in an effort to impress LDP Diet members with their fund-raising powers and to win the prime ministership. The Kōmoto Toshio faction, one of the party's weaker factions, had been collecting large amounts of money for the party presidency race since 1978. The Tanaka faction, the LDP's most powerful and richest in the early 1980s, was reporting low levels of fund-raising as it sought to keep a low profile while Tanaka's legal problems continued. The Tanaka faction's senior Diet members were collecting large amounts of money, but reported the amounts not by faction but by individual politicians.

Table 3.4 indicates the reported incomes of seven of the LDP factions for the 1987–1989 period. Former Prime Minister Takeshita's faction, the financial successor of the former Tanaka faction, was rocked in the late 1980s by serious political funds scandals. After the Recruit Cosmos scandal toppled

TABLE 3.1
Party revenues and expenditures, 1989 (in millions of yen)

Party	*Revenue 1989*	*Expenditure 1989*
JCP	29,888	31,430
LDP	24,616	23,399
CGP	14,942	13,925
JSP	5,550	6,080
DSP	4,225	3,554
SDF	60	61
Party Political Fund-Raising Organizations, 1989		
Kokumin Seiji Kyōkai (LDP)		12,598
Seiwa Kyōkai (DSP)		825

Source: Home Affairs Ministry, *PFCL 1989 Report* (*Asahi Shimbun*, September 14, 1990).

TABLE 3.2
General sources of party revenues, 1989, in percent

	Corporate Contributions	*Party Dues*	*Business Income*	*Other*	*Loans*
LDP	54.1	18.3	6.0	1.3	20.3
DSP	40.8	7.8	12.1	8.0	31.3
JSP	3.3	30.9	43.2	13.6	9.0
JCP	1.1	4.2	92.4	2.3	--
CGP	--	6.4	75.5	11.1	7.0
SDF	55.9	1.9	2.4	39.8	--

Source: Home Affairs Ministry, *PFCL 1989 Report, Asahi Shimbun* (September 3, 1990).

TABLE 3.3
LDP sources of revenue, 1989

Industry	*Percent of LDP Funds*
Banks	29.1
Construction, Real Estate	15.2
Electric and Communication	7.1
Heavy Industry and Metal	6.5
Automobile	6.4
Trading Companies	5.7
Labor Unions	5.7
Insurance	5.2
Stock Exchange/Brokers	4.2
Pharmaceutical	2.8
Transportation-Railroads	2.8
Others	9.3
	100.0

Source: Home Affairs Ministry, *PFCL 1989 Report, Nihon Keizai Shimbun* (September 14, 1990).

the Takeshita prime ministership in 1988, the Takeshita faction reported relatively small amounts of funds raised. Of the seven factions listed, four are major fund-raisers (Abe, Miyazawa, Takeshita, and Nakasone), each raising over 3.3 billion yen in the three-year period; three are relatively minor fund-raisers (Kōmoto, Nikaidō, and Watanabe), raising less than 2.6 billion yen.

As the previous discussion indicates, large sums of political funds are raised by individual senior leaders in the various factions. Table 3.5 displays the top thirteen LDP individual fund-raisers. Heading the list is Hashimoto Ryutaro, an LDP secretary-general in 1989, who is often mentioned as a future prime minister, as are several other names on the list. One sure way of being mentioned as having the qualities needed for party leadership is to have clearly demonstrated the skills of a very successful money raiser. A similar list from 1984 contained the names of all the current faction leaders.[5]

Finally, Table 3.6 presents the reported political contributions of Japanese corporations and banks in 1989. Listed are those businesses ranking among the top thirty-five in terms of total political donations. When the list is compared with the 1984 political funds report, banks have replaced Japan's heavy industries as the financial godfathers of LDP fund-raising efforts. In 1984 Nippon Steel and Mitsubishi Heavy Industries were the second- and fourth-ranked contributors. Five years later all of the top twelve and nineteen of the top thirty-five corporate contributors to the LDP were banks. Of the top thirty-five, all but three gave money to both the LDP and the DSP. It is significant that corporate contributions are overwhelmingly in favor of the LDP; only small contributions, largely symbolic, are made to the DSP.

A hundred billion yen represents a huge amount of money—almost $770 million. Even if the Political Funds Control Law report had contained an accurate portrayal of the nature of Japanese political financing, the implications would be disturbing—but according to many informed observers, these figures represent only one-third to one-fourth of the *real* totals to begin with! Just what is it about Japanese party politics that requires such enormous amounts of money? We turn to that question in the next section.

AN EXPENSIVE STYLE OF POLITICS

The financial restrictions incorporated into the Japanese election laws described in the previous chapter might lead one to anticipate that elections would be very inexpensive in Japan. But the reality of the situation is just the reverse. The government has attempted to reduce the costs of elections both by subsidizing the cost of campaigns and by prohibiting certain types of campaign activities.[6] In the 1975 election law revision package, the government increased its direct subsidy to Japanese parties and candidates by paying every candidate the costs of using an election campaign automobile, printing posters, and placing five advertisements in newspapers, in addition to the free franking privileges for two campaign leaflets per candidate. Yet, upon examining the total picture of a Japanese campaign, we find that these subsidies and restrictions have not controlled the problem of extraordinarily expensive elections. What has been accomplished is the designation of most

TABLE 3.4
LDP factional political funds 1987-1989 (in millions of yen)

Faction	*1987*	*1988*	*1989*
Takeshita	1,969.6	830.7	1,053.0
Abe	1,285.6	2,852.0	1,569.8
Miyazawa	2,263.3	1,457.9	955.9
Nakasone	1,386.2	1,239.4	1,153.6
Kōmoto	811.7	998.7	871.3
Nikaidō	871.4	203.3	63.9
Watanabe	617.3	810.1	720.6

Source: Home Affairs Ministry, *PFCL 1989 Report, Asahi Shimbun* (September 14,1990)

TABLE 3.5
Political funds collected by individual politicians, 1989 (in millions of yen)

Rank	*Politician*	*Faction*	*Contributions Received*
1	Hashimoto Ryūtarō	(Takeshita)	538.6
2	Yamaguchi Toshio	(Watanabe)	524.6
3	Mori Yoshirō	(Abe)	448.2
4	Katō Mutsuki	(Abe)	311.1
5	Ishihara Shintarō	(Independent)	266.7
6	Obuchi Keizō	(Takeshita)	233.3
7	Kōno Yōhei	(Miyazawa)	213.4
8	Katō Koichi	(Miyazawa)	190.7
9	Watanabe Kōzō	(Takeshita)	162.1
10	Hata Tsutomu	(Takeshita)	161.2
11	Mitsuzuka Hiroshi	(Abe)	143.5
12	Ozawa Ichirō	(Takeshita)	69.6
13	Nishioka Takeo	(Miyazawa)	41.2

Source: Home Affairs Ministry, *PLCL 1989 Report* reprinted in *Nihon Keizai Shimbun* (September 14, 1990).

campaign expenses as illegal. Although all parties must raise funds to compete in elections and to maintain their party organizations, the problem is especially acute for the Liberal Democratic party. The Socialist parties, the JSP and DSP, rely on their labor union supporting organizations to carry their efforts, and the JCP and Kōmeitō have their efficient grass-roots organizations. Clearly, the conservative party has the greatest need to resort to money politics. Consequently, in the discussions of money politics in the remainder of this chapter, the references (unless otherwise noted) are to the LDP or conservative independent candidates and their financial practices.

Candidates for the Japanese Diet are, by law, limited to a certain maximum level of expenditures. This limit is usually computed on the basis of a flat sum plus so many additional yen per voter in the constituency. But the limit is almost universally ignored by candidates, and the disclosure reports to the Home Affairs Ministry are usually carefully falsified. Particularly among LDP and JSP candidates, it has become a tradition to send in a disclosure report listing expenditures slightly under the legal limits while actually spending many times the reported amount. Yet no member of the Diet has ever been

TABLE 3.6
Major Corporate Political Funds Contributors, 1989 (in millions of yen)

Rank	*Corporation*	*Total Contributions*	*To LDP*	*To DSP*
1	Fuji Bank	91.8	85.6	6.1
1	Daiichi Kangyō Bank	91.8	85.6	6.1
3	Sumitomo Bank	91.6	85.5	6.1
3	Sanwa Bank	91.6	85.5	6.1
5	Nihon Kōgyō Bank	91.4	85.2	6.1
5	Long Term Credit Bank of Japan	91.4	85.2	6.1
7	Tokyo Bank	90.8	84.7	6.1
8	Tōkai Bank	90.1	84.1	6.0
9	Mitsubishi Bank	88.5	85.6	2.8
10	Nippon Credit Bank	86.8	81.0	5.8
11	Taiyō Kōbe Bank	86.4	80.6	5.8
12	Daiwa Bank	84.6	78.9	5.6
13	Sony	84.5	77.5	7.0
14	Mitsui Bank	84.1	84.1	--
15	Shin Nippon Steel	79.0	75.0	4.0
16	Kyowa Bank	78.6	73.4	5.2
17	Saitama Bank	70.4	65.8	4.5
18	Mitsubishi Corporation	69.6	69.1	0.5
19	Mitsubishi Electric	67.4	66.4	1.0
20	Hokkaidō Shokutaku Bank	65.4	61.0	4.3
21	Takenaka Construction Company	61.8	58.3	3.4
22	Marubeni Corporation	61.8	61.8	--
22	C. Itoh and Company	61.8	61.8	--
24	Mitsui Company	60.0	59.0	1.0
25	Nippon Life Insurance	59.9	54.8	5.0
26	Sumitomo Trust Bank	59.2	57.0	2.2
26	Yasuda Trust Bank	59.2	57.0	2.2
26	Mitsubishi Trust Bank	59.2	57.0	2.2
30	Kashima Construction Co.	58.1	49.5	4.2
31	Mitsubishi Heavy Industries	55.5	47.1	8.4
32	Dai-Ichi Seimei Insurance	54.4	50.9	3.4
33	Ohbayashi Construction Co.	54.3	50.9	3.4
34	Toyota Motors	54.0	46.8	7.2
35	Kawasaki Heavy Industries	53.8	50.3	3.5

Source: Home Affairs Ministry, *PFCL 1989 Report, Nihon Keizai Shimbun* (September 14, 1990).

prosecuted or denied a seat because of these practices. The 1977 House of Councillors election imposed a 21 million yen limit on expenditures, but incumbent JSP member Sasaki Shizuko from Ōsaka announced in late March that she would not seek reelection because she could not raise the 100 million yen needed to finance a "bare-bones" campaign. In the national constituency, 500 million yen ($1.7 million) was considered a necessity for a successful 1974 campaign; by the 1980 election, that figure had risen to 700 million yen. These extremely costly campaigns were a direct result both of the use of the medium-sized constituency system in House of Councillors prefectural district elections and of the severe burden placed on national constituency candidates to build a successful campaign in a nationwide election district prior to 1983.

With respect to the lower house races, insiders have estimated that any incumbent would need at least 40 million yen to retain his or her seat but that most spend at least 100 million yen, whereas a newcomer would need at least twice that figure.[7] These estimates are still a good guess despite inflation. As a former LDP construction minister noted, "You cannot win an election unless you spend about 100 million [yen] during the six months just before the election is called, and more than 100 million [yen] during the official campaign period."[8] A candidate can incur significant expenses during the above-mentioned precampaign periods. Many politicians will also hold periodic preelection speech meetings, which cost 3 to 5 million yen each. Five to ten of these meetings will be held in an election year, for a total cost of 30 to 50 million yen.[9]

Being a Diet member can be a very expensive occupation. The *Asahi Shimbun* ran a series of articles in 1989 on the expenses associated with such a career in politics. A survey discovered that the average LDP Diet member or his or her representative attended over 30 ceremonies, receptions, or funerals each month. One Tokyo member claimed to have "attended" over 300 such events on the average each month. In addition, politicians are expected to attend seasonal parties, and about one in every six reported attending over 200 such parties a year. Each of these events requires a "gift" or contribution from the politician: funerals 10,000 yen ($76), weddings 30,000 yen. The average LDP Diet member claimed to spend about 1 million yen a year on parties. When class reunions and store openings in a member's district are added, the *Asahi Shimbun* noted that for the average Diet member, such political costs were a little less than 100 million yen a year ($770,000).[10] Diet members received slightly over 18 million yen a year in salary and bonuses ($140,000). The government pays for only two secretaries, but most members hire more than two.

With a significant gap between government-provided money and the political expenditures of the office, the typical LDP Diet member must find money from other sources. The *Asahi Shimbun*'s survey noted that about 39 percent of these funds came from corporate contributions, 17 percent from fund-raising parties, 15 percent from individual contributions, 12 percent from the government salary or subsidies, 9 percent from the member's factional leader, and 8 percent from loans.[11]

Elections are most expensive when the LDP or conservative independent candidates are in conflict within the same constituency. In such cases, which occur in all 130 constituencies, the real battle is among the conservatives and not between the conservatives and opposition parties.[12] In the most extreme cases, these conflicts may result in an ever-escalating pattern of money politics and even vote-buying. In the 1979 lower house elections, for instance, the race in Chiba's second constituency drew the media's attention because of widespread charges of vote-buying by the conservative candidates. As described by the press, the political culture of the second district is one in which all candidates are expected to buy votes. LDP Diet member Toru Uno was subsequently charged with spending 260 million yen to buy approximately 110,000 votes at 2,000 yen per vote. Some reports indicate that all three conservatives paid for many of their votes. On the House of Councillors level, another conservative candidate's regional campaign manager was convicted of vote-buying during the 1974 elections, when he paid 21 million yen to local campaigners in fifteen western prefectures.

The LDP gave to each of its 311 official candidates in the 1986 lower house elections a maximum of 30 million yen. All of its candidates received 5 million yen each, and those who had previously served in a cabinet received another 5 million. "Backbenchers" (those without cabinet service) received a maximum of 5 million yen from the party. In a special grant, members from a constituency in which the number of seats had been reduced for the 1986 elections received a maximum of 30 million yen.[13] The LDP in 1990 collected enough money that it allocated 25 million yen for each of the endorsed incumbents through the factional bosses.

Various sources estimate the LDP and its candidates spent more than 200 billion yen ($1.3 billion) in campaigning for the 1990 lower house elections.[14] The LDP was much better prepared financially for these elections because it was able to instill a sense of crisis into its fund-raising that was based largely on the JSP victories in the 1989 HC elections. The business world responded—for example, Keidanren chairman Saito declared total support for the LDP in terms of fund-raising and voter mobilization. In order to evade the limits on corporate donations, a system of bank loans was secured in 1990 based on the expected contributions from individual corporations over a three-year period. The LDP asked its business allies for 20 billion yen in loans; the nine leading city banks provided 12 billion yen of that total by themselves. It was reported that the LDP used its Tokyo headquarters building as collateral.[15] Finally, one must remember that the LDP holds periodic internal campaigns for the post of party president, who, of course, also serves as prime minister of Japan. This internal conflict among the major factional leaders requires the organizational and financial support of hundreds of thousands of potential voters among the paying members, but for many the dues are paid by one of the factional leaders. All in all, conservative politics are expensive politics.

FUND-RAISING IN JAPAN

Each of the six political parties has its own special fund-raising methods (a subject that will be examined in greater detail in later chapters). By and large, the two Socialist parties rely on their supporting labor union federations for the bulk of their funds. Both the JSP and DSP can count on former Sōhyō and Dōmei unions for about 400 to 500 million yen, respectively, during a campaign such as the October 1979 lower house contest. The DSP receives a major portion of its funding from corporations and other organizations, which also give larger amounts to the LDP. Kōmeitō and the JCP raise less money but have the best grass-roots organizations in the nation. The JCP claims that nearly 90 percent of its funds are raised by selling party publications, including *Akahata,* its daily newspaper.

Our major focus in this context, given the sheer magnitude involved, must necessarily be directed to the LDP's fund-raising techniques. The primary source of LDP funds remains corporate Japan. During the late 1970s Japanese business gave an officially reported total of about 9 billion yen a year to the LDP. Again, this is the official figure derived from the PFCL reports, but it is also only "the tip of the iceberg."[16] In addition, an estimated three to four times that total is transferred from the business community to factional leaders and politicians during a given year. The LDP established a special organization, Kokumin Seiji Kyōkai, to facilitate the collection of corporate money for the LDP. This organization and its techniques will be discussed in the latter half of this chapter, where the reform of the PFCL is presented in detail.

Politicians, mostly conservatives, have developed ingenious methods to raise funds—often by evading the spirit, if not the intent, of the PFCL. One technique adopted from the United States in the mid-1970s is the fund-raising party, which is usually a technique used by the conservatives. During the last two years of the 1970s, as the parties planned for the October 1979 elections, a fund-raising party occurred every three days in Japan. Even so small a group as the NLC managed to raise 295 million yen by holding nine such parties. Contributions to such parties are often provided by corporations. In 1979, it was revealed that the giant communications corporation KDD had, in one instance, purchased 200 tickets at 10,000 yen each for one politician—in short, a 2 million yen contribution. In December 1980, Prime Minister Suzuki gave a speech at a fund-raising party in Ōsaka, where 2,000 business men gave 50,000 yen each for a total of 100 million yen. On the average, a successful fund-raising party can bring 20 million yen to a politician's coffers, and an especially influential politician can expect to raise 50 million yen. Fukuda Takeo's policy study group, Seiwakai, held a party in December 1979 in both Tokyo and Ōsaka for 30,000 yen per guest and reportedly netted several hundred million yen.[17] And on June 20, 1985, a fund-raising party was held for LDP Vice-President Nikaidō Susumu at the Hotel New Otani. An estimated 8,000 supporters attended the affair, which was sponsored by the Mokuyō Club of the Tanaka faction, and over 30,000 tickets priced at 30,000 yen each were sold to raise an estimated 900 million yen—a record at the time for the most money raised at a single Diet member's fund-raiser. These fund-raising parties have become so important for the LDP that one-third of the 1984 revenue of the Fukuda faction was generated by such parties, as was 507 million yen of the Nakasone faction's income that year. Half of the Kōmoto faction's income in 1984 was also "party"-generated.

As rumors of a pending House of Representatives election began to circulate in early 1983, the major Tokyo hotels were booked up by politicians reserving space for fund-raising parties. Prices for a single ticket to such a party honoring or encouraging a politician ranged from 20,000 yen to 30,000 yen in 1982-1983. Even on the prefectural level, parties are significant fund-raisers. In 1978 Aichi Prefecture Governor Nakaya held such a party on

October 25 and sold 11,320 tickets at 20,000 yen each. The party grossed 180 million yen and had only 30 million yen in expenses. Thirteen companies and organizations bought more than 100 tickets each. The Toyota Motors group, based in the area, purchased 1,000 tickets; the Tōkai Bank, Nagoya Railways, and others bought 500-plus tickets each. Even the electric and gas companies, which had left the fund-raising game in 1975, purchased large blocks of tickets for the Nakaya party.[18] As another example, the Socialist mayor of the city of Sendai in Miyagi Prefecture held a fund-raising party in late 1981. One thousand tickets at 20,000 yen each were sold to more than twenty construction companies scheduled to receive contracts on the new Sendai subway. The Tōhoku Construction Industry Council allocated the tickets to its member companies according to their size. The biggest companies bought 100; the middle group, 50; and so forth.[19]

An understanding of the political accounting of these fund-raising parties is instructive. According to the PFCL, politicians are not required to report "party earnings," although the Home Affairs Ministry urges them to do so. If the fund-raising party is sponsored by a political organization (*seiji dantai*), the organization does have to report the funds raised. In the spring of 1981, twenty-two such parties were held by LDP Diet members, but only ten such members reported their expenditures and income. Twelve of the parties were sponsored through "promoters meetings" or an "executive committee" (*shikkō inkai*) and thus were not required to report as political organizations.[20]

Among the opposition parties, the JCP and CGP do not hold fund-raising parties. The JSP's parties are almost always held in the election districts and are almost never reported to the Home Ministry. Many DSP parties are held, but the accounting for these parties is seldom reported.[21]

Under the PFCL, moreover, contributions to individual politicians can either be retained under the politicians' personal control, donated to a designated political organization, or channeled automatically into support groups. If the last course is followed, the money need not be reported. Of the 887 reporting politicians in 1981, 604 did just this; another 191 used the designated organizations method; and only 92 retained control of the money.[22]

Recent scandals have exposed some of the "kickback" practices in which needed money is delivered to conservative politicians. Matsuno Raizo, a former director general of the Defense Agency, admitted he had received 500 million yen from Nisshō-Iwai Company between 1967 and 1971.

Much money seems to flow to LDP politicians as "gifts" for services performed by the politicians. Japan is a society in which gift-giving (and money-giving) is commonplace upon introductions or requests for assistance from other more senior or prestigious people. This custom is especially prevalent in politics. One former cabinet minister from the Tanaka faction noted that "whether or not you are able to persuade a government department to do something you want is directly related to your ability to raise political funds." Another Tanaka HR member told the *Asahi Shimbun* that "politicians now say 'I will arrange for you to get your contract and you will give me 1 million [yen].'" When Itō Hiroshi, former managing director of the great

Marubeni trading company, decided to give Prime Minister Tanaka some money when he asked Tanaka's assistance on airplane sales to All-Nippon Airlines, the decision made was that 500 million yen seemed appropriate.[23]

Although construction industries are legally prohibited from contributing to governmental officials, many are making substantial regular contributions based on a percentage of the contracts they are awarded.[24] Other associations, such as the Japanese Federation of Tax Accountants Association in late 1977, made substantial contributions to both LDP and opposition Diet members while a revision to a tax accountant law was in the Diet. Some politicians were paid up to 500,000 yen in the way of "transportation fees" prior to the 1979 general elections.[25]

One of the interesting coincidences of the Japanese economy is the sharp rise that occurs in the Tokyo stock market prior to each election. A traditional method of fund-raising involves providing politicians with inside information on stock market transactions and then permitting the market to be manipulated by brokers to provide "quick in–quick out" transactions guaranteeing quick profits for the politicians. One such stock doubled in value within ten days in the year prior to the 1979 elections, only to return to its original price twenty days later.[26] Some politicians are offered land at extremely low prices and through low-cost loans; then, when quick funding is needed for an election, the land will be purchased by corporations at extremely inflated prices. The result in such cases is a large, unofficial campaign contribution.

The aforementioned KDD scandal provided some insight into two of the more bizarre methods of transferring corporate money to campaigns. KDD apparently persuaded art dealers to buy back art items sold to KDD for far in excess of the purchase price, whereupon the politicians converted the "gifts" to cash and KDD paid the difference. Most of these gifts were made to Diet members connected with the Posts and Telecommunications Ministry—the supervising ministry of KDD. The KDD was charged with compensating art dealers who purchased the name cards of politicians at prices of up to 1 million yen per card. The name cards were addressed to top KDD officials who later purchased inexpensive paintings priced at several million yen apiece. The difference was an unreported contribution to the politician.[27]

BACKGROUND FOR THE PFCL REFORMS OF 1975

On November 3, 1975, representatives of Japan's conservative Liberal Democratic party and the nation's largest corporations and banks announced an agreement to collect political money totaling 5.2 billion yen ($17,331,000) from the business community and donate it to the conservative party of Prime Minister Miki Takeo before January 1, 1976. As in the past, the total amount was to be divided among various business organizations, such as the Iron and Steel Federation and the Federation of Bankers Associations in Japan. Then individual corporations were assessed their portion according to such criteria as capitalization and recent earnings. Subsequently, the quota of the Automobile Manufacturers Association was reported to have been set at 500 million and that for the less prosperous Shipbuilders Association of Japan at 150 million, whereas the Bankers and the Iron and Steel federations were assigned to collect 500 million yen each. The real significance of the announcement was to signal to all concerned that the Liberal Democrats and big business had done their penance following the 1974 election scandals, and that they were returning to "business as usual" in *seiji kenkin*—that is, money politics.[28]

The setting for this interesting and instructive series of events was constructed by the LDP and business leaders early in 1974, as the July House of Councillors elections loomed as a possible turning point in the postwar conservative dominance of the national Diet. The upper house elections are contested on two different levels: One set of Councillors is elected to local constituencies based on prefectural boundaries, and a smaller group is elected on the national level. It was the latter group that placed such a tremendous financial burden on the LDP that the party was compelled to turn to business for additional assistance. The corporations were also asked to adopt specific candidates and to sponsor their campaigns, and some corporations ultimately functioned as political organizations providing money, organization, meetings, contacts, and votes for their candidates. Direct corporate sponsorship was a logical extension of the role played by business as the financial godfather of the Liberal Democratic party. For instance, the huge Mitsubishi company was asked to sponsor a little-known former bureaucrat named Saka Ken for an anticipated easy victory. A Saka supporters' organization (*kōenkai*) was formed and staffed entirely by Mitsubishi personnel, and Saka was packaged and marketed to the public in much the same way as were hundreds of other Mitsubishi products. In addition, Hitachi, the electronics giant, sponsored a female television model named Santo Akiko, and it was reported by the *Asahi Shimbun* that Hitachi management had pressured retail store outlets, employees, and subcontractors to support the Santo candidacy.

Tremendous amounts of money were spent both by the LDP and by corporate supporters of the sponsored candidates. However, the strategy backfired when the Japanese media began to explore the unique role played by the corporate "parties." The adverse public reaction ultimately spelled the failure of several of these corporate candidates, including the "unbeatable" Saka, to win seats.[29]

The LDP had successfully weathered other electoral storms during the 1967–1974 era without being forced beyond vague promises to reform its methods of political financing. Each time, a reform bill was allowed to die in the Diet when the LDP sensed that the public's attention had drifted to other subjects. However, the 1974 scandals proved to require more than the usual conservative reaction to demands for reform. The hue and cry of the opposition parties, mass media, and certain articulate sectors of the general public forced the LDP and its business allies into a masterful performance of symbolic politics.

Correctly evaluating the initial intensity of demand for positive steps toward reform, the LDP and the business community offered the first gesture of response. The president of the most powerful business organization, Keidanren, announced that it would no longer assess its member corporations for political donations to the National Association (Kokumin Kyōkai), an organization whose sole purpose was to funnel business money into the coffers of the LDP. Other corporate giants followed the Keidanren lead, and the electric companies, the iron and steel industry, and the banks all announced that they would suspend payments to the LDP until effective reforms were implemented.

The National Association, the recipient of so many billions of yen in donations to the LDP over the years, was now tainted. It was reorganized out of existence and replaced by a "new image" organization called the National Political Association (Kokumin Seiji Kyōkai). The crowning touch was the selection of the respected former head of NHK (the national public broadcasting corporation), Maeda Yoshinori, as chairman of the new organization. Maeda came to the chairmanship with many interesting ideas on how to reform the processes by which political funds were collected by the parties. For example, he proposed that the new organization funnel money not only to the LDP but to other Japanese political parties as well. Maeda saw the new organization as the possible model for a system of funding to the nation's parties based primarily on contributions from individuals, and proposed that the new National Political Association establish its financial base on the small donations of 600,000 individuals rather than on the concentrated wealth of the corporate giants.

As many other observers have noted, 1974 was not a very good year for the LDP. During the last three months of that year, the party was rocked by the widening financial scandal involving Prime Minister Tanaka Kakuei. By late November, it was obvious that Tanaka would have to be replaced to avoid further embarrassment and public scrutiny of the complex financial web that had entangled the LDP and the business sector.[30] A series of manipulations by senior party leaders, Shiina Etsusaburō in particular, bypassed the normal process of selecting a new LDP president and, hence, a prime minister. Such a freewheeling party election would only have intensified the party's image as a money-drunk organization.[31] From the ranks of the smaller LDP faction leaders, Miki Takeo, the "cleanest" of the factional leaders, was appointed by Shīna to be the next party president. Miki was the perfect choice as, in symbolic terms, he communicated the uncorrupt image the party needed to present to the Japanese public as a long year ended. Was there anyone better? Had Miki not resigned as deputy prime minister in protest over the excesses of the July election campaign? He seemed the right man at the right time to lead the party and the nation to real reform of the political-financial processes. In one of his first statements as the new prime minister, Miki said, "I will carry out fundamental reform in the matter of how political funds are collected and used."[32] The Japanese public breathed a sigh of relief, and even cynical political critics noted that the prime minister and his party seemed to be sincere. As 1974 ended, the feeling, in general, was that genuine reform would finally take place and that a new style of politics was on the way.

However, the public's attention span concerning political problems tends to be remarkably short, especially in areas relating to political parties and election details. As the early months of 1975 passed, it became clear that the Japanese public was more interested in pocketbook issues than in abstract questions of election law. Inflation, recession, and other economic questions were real issues encountered daily; election details were of interest only for a few days every year or so, and then only for a small percentage of the population.

It now seems clear from all available information that both Maeda and Miki were sincere in their desire to make reforms in the wide use of political money. However, both quickly realized that forces far more powerful held the actual control over their respective organizations. In May 1973 the LDP Executive Board had stated that there should be no restrictions on the amount of donations to political parties, but by early 1975 public pressure had forced the party into supporting some type of restrictions. The heart of the Miki plan was his proposal to end all corporate contributions after a three-year grace period and to shift to individual contributions as the financial base of the LDP. But this proposal was far too radical for the party mainstream, and on February 6, 1975, the LDP Election Research Council reported that the Miki plan was probably unconstitutional and that corporate donations should not be banned. Instead, it recommended limits on corporate contributions, tax credits to encourage individual contributions, and compulsory publication of funds received and expended. The report suggested maximum total contributions of 200 million yen each from companies capitalized at over 5,000 million yen. In addition, donations to individuals and factions up to 600,000 yen a year would not have to be disclosed. LDP Vice-President Shiina and other powerful leaders opposed Miki's radical proposals and endorsed the council's recommendations; thus, for all practical purposes the Miki plan was dead. In another symbolic gesture, however, the LDP Executive Committee resolved to meet operating expenses through individual contributions and membership fees within five years.

It was, of course, the far weaker LDP plan and not Miki's "radical" plan that was submitted to the Diet early in the summer of 1975. However, as other issues dominated the press, and as the pressure decreased, the party watered down the original proposal even more before it was brought up for debate in the House of Representatives. The new plan included a series of graduated steps that allowed a large corporation to give up to 100 million yen a year—500 percent higher than the figure specified in the early 1975 plan. In addition, the limit on donations to a faction or an individual candidate not requiring specific reporting was raised from 600,000 to 1 million yen.

The LDP "reform revision" essentially made legal and legitimate various practices that had received heavy criticism during the previous year. Financial conduits such as the National Association, created to collect and donate billions of yen to the LDP, were now legalized, and each political party was allowed to designate one such organization to handle its fund-raising activities. Corporate contributions were completely legalized and thus legitimized; even de facto quotas were established, thus probably making it more difficult for corporations to avoid giving financial support to the LDP. The annual ceiling for political contributions by companies whose capitalization exceeds 5,000 million yen is 30 million yen; for those between 1,000 million and 5,000 million yen it is 15 million yen; and for those capitalized under 1,000 million yen it is 7.5 million yen. But for the growing number of giant corporations, the ceiling rises 5 million yen for each 5,000 million yen in capitalization over 10,000 million yen, to a maximum of 100 million yen. Labor unions are given ceilings based on total membership; unions claiming over 100,000 members are allowed to contribute a total of 30 million yen; then the limits gradually fall, ending in those smaller unions of fewer than 50,000 members, which cannot give more than 1.5 million in a single year.

These so-called restrictions are a very light burden for the LDP-business alliance to bear. Nippon Steel, with capital funds over 230,000 million yen, is limited to a total contribution of 100 million yen to parties and another 50 million yen to factions and other organizations. When Nippon Steel Corporation complained to the *Mainichi Shimbun* that it used to give between 2 billion and 2.5 billion yen a year in political donations and now was limited to only 150 million yen a year because of the Political Funds Control Law, Takeuchi Kiyoshi, an LDP House of Councillor member, said, "Money collection means went underground."[33] Mitsubishi and Fuji Bank contributions to parties are "restricted" to only 78 million yen a year. Given that in 1974 the National Association received 400 million yen each from the Tokyo Bankers Association and the Japan Steel Association, the restriction that the LDP imposed on itself does not seem to be the cause of much discomfort for the conservatives. As President Nagano Shigeo of the Japan Chamber of Commerce and Industry reflected on December 8, 1975, "This [revision law] means that the LDP will have to collect relatively small amounts from a larger number of companies."[34] In order to effectively broaden its financial base, the LDP announced in December 1975 the creation of the Jiyū Seiji Renmei (Free Politics League), whose purpose is to serve as a fund-raising body among medium- and small-sized businesses. For some time, the LDP has been concerned about the Japan Communist party inroad into the smaller-sized Japanese businesses and, hence, the amount of political funds being collected by the Communist party organ, Minsho.[35]

Almost immediately following passage of the revision of the Political Funds Control Law, the major pillars of the conservative party announced that they would resume donations, retroactive to the day on which they suspended contributions in October 1974. The Tokyo Bankers Association contributed its own backlog of membership fees to the National Association totaling 240 million yen. President Itakura of the Bankers Association justified the resumption of the contributions by the bankers by saying, "Banks should endeavor to help the sound expansion of a political party which supports the just cause of parliamentary democracy."[36] Less charitable critics saw the contributions as an exchange for the government decision to sharply reduce the interest rates that banks had to pay on demand deposits. The private railroad companies, also former major contributors, resumed their contributions and donated about 150 million yen only two days before the 25 percent fare increase approved by the government went into effect on December 15, 1974.

Meanwhile, on July 2, the "reformed" National Political Association was rocked by its new chairman's resignation. Maeda Yoshinori had become increasingly aware that the new organization was a "farce"—a mere public relations ploy by the conservatives to take pressure off the party during those trying days in 1974. The new chairman and some of his staff were true reformers, but the old National Association's board of directors had come to the new organization almost completely intact. Consequently, each of Maeda's reforms was quietly defeated in the privacy of association board meetings. By summer, LDP Secretary-General Nakasone and other LDP leaders correctly surmised that Maeda's function was no longer necessary, and they moved to "normalize" their fund-raising channels. In early July, after Nakasone ordered Maeda to have the National Political Association collect money only for the LDP, Maeda and his supporters quit. The *Mainichi Shimbun* commented that "Maeda's ideals had been mercilessly crushed by the hard realities of politics."[37] Perhaps it would be more accurate to say that Maeda was just another victim of a masterful pattern of symbolic politics, along with most of the Japanese public.

Throughout most of the summer and fall of 1975 many believed a Diet dissolution was imminent, to be followed by a general election. However, it was very clear that the powers in the LDP did not want a general election until some time in 1976, because the party coffers were empty and the party still owed over 10 billion yen from the last election. In 1974, as in previous elections, the LDP borrowed money from banks in exchange for promissory notes usually signed by the party secretary-general and later repaid by the nation's corporations, each of which was allotted a share of the total cost.

However, following the 1974 elections, the flow of business contributions ceased almost completely and the party was not able to pay off its loans. The conservatives had to clear past debts before they could begin to prepare for the next election. And, as the revision of the Political Funds Control Law would not go into effect until January 1976, there was still time to appeal to their old business allies for sufficient funds to pay off the old debt. One-half of the debt was allocated to the large business associations. But the problem of the second 5 billion yen proved more difficult. At first, the suggestion was made that the banks could merely write off the sum as a bad debt or, perhaps more politically, as a contribution. On December 13, 1974, however, Prime Minister Miki announced that the several party factions would be asked to pay off the 5 billion yen.[38] Of course, the LDP factions receive their funds from exactly the same source their party does—the business community.

The LDP tried a series of *seikei bunka paatii* (political, economic, cultural parties—the Japanese version of the $100-a-plate political dinner) in major cities during that year, and it grossed several hundred million yen. A young Tokyo LDP Diet member attempted a fund-raiser with many television personalities and managed to attract over 10,000 citizens paying 700 yen each to attend the event. But after all the expenses were deducted, only 1 million yen were left.[39]

Thus, in November and December 1975, certain top leaders of the LDP, including the "clean" prime minister, criss-crossed the nation attempting to pressure business associations and corporations to give huge sums of money before the new law went into effect on January 1, 1976. This period of frantic questing is reminiscent of the last months before the U.S. 1972 campaign funds law went into operation, when Republican leaders were rushing around trying to collect as much as possible before the names of contributors had to be reported. It is somewhat ironic that despite the contributions by Japanese corporations of billions of yen to the conservatives, the *Nihon Keizai Shimbun* (a leading economic journal) reported that, for the half year ending September 31, 1975, one out of every three Japanese corporations listed in the first and second sections of the Tokyo Stock Exchange were operating in the red, and most of the others recorded extremely small profits.[40]

Meanwhile, in the time since Miki has assumed office, some major shifts have occurred in his public position regarding *seiji kenkin*. In 1974 he argued that "if the party continues receiving political contributions from business interests, it will become an agent representing business interests." Only a year later, he said in defense of the LDP request for corporate financial assistance that "the party is laboring under heavy debts and I am only willing to accept offers to help lessen this burden. It is true that a political party needs a huge amount of money for its activities. However, this does not mean that it is obliged to return favors to donators."[41]

The LDP strategy of symbolic response to the demands for reform was completely successful. As 1975 closed, public support for the LDP had risen to 44.3 percent, according to a *Kyōdo News* public opinion poll. Yet the very same poll revealed that support for Miki, the reformer prime minister, had dropped to a low of 31.6 percent.[42] The public was clearly more interested in inflation, education, strikes, pollution, and defense issues, and either was sufficiently satisfied by the LDP's gestures in the area of political money or cared little about the subject in the first place. The tactic of suspending corporate contributions, the creation of a "reformed" new funding channel with a "reform" image figurehead leader, the selection of a "clean" prime minister, and the highly publicized revision of the political funds law, in combination with a series of announcements of new fund-raising ideas, had "poured oil on troubled waters" and allowed the LDP to ride out the storm with little long-term damage.

The revisions to the Political Funds Control Law have significantly reduced the pressure to solve the continuing problems of political finance in Japan. Many of the problems have been legitimized by the revisions, and the public appears to be satisfied with the reforms, at least for the moment.

The LDP has adapted well to the 1975 restrictions. Keidanren officials estimated that it gave the LDP 15 billion yen for the 1980 elections and noted that "there are a lot of corporate and industry associations that have not yet reached the donation ceiling set by the PFCL."[43]

Member corporations could make an aggregrate donation of 25 billion yen every year if each member corporation was willing to make its maximum donation. Leading corporate contributors to the LDP continue to be the banking, construction, steel, and electric power industries. The Japanese Federation of Construction Organizations contributed 760 million yen in 1979 and 630 million yen in 1978, while the LDP has kept public works construction projects well funded by the government. In addition, during the 1970s the so-called protected industries (such as banks; insurance, electronic, automobile, and security companies; and railroads) continued to be major supporters of the LDP. The conservatives did suffer a reduction in funds until 1979, but a strong resurgence occurred in that election year. Quite simply, when the party needed money, funds appeared.[44]

During 1980, the leading corporate contributors to the LDP were as follows:

1. Civil engineering and construction industry (46 companies for a total of 850 million yen)
2. Banks (13 major banks for 800 million yen)
3. Steel industry (5 companies for 630 million yen)
4. Electric machinery and appliance industry (18 for 530 million yen)
5. Local banks (63 banks for 530 million yen)
6. Private railways and transport companies (510 million yen)
7. Insurance companies (480 million yen)
8. Automobile industry (370 million yen)
9. Trading houses (350 million yen)
10. Securities houses (270 million yen)

Hirose Michisada, the chief researcher for the *Asahi Shimbun*, observed that the civil engineering and construction industries replaced the steel industry and city banks at the top of the list in 1976, just when large-scale public works spending began to stimulate the economy. But because the LDP still single-handedly controls the national government, 93 percent of corporate Japan's 1980 political contributions went to the ruling party. The 6.5 percent contributed to the DSP is an insurance policy in case the LDP loses its pure majorities during some election in the future.[45]

Among "corporate Japan's" political contributions of 49 billion yen during 1984, almost 300 million yen were donated to the opposition parties. Nevertheless, the LDP received more than 90 percent of the business world's monetary gifts to parties. The Japanese Medical and Dental Associations gave a combined 1 billion yen. And the political contributions from other economic sectors included 1.22 billion yen from the commercial banks (36 percent of the total political money raised in 1984); 450 million yen from the steel and machine industries (13 percent); and 380 million yen from the electrical machinery/telecommunications industries (11 percent).

By 1985, the LDP was still able to fund its lower house campaigns by floating large bank loans and then paying them off over a three-year period—

ironically, with the help of large contributions from the banking community. Corporate Japan still feels restricted by the limits on how much a corporation may give in political contributions in a reporting year, and both the LDP and the business sector would like to liberalize that part of the law. The business sector would also like to do away with the constant schedule of fund-raising parties that has resulted from the limitations on corporate contributions. As the opposition parties are strongly opposed to any such changes, any significant change in the near future is unlikely.

As the required 1981 review of the PFCL approached, money critics of the law noted that major loopholes still existed. No one was required to report donations of less than 1 million yen a year. Many politicians have established multiple supporting organizations to collect as many of these smaller donations as possible. Conservative politicians, in particular, use multiple fund-raising organizations to conceal the sources of their funds.[46] For instance, Katō Mutsuki, of the Tanaka faction, used an organization named Jōzankai to raise 147 million yen in 1980. No names of the companies giving money were reported by this group. However, other fund-raising organizations used by Katō reported the following: (1) Seikei Kondankai (Political and Economic Discussion Council): 500,000 yen from the head of the Tokyo Metropolitan Truck and Bus Association; (2) Sōgō Seikei Konwakai (Overall Political and Economic Discussion Club): 1.4 million yen from Nippon Express Co.; and (3) Kindai Kōtsū Seisaku Kenkyūkai (Modern Transportation Policy Research Council): 1 million yen each from the Aichi and Ōsaka Truck and Bus Political Leagues.

Politicians seem to love these lofty names for their fund-raising organizations. Nikaidō Susumu, one of the leaders of the Tanaka faction and LDP secretary-general under both Suzuki and Nakasone, has included the following among his fund-raising groups: Group 21, New Century Planning Research Council, Japan National Land Planning Council, and the New Foreign Policy Research Council. These and other such groups collected a total of 120 million yen in 1980, but no corporate names were disclosed.[47] More significantly, individual politicians are not required to make public the means by which they acquired a political donation or expended it. The proposition requiring all political organizations to report collections and expenditures died in the 1980 Diet session. Indeed, it is unclear as to how money raised by political fund-raising parties is accounted for under the current law. Finally, under the PFCL, only those politicians actually receiving illicit donations are punishable, and the politician's aides are the only ones prosecuted, as in the Fujima Hospital scandal in 1980.[48]

By early 1981 the LDP, feeling confident following its victory in the 1980 double elections, figured it was time to consider rolling back some of the restrictions placed in the 1975 revisions. The LDP's Election System Study Committee recommended raising the ceilings for corporate contributions to parties, increasing individual contribution limits, and lowering ceilings for contributions in election years. Thus the party that had once proclaimed its desire to shift from corporate funding to individual funding now largely argues the need to ease the restrictions on corporate funding. In 1979 individual contributions made up only 9 percent of the party's official revenue, and many of those dues were paid by factional leaders from corporate money.[49] The other parties, with the exception of the DSP, want to ban corporate funding; the JCP would prefer to ban union funding as well. Ultimately, in the absence of the LDP's support, major revision of the PFCL failed to pass in 1981.

When the 1982 PFCL reports were issued in September 1982, the Japanese press wrote at length on the existing loopholes of the law. The *Japan Times* indicated that the reports gave a reasonably full accounting of the flow of money to established political parties but also pointed out that they suffered a major weakness in the area of money directed at factions and individual politicians. An April 1981 revision in the law required politicians to report political money and private money separately, but only 281 of 754 incumbents reported political funds in the following year.[50] The *Asahi Shimbun* said that little information existed as to where factional money came from, and the existing reports are not believed to be true; indeed, "the sources of political funds are generally veiled in the financial statements."[51]

One can find in these chronicles of the money problems of the LDP many clues that point to serious illnesses infecting the Japanese body politic. The conservatives rely on corporate generosity because they have no real base in the Japanese public. The LDP local infrastructure is quite weak, and most citizens feel that their stake in the Japanese political game is not important enough to warrant contributions to a preferred political party. In addition, the Japanese electoral law, that complex and tremendously restrictive set of rules, does everything possible to prevent the average Japanese citizen from becoming involved in the political process. Japanese voters are spectators rather than participants; they are less involved than other democratic voters anywhere in the world.

Most democratic nations have discovered that financial support of parties is closely tied to direct, active citizen participation in the nation's political process and to a sense of a stake, psychological or otherwise, in the outcome of elections. Because the LDP has dominated almost without a break since its creation in 1955 and because the electoral laws inhibit active citizen involvement in elections, the average voter is usually bored by the elections. Public opinion surveys, as well, continually discover that most Japanese do not have a deep interest in politics and elections. Therefore, why should they give money to support a party, especially a business-oriented and business-financed party?

Those who, like Miki and Maeda, have dreamed of shifting the burden of LDP finances from the shoulders of big business to the average citizen are doomed to disappointment for the foreseeable future. Kōno Yōhei's NLC also hoped to build on a base of individual contributions, but it failed to provide enough money for political activities. Reform in *seiji kenkin* can be undertaken only as part of a sweeping reform—a reform that alters the very foundations of Japanese politics. Anything short of such a "revolution" is likely to produce only variations on the present theme. As one Tokyo newspaper lamented following the resumption of the LDP-business financial ties, "Nothing has changed."[52] But one thing *has* changed—a golden opportunity, the best opportunity since 1955, to effectively reform Japanese politics has been lost.

THE RECRUIT COSMOS SCANDAL

An earthshaking scandal (Recruit Cosmos) exploded in 1988–1989 and demonstrated the magnitude of money that could be collected by politicians with influence. The president of Recruit, Ezoe Hiromasa, sought to buy political access for his relatively new set of companies through massive political funds contributions and sweetheart stock deals to key governmental personnel. Additionally, Recruit also bought many tickets for key politicians' fund-raising parties, in one such case contributing 14 million yen to the "reform" prime minister, Kaifu Toshiki. Finally, the Recruit company would loan its employees to politicians to use during election campaigns.

Prime Minister Takeshita admitted that in the months prior to assuming office he received 151 million yen ($1.6 million) from Recruit in preissue stock shares in Recruit Cosmos, a property holding company about to be traded on the Tokyo Stock Market, and in the purchase of tickets to his fund-raising parties. Takeshita later admitted that he received another 50 million yen ($381,000) from Recruit that he had forgotten to report. Over 1.3 billion yen ($10 million) in total was donated to a variety of politicians by the Recruit company.[53]

Takeshita and four LDP cabinet ministers were forced to leave the government. More than a dozen people were arrested, including two former vice-ministers and the former chairman of Nippon Telegraph and Telephone. All of the major LDP faction leaders except Kōmoto were involved in the scandal in one way or another. Additionally, this scandal was unique because major opposition party politicians were also the recipients of Recruit money; both DSP party leader Tsukamoto Saburō and CGP chairman Yano Jun'ya had to resign their party chairmanships. The personal secretaries of Abe and Miyazawa resigned, and Takeshita's secretary took his own life when the scandal began to envelop his boss.

Kuroda and Miyagawa suggest that the Recruit scandal was the most important of the many political funds scandals of the postwar era. Among its direct outcomes were the 1989 upper house defeat of the LDP; the rising sense of ethical standards that toppled not only Takeshita but his successor, Uno Sōsuke in 1990; and the perception that the LDP was vulnerable for the first time to losing control of the reins of government on the national level. The scandal also showed many how "lobbying" in Japan was accomplished when special interests lacked normal access to the decisionmaking networks of the LDP, bureaucracy, and favored interest groups.[54]

Along with the proposed reforms of the national HR election system, the Election System Council in 1990 also recommended a series of reforms to the political finance laws. One proposal was that each Diet member be limited to only one fund-raising committee in his or her home district and one in Tokyo and that all donations under 1 million yen would not have to be reported, a measure specifically addressing the pattern of Diet members having several fund-raising committees and using them to collect many small contributions from the same person or corporation and thus evading the requirement that all donations over 1 million yen be reported to the government. The council also recommended that Diet members be required to list all donors by name for contributions over 10,000 yen to committees other than the two proposed. A ban on the giving of money by corporations and unions to any organizations other than political parties seeking seats in the Diet was also suggested. Finally, the committee urged that when a secretary of a Diet member is found guilty of violating the PFCL, the member would lose his or her Diet seat and be banned from running for the Diet for a period of five years.[55] As of early 1991, these proposals were still being debated, and it is quite uncertain that these or any other reforms will be implemented.

NOTES

1. "Vox Populi, Vox Dei," *Asahi Shimbun* (June 22, 1980).

2. See Ronald J. Hrebenar, "The Politics of Electoral Reform in Japan," *Asian Survey* 18, no. 10 (October 1977), pp. 978–996. The original source is *Mainichi Daily News* (December 28, 1975).

3. *Asahi Evening News* (September 2, 1982).

4. Gerald L. Curtis, *The Japanese Way of Politics* (New York: Columbia University Press, 1988), p. 189.

5. How do ambitious faction members use money to gain supporters for a future run at the LDP presidency? Gerald Curtis notes how Takeshita used the huge amount of political funds he collected in 1984. Takeshita saved 550 million yen for future political activities. He then gave the rest in units of 5 million to 10 million yen to members of the Tanaka faction and units of 100,000 to 1 million yen to members of other factions. Finally, he gave 92 million yen to his faction and 2 million yen to Nikaidō, the senior member of his faction. Ibid., pp. 182–183.

6. The amount of public money expended in the 1990 lower house elections in subsidies to parties and candidates and direct election management costs totaled approximately 35.3 billion yen. PFCL 1990 Report.

7. *Japan Times* (April 5, 1979). Curtis concludes that a well-established LDP incumbent probably spends about the equivalent of $1 million in his reelection campaign to the House of Representatives. A new LDP candidate will spend much more than that to have a chance to win a seat. Curtis, *The Japanese Way*, p. 176.

8. *Mainichi Daily News* (January 19, 1980).

9. Masanori Tabata, *Japan Times* (September 20, 1979).

10. *Asahi Shimbun* (April 5–11, 1989). Curtis estimates that the typical LDP Diet member needs an extra 5 million to 10 million yen a month to cover extra political costs, and that in an election year, those totals would have to be 200 to 300 percent higher. Curtis, *The Japanese Way*, p. 177.

11. *Asahi Shimbun* (April 5–11, 1989).

12. See Gerald Curtis, *Election Campaigning Japanese Style* (New York: Columbia University Press, 1971); and J.A.A. Stockwin, *Japan: Divided Politics in a Growth Economy* (London: Weidenfeld & Nicolson, 1982).

13. *Asahi Evening News* (June 10, 1986).

14. *The Economist* (May 5, 1990).

15. *Mainichi Shimbun* (April 10, 1990), and *Asahi Shimbun* (December 10, 1989).

16. *Japan Times* (September 20, 1979).

17. *Mainichi Daily News* (January 19, 1980), and *Asahi Shimbun* (September 9, 1982).

18. *Asahi Evening News* (May 8, 1982).

19. *Mainichi Daily News* (April 15, 1982).

20. *Asahi Shimbun* (September 9, 1982).

21. Ibid.

22. *Japan Times* (September 19, 1982).

23. *Asahi Evening News* (June 17, 1982).

24. *Mainichi Daily News* (June 14, 1980, and January 15, 1980).

25. *Mainichi Daily News* (February 3, 1980).

26. *New York Times* (August 4, 1979).

27. *Mainichi Daily News* (January 21, 1980), and *Asahi Evening News* (January 7, 1980).

28. Much of this section was originally taken from Ronald J. Hrebenar, "Political Money, the LDP and the Symbolic Politics of Reform," *Japan Interpreter* 10, no. 3 (September 1976), pp. 66–73. See also Frank Baldwin, "The Kokumin Kyōkai," *Japan Interpreter* 10, no. 1 (September 1976).

29. See Michael K. Blaker, *Japan at the Polls: The House of Councillors Election of 1974* (Washington, D.C.: American Enterprise Institute, 1976).

30. James L. Huffman, "Kinmyaku and Jinmyaku," *Japan Interpreter* 9, no. 4 (Spring 1975).

31. See Daniel I. Okomoto, "LDP in Transition: Birth of the Miki Cabinet," *Japan Interpreter* 9, no. 4 (Spring 1975).

32. *Japan Times* (October 19, 1975).

33. *Mainichi Daily News* (January 21, 1980).

34. *Asahi Shimbun* (November 7, 1975).

35. Ibid.

36. *Mainichi Shimbun* (September 8, 1975).

37. *Mainichi Shimbun* and *Mainichi Daily News* (July 25, 1975).

38. *Japan Times* (November 7, 1975).

39. Ibid.

40. Reported in *Japan Times* (December 18, 1975).

41. *Japan Times* (November 5, 1975).

42. *Japan Times* (December 15, 1975).

43. *Mainichi Daily News* (January 21, 1980).

44. *Mainichi Daily News* (June 15, 1980).

45. *Asahi Evening News* (August 13, 1981).

46. Another unintended outcome of the 1975 Political Funds Control Law revisions was to make the process of collecting political finances much more the task of the individual Diet member. As the Recruit Cosmos scandal demonstrated, money is flowing to many more politicians than most previously thought to be the case. Previously, money flowed more to the LDP and the faction bosses; now it is often going to senior faction second-level leadership and the "backbenchers" of the party. Sources of money in the Diet members' constituencies have become much more

important, and that pattern has increased the likelihood of political scandal. Curtis, *The Japanese Way*, pp. 186–187.

47. *Asahi Evening News* (June 15, 1980).

48. *Japan Times* (December 9, 1980).

49. *Mainichi Daily News* (February 23, 1981).

50. *Japan Times* (September 15, 1982).

51. *Asahi Shimbun* (editorial, September 9, 1982).

52. Minoru Shimizu, "Revival of LDP-Business Collusion," *Japan Times* (October 16, 1975). In a *Mainichi Shimbun* editorial on July 27, 1975, the comment was made that the LDP reform effort "was after all a farce."

53. *The Economist* (April 29, 1989).

54. Yasumasa Kuroda and Takayoshi Miyagawa, "The Recruit Scandal in the Japanese Diet: Its Nature and Structure," paper presented at the 1989 meeting of the American Political Science Association, August 31, 1989, Atlanta, Georgia.

55. *Tokyo Report* (May 2, 1990).

PART TWO

The Parties of the Left

4

The Japan Socialist Party: Resurgence After Long Decline

J.A.A. STOCKWIN

Except for a brief period as one element in a coalition government in 1947 and 1948, the Japan Socialist party (JSP) has never been in power at the national level. Until the late 1980s, therefore, it was (and sometimes still is) often dismissed as being of little significance in the politics of contemporary Japan. Inspecting its electoral performance, we see that although it enjoyed the support of about one-third of the voting public in the late 1950s, this proportion had apparently declined to about one-fifth in the early 1980s. Indeed, it is evident that over many years the JSP suffered from a wide variety of problems, most of which appeared to be chronic. Its image was generally lackluster and even old-fashioned, so that many Japanese regarded it as poorly organized, indifferently led, narrowly based, doctrinaire and irresponsible in policy, lacking in autonomy, poor in human talent, and overly prone to ideological and factional division. There is a story (though perhaps it is apocryphal) that the late chairman of the Chinese Communist party, Mao Zedong, once said that he had never encountered a party so strange and difficult to understand as the JSP. Up until the late 1980s, many Japanese would have endorsed his sentiment; indeed, some would still do so.

The late 1980s, however, saw a sudden and unexpected improvement in the fortunes of the JSP, and even though the implications of this improvement for its future electoral performance were by no means clear as the 1990s began, the party had clearly entered into an arena of opportunity such as it had not experienced since the 1950s. In September 1986, Doi Takako, the first woman ever to lead a Japanese political party, became chairman (*iinchō*) of the JSP. In the July 1989 House of Councillors elections, held in an atmosphere of electoral disillusionment with the LDP government occasioned by the Recruit scandal, revisions to the taxation system, the lifting of some agricultural protection, and other issues, the LDP was convincingly defeated, with the principal beneficiary being the JSP. Twelve of its successful candidates were women.

Early hopes following these HC elections that the LDP would be again defeated and the JSP (or a JSP-led coalition) would be swept to power in the subsequent House of Representatives elections were not fulfilled. The lower house elections of February 1990 were won without difficulty by the LDP, even though its majority was reduced. The JSP, however, won 50 extra seats in the election, at the expense principally of the smaller opposition parties. It therefore began the 1990s in a stronger position than it had occupied for more than two decades.

Yet even before its recent resurgence, there was also a more positive side to the JSP—a side that, although it should not be exaggerated, may serve to modify slightly the bleak picture of chronic decline. From the 1950s onward the JSP always remained the largest of the various parties of opposition, regularly managing to win more than twice as many House of Representatives seats as those obtained by any other opposition party. It maintained a nationwide organization of reasonable (though hardly impressive) effectiveness based largely on what used to be Japan's largest labor union federation, Sōhyō, now dissolved into the Shin Rengō (New Rengō) federation.

Unlike the Kōmeitō and the Japan Communist party (JCP), the JSP's support since the 1960s has not been heavily concentrated in metropolitan areas. Perhaps the main reason for this was that the public-service unions forming the core membership of Sōhyō had enough members spread throughout the country to provide the party a chance of parliamentary representation (given the multimember constituency system)[1] in many rural and semirural constituencies. It also differs markedly from the Kōmeitō and the JCP in its form of organization. Whereas the latter parties have centralized authority, thus providing lower party echelons with relatively little independent voice, the JSP has an organizational structure that militates against the imposition of strong central authority and thus permits formally subordinate groups of various kinds to function with considerable freedom.

In some ways, however, this loose structure was disastrous for the JSP, as factional disputation could not be curbed and the party leaders often appeared to preside but not to rule. These difficulties, in turn, had a conservative effect on the making of public policy, inasmuch as the compromises once hammered out between fractious groups were too delicate to risk amending and updating. The party frequently appeared on the brink of splitting asunder, and indeed it has done so on a number of occasions in its turbulent history. On the other hand, there may also be some advantage to the organization of the JSP as compared with the authoritarian approach of its smaller rivals. Whereas the JCP and the Kōmeitō impose a uniformity of approach on a highly committed membership, therefore tending to restrict their appeal to the alienated and suggestible, the JSP has presented a more "comfortable" and familiar image, which, though not enormously attractive, has also not been particularly demanding for the individual supporter.

In the Japanese political context, the JSP has been recognized as indigenous, even traditional, despite its leftist rhetoric. Indeed, strange as it may seem, the party that has most resembled the JSP in structure is not the JCP (with which it might seem to have the most in common ideologically) but the Liberal Democratic party (LDP), which is likewise loosely organized and gives much leeway to the maneuverings of interest groups and factions. In a curious and suggestive way, moreover, the linkages that prevail between the LDP and the public sector have had a parallel in the linkages between the JSP and the public-sector unions.

In the past, the JSP has been of further significance in that it has been a genuine party of opposition. Felicitously (or notoriously, depending on one's point of view), government policymaking has for the most part been controlled since the end of the Allied Occupation by a broad combination of public servants, conservative politicians, and representatives of powerful private-interest groups. Since 1955 almost all of Japan's conservative politicians have been concentrated in a single political party—the LDP—which until its defeat in the House of Councillors elections of 1989 had had the happy fortune to win every general election (though occasionally by narrow margins). The Japanese electorate is not unique in having continued to place the same political party in office at national level over a period measured in decades.[2] In such circumstances as these, observers are apt to forget about the opposition parties because they do not control policymaking and may have no apparent prospect of doing so.

Nevertheless, even though the opposition may have little prospect of coming to power, it is of interest insofar as it articulates alternative perspectives on policy and represents interests normally excluded from representation in government. In this connection, however, we must acknowledge that a strong tendency in an opposition long excluded from power (as well as in interest groups similarly excluded) is to attempt to reach accommodations with those permanently in control of the mechanisms of policymaking. When the realistic alternatives include replacing the ruling party or parties in office, the incentive to do so is much lower than when the bleak alternative to accommodation is permanent exclusion from any influence whatsoever on policy decisions.[3]

The strategy of forging links with the ruling establishment was much in evidence among the centrist parties during the 1980s. One party that has shown little sign of making compromises with authority is the JCP, but, as we have seen, that party appeals to a narrow and committed clientele (as well as some who cast protest votes by voting for it). The largest opposition party, the JSP—although it has always frequently made tactical accommodation with the government—is still seen as the heir to a tradition of politics different from that prevailing in Japan since the end of the Occupation. Indeed, the recent resurgence of the party's fortunes presents the JSP with a dilemma of adjustment to new circumstances. For long it was pilloried—not always justly—as the party of "opposition to anything" that the LDP government proposed. Now, however, it has to temper an oppositional stance with the ability to present credible alternative policies, and the extent to which it can find and articulate these is likely to be the key to success if it is to transform itself into a party capable of governing Japan.

The ideological distinctness of the JSP proceeds in part from the Marxist framework and language in which many of its pronouncements have in the past been couched. Unlike the West German Social Democratic party, the JSP in the late 1950s failed to shake off the major Marxist elements in its heritage—hence the defection of its right wing, which formed the Democratic Socialist party (DSP) in 1959–1960. Even so, much of its Marxist orientation remained at the level of rhetoric, and other elements vied with it for attention within the party. In any case, it seems unlikely that the majority of those who voted for the JSP in the 1950s and 1960s did so out of sympathy with the Marxism contained in its message. More important was the image that the party was able to cultivate as champion of the democratic and pacifist reforms of the Allied Occupation, particularly of the earlier stages of the Occupation before a conservative reaction had set in.

Many of the JSP's policies were conceived in reaction against the conservative governments of the 1950s, particularly against the power of what the JSP chose to call "monopoly capital." It repeatedly inveighed against rearmament, which (in its view) defied the "Peace Constitution," Japanese membership of an anti-Communist alliance of nations led by the United States, erosion of the powers of the National Diet, antilabor legislation (including the withholding of the right to strike from public-sector workers), exclusion of labor unions in general from central decisionmaking, attempts by the Ministry of Education to increase its control over the teaching profession and the curriculum, and so on. Its general strategy was to paint the LDP government as reactionary and strongly antidemocratic as well as potentially militaristic. The argument that successive conservative governments were engaged in a conspiracy to subvert the postwar democratic reforms had a certain appeal, particularly among urban intellectuals and workers in the period before rapid economic growth had added so conspicuously to general prosperity.

The policy choices confronting policymakers in Japan of the early 1990s are far more complex than those in the early 1960s. In essence, both Japan and the world environment have changed enormously, and the JSP is belatedly attempting to modernize its notably old-fashioned image to fit contemporary realities. The bonus of new seats won in the upper and lower house elections of 1989 and 1990 have brought into the National Diet numbers of JSP Diet members from different backgrounds and with more varied ideas than the heavily union-influenced parliamentarians who dominated the party in the past. Some of the main policy positions of the JSP still strike many observers as either too ideological or too opportunistic, and the tendency to repeat slogans rather than think policy through, including its likely consequences, has not entirely disappeared. Nor have the defects of party organization been clearly remedied. Nevertheless, the party looks in much better shape as the 1990s unfold than it has for three decades.

We shall be seeking in the rest of this chapter to answer the question of whether the JSP is now capable of developing into a genuine challenger for political power. Even though the euphoria generated by its successes in

July 1989 dissipated following the election results of February 1990, at least the party is no longer relegated to the status of political irrelevance, as was largely the case, for instance, after the elections of 1986.

PARTY HISTORY

History has weighed heavily on the JSP and, at crucial points in its development, has inhibited certain necessary changes. The party was founded in November 1945, but its founders came bearing miscellaneous intellectual baggage from the prewar period—notably from the initial period of left-wing party building in the latter half of the 1920s. That period saw the emergence of a three-way split in the socialist movement, thus also reflecting labor union divisions. The reasons for this split, and even some of the leading personnel involved, were carried over into the postwar JSP and formed the background of persistent factional conflict within that party. Indeed, much of the factional division in the JSP during the first two postwar decades becomes comprehensible when one realizes that the party as formed in 1945 was a loose amalgam of the Shamin-kei on the right, the Nichirō-kei in the center, and the Rōnō-kei on the left.[4] Each of these groups derived from separate small parties that had briefly come into existence in the late 1920s. The ideological differences among the three are too complicated to describe in detail, but the strands of thinking about labor unionism differed radically between the right- and left-wing groups. The Shamin-kei represented a form of thinking about the role of unions that assumed that workers' interests could best be secured through cooperation between labor and management on the basis of an enterprise union structure. The Rōnō-kei, on the other hand, took a far more confrontational stand, seeking to foster industrial unionism and to "take on" government and management across a range of policy issues. The differences between the two extended in the postwar period to fundamentally contrasting views about foreign and defense policy, and particularly about the peace settlement that ended the Allied Occupation in 1952. The Rōnō-kei was deeply opposed to the pro-U.S. anti-Communist foreign policy line of post-Occupation governments, and advocated a nonaligned or neutralist foreign policy, to be guaranteed by the major powers.[5] It was also strongly opposed to any rearmament by Japan, however disguised by euphemistic language. On all of these issues the Shamin-kei was the most muted in its criticism of the government, and both its domestic and foreign policy attitudes were influenced by an acute suspicion of and hostility to anything that smacked of communism.

On most of these issues, the Nichirō-kei supported policies falling somewhere in between the policy lines espoused by the other two parties, such that its attitudes were less clearly defined. In any case, as it had provided much of the leadership of the 1930s Shakai Minshutō (Social Masses party), which had developed close links with various ultranationalist groups, its influence was much weakened in the democratic atmosphere of the late 1940s and 1950s.

In great contrast to its impotence in later years, the JSP in the first few years after its foundation was generally recognized as a realistic contender for political power. In the first postwar general election for the House of Representatives, that of April 1946, the JSP won 92 seats (with 17.8 percent of the vote) to become the third largest party; then, in the second election, just a year later, it actually turned out to be the largest party, with 143 seats (on 26.2 percent of the votes cast). The reason it could reasonably expect to participate in government at this stage was that the conservative camp was highly fragmented. With conservative unity established after 1955, even considerably better results (as in 1958) left power a long way from its grasp.

In the fluid political situation of the immediate postwar years, virtually any coalition arrangement that could guarantee a majority in Parliament seemed possible, although this is not to say that any coalition would prove able to provide effective government. In June 1947 a coalition government consisting of the JSP, the Japan Democratic party, and the People's Cooperative party was launched under the prime ministership of Katayama Tetsu, a Socialist. This government was a chaotic affair, faced by a tumultuous political situation in the country at large as well as by severe internal strains that quickly tore it apart. An attempt by the Socialist element within the coalition to nationalize the coal mines did much to threaten the coalition's unity, and attempts to control the galloping inflation failed. At the same time, a number of the most significant reforms of the Occupation were implemented during the coalition's tenure of office.

The worst result of its period in government was the exacerbation of already serious policy and personality differences between its left and right wings. The balance of intraparty power in the Katayama government was heavily in favor of the right (particularly the Shamin-kei), but by the time of the cabinet's collapse in February 1948, the Left (mainly Rōnō-kei) was substantially in revolt against the right-of-center leadership. Indeed, the government's fall was precipitated by the decision of the Left to vote against the budget.

The Katayama cabinet was succeeded by another coalition in which the same parties participated, but the leader this time was a prime minister, Ashida Hitoshi, from the Japan Democratic party. This administration struggled on, through a series of crises, until its resignation in October 1948. Thus ended the JSP's one and only positive experience of participation in office, which it enjoyed up to the time of this edition in 1991.

Some idea of the turbulence of the JSP during the Occupation years is suggested by the number of splits and defections it suffered during that period—a period that, in a sense, replicated the troubled history of Japanese socialism in 1926–1932.[6] The first defection took place in January 1948, when a right-wing group led by Hirano Rikizō, previously dismissed as minister of agriculture, broke away. This was followed by a left-wing splinter in September 1948, when Kuroda Hisao and his faction left the JSP (some were dismissed from it) after voting against the Ashida government's budget. This, in turn, led to the formation of a left-wing mini-party, the Rōdōsha Nōmintō (Labor-Farmer party), which rejoined the (by then) reunited JSP in 1957.

In January 1950 the JSP briefly split into three separate fragments roughly corresponding to the Shamin-kei, Nichirō-kei, and Rōnō-kei divisions previously mentioned, but they came together again in April of the same year. A far more serious and durable split occurred in October 1951, when the party divided into two over the San Francisco peace settlement, with the Left strongly opposing it and rejecting any form of rearmament, whereas the Center and Right were prepared to give it qualified approval.[7] Two separate parties, both calling themselves Nihon Shakaitō (Japan Socialist party)[8] but generally known as the Left Socialist party and the Right Socialist party, were in existence for four years between October 1951 and a painfully effected reconciliation in October 1955.[9]

Underlying the numerous splits and defections that occurred in the first postwar decade was a steady shift in the balance of power from the Right, which was initially dominant, toward the Left. This was partly a reaction against the chaotic experience of the Katayama and Ashida governments, in which the JSP had participated under a right-wing leadership. The party was drastically repudiated by the electorate in the aftermath of the Ashida government's collapse, and it recorded by far its worst electoral result up to the present time in the lower house general elections of January 1949.

A further and more significant reason for the rise of the Left in this period relates to the struggle for control over the labor union movement, which was going on at the time between the Communists and various kinds of Socialists. During the early part of the Occupation, the JCP made a strong bid for control over the newly formed unions, but by 1949–1950 control of many unions and union federations had been wrested from the hands of the Communists by union leaders closely aligned with the Rōnō-kei, or left-wing faction of the JSP. The formation of the Sōhyō federation of labor unions in 1950—ironically, with strong support from the Occupation authorities—was a high point in the establishment of left-wing Socialist control. As can readily be seen from Table A.1, during the period of two Socialist parties (1951–1955) the electoral strength of the Left Socialists increased more rapidly than that of the Right Socialists, so that at the time of reunification in October 1955, the Left was in a substantially more dominant position than it had been at the time of the 1951 split. The organizational advantages accruing to the Left from increasing close links with Sōhyō-affiliated unions, in competition with the Right, whose base of support was more heterogeneous and whose links with the union movement were weaker, were clearly reflected in the patterns of Left Socialist electoral advance. Over the long term, however, the advantages were less sure. By the 1960s the Sōhyō unions had become the established base of support for the JSP to the extent that the organizational structure of the party itself was allowed to atrophy, and the party became identified in the public mind with a restricted set of union interests. The bulk of the unions affiliated with Sōhyō were based on workers in the public sector, who had sectional grievances against the government because of the restrictions on the right to strike and organize introduced in 1948. The leftist radicalism of the Sōhyō unions was much stimulated by these grievances, which were of limited interest to those not directly concerned.

The ideological divide between the right and left wings of the JSP ran very deep and has continued to bedevil the party to the present day. The parameters of the argument were quite clearly set out in the Inamura-Morito debate, which took place in 1949. Essentially, the debate was about whether the JSP should be a "class-party," as argued by the Left, or a "mass-party," as the Right believed it should be. Connected with this issue were arguments about revolutionary versus evolutionary approaches to political change and disagreements about whether the party should concentrate on parliamentary or "extra-parliamentary" activities. The intellectual origins of the respective ideas of the two sides were of course quite diverse. Morito Tatsuo, the right-wing spokesman in 1949, derived many of his ideas from the British Labor party, the Fabians, and Christian humanitarianism; hence he was committed to gradual reform, parliamentary democracy, and the creation of a base of support that would extend well beyond the working class, strictly defined.

The intellectual antecedents of the Japanese Left, on the other hand, could be traced back to the German Marxism of the 1920s, although the Left had many quarrels with Marxism-Leninism, at least as interpreted by the JCP. Its differences with the Communist party, which were genuine, were sharpened during the struggle for control of the union movement during the late 1940s. The Left consisted, however, of "Socialists first and Democrats second," whereas many on the Right were inclined to place their priorities the other way around. The leftists were also broadly within the lines of the Rōnō school[10] of Japanese Marxism of the prewar period, which held that a single-stage revolution was possible in Japanese circumstances, as opposed to the two-stage revolution advocated by the Communists. Perhaps even more significant than the actual arguments used was the fact that the Rōnō school had long ago rejected any kind of international Communist control of their activities and therefore constituted a distinctly national Marxist tradition.

This tradition proved crucial in guiding the dominant political perceptions of the JSP over the succeeding two or three decades. As a mode of thinking it was not entirely inflexible, nor did it remain unmodified by pragmatic considerations of political competition and the pursuit of power. It did, however, mold political perceptions in significant ways. Although it is difficult to disentangle rhetoric from practice, the Rōnō tradition tended to narrow the target of the party's appeal to those definable as "working class." This tradition also resulted in a confrontational approach to "monopoly capital" and to the government-business establishment in general. Faced by an apparently permanent conservative majority in Parliament, the party and associated groups, including labor unions, were quick during the 1950s and 1960s to take to the streets in massive demonstrations rather than confine themselves to parliamentary debate. Moreover, in foreign policy an ostensibly neutralist program was repeatedly pulled in the direction of sympathy toward Peking and, to a slightly lesser extent, Moscow, and in the direction of hostility (at times extreme) toward the United States.

Foreign and defense policy was indeed a most crucial source of JSP concern, to the extent that it was almost constantly at loggerheads with the ruling establishment. It remains the policy area in which the JSP image is most clearly established and best known. The party's long-standing position as champion of the "Peace Constitution," as well as advocate of the notion that Japan should repudiate the Security Treaty with the United States and phase out the Self-Defense Forces in order to become both unarmed and nonaligned, serves as a mark of identification. Over the years, the security policy has also been the source of much disagreement within the party itself.

The origins of this policy can be traced at least as far back as the "three peace principles" accepted by the JSP in December 1949 during the national debate over the prospective peace settlement. The peace principles were as follows: "a peace treaty with all the belligerent powers" (as distinct from a treaty signed only by the anti-Communist nations that had fought against Japan), "permanent neutrality," and "no military bases to be given to a foreign power." The outbreak of the Korean War and the authorization by General Douglas MacArthur of a quasi-military "Police Reserve" made the issue of rearmament a focus of intense political controversy. In January 1951 a fourth principle was therefore added to the three peace principles already endorsed by the JSP: "opposition to rearmament." The principles, however, were rejected by the Shamin-kei, and this rejection became the basis for the four-year Right-Left split in the JSP that began in October 1951. This scenario, then, was the background to the endorsement of "positive neutrality" as an alternative to the pro-U.S. foreign policies of the government in the late 1950s.

The political compromise hammered out in 1954 and 1955 between the Left Socialist party and the Right Socialist party was achieved in an atmosphere of optimism occasioned by the rapidly improving electoral fortunes of the two Socialist parties in the first half of the 1950s. It was also facilitated by the fact that both parties were led by their moderate wings and that political tensions were relatively relaxed at the time of the negotiations. The appearance of unity, however, was to prove relatively short-lived. The Sōhyō labor federation itself had split in 1954, after a substantial section of its private industry union membership had revolted against what it saw as the unduly confrontational policies of the then current Sōhyō leaders. The formation of the Liberal Democratic party shortly following the Socialist reunification was demoralizing to the Socialists, because it meant that governmental office was removed much further from their grasp. The policies of the Kishi Nobusuke government, which emerged in 1957, were also particularly provocative to the JSP across a range of issues, both domestic and foreign, while international tensions also increased to some extent after the relatively relaxed period of the middle 1950s.

From the time of Kishi's abortive attempt to revise the Police Duties Law in 1958, mass demonstrations against the government became the order of the day for the Socialists. These demonstrations culminated in mass protests against revision of the Japan-U.S. Security Treaty in May-June 1960, thus forcing the prime minister to cancel President Eisenhower's visit and indirectly leading to Kishi's resignation. The events of 1960 were in a real sense a turning point in Japan's postwar politics, in that they marked both a watershed between the politics of Left-Right confrontation on highly charged political and foreign policy issues and a more incrementalist politics based on rapid economic growth and expanding shares.

It was becoming clear even before 1960 that the expansion of JSP electoral support that had been taking place throughout the 1950s was tapering off. Moreover, the party was conspicuously weak at the grass-roots level, having become heavily reliant on the surrogate organization provided by Sōhyō-affiliated unions. Its performance in elections for local government assemblies and local chief-executive positions was proportionally much weaker than its performance in elections for the National Diet. But even at the national parliamentary level, the party appeared unable to jump the barrier of just over one-third of the lower house seats. Evidence was accumulating that younger voters were less enthusiastic about the party than they had been a few years earlier.

The late 1950s also saw a gradual drift to more extreme left-wing positions by the carefully chosen "moderate" leaders of the reunited party. The party secretary-general, Asanuma Inejirō, created a furor in Japan when, in March 1959, in the course of a JSP mission to China, he made the remark that "American imperialism is the common enemy of the peoples of Japan and China." The fact that Asanuma was a veteran leader of Nichirō-kei (i.e., centrist faction) origin clearly indicated how polarized Japanese politics had become by the late 1950s, as the Kishi government proceeded with its revisionist program. The JSP was coming increasingly under the influence of an intellectual pressure group called the Shakaishugi Kyōkai (Socialism Association), led by Professor Sakisaka Itsurō of Kyūshū University. Sakisaka's group espoused an extreme version of the Rōnō school of Marxist analysis referred to earlier, which, although it was critical of the Japan Communist party on many points of doctrine, had also completely rejected the possibility of achieving socialism through democratic parliamentary methods.

The influence of the Shakaishugi Kyōkai and the leftward drift of the JSP leadership was too much for the right-wing Shamin-kei group led by the former union boss, Nishio Suehirō, who was uncompromisingly anti-Communist. In October 1959 Nishio pulled his faction out of the party and was followed by some members of the Nichirō-kei. The next year they founded the Democratic Socialist party (DSP).[11] The background to this split was related in part to the defections of right-wing unions in 1954 from the Sōhyō federation. During the late 1950s a number of long-drawn-out strikes by left-wing unions had resulted in the creation of "second unions," which sought to negotiate compromise agreements with management. Relations between first and second unions were naturally extremely strained, and these strains were reflected in the divisions both at the union federation level and within the JSP. Sakisaka's organization had been particularly active in promoting union intransigence in the strike at the Miike coalfields in Kyūshū, where

TABLE 4.1
JSP multiple candidatures (1958, 1979, and 1990 HR elections)

1958			*1979*			*1990*		
A	*B*	*Total*	*A*	*B*	*Total*	*A*	*B*	*Total*
46 (40%)	91 (79%)	115	9 (7%)	27 (21%)	130	15 (11%)	23 (18%)	130

Note: A = constituencies in which the JSP won two or more seats.
B = constituencies in which the JSP put up two or more candidates.
Total = total number of lower house constituencies.

Sources: Data calculated from *Asahi Nenkan* (1959 and 1980), Mainichi Shinbunsha, *'90 sosenkyo* ('90 Elections), Tokyo, 1990, pp. 14-19.

relations between first and second unions became violent at times. By 1959, therefore, the task of holding together a party composed of such diverse and mutually antagonistic elements had become impossible.

Even though the DSP did not prove as electorally successful as some had predicted it would be, the loss of its right wing seriously depleted the parliamentary ranks of the JSP. Moreover, the traumatic experiences of the May-June crisis of 1960 over revision of the Japan-U.S. Security Treaty, and the November 1960 assassination of JSP Chairman Asanuma Inejirō by an ultranationalist, forced the party to reassess many of its basic policies. Under a new leader, Eda Saburō, the party was introduced to a new doctrine of gradualism (though still with Marxist overtones) known as "structural reform." The emergence of this doctrine, with its nonrevolutionary emphasis on slowly altering the balance of power between labor and capital, was also closely connected with factional realignments and struggles for leadership.

Eda's grip on the sources of power in the JSP proved temporary and fragile.[12] By the end of 1962 he was already being eased out of the leadership; and by May 1965, with the election of Sasaki Kōzō as chairman, the Left was once more firmly in control. The early 1960s, however, saw a remarkable substitution of moderate for extreme policies on the part both of the government (under Ikeda Hayata) and of the principal party of opposition, the JSP, under its moderate chairman, Kawakami Jōtarō.

The second half of the 1960s, however, was a different story. The Vietnam War and associated issues re-created tensions between the government and opposition over policy toward the United States. Fears that Japan was increasingly being used by U.S. forces as a staging post for its operations in Vietnam, and that Japan's security was therefore being jeopardized rather than enhanced by the Japan-U.S. Security Treaty, prompted an extremely confrontational stance by the JSP leaders against the Satō government. The questions of continued U.S. occupation of Okinawa, bad relations between Japan and China, the prospect of a further renewal of the Security Treaty in 1970, and the eruption of student radicalism on campuses throughout the nation in 1968-1970 further added to the political turmoil as well as to the extremism of the JSP leadership.

For the party also, the 1960s were a period of electoral decline, particularly toward the end of the decade (see Table 4.1). In the lower house general elections of December 1969, the JSP lost 50 seats and its total fell from 140 to 90 as a result of the decline in its proportion of the total vote by 6.5 percent. Admittedly, the working of the multimember constituency system produced a greater loss of seats than was really warranted by the loss of votes. Nevertheless, this event was recognized within the party as a disastrous defeat, and once again the party was forced to take stock.

As with the scenario in 1960, when the JSP was weakened by the formation of the DSP, the electoral decline of the late 1960s must be analyzed not only in terms of popular reaction against the party's policies (a factor that was demonstrably involved) but also in terms of the undermining of JSP support by the emergence of new political forces. Not only the formation of the DSP in 1960 but also the emergence of the Kōmeitō in the late 1960s and the electoral resurgence of the JCP a little later made inroads into the electoral support of the JSP as well as of the LDP. A particularly striking fact is that erosion of JSP support occurred most heavily in those metropolitan areas of the Pacific coast which had been the Socialist heartland in the 1950s. According to one study, just 50 percent of the seats classifiable as "metropolitan" went to the JSP in the lower house elections held in 1958; the figures were 24.7 percent for the 1967 elections and a mere 19.7 percent for the elections of 1972. The corresponding figures for "urban" seats were 34.0 percent (1958), 28.1 percent (1967), and 23.5 percent (1972); for "semiurban" seats, 34.2 percent (1958), 30.8 percent (1967), and 28.3 percent (1972); and for seats classified as "rural," 31.8 percent (1958), 30.3 percent (1967), and 23.3 percent (1972).[13] In other words, while the number of JSP seats had decreased in all categories, the party lost ground more heavily in Japan's biggest cities, particularly Tokyo, Ōsaka, and Yokohama, than in other parts of the country. Indeed, by 1972 the party was doing marginally better in rural and small-town Japan than in the larger cities and towns. These latter were precisely the areas in which the Kōmeitō, the JCP, and, to a lesser extent, the DSP were picking up support.

Kōmeitō and Communist successes were premised on a vigorous and precise approach to organization in which the membership of large numbers of committed individuals was a major factor. This the JSP, with its continued reliance upon surrogate organization by Sōhyō-affiliated labor unions, could not match. Although it could maintain a good part of the support of those who had been attracted to its cause in the late 1940s and the 1950s, it had difficulty persuading new voters to rally to its side, particularly those who might have been expected to grant their support on the basis of their residence in singularly alienating conditions in large metropolitan apartment blocs or other, often low-quality, housing.

The JSP was also ill-equipped to take advantage of the new style of progressive politics that was emerging in the early 1970s, centering on issues of environmental pollution and related questions and involving the emergence of citizens' movements as a vital and to some extent unpredictable political force at the grass-roots level. Nevertheless, Socialist backing was an important element in most of the newly emerging "progressive local authorities," which made their appearance around this time in the larger cities and urban prefectures. Sometimes, as in Kyōto during the campaign prior to the 1974 elections for governor, the Socialists found themselves outclassed organizationally by the Communists, such that participation in progressive coalitional arrangements at the local level was not always a comfortable experience for them.

If the 1960s were a period of rapid and disturbing decline for the JSP, the 1970s saw a certain consolidation of its electoral strength, even though the overall trend still appeared to be one of gradual diminution. It was difficult to find a commentator prepared to argue that the JSP had come close to sorting out its problems or turning itself into a vital and dynamic party of opposition. Indeed, the prevailing image was one of stagnation and conservatism of outdated policies and attitudes, although fundamental intra-party ideological divisions remained. To some extent, however, it was true that things were not as bad as they had been in the 1960s. For one thing, after the turbulent leadership politics of the 1960s, greater stability of leadership was achieved in the 1970s. Between 1970 and 1977 the top two party posts of chairman and secretary-general were in the hands, respectively, of Narita Tomomi and Ishibashi Masashi, neither of whom had strong factional connections. In other words, they were free to exercise the arts of compromise and reconciliation between the Left and the Right.

The stability, however, was only relative. During the early and middle 1970s Eda Saburō was actively exploring the possibility of creating a new left-of-center coalition (or even a single party) combining the DSP, the Kōmeitō, and sympathetic sections of the JSP. The problem with this approach was that it could succeed only at the cost of splitting the JSP once again, as the left wing of the JSP was most unlikely to accept such an arrangement. The official JSP policy, which reflected the need felt by the Narita-Ishibashi leadership to conciliate the Left as well as the Right, was that the party should work for an alliance of all opposition parties including the JCP. However unrealizable such a program might have appeared, it at least had the merit that it did not provoke internecine strife among the various factions of the JSP.

While Eda and his supporters were exploring an alternative "opening to the center," Sakisaka's extreme left-wing organization, the Shakaishugi Kyōkai, was revealing substantially increased strength at party congresses. Although it remained weak among JSP Diet members, the Shakaishugi Kyōkai by the mid-1970s commanded impressive support among rank-and-file activists.

The year 1977 was a time of crisis for the JSP, torn as it was between the fissiparous tendencies of the Eda group on the Right and the Shakaishugi Kyōkai on the Left. An ironic result of the latter's emergence as a major force within the party was that Sasaki and Eda, rivals for leadership in the 1960s, found themselves working together to prevent its takeover of the JSP. The Atarashii Nagare no Kai (New Current Society), a grouping of various anti-Kyōkai elements, had been formed essentially for this purpose, but in early 1977 it appeared to have its back against the wall in the face of ample evidence of Kyōkai resurgence. In the spring of 1977 Eda finally defected from the party, to be joined later in the year by Den Hideo and a few others. The defections that occurred during the year were not large in number, but they resulted in the formation of a new mini-party, the Shakai Minshu Rengō (Shaminren), or Social Democratic League. Eda, however, died shortly after leaving the JSP and did not live to see the formation of the new party.

Narita and Ishibashi also tendered their resignations from the two top posts in the JSP in the summer, and Narita proposed Asukata Ichio, the progressive mayor of Yokohama, as his successor. Asukata represented an adventurous prospect given that, although he had been a Socialist Diet member up until the early 1960s, it was his more recent career as an innovative and radical mayor of one of Japan's largest and most polluted cities for which he was best known. His political philosophy was based on notions of administrative decentralization and local initiatives, which contrasted markedly with assumptions about the building of socialism through central control prevalent especially on the Left of the JSP. Nevertheless, Asukata was a politician strongly influenced by Marxist categories of analysis.[14] He initially refused the nomination because of the atmosphere of intraparty acrimony in which it was introduced. By holding out for three months he was able to become party chairman with the image of a unifying leader, rather than the partisan figure he might have appeared to be had he accepted nomination at the September congress of the party. He was also able to have his own conditions for nomination accepted.[15]

After the traumatic year of 1977, when arguably a most serious intraparty split was narrowly avoided, the JSP appeared to take on a new lease on life under the chairmanship of Asukata. The new chairman put a great deal of effort into the creation of mass party membership; and although the initial aim of 1 million members was from the start quite unrealizable, the number of individual members of the party rose gradually. Asukata also instituted a system whereby the party chairman was elected by the total membership of the party instead of by delegates to the party congress—a system that paralleled one newly introduced into the LDP. Both of these reforms, as well as Asukata's policy line of administrative decentralization, infused a certain amount of new life and purpose into the party as a whole, which for a long time had been running through a process of constant maneuvering among factions of Diet members.

Asukata's reforms did not, however, effect a radical breakthrough in the chronic structural, organizational, and ideological problems of the JSP, which by the end of Asukata's period in office in 1983 seemed only marginally less demoralized than it had been when he assumed office. The party fared poorly in the lower house general elections of 1979 and 1980, as well as in the upper house elections of 1980 and 1983. Many of the progressive local administrations (*kakushin jichitai*), which had dominated the big-city scene in the early and middle 1970s and had formed such an important bulwark of Asukata's political philosophy, had been replaced by administrations of a conservative coloring by the early 1980s. Plainly, there was a conservative mood in the country that was not especially receptive to the messages that the JSP had to offer, even if the JSP had been able to overcome the structural problems that had weakened its impact over the years. Moreover, Asukata himself was widely criticized both within the party and outside it for his indecisiveness and lack of an appealing image. Several political decisions between 1980 and 1983 harmed his reputation, and in the summer of 1983 he announced his resignation. Ishibashi Masashi was elected, unopposed, as his successor.

Ishibashi proved to be a vigorous and reformist leader. Determined—as he reiterated at every opportunity—to transform the JSP from a party of perpetual opposition into a party ready to participate in power, he set out to galvanize the JSP into modernizing itself, which meant relinquishing many of its ancient shibboleths. The road to reform was not easy, however, and like other chairmen before him, he faced strong resistance from the left wing. Sometimes the result was an uneasy compromise. For instance, the party congress of February 1984 came up with a policy position regarding the Self-Defense Forces, which held that they were unconstitutional but also, as their existence was based on parliamentary approval, that they should be considered "legal." The party also softened somewhat its previous hostility to nuclear power stations.

The most important change promoted by Ishibashi was the rewriting of the party's 1955 platform, "The Road to Socialism in Japan," which was a document heavily infused with Marxist concepts and rhetoric. After much difficult debate, a modernized platform replacing the 1955 document was approved by the party congress in January 1986.

In July 1986 simultaneous elections were held for the upper and lower houses of the National Diet. The elections produced a sweeping victory for the LDP under Nakasone Yasuhiro, and the JSP was crushingly defeated, seeing its lower house seat total reduced to 86. Ishibashi accepted responsibility for the defeat and resigned the party chairmanship. In his stead the party chose Doi Takako, a JSP lower house Diet member since 1969.

The choice of a woman as leader of a political party for the first time in Japanese history caused an immediate sensation in the mass media, which thrives on political sensations. Her election, however, was no nine-day wonder. Over time, she developed a strong profile as a political leader skilled in communication, with a gift for presenting political issues to ordinary people in ways that could be readily understood. Even though her capacity to reform the party has arguably proved limited, there seems little doubt that the upsurge in support for the JSP apparent in 1989–1990 owes much to the charisma that she has been able to establish.

Doi Takako was born in 1928 as the second daughter of a medical doctor working in Kōbe. Before entering Parliament in 1969, she taught constitutional law at Dōshisha University in Kyōto and has spoken frequently on constitutional issues as party leader. Her intellectual background should hardly be seen as radically reformist in terms of the party's history, and her style has been to speak out trenchantly in defense of the peace clause of the 1946 constitution, against government proposals for taxation reform and against the lifting of agricultural protection, particularly of rice. On the other hand, as party leader she has clearly developed a feel for what works politically, and her performance in election campaigns has been impressive. Her careful cultivation of the women's vote, though an obvious strategy for a female leader, has paid off well. The party's official description of her as essentially an ordinary person, without pretension, appears not to be too far from the truth.[16]

A few months after Doi Takako was given the leadership of the JSP, the importance of taxation reform as a political issue from which the party could derive electoral advantage became apparent. Early in 1987 the durable Nakasone government, given confidence by its strong performance in the double elections six months previously, proposed to introduce a form of value-added tax (*uriagezei*), despite the fact that the prime minister had made what appeared to be a promise in the electoral campaign that he was not thinking of introducing any new large-scale indirect taxes. In March 1987 a JSP candidate reaped the benefit of popular anxiety about the value-added tax by overturning the previous LDP majority in an upper house by-election in Iwate Prefecture in the north of Honshū. The Nakasone government later withdrew the proposal.

Following Nakasone's retirement from the prime ministership and his succession by Takeshita Noboru in November 1987, the new Takeshita government in March 1988 announced proposals for a new kind of indirect tax, to be called "consumption tax" (*shōhizei*). In the face of determined opposition led by the JSP, the related bills were "forced" through the lower house during November 1988 (in other words an affirmative vote was taken in the absence of Diet members from the JSP and some other parties) and through the upper house in December. A consumption tax of 3 percent thereby came into effect on April 1, 1989.

Beginning in the summer of 1988, Japanese politics in general and the Takeshita administration in particular were increasingly traumatized by what became known as the "Recruit scandal." The ambitious head of a company specializing in employment information saturated the political world with unlisted shares in a subsidiary company, Recruit Cosmos. The shares could be sold at a profit once the company was listed on the stock exchange, but the whole operation was highly questionable under Japanese law. Revelations concerning the Recruit scandal came cumulatively, and politicians of almost all persuasions were found to be implicated. In November a JSP Diet member, Ueda Takumi, admitted that his secretary had accepted Recruit Cosmos shares, and Ueda promptly relinquished his seat in the Diet to accept responsibility. This prompt action by one of its parliamentarians enabled the party to escape the opprobrium that came to attach more and more to other parties, and in particular to leading members of almost every faction in the LDP. Public opinion polls revealed rapidly declining support for the Takeshita cabinet, and in April Takeshita announced his resignation, being succeeded in June by Uno Sōsuke.

Uno had scarcely taken up the reins of prime ministerial office when allegations began to be made about inappropriate activity in his private life. It is hardly surprising, therefore, that when the House of Councillors elections were held in July, the LDP found itself at the nadir of its support.

When the election results were announced, the JSP was for the first time the largest party by numbers of seats, having won 35.1 percent of the vote in the national (proportional representation) constituency, and 31.6 percent in the prefectual constituencies. For the first time in its history, the LDP was forced into a minority position of 109 seats out of 252. The effective total of JSP seats was further augmented by the success of several candidates standing under the label of the recently formed Rengō (Alliance) labor union federation. Doi Takako, quoting a poem by the turn-of-the-century feminist poet Yosano Akiko, announced: "The mountains have moved."[17]

Apart from the Recruit scandal, the issue of consumption tax, and the prime minister's private life, an issue that undoubtedly swung many votes from the LDP to the JSP (and Rengō) in agricultural areas was the earlier decision to lift agricultural protection on some agricultural products, notably beef and citrus fruits. Thus in the 26 single-member constituencies, which were mostly rural/agricultural prefectures away from the big cities, an LDP majority of 25 out of 26 was converted to a JSP/Rengō majority of 23. Another feature of the election was the unprecedented number of women candidates standing for the JSP, of whom 12 were elected. This was known in the press as the "Madonna strategy" and gained the party a great deal of (mostly favorable) publicity.

With the substitution of Kaifu Toshiki for the hapless Uno as prime minister following the elections, the LDP gradually managed to restore a degree of normality to its affairs, and little by little the steam went out of the various issues that had lost the party the upper house elections. Thus, although it lost seats in the House of Representatives elections of February 1990, it emerged with a healthy majority. The JSP did not fulfill its promise of winning the elections (which was in any case unlikely) but it succeeded in increasing its seat total from the abysmal 86 lower house seats it had been reduced to in 1986, up to 136 seats in 1990.

The elections of 1989 and 1990 thus ushered in a period in which the JSP, though it had failed to convince the electorate that it was capable of governing the country, had asserted convincingly its primacy among the opposition parties—a position that it had once occupied but that over many years had appeared to be slipping away from it. The long years in the remote political wilderness had bred low morale and a certain complacency within its ranks. The task facing the Doi leadership as a result of its political resurgency was to convert the party from a "party out of power" (*yatō*) to a party capable of mounting effective opposition and, ultimately, of achieving power.[18]

One manifestation of the changes being wrought in the party by its electoral successes was the formation of a body called the New Wave Society (Nyū Uēbu no Kai), consisting of 28 out of the 50 lower house Diet members newly elected in the February 1990 elections. Nine out of the 28 were lawyers and others followed a variety of occupations, but the labor union representation was minimal. The New Wave Society, which maintained close links with the Shaminren (Social Democratic Federation) was actively exploring ways of reforming the party structure and policies in such a way as to make it a party of true opposition and potentially of government.

An indication of how the JSP leadership conceived the party's role and strategy in the early 1990s was given by the participation of its vice-chairman, Tanabe Makoto, alongside the chairman of the Takeshita faction of the LDP, Kanemaru Shin, in the Kanemaru-Tanabe mission to North Korea in September 1990. The JSP had long maintained links with North Korea, despite the absence of diplomatic relations between Japan and that country. The mission was successful in securing the release of two Japanese fishermen incarcerated in North Korea since 1983 and opened up the possibility of normalizing relations between the two countries. This was an example of the JSP offering to "share" its links to the North Korean regime with the ruling party in Tokyo in return for a part of the action in an important diplomatic démarche.

PARTY STRUCTURE AND ORGANIZATION

The formal organizational structure of the JSP incorporates substantial elements of democracy. The most important democratic element in the party organization is the Congress, which must be held at least once per year (although provision is also made for extraordinary congresses). The Congress acts as more than a sounding board for rank-and-file opinion, given that major party posts are determined by Congress votes and Congress resolutions are expected to be taken seriously by the leadership. The role of the party Congress in the JSP is much greater than the role of the equivalent body in the LDP, partly, no doubt, because the JSP is out of office. The main organs whose members are chosen by the Congress are the Central Executive Committee, the Control Commission, and the Central Committee. Of these, the Central Executive Committee (CEC) is by far the most important; in effect, it constitutes the party's central governing body. The Control Commission is supposed to deal with matters of party discipline, and the Central Committee, which is supposed to take over from the Congress when it is not in session, in fact plays a minimal role.[19]

In one respect, the character of the party Congress has been subject to crucial fluctuations. Delegates to the Congress include officials of central party headquarters and representatives of local branches. Until 1962 it was normal for Diet members to qualify automatically as delegates to the national Congress in Tokyo. From 1962, however, they could become delegates only if elected from local branches. This change took on considerable importance in view of the general tendency for Diet members to be relatively conservative and pragmatic in contrast to rank-and-file branch activists, who tend to be more militant and concerned with ideological purity. This exclusion of JSP Diet members became a particular problem in the mid-1970s, when a large number of Shakaishugi Kyōkai members and sympathizers were being elected to the Congress, whereas the Kyōkai enjoyed the support of only a tiny minority of Diet members. In 1977, as a result of the serious intraparty crisis of that year, the situation more or less returned to that existing before 1962, and the influence of the Shakaishugi Kyōkai in the party Congress subsequently declined.

As is common in Japanese political organizations generally, strenuous efforts are made to avoid open contests in the election to party posts at each Congress. In the JSP these efforts are a reflection less of the cultural norm of consensus than of the crucial necessity of prearranging selection to posts if damaging factional and Left-Right wrangles are to be avoided on the floor of the Congress. The party's worst crises (e.g., those in 1949–1951, 1959–1960, at various times during the 1960s, in 1977, and again in 1982) tend to occur when either the Left or the Right is seen by the other to be seeking to monopolize executive positions. A balanced ticket has therefore been a practical necessity if damaging conflict and, ultimately, the splitting of the party are to be avoided. Unfortunately, however, a balanced ticket is not always the best way of producing innovative, appealing, or even clear and comprehensible policies given the gulf that, for much of its history, has divided the JSP between Marxists and democratic socialists. This, in a sense, has been the party's ultimate dilemma.

The CEC, as the party's chief executive body, is responsible for general policy formulation and oversight of party organization. As the party rules describe it: "The Central Executive Committee represents the party as its highest executive organ, and is responsible to the National Congress and the Central Committee."[20] It meets frequently, and much of its work is done in functional branches (*kyoku*) and committees. The role of the chairman of the Executive Committee (often simply referred to as "party chairman") in relation to the committee itself is controversial. The determination to maintain intraparty democracy and rank-and-file influence has often meant a relatively weak role for the chairman. One of Asukata's main conditions for accepting the party chairmanship in 1977 was that the chairman should be able to break deadlocks in the CEC—deadlocks that had sometimes paralyzed its effectiveness in the past.[21]

Under the leadership of Doi Takako, the party has not radically changed its organizational structure, and as before effective control of the party has depended on the ability of the chairman, secretary-general, and a small number of other principal party officials to work closely together. Thus in 1990 Doi Takako (chairman), Yamaguchi Tsuruo (secretary-general), and Tanabe Makoto (vice-chairman) formed a close-knit team able to cooperate in the formulation of party strategy.

A proposal under active discussion in the party during 1990 was the formation of a "shadow cabinet" system, based on the British model, whereby ministerial portfolios would be "shadowed" by JSP Diet members specifically appointed for the purpose. The establishment of such a system would enable those so appointed to acquire expertise in the relevant policy area, and the party as a whole would be able to project a more convincing image to the electorate as a party that really thought about policy. Procedures for appointment were contentious, as they bore on the basic power structure (including the factional structure) within the party.

Leadership

The leaders of the party at the national level include the chairman of the CEC (the party chairman), a small but variable number of vice-chairmen (usually between two and four), the secretary-general, the chairman of the Control Commission, chairmen of the branches and committees of the CEC, and a number of party advisers, or elders (*komon*). Throughout most of the party's history the National Congress elected the chairman, but Asukata instituted a process of election among the party membership at large.

Leadership selection in the JSP has been a question to which enormous attention is paid within the party; indeed, the choice of chairman and secretary-general, as well as the distribution of top posts generally, has often been obsessively contested among various factions and other intraparty groups. Even though the number of posts and the degree of power, opportunity, and prestige they carry are less than those associated with the LDP, there are marked similarities between the scramble for position in the JSP and that in the LDP. Despite the difference between the two parties in the greater role accorded by the JSP to the National Congress, they are very much alike in adhering to the practice of rotating positions so as to satisfy the aspirations for office of the different intraparty groups. Moreover, although this rotation occurs as a result of regular contests, maneuvers, and calculations about a shifting balance of power, there is the unwritten expectation that ultimately all interested groups will be given some share in the power available. In the JSP the failure, even over a relatively short term, to fulfill such expectations creates disruptive friction and strife, as we have seen. It may also be noted that this system of leadership selection differs greatly in practice from that employed by either the Kōmeitō or the JCP—especially in the case of the former, in which the tenure of top positions by the same individuals has been of much greater duration.

The party chairman plainly occupies a key position in the party, even though the chairman commands far less power and fewer resources than the president of the LDP. It is difficult to generalize about the ten chairmen and the one acting chairman experienced by the party between 1945 and 1990.[22] Nearly all of these individuals came to the chairmanship after long experience in the party or, in the case of the earlier postwar incumbents, in the prewar Socialist movement, which would include left-wing parties and labor and tenant organizations. Asukata was an exception: Although he had been a Socialist Diet member until the early 1960s, he was fully occupied in his post as mayor of Yokohama between 1963 and 1978. He was therefore the only chairman who could be said to have been brought into the party from the outside. Eda Saburō, acting chairman for a few months following the assassination of Asanuma in October 1960 and a key contender for the chairmanship throughout the early 1960s, was somewhat exceptional in having been very little known outside the party until 1960, and then for having sought the wholesale reform of the party's policies and image without first serving a long leadership "apprenticeship." It should be noted, however, that this experiment was ultimately not successful.

The chairmen up to the late 1960s—namely, Katayama Tetsu, Suzuki Mosaburō, Kawakami Jōtarō, Sasaki Kōzō, and Katsumata Seiichi—were all faction leaders of long standing, and Asanuma Inejirō, though not technically leading a faction (he belonged to the Kawakami faction), had essentially come from the same mold as other faction leaders (Katayama's case is also perhaps a little doubtful). Narita Tomomi (the chairman from 1969–1977), like his long-standing deputy in the position of secretary-general, Ishibashi Masashi, had always avoided strong factional identification, and this was also the case with his successor, Asukata Ichio. The two most recent chairmen, Ishibashi Masashi and Doi Takako, have also not been closely identified with established factions, so that the party may be said to have established a definite pattern in this regard, whereby chairmen derive their acceptability from their believed neutrality, or at least nonpartisanship, in factional contests. Such neutrality has not precluded chairmen from vigorously pursuing fundamental reforms to policy and organization.

In the case of Doi Takako, a new element has entered into the situation, namely that her national popularity has clearly been a major element creating the party's impressive electoral showing in the 1989 and 1990 elections. Her popularity stems partly from the fact that she is the first woman to lead a political party in Japanese history and partly from her demonstrated capacity to articulate policy in no-nonsense ways that ordinary people can understand. Support for her, however, among JSP Diet members met by the present writer in summer 1990 appeared to be by no means universal, with some arguing that she did not sufficiently consult with them, and others regarding her as an obstacle, because of her firm views on certain issues, to needed reform of party policy. Even so, most conceded that any move to replace her as leader would remove a prime factor in the party's newfound popularity with the electorate. Despite this, JSP Vice-Chairman Tanabe replaced Doi in July 1991.

Factionalism

As should now be abundantly clear, factionalism has been a pervasive feature of the JSP since its inception. Much has been written about factionalism in Japanese political parties,[23] and it is easy to regard JSP factionalism simply as a further example of a common phenomenon. In some ways, of course, one may reasonably regard JSP factions merely from the standpoint of Japanese political culture and refrain from much further exploration. Factions in the JSP exhibit symptoms of traditional *oyabun-kobun* (surrogate parent-surrogate child, or "boss-henchman") relationships, compete for intraparty posts for their members, serve as channels for funding to help members fight elections, and seek to influence the party leadership and party policies in various ways. Hence they resemble the factions in the LDP, except that their contests are political sideshows whereas those in the LDP occupy center stage.

Important and interesting differences do exist, however. First, conflicts of policy and ideology appear to assume a greater importance for the JSP factions. Parallels may be found in other countries, where the parties of the Left appear to be more prone to factional division based on ideological difference than do the parties of the Right. Second (and equally obvious), the discipline of power, which is present in the LDP, is absent in the case of the JSP. This is not to say that factionalism is absent in the first and present in the second but, rather, that for the JSP there is no restraint on factional disruption imposed (as for the LDP) by the desire to retain power. A comparison of the history of splits and defections in the two parties is at least suggestive in this regard.[24]

The third difference concerns the significant change that occurred in the character of factionalism in the JSP from the 1940s and 1950s to the 1970s and 1980s. JSP factions in the later period appear to be more amorphous and fluid than they had been in the earlier period. One possible reason for this stems from the election system. It has long been recognized that in the larger parties the multimember constituency system tends to create or at least exacerbate factional divisions by forcing candidates of the same party to stand against each other in the same constituency. Clearly, the larger the party is, the more likely this factor will operate—and the LDP is the example usually given. The JSP is a party whose Diet representation has declined over the period in question (i.e., 1955–1990). Thus it is at least possible that the apparent change in the character of factionalism might be casually connected with a decline in the number of constituencies in which more than one JSP candidate is running.

From Table 4.1 it can readily be seen that multiple candidacies on the part of the JSP drastically declined between the 1958 elections (when the JSP representation was at its height) and those of 1979. Whereas in 1958 the party put forward more than one candidate in almost four-fifths of all lower house constituencies, the proportion had fallen to just over one-fifth in the 1979 elections. Constituencies in which more than two Socialists were successful amounted in 1958 to two-fifths of the total, but in 1979 to less than one-tenth. Moreover (although this is not shown in the table), eight constituencies in 1958 elected three Socialists, but in 1979 only one, and in 1990 none. Interestingly enough, by 1990, despite the JSP resurgence, the proportion of multiple candidacies and seats did not greatly differ from 1979. This shows that by comparison with the late 1950s, JSP electoral support remained widely spread rather than concentrated in urban areas. Whereas in the late 1950s the JSP was similar to the LDP in presenting several candidates in many constituencies, in more recent times it elected one candidate in nearly all constituencies (93 percent in the 1990 elections), but more than one in rather few (11 percent in 1990). We are unable to establish with complete certainty a connection between this and a change in the character of JSP factions. We suggest, however, that a connection does exist, and that it can be described in the following way.

Factionalism exists to some extent in all Japanese political parties, although in one or two instances it is actively suppressed. In the smaller parties factions are somewhat amorphous groupings around particular leaders, but in the LDP they constitute highly organized machines designed for the pursuit of political power. Among the reasons for which LDP factions need to be organized as sophisticated political machines is the necessity to pit competitive political campaigns against the campaigns of other candidates from the same party. As elections are extremely expensive, factions, rather than the party itself, serve as the main channels of funding to candidates. Factions in the JSP were never organized with the degree of sophistication attained by LDP factions, but up to the 1970s they were cohesive and had a strong sense of identity and separateness. It was unusual to find two members of the same faction fighting the same constituency, and factions not only took on electoral tasks for their members but also competed in struggles for party leadership.

As can be seen from Figure 4.1, the party at its inception in 1945 consisted essentially of four factions, three of which were previously identified as Rōnō-kei, Nichirō-kei, and Shamin-kei. (The agriculturally based Hirano faction left the party in January 1948 and was henceforth of no significance.) By the time of JSP reunification in 1955, the party contained five factions, three of which (those led by Suzuki, Kawakami, and Nishio) were lineal descendants of the three just mentioned. Apart from these, the left-wing Wada faction was the following of Wada Hiroo, a former official of the Ministry of Agriculture and Forestry and, later, minister of agriculture. Because of the bureaucratic origin of its leader and some of his closest associates, this faction was known in the press as a "bureaucrat's" faction. On the extreme Left there was now also a small grouping called the Heiwa Dōshikai (Peace Comrades Association), headed at that time by the leader of a repressed minority caste, Matsumoto Jiichirō. Apart, perhaps, from the Heiwa Dōshikai, these factions had strong leader-follower characteristics, much like the factions in the LDP.

In 1959–1960 the Nishio faction and part of the Kawakami faction defected and formed the DSP. Within the JSP, the emergence of "structural reform" as a new doctrine promoted by Eda Saburō and others was the focus for major factional realignment. Following Suzuki's retirement, his faction split between the followers of Sasaki Kōzō, who opposed it. The remnants of the Kawakami faction and the Wada faction (which became the Katsumata faction after Wada's death in 1967) largely supported structural reform, whereas the Heiwa Dōshikei split between supporters and opponents, and the Shakaishugi Kyōkai, which was becoming a force in the party from the early 1960s, saw it as ideologically revisionist and strongly opposed it. During the 1970s the main political alignments related to a division between a broadly leftist alliance backing the chairman, Narita Tomomi, and the Atarashii Nagare no Kai, which sought to combat the increasing influence of the Shakaishugi Kyōkai.

FIGURE 4.1
Factional history of the Japan Socialist party

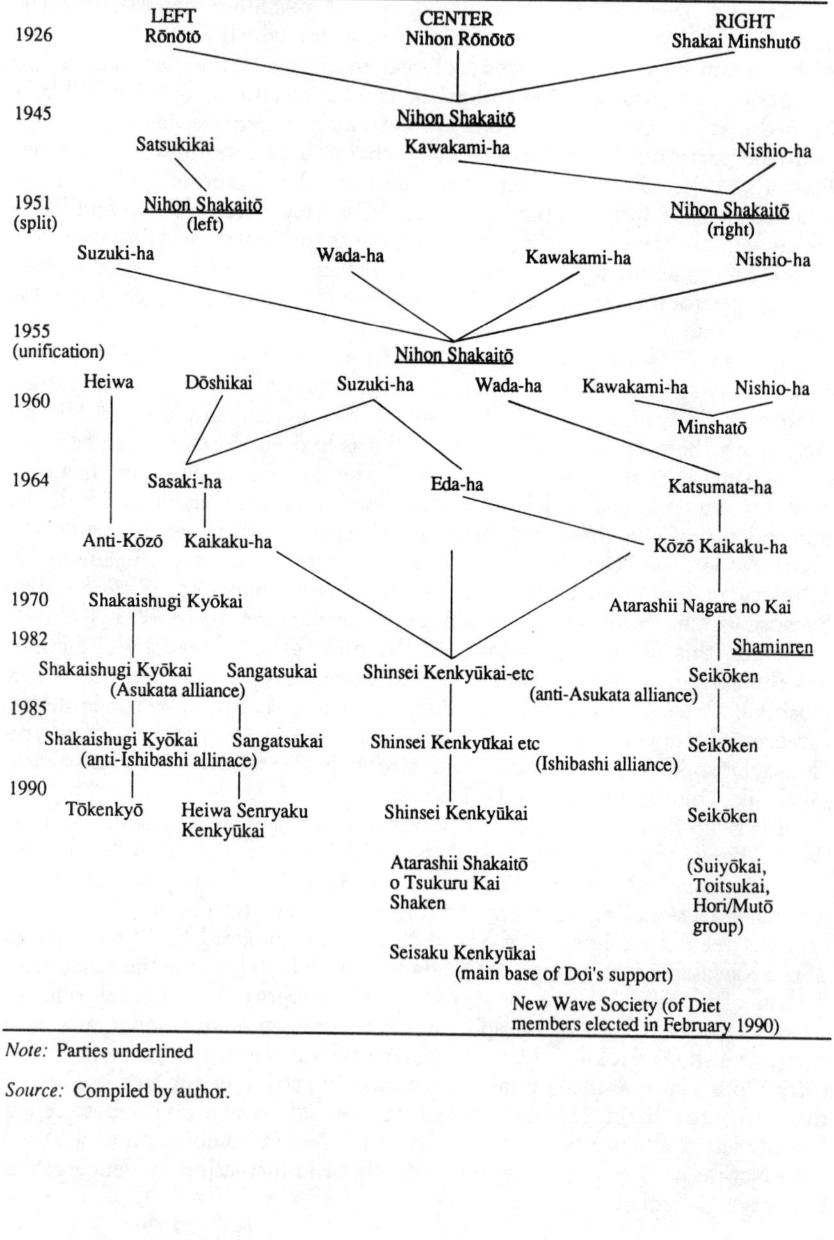

Note: Parties underlined

Source: Compiled by author.

As the appointment of Asukata as chairman and the defections that occurred during 1977 brought about a further factional realignment, the situation by 1982 was exceedingly complicated. Broadly speaking, an "Asukata alliance" of Left and Center confronted an "anti-Asukata alliance" of Center and Right. Even more broadly speaking, the Ishibashi regime was based on the Right and elements of the Center against the Left, but the factional situation was very fluid and not wholly dependent on ideological factors. The factional situation has not fundamentally changed under Doi Takako, except that the far left has much declined, especially after the death of its principal mentor, Professor Sakisaka Itsurō, in 1985. Doi, like Ishibashi, is sustained essentially by a center and right-of-center alliance, but is herself almost entirely nonfactional. The most interesting development since the February 1990 elections has been previously mentioned: the formation of the New Wave Society of newly elected JSP Diet members with close links to Eda Satsuki and the Shaminren. Whether this should be called a faction is a matter of definition, but its members generally say it is not a faction in the old sense.[25]

In Table 4.2 is a compilation of skeleton information, largely serving an illustrative purpose, on the various groups and factions that existed in the JSP in the late 1980s and 1990. JSP factions are much more shadowy organizations than factions in the LDP, and far less information is available about them in the press. Their comparatively amorphous nature is illustrated by the fact that different JSP Diet members will provide intraparty-factions lists that are somewhat inconsistent with each other. Factions are normally designated as study groups rather than leader-follower groups, but leadership is not unimportant. It should be clear from Figure 4.1 and Table 4.2 that the relatively firm factional and ideological divisions of twenty-five and thirty years earlier have become jumbled and confused, and the remnant of the far Left is perhaps the only group attempting to maintain much continuity with the past.

Factionalism is thus less rife within the JSP than it once was, but it still constitutes a problem for the Doi leadership and for attempts to reform party policy. Appointments to policy organs, particularly the Policy Deliberation Council (Seisaku Shingikai), are still largely made along factional lines, and this continues to result in sterility in policy discussion.[26]

Interest Group Ties, Party Finances, and Membership

For many years the principal organization and financial backing for the JSP was provided by the Sōhyō federation of labor unions. The recent amalgamation of the various labor union federations into a single organization, Shin Rengō, was one of the factors prompting the JSP to seek to broaden its base of support.[27] Although Sōhyō, as Japan's largest union federation with over 4 million members, was in some ways a powerful and effective backer, the dominant influence within Sōhyō of public-sector unions severely limited the JSP's appeal, given the parochial nature of the interests and grievances of those unions. In any case, however, several of the enterprises

TABLE 4.2

JSP factional composition, late 1980s and 1990

Note: L to R: name of faction [translation] (former name). Number of JSP Diet members affiliated. Leading member(s).

A. Right-wing factions:

Suiyōkai [Wednesday Society] (former Eda faction). 28. Tanabe Makoto, Yamaguchi Tsuruo.

Tōitsukai [Unity Society] (former Kawakami faction). 9. Kawakami Tamio, Kawamata Kenjiro.

Hori/Muto Group. 5. Hori Masao, Mutō Sanji.

These three are also grouped together as Seiken Kōsō Kenkyūkai (Seikōken) [Political Power Structure Study Group]. 55.

These groups are ideologically most in sympathy with European social democratic and labor parties and worked assiduously for revision of the party platform, finally achieved in 1986, along social democratic lines. Apart from the three groups listed above, some members of the former Atarashii Nagare no Kai [New Current Society] also belong to Seikōken. These groups have constituted the core backing for the successive chairmanships of Ishibashi and Doi.

B. Centrist factions:

Seisaku Kenkyūkai [Policy Research Group] (former Katsumata faction). 9. Ishibashi Masashi, Itō Shigeru, Kadoya Kenjirō.

This group can trace its history back to the faction led by Wada Hiroo, a former civil servant and early postwar minister of agriculture, and later by Katsumata Seiichi, who was party Chairman briefly in the late 1960s. Ideologically it was formerly regarded as "moderate left" within the party, but is now generally seen as "centrist."

Shakaishugi Kenkyūkai (Shaken) [Socialism Research Group] (former Sasaki faction). 10. Hirose Hideyoshi (retired before 1990 lower house elections).

This group inherited a pro-China position from its former Chairman, Sasaki Kōzō, in the late 1960s, when it was regarded as extremely radical. Not much of this still remains. It has expended much energy combatting the far left. Once a powerful faction, but now in decline.

Atarashii Shakaitō o Tsukuru Kai [Society to Create a New Socialist Party]. 20. Yamamoto Masahiro, Ogawa Jinichi, Ōhara Tōru.

Shinsei Kenkyūkai (Shinseiken) [New Life Research Group]. A rather heterogeneous and amorphous centrist grouping, with some tendency to lean to the left. 14. Shimazaki Yuzuru.

C. Left-wing factions:

Heiwa Senryaku Kenkyūkai [Peace Strategy Research Group]. 32 (but some overlapping membership with other groups). Shitoma Hiroshi, Yadabe Osamu.

This is the former Sangatsukai [March Society], which was in essence the representatives in the National Diet of the former Shakaishugi Kyōkai [Socialism Association], the latter being strong in some constituency parties but weak in the National Diet.

Tō Kensetsu Kenkyū Zenkoku Renraku Kyōgikai (Tōkenkyō) [National Liaison Council for Party Construction Research]. 4. Takazawa Torao, Shibutani Sumio.

This is the remnant of the former Shakaishugi Kyōkai, originally founded by the late Professor Sakisaka as a Marxist-Leninist, strongly pro-Soviet ideological organization, quite distinct, nevertheless, from the Japan Communist party. It was strong in constituency branches in the 1970s, but has since declined, particularly since the death of its founder in 1985. It still has a following in some party constituency branches.

D. Nonfactional grouping:

Nyū Uēbu no Kai [New Wave Society]. 28.

This group, founded by 28 JSP Diet members newly elected in the lower house elections of February 1990, is dedicated to preparing the party as a genuine alternative government. Several of its members are lawyers, and the feature that most sharply distinguishes it from the rest of the party is the almost total absence of former labor union officials in its ranks. It has established close links with the Shaminren, led by Eda Satsuki, son of the late Eda Saburō.

Sources: Information given by persons connected with the JSP during several visits by the writer to Japan, the latest being in the summer of 1990; *Asahi Shinbun* (September 19, 1989), *Asahi Jānaru,* (August 11,1989), pp. 14-18.

whose workers were powerful within Sōhyō were privatized during the 1980s, thus reducing the size and effectiveness of public-sector unions as a whole. Indeed, this was one factor in the dissolution of Sōhyō and formation of a single major union center.

Despite the dissolution of Sōhyō, union support for JSP Diet candidates remains important, essentially for three reasons. One is that many JSP candidates receive their principal organizational support from unions that are strong in their constituency. Often it is a case of the union giving support for a candidate who has emerged from the ranks of its own officials, which leads us to the second reason why unions are influential. Many JSP Diet members are former union officials (in the past at times over half of them have been). This has had the effect of restricting the opportunities for talented people not of union background to be chosen as Diet candidates.

The third reason concerns funding. Although the actual amount of money received by the party is impossible to estimate with any accuracy (as in the case of the LDP), membership dues have clearly made up only a relatively small part of total funding. Much of the supplement has come from the union movement, but the party has received money from a variety of sources as well, including a certain amount from business firms.

It would be incorrect to suggest that the JSP is completely dominated by labor unions, as a variety of other interests in small business, the professions, the intellectual community, and even the farming sector[28] give it a certain amount of support. Although it is almost always politically useful for interest groups to make contacts with the LDP and the government bureaucracy, the JSP role in Diet committees and elsewhere has always meant that some interest groups consider it worthwhile to cultivate the JSP to some extent.

One issue that has much exercised the JSP over the years is the question of individual membership. During the early 1970s party membership, never high, had fallen to perhaps as low as 30,000. Successive party chairmen sought to increase membership, and Asukata talked of having a million members of the JSP eventually. Even though much of the effective organizational support for the party came from unionists who were party backers, and on occasion from workers but who were not formerly enrolled as workers, it was embarrassing to have a far lower level of membership than parties electorally much weaker, such as the Kōmeitō and the JCP. During the 1980s, the number of members began to creep upward, and this process was much accelerated when in 1988 Doi Takako announced a scheme for "cooperative party members" (*kyōryoku tōin*), who for a membership fee of 500 yen per month were given a vote in JSP chairmanship elections. According to one report, membership numbers had advanced to an unprecedented 125,000 by the summer of 1989.[29]

Electoral and Campaign Styles

Until the upper and lower house elections of 1989 and 1990, JSP organizational ability was conspicuously lacking by comparison to that of several other parties. The typical campaign by a JSP candidate was based, not unlike the campaigns of LDP candidates, upon *kōenkai* (personal support groups) composed of individuals who were influential locally and thought able to deliver a certain number of votes. These individuals were predominantly labor unionists, but some Diet members had *kōenkai* with memberships quite diverse in composition. Of course, as the JSP has for many years polled more than 10 million votes in general elections, those who vote for it extend well beyond the ranks of unionists and their families. Indeed, studies have found that those who vote for the JSP are particularly hard to categorize beyond the fact that they tend to be concentrated in the middle age groups and the less well off sections of the community.[30]

The campaigns of 1989 and 1990 contained much the same elements as previous campaigns but with the additional factors of a popular and forceful leader, a considerable number of women candidates, and burning issues (such as the Recruit scandal, agricultural protection, and consumption tax), adding emotional heat to the campaign. It is worth noting that in preparing for the lower house elections of February 1990, the party found it difficult to decide how many candidates to put forward. In the end it advanced 149 candidates (of whom 136 were elected). This was rather more than in previous elections but still far short of half the total seats in the house (256, or one-half of 512). With previous experience in mind, party leaders were fearful of fielding too many candidates in the multimember constituencies, in case they would split the party vote and many of them fail to be elected.

A further reason seems to have been that the JSP had real difficulty in finding suitable candidates. In any event, the party still relied heavily on its traditional sources of recruitment for Diet candidates: former labor unionists and local party officials. Of the 55 newly elected JSP Diet members in February 1990, no fewer than 19 (34.5 percent) came from labor unions and 7 (12.7 percent) from the ranks of local party officials. Of the rest a quite impressive 9 (16.4 percent) were lawyers, 5 (9 percent) were from the mass media, 4 (7.3 percent) were from agriculture, with the remaining 11 (20 percent) being miscellaneous others. Unprecedentedly, 6 (10.9 percent) of the 55 were women.[31]

The kind of appeal made by JSP candidates in elections was traditionally very confrontational. This was particularly marked during the 1950s and 1960s, when the JSP lost no opportunity to attack the government for its defense and foreign policies, for its alleged attempts to subvert the constitution, for the influence of "monopoly capital," and for its antilabor policies in general. Eda Saburō in the early 1960s attempted to develop a less rhetorical and more down-to-earth campaigning style, discussing issues that touched people's everyday lives as he aimed to appeal to the concerns of people in a rapidly emerging consumer society. Such an approach was only fitfully followed by his successors, but the issues of the late 1980s and early 1990s lend themselves much more to the kind of approach that Eda pioneered a quarter of a century earlier. Doi Takako has in effect taken up his mantle, though her speeches lack nothing in forcefulness, and she continues to press home the party's traditional message in defense of the constitution and against what are conceived to be the narrow interests of big business (as on the tax issue, or on the lifting of agricultural protection).

For the most part, therefore, JSP parliamentary candidates now seek to appeal to the voters on the basis of issues that concern their real interests. They also of course resort to the time-honored technique of using local connections and the organizational backing of sympathetic unions. The attempt to turn the JSP from a union party to a "citizens party" has moved a certain distance, but conservative forces within it remain strong. Only if it decides to contest enough seats in lower house elections, so that a JSP government is a real possibility, is the party's campaigning performance likely to change fundamentally.

Parliamentary Behavior

Much as in the case of electoral campaigns, the parliamentary behavior of the JSP has undergone some modification since the 1950s and 1960s. (It must be noted, however, that fluctuations have also resulted from the changing balance of forces within the National Diet.) Throughout much of the 1950s and 1960s the party engaged from time to time in disruptive tactics in the

Diet with a view toward preventing or delaying the passage of controversial legislation. Tactics included boycotts (whether of particular Diet committees, or of the plenary session), various methods of filibuster such as "cow-walking" (i.e., walking with deliberate slowness through the chamber), and, as in the famous episode in May 1960 when the party was seeking to prevent passage of the revised Mutual Security Treaty, physically preventing the Speaker from putting a motion to the vote.

There were several reasons for such tactics. First, from the party's point of view the Liberal Democrats were engaged in a dangerous program of reactionary change with regard to the constitution, foreign and defense policy, union legislation, education, the economy, and so on. It was crucial that the government be frustrated in its endeavors, however unorthodox the method. Second, as we have already seen, the left-wing factions of the JSP were by no means wholeheartedly committed to parliamentary methods, which some Socialists saw through Marxist eyes as institutional devices designed to further the interests of the capitalist class. Some also believed in "parliamentarism plus"—that is, the use of the National Diet backed up by the use of extraparliamentary demonstrations. A third reason (though it may have been as much an excuse as a genuine reason) was that the party, especially during the Security Treaty revision crisis, was prepared to criticize the principle of majoritarianism as constituting a "tyranny of the majority." Such a resort to the traditional Japanese principles of decisionmaking by general consensus rather than by the view of the majority prevailing suited the JSP's interests during the period of long-term LDP majority rule. Fourth, as the government, according to the rules of the National Diet, did not have complete control over the parliamentary timetable, there were occasions on which actions by the JSP resulting in delay of the passage of legislation could actually result in the failure of such legislation.[32]

During the period from 1976 to 1980 in the House of Representatives and from 1974 to 1980 in the House of Councillors, the LDP majority was reduced to the point where it lost its control of a number of parliamentary committees. As a result, the opposition parties were, to some extent, given the capacity to influence policy by working within the parliamentary system. Since by this time the JSP was merely *primus inter pares* among the opposition parties themselves, it was motivated both to work within the system and to operate in coordination with the other opposition parties. Although the difficulties of coordinating strategy with the other parties of opposition were considerable, inasmuch as policy could be effected only if all the opposition parties acted together in a given committee, occasional successes were achieved.

Following the LDP victory in the 1980 double elections, this situation no longer applied. (The LDP, however, lost control of upper house committees following the 1989 elections.) The JSP still sometimes leads committee boycotts, but in practice now accepts parliamentary procedures and rarely attempts to subvert them. Its strong position in the upper house, however, now gives it an excellent opportunity to block any contentious legislation (for instance, relating to overseas dispatch of the Self-Defense Forces) of which it strongly disapproves.

The JSP in Local Politics

The position of the JSP in local politics has in the past generally been weak, and even in the period during the 1970s when "progressive local administrations" were common in large cities and elsewhere, the JSP had to share participation with other opposition parties. The party faced the dilemma at that time that when the opposition as a whole appeared to be capable of using local politics as a springboard for power at the national level, the JSP was conspicuously giving ground to the other opposition parties in the larger cities, where the new developments were taking place.

From the late 1970s most of the "progressive local authorities" (meaning chief executives—governors of prefectures and mayors of cities, towns, and villages) were defeated, as a new conservative trend manifested itself in local politics. Since then a common pattern throughout the country has emerged, whereby chief executives are elected with the backing of all or nearly all the major and minor parties. This puts the LDP and the JSP (as well as other parties) on the same side in joint sponsorship of a single candidate. The JSP resurgence from the late 1980s, however, has once more boosted JSP fortunes in a number of local governments, though the LDP and conservative independents retain a commanding position if the total picture is taken into account. With the JSP now able to take the initiative given the improvement of its fortunes, it will be up to it to ensure that coalitions entered into work to its advantage.

PROBLEMS AND PROSPECTS FOR THE FUTURE

The problems facing the JSP have been canvassed extensively in the course of this chapter. Many of these problems arguably date to the time of the Katayama and Ashida coalition governments of 1947–1948, to the failures of those governments, and to the leftist reaction within the JSP that they provoked. The dominance of the left wing from the early 1950s could scarcely fail to relegate it to a prolonged stay within the political wilderness in conditions of rapidly increasing prosperity. Indeed, the failure of the JSP to attain a share in power at the national level since 1948 may be seen as the reverse side of the coin of conservative success. The conservatives succeeded in forging an alliance of forces that remained sufficiently popular with the electorate to ensure its continued tenure in office. As the 1990s began, this alliance showed signs of crumbling, but it is too early to declare its demise.

Our statement regarding the inverse relationship between the JSP and the LDP, however, is not particularly helpful if one is trying to estimate the future prospects of the JSP. Although it is obviously true that a logical connection exists between the past failure of the JSP and the success of the LDP, the crucial question is "Why?" in each case. Where the Socialist party is concerned, the answer will be divided into three parts: policy, organization, and environment; then the connections between them will be shown.

The most common accusation directed against the JSP is that its policies have been "extreme" or "unrealistic." The party's policy of unarmed neutralism has often been cited as proof of both extremism and unrealism. In practice, however, there is ample evidence that if the party ever came to power, it would act with a measure of pragmatism on defense. (This is not the same as saying that it would retain all the current defense arrangements intact.) Over many years the JSP has articulated deeply felt fears held in large segments of the population about the possible consequences of allowing the military to make a political comeback, given the pre-1945 record of the armed forces in politics. The late 1990 debate about sending a contingent from the Self-Defense Forces to the Persian Gulf once more showed the continued presence of anxieties of this kind.

Rather than extremism, the problem with JSP policy has been its tendency to incoherence. The party platform of 1955 and certain later basic statements of policy were a compromise between Left and Right, but because of the continued salience of the Left-Right division, the platform proved extremely difficult to revise. Ishibashi's great achievement as JSP chairman was to promote acceptance of a revised statement of fundamental policy.[33] Another example of incoherence has been the party's tendency to promise high levels of agricultural protection in the countryside and cheaper food in the cities. Since the 1960s the party's support has been no greater in the cities than in the countryside, so that this problem is unlikely to be easily resolved, except by far greater efforts being devoted to hammering out practical and coherent policy solutions than have been expended hitherto.

At the deepest level, policy incoherence stems from the continued division within the JSP between Marxist and non-Marxist thinking. The party could never convince the electorate about the effectiveness of its policies when it was unsure whether its ideology was based on the principles of Marxism or of social democracy. Since the late 1980s, however, the Soviet model of political and governmental organization has been in rapid decline, even dissolution. With it Marxism and, in particular, Marxism-Leninism have almost everywhere lost much of the appeal they once had. This in turn has been reflected in the decline of the Marxist Left within the JSP and quite suddenly has made it easier for the party to restore in its policies the cohesion that was lacking for so long. The process is far from complete, but the first steps have been taken.

Organization, too, has long been a problem, in part because of the party's need to rely so heavily on labor union support for funding and in election campaigns. The privatization drive by government in the 1980s has shaken up the union movement and is an important factor leading to the formation of a single major union federation. It has also created at least the opportunity for the JSP to broaden its base beyond the ranks of a narrow segment of union activists. Whereas, as we have seen, the party still recruits a high proportion of its candidates for election from labor unionists, there is increasingly a leavening of candidates from other walks of life, for instance, from law. Moreover, the novelty of choosing significant numbers of women candidates appears to be remarkably popular.[34]

Thus we are led to the question of environment, which has two aspects. First of all, working-class consciousness, which has sustained a number of social-democratic and labor parties in Western Europe and elsewhere, is weak in Japan, partly because of increased prosperity and partly because of the deliberately inculcated Japanese style of "cooperative" labor-management relations. Between the 1960s and the 1980s the JSP, because of the narrowness of its organizational base and of its appeal, allowed other parties such as the Kōmeitō, the JCP, the DSP, and the LDP itself to pick up votes of less prosperous sections of the workforce, particularly those in small and medium firms. The election results in 1989 and 1990 suggest that changes in government policy on taxation and other issues have reduced the appeal not only of the LDP but also of those centrist parties that accommodate themselves to LDP policies. What still remains is for the JSP to reform itself into a really credible alternative party of government with a set of practicable and convincing policies, as well as personnel and leadership to match.

Second, the political environment was radically changed by the formation of the Liberal Democratic party out of previously warring conservative factions in 1955. The coalition governments of 1947–1948, in which the Socialists participated, were possible only because of the failure of the conservatives to unite into a single party. Socialist participation in a coalition government was always eminently possible until the door was finally closed in 1955 in the greatest conservative master-stroke of the postwar period—and indeed, a minority conservative government needed some Right Socialist backing for a few months in 1954.

The JSP, given its roots in the postwar democratic reforms and a nationwide and indigenous organizational base on which to build, may still prove capable of developing the kind of alternative policies and even the alternative government that would be needed if statist tendencies and political corruption are to be checked or put into reverse. The election of a woman as party chairman, whatever its immediate motives, has proved an imaginative act because Doi Takako, with her personality and gender, has found rapport with large numbers of ordinary people. The changes set in train by her predecessor and continued under her leadership, combined with opportunities fortuitously provided in the late 1980s by the LDP itself, have enabled the JSP to lift itself above the stagnant demoralization into which it had fallen. For the JSP, the 1990s are a decade of opportunity, but much more work needs to be done if that opportunity is to be seized.

NOTES

1. Most constituencies in the lower house elect from two to six members, while each voter has a single, nontransferable vote. Thus candidates are commonly elected with less than 20 percent of the vote in a given constituency.

2. Apart from the long tenure held by social-democratic parties in some Scandinavian countries, Australia had an uninterrupted period of rule at the federal level by a coalition consisting of the Liberal and Country parties between 1949 and 1972, and again between 1975 and 1983.

3. It may be noted that the Trade Union Congress in Britain, after deliberately minimizing its dealings with government during the first Thatcher administration,

softened this policy after Thatcher was elected to a second term in office with a large majority.

4. A fourth element, the Nichirō-kei, an agriculture faction led by Hirano Rikizō, left the party in 1947 and may be disregarded for our present purposes.

5. See J.A.A. Stockwin, *The Japanese Socialist Party and Neutralism* (Melbourne: Melbourne University Press, 1968).

6. The standard works in English on the prewar and early postwar Socialist movements are as follows: George O. Totten, *The Social Democratic Movement in Prewar Japan* (New Haven and London: Yale University Press, 1966); and Allan B. Cole, George O. Totten, and Cecil H. Uyehara, with a contributed chapter by Ronald P. Dore, *Socialist Parties in Postwar Japan* (New Haven and London: Yale University Press, 1966).

7. For details, see Stockwin, *The Japanese Socialist Party,* Ch. 4; Cole et al., *Socialist Parties,* pp. 32–36.

8. During the early years of its existence, the JSP was officially known in English as the Social Democratic party of Japan.

9. For details, see Stockwin, *The Japanese Socialist Party,* Ch. 7; Cole et al., *Socialist Parties,* Ch. 3.

10. Deriving from the writings of Yamakawa Hitoshi and others in the prewar period, the Rōzō school had taken issue with the two-stage revolution theories of the Kōza school. The two were essentially schools of Japanese historiography, whereas the Rōnō-kei, though sharing the same kinds of ideas, was a factional grouping within the JSP.

11. The best source in English on the 1959–1960 split is D.C.S. Sissons, "Recent Developments in Japan's Socialist Movement," *Far Eastern Survey* (March 1960), pp. 40–47, and *Far Eastern Survey* (June 1960), pp. 89–92.

12. That is, Eda was temporary chairman, from November 1960 to March 1961, following the killing of Asanuma. He subsequently occupied the position of secretary-general for a period.

13. J.A.A. Stockwin, *Japan: Divided Politics in a Growth Economy* (London: Weidenfeld & Nicolson, 1975; New York: W. W. Norton, 1975).

14. Terry E. MacDougall, "Asukata Ichio and Some Dilemmas of Socialist Leadership in Japan," in Terry E. MacDougall, ed., *Political Leadership in Contemporary Japan* (Ann Arbor: University of Michigan, 1982), pp. 51–92.

15. MacDougall, "Asukata Ichio," p. 64. The conditions were as follows: (1) direct election of the party chairman by the entire party membership; (2) giving top leadership the authority to break deadlocks in the CEC and the chairman authority to break deadlocks among the top three leaders; (3) opening the party to advisers and specialists from outside its ranks, by creating advisory panels.

16. According to a party handbook, she lives the thrifty life of an average "salaryman," likes tennis and swimming, and claims as her favorite record "Ella Fitzgerald in Berlin." Nihon Shakaitō, *Dētabukku Shakaitō* [Socialist party data book] (Tokyo: Nihon Shakaitō, 1990), p. 5.

17. For the text of the poem and a view of the use of it by the JSP chairman, see Fukushima Hiromi, "Yama no ugoku hi wa kuru ka" [Will the day come when the mountains move?], *Keizai Hyōron,* special issue on the JSP (October 1989), pp. 112–113.

18. See Nakamura Kenichi, "Teikō seitō kara taikō seitō e no shohōsen" [From a party of resistance to a party of opposition: A prescription], *Asahi Jānaru* (July 20, 1990), pp. 22–24. Yamaguchi Jirō, "Shakaitō wa 'taikō seitō' ni dappi subeshi" [The JSP must turn into an opposition], *Ekomomisuto* (October 9, 1990).

19. Cole et al., *Socialist Parties*, p. 247.

20. "Nihon Shakaitō kettō 20 shūnen kinen jigyō hakko iinkai" in *Nihon Shakaitō 20 nen no kiroku* [The twenty years' record of the Japan Socialist party] (Tokyo: Nihon Shakaitō, 1965), p. 428.

21. MacDougall, "Asukata Ichio," pp. 54, 64.

22. A useful table, giving the dates and backgrounds of most of these JSP chairmen, can be found in MacDougall, "Asukata Ichio," p. 92.

23. See, for instance, J.A.A. Stockwin, "Factionalism in Japanese Political Parties," *Japan Forum* 1, no. 2 (October 1989), pp. 161–71.

24. Pressure from industry upon the LDP to remain as one party may also have significantly assisted that party to stay together. Similar union pressure on the JSP has also been observed but is evidently less effective.

25. Interviews at New Wave Society seminar at Tsumagoi village, Gumma prefecture, July 26–27, 1990.

26. Nishii Yasuyuki and Nishimae Teruo, "Shakaitō kenkyū: sono jinmyaku, soshiki, seisaku" [A study of the Socialist party: Personnel relations, organization, policy], *Asahi Jānaru* (August 11, 1989), pp. 14–18.

27. See Fujii Shōzō, *Rengō no tanjō* [The birth of Rengō] (Tokyo: Rōdō Junpōsha, 1989).

28. For instance, the member for Yamagata No. 1 constituency, Endō Noboru, first elected in February 1990, was first and foremost a representative of the local agricultural interest. Interview, July 29, 1990.

29. Nishii and Nishimae, "Shakaitō Kenkyū," p. 15.

30. According to one study: "Among JSP voters there are many who are of an 'indeterminate' (*chūkanteki*) type, and indeed they include not one type in particular but all types of people. There are many manual workers (though not as many as among *Kōmeitō* voters) but manual workers are a minority. JSP voters include the largest proportion of labour unionists of the voters for any party, but even so unionists are quite a small proportion of JSP voters, and even among unionists less than half actually vote. In their demographic characteristics, such as education, age, degree of satisfaction, housing and class consciousness, they are 'indeterminate.' They have no particularly outstanding characteristics. The fact that there are many JSP voters among middle aged people shows that it is becoming a party of 'nostalgia.'" Ogawa Kōichi, Hasuike Minoru, Araki Toshio, and Abe Shirō, *Daitoshi no kakushin hyō: to Sapporo to Sendai no baai* (Tokyo: Bokutakusha, 1975), p. 356.

31. Calculated from data in Mainichi Shinbunsha, *'90 Sōsenkyo* ['90 general election] (Tokyo: Mainichi Shinbunsha, 1990), pp. 19–48.

32. See Hans H. Baerwald, *Japan's Parliament: An Introduction* (Cambridge, Cambridge University Press, 1974).

33. For text of this policy, see *Dētabukku*, pp. 288–297.

34. For instance, Itō Hideko (Hokkaidō No. 1) won the largest number of votes (261,170) gained by a single candidate in the lower house elections of February 1990. Doi Takako (Hyōgo No. 2) came in third, with 225,540 votes. *Dētabukku*, p. 39.

5

The Japan Communist Party: The "Lovable" Party

PETER BERTON

The Japan Communist party (Nihon Kyōsantō, or JCP) has not played a decisive role in the political life of Japan, nor is it likely to do so in the foreseeable future, barring either catastrophic economic and social collapse or Soviet occupation. The JCP currently captures about 8 percent of the popular vote in national elections, but because the electoral system favors the incumbent Liberal Democratic party (LDP), the JCP ends up with proportionately fewer seats in the two houses of the National Diet than it deserves on the basis of the popular vote. The party has never held political power in Japan, not even as a junior coalition member. And yet we would do well to remember how few members the Bolsheviks had on the eve of the October Revolution.

The JCP also has more active members, more affiliate groups and front organizations, a larger budget, many more subscribers to its party publications, and a better organization than most other parties in Japan. Thus the Japan Communist party perhaps deserves closer scrutiny than other Japanese opposition parties of its size.[1]

HISTORICAL BACKGROUND

The Japanese Communist movement is part of a larger social movement that has developed since the end of the nineteenth century. Its influence represents an amalgam of Marxism, Christian humanism, socialism, and anarcho-syndicalism. Some of the early Communists were also influenced by Russian social thought and, in particular, Tolstoyan humanism.[2] More directly, however, the Communist party came into being as a result of the Russian Revolution and the subsequent establishment of the Third Communist International, widely known as the Comintern. Meetings between Japanese revolutionaries and Comintern functionaries in Bolshevik Russia as well as in Shanghai led to the formation of the Japan Communist party.

The JCP was formally organized on July 15, 1922, at the home of one of its founders in the middle-class district of Shibuya in Tokyo. But nine months earlier, a manifesto and regulations of the Japan Communist party had been published in a Soviet journal in Irkutsk in Siberia.[3] This event has symbolic implications given that the most important documents of the Japanese party during the prewar period were, in fact, "Made in the USSR." The JCP was also known as the Japanese Branch of the Communist International and was in reality directed and manipulated by Moscow.

From the beginning, the JCP was a small, conspiratorial group bent on abolishing the Emperor system, militarism, and capitalism. But the match was very uneven. The powerful, centralized Japanese state, which operated in a small territory and a closely knit society, had at its disposal a vast apparatus of law enforcement and efficient civil and military intelligence services. The prewar history of the party is thus a sad story of organization, repression, restarts, mass arrests and imprisonment, new instructions from the Comintern, arrival and prompt arrest of the replacements trained in Moscow,[4] recantation by prominent leaders, and long prison terms for unrepentant Communists.

POSTWAR DEVELOPMENTS TO 1955

In early October 1945 the present author happened to be in front of Tokyo station, near his office in the Civil Intelligence section of the Allied Occupation Headquarters, when he saw truckloads of emaciated Japanese waving red flags and shouting as if in intoxicated delirium. They were Communist political prisoners released from jails by order of General MacArthur—the hard-core survivors of Imperial Japan's thoroughly efficient repression by the Thought Police and the Army Gendarmerie. For many of them, freedom came after long periods (in several instances, as many as eighteen years) of detention.[5] A few weeks later, on December 1, 1945, the Japan Communist party was officially revived at its Fourth Party Congress. In February 1946, following the return to Japan from Yenan of Nosaka Sanzō (the Japanese delegate at the Comintern headquarters in Moscow during the 1930s),[6] the Fifth Party Congress was convened. The party leadership claimed that in the intervening three months, membership rose from an estimated 1,000 members to 7,000. In April, during the first postwar election, the party managed to elect six members to the 464-seat House of Representatives and began to participate in electoral politics. Nosaka's idea was to create a "lovable" Communist party and to proceed along a parliamentary road to power—not an unreasonable position given the reality of U.S. military occupation.[7]

In the 1949 national elections the party received 3 million votes, or almost 10 percent of the total vote (up from 2.1 million, or 3.8 percent, and 1.0 million, or 3.7 percent, in the 1946 and 1947 elections, respectively), and elected 35 of the party's candidates. This increase in the number of seats came entirely at the expense of the Socialists, whose popularity plummeted following the failure of their coalition government. (As it happened, it would be twenty years before the JCP would again receive 3 million votes, which by then represented only 6.8 percent of the total vote.)

In January 1950, shortly after the JCP achieved its greatest electoral success, the Communist Information Bureau (Cominform) issued a blistering attack against Nosaka's peaceful parliamentary tactics, urging the party to adopt a militant line. Stalin had his own reasons for insisting on this policy change, which went against the best interests of the JCP.[8] The party mainstream under Party Secretary General Tokuda Kyūichi[9] hesitated, but an "Internationalist" faction, which ironically included the present supreme leader Miyamoto Kenji (now an advocate of a soft parliamentary line), urged the adoption of the Cominform instructions to pursue a violent leftist course. The party leadership eventually succumbed to pressure from Moscow and Peking and, especially after the outbreak of the Korean War some six months later, took a direct turn toward the Left.[10] General MacArthur ordered the Japanese government to purge the entire Central Committee of the party, which then set up an underground organization, with the top leaders and a number of middle cadres going illegally to Peking.

The underground party tried to stage some acts of terrorism and industrial sabotage to help the Communist Korean War effort, but these were sporadic and ineffectual. This suicidal policy had immediate results at the polls, however. The Japanese public's reaction was to throw out all 35 JCP Diet members in the next election to the House of Representatives in October 1952.

In 1953 Stalin died, the Korean War came to an end, and Soviet and Chinese policy gradually became more moderate. The Japan Communist party followed suit.

THE MIYAMOTO LINE: A PARTY DICTATOR SELLING PARLIAMENTARY DEMOCRACY

Since the mid-1950s the JCP's development and policies have borne the imprint of its undisputed leader—namely, Miyamoto Kenji, who was eighty-three years old in 1991.[11] This period represents more than half of the party's almost seventy-year history. A graduate of Tokyo Imperial University, the most prestigious institution of higher learning in Japan, Miyamoto was a prominent literary critic in his twenties and, along with his famous late wife, Yuriko, a noted member of the Proletarian School of literature. Miyamoto joined the JCP in May 1931, was arrested in December 1933, and spent twelve years in prison. An unusual aspect of his case was that he was accused of "lynching" a suspected police infiltrator. Upon release from prison in October 1945, Miyamoto returned to active party work; he was one of seven Central Committee members at the first postwar party congress. But he was not a member of the "Mainstream" Tokuda faction, and it was not until the mid-1950s that Miyamoto maneuvered himself into center stage in the aftermath of the militant-line debacle. He steered party fortunes through consolidation and the establishment of "a new people's democratic revolutionary policy," which led to rapid growth in JCP membership, electoral successes, attempts to form united fronts with other opposition parties, and an independent stance in the international Communist movement.

Over the past two decades, Miyamoto's closest associates have been the Ueda brothers:[12] Ueda Kōichirō (sixty-four years old) and his younger brother Fuwa Tetsuzō (sixty-one years old, born Ueda Kenjirō), both of whom joined the JCP while still students at the prestigious First Higher School. The brothers moved on to the elitist Tokyo University, the elder majoring in economics (Miyamoto had graduated from the same department a generation earlier) and the younger brother in physics. Upon graduation, Fuwa became an official of the iron and steel workers union, where he stayed on for eleven years, at the same time helping his brother with theoretical assignments at the JCP headquarters. In May 1964, Fuwa quit his union post and became a full-time staff member at the party headquarters working under his brother. Fuwa's career in the JCP was phenomenal: In six years he rose from candidate member of the Central Committee to become the director of the Secretariat and member of the Presidium in 1970. While heading the Secretariat for a dozen years, he became a member of the Standing Committee, then its acting chairman, and, in 1982, its chairman, at which point Miyamoto moved to the post of chairman of the Central Committee. A bright organizer with a theoretical bent, Fuwa is the author of many JCP documents that have tried to refurbish Marxist-Leninist theory by making it palatable to the Japanese electorate. In the past decade and a half he has turned his attention to relations with the Euro-communist parties, and, more recently, to Mikhail Gorbachev's perestroika and new thinking. The party is fortunate to have vigorous younger men among its top leaders. With Fuwa as anointed crown prince, the JCP is likely to continue its soft line following Miyamoto's departure.[13]

Evolution of Policy

How does one characterize Miyamoto's policies in the postmilitant period, 1955 to the present (1991)? Were they influenced by the Soviet, Chinese, Eurocommunist, or other models? Have they changed over time? And, if so, what factors were responsible—domestic, external, or intra-Communist?

Overall, Miyamoto's policies can be characterized as a continuous soft line when compared with the hard, militant line of the prewar and 1950–1955 periods. But during the past thirty years or so, one notices an evolution from an almost grudging acceptance of parliamentary tactics to an appreciation of the transformation of postwar (especially post-Occupation) Japan into an advanced industrial (in many respects even postindustrial) democratic society, in which neither the Soviet nor the Chinese—only the Eurocommunist model—has any relevance.

For convenience, let us consider the evolution of the Miyamoto line over three periods: (1) 1955–1961: consolidation of power and rejection of Togliatti's structural reform theories; (2) 1961–1968: growth, rejection of the Soviet and Chinese models, and declaration of independence; and (3) 1968 to the present (1991): nationalism and growing convergence with Eurocommunism.

Consolidation, 1955–1961. This was a complex and controversial period in JCP history. A number of young cadres returned from their refuge in Peking, and the party emerged from its militant episode with two competing factions. Eventually Miyamoto switched from the "Internationalist" to the "Mainstream" faction in a successful bid to become secretary-general. But the JCP was not the only party in turmoil. The international Communist movement itself was undergoing a metamorphosis that began with Nikita Khrushchev's de-Stalinization speech at the Twentieth Congress of the Communist Party of the Soviet Union (CPSU) in early 1956. This was followed by Palmiro Togliatti's "polycentrism" and structural reform theories,[14] the Polish and Hungarian revolts, and further Yugoslav shifts to the right—all leading to the break between Moscow and Peking that shook up the entire movement.

The JCP was much affected by the epochal changes in international communism. Many Japanese Communists and Socialists alike were attracted to Togliatti's position. Others saw the principal enemy to be "U.S. imperialism"; they believed in a kind of "national liberation" along the lines of the Chinese model with at least the option of violent action, although most agreed that under prevailing Japanese circumstances a militant, violent line was counterproductive. These personal rivalries, factional struggles, and foreign influences were resolved after a fashion at the Eighth JCP Congress in July 1961 with the expulsion of the advocates of structural reform and the victory of Miyamoto and his allies. West European ideas were thus rebuffed, and "U.S. imperialism" (along with Japanese monopoly capitalism) was proclaimed as the principal enemy (clearly a Chinese position in opposition to Soviet "peaceful coexistence" and détente). At the same time, the JCP cautiously returned to the peaceful parliamentary tactics of Nosaka's "lovable" party, advocating a "united national democratic front" in a National Diet considered to be an important "tool" of the people. In the international Communist arena, the JCP, although clearly sympathetic with the Chinese position, was hewing cautiously to a neutral line and endorsing the ambiguous 1960 Moscow Statement, all the while enshrining in the party program "the camp of socialism headed by the USSR."

Rejection of the Soviet and Chinese Models, 1961–1968. This was a traumatic period for the JCP leadership, which first had to take sides and then had to break umbilical ties to both Moscow and Peking. It was also a period of mass expulsions and of threats to the party posed by splinter groups favoring the CPSU and the Chinese Communist party (CCP). It is a measure of Miyamoto's political talent that he kept the party together while presiding over the period of its greatest growth in membership, which, in turn, toward the end of these years, was translated into dramatic gains at the polls. Two JCP congresses, in 1964 and 1966, consolidated Miyamoto's power, reiterated the policy of pursuing peaceful parliamentary tactics, and proclaimed the party's independence from outside influence and control. At the same time, *Akahata*, the party organ, reprinted Chinese articles on the People's War and violent revolution, including Lin Piao's famous 1965 manifesto—a violent revolutionary formula that was considered unacceptable only "under present circumstances." The JCP's relations during this period were heavily tilted toward Asian Communist parties, with very few personal ties to the parties of Western Europe.

Most important, this period saw the severance of the JCP's ties with the two fraternal Communist superparties: first with the CPSU in 1964 over the Partial Nuclear Test Ban Treaty, which the Soviet Union had initiated and which the JCP repudiated in support of the Chinese position, and then with the CCP in 1966–1967 over Mao Zedong's insistence that the JCP join an anti-U.S. and anti-Soviet united front. The Japanese party was now essentially on its own.

Nationalism and the Eurocommunist Model, 1968 to Present (1991). The Soviet invasion of Czechoslovakia graphically demonstrated to the JCP leadership the need to emulate the Italian Communist party (PCI)—that is, to draw away from the Soviet Union and pursue a more peaceful, parliamentary road to power.

In July 1969, a member of the Standing Committee of the JCP Presidium declared that if the party came to power, it would permit the free functioning of opposition parties, unless they resorted to unlawful means. This statement, made in an election year, may have been intended simply to improve the party image, but the same criticism of one-party dictatorship showed up the following year in an official party program submitted to the Eleventh JCP Congress. (To create an image of an "open" party, the congress for the first time was thrown open to the public and the press.) In its next two congresses, in 1973 and 1976, the JCP continued to advance its autonomy and independence on the one hand, and its commitment to peaceful change on the other.

To stress the relevance for Japan of the West European model (and thus the irrelevance of the Soviet and Chinese models), the JCP, in commemoration of its fiftieth anniversary in July 1972, staged an International Conference on Theory devoted to the problems encountered by Communist parties in advanced capitalist countries. The Italian, French, Spanish, British, West German, and Australian parties sent delegates. The topics discussed included parliamentary and constitutional experiences; united front tactics; methods for making the transition from capitalism to socialism in a democratic setting, including structural reforms; and the question of terminology, such as the proper rendering of the phrase *dictatorship of the proletariat* in various languages. In fact, at the Twelfth JCP Congress the following year, the JCP dropped the word *dokusai* (dictatorship) in favor of *shikken* (regency or exercise of power) in translating *dictatorship of the proletariat,* and at the Thirteenth JCP Congress in July 1976 that phrase was dropped altogether in favor of *working class power. Marxism-Leninism* itself suffered the fate of *dictatorship of the proletariat.* At the 1970 Eleventh JCP Congress, rules were amended to make Marxism-Leninism only a "theoretical basis" and not a "guide to action."[15] The term was given the coup de grace six years later, at the Thirteenth JCP Congress, when references to Marxism-Leninism were either eliminated completely or replaced by *scientific socialism* in the party's program and constitution. The Central Committee tried to explain that, while the terms were essentially synonymous, it had been almost a century since Marx and Engels were active and more than half a century since the death of Lenin, and therefore *scientific socialism* constituted more than just the theories of Marx, Engels, and Lenin. Furthermore, aware that in Japan, Marx and Engels were less controversial than Lenin, the party cleverly dissociated itself from the latter (and in the process from Russia and, by implication, also from China), at the same time stressing Japan's position as an advanced industrial country.[16]

Repeated declarations of independence by the JCP were officially formalized in 1973 at the Twelfth JCP Congress through an amendment to the basic party program of 1961 designed to eliminate the reference to the USSR in the phrase "the camp of socialism *headed by the USSR*" (emphasis added). The JCP also tried to dissociate itself from student violence by branding such activities as Trotskyist. Miyamoto even declared that "violence, along with sex, drugs, and gambling, was one of the four sins."[17]

Along with eliminating this or that offending term, the JCP sought to promote the image of a party devoted to the preservation and expansion of freedoms in Japan. This was necessary partly to erase the totalitarian image of communism and partly to counteract the LDP slogan, "Defend the Free Society."

In the spring of 1976, Fuwa published a nine-part essay entitled "Scientific Socialism and the Question of Dictatura—A Study of Marx and Engels," in which he stressed "the institutions of a democratic state, with the Diet as an organ of supreme authority of the country in name and reality" (previously, the Diet had been termed only a "tool" of the people).[18]

Fuwa's essay was followed by a draft of the far-reaching "Manifesto of Freedom and Democracy," which was officially adopted on July 30, 1976, at the Thirteenth Extraordinary Party Congress. The Manifesto mentions approvingly the American Declaration of Independence and the French Declaration of the Rights of Man. The third section ends with this eloquent declaration of JCP independence:

> The Communist Party of Japan reiterates that it will make no model of the experiences of any foreign countries, such as the Soviet Union and the People's Republic of China. As a consistent defender of freedom and democracy of the people, it will correctly inherit the original stand of scientific socialism; it will seek a creative development of socialism under the condition of a highly developed capitalist country, Japan; and it will continue to pursue a unique way to an independent democratic Japan and a socialist Japan, hand in hand with the people.[19]

The JCP was dealt a great blow in the press and in the Diet by the official reopening of the "lynching case"—the accusation that back in the 1930s Miyamoto had taken part in the murder of a JCP member who was thought to be a police spy. If Miyamoto was guilty of murder, he was serving time before and during World War II as an ordinary criminal and not as a political prisoner eligible to be released by order of the U.S. Occupation authorities. In any case, this bad publicity was obviously not helpful to the JCP in an election year.

Electoral Reverses Since 1976

The elections to the lower house in December 1976 and to the upper house in July 1977 reversed the upward trend of JCP representation and halved the party's delegation in the National Diet.[20] What were the reasons for the party's electoral successes in the late 1960s and early 1970s, and for the reverses in the mid-1970s? The JCP's electoral record is analyzed in a later section of this chapter, but a few major factors should be mentioned here. The adoption of an independent, nationalist, and Eurocommunist line after 1968 has helped the party to grow and, more important, to capture a segment of the floating and protest votes. The JCP has also been effective on the local level—especially in urban areas—in helping citizens to cope with the complexities of daily living and to deal with local authorities.[21]

Paradoxically, the very success of the party has sown the seeds for subsequent failure. So long as the JCP was an insignificant political force, it attracted the floating and protest votes and competed with other opposition parties for votes on the Left. But as soon as it was perceived as a potential force (it emerged in 1972 as the second-largest opposition party in the lower house, and for a while it *was* the largest opposition party in the Tokyo Municipal Assembly), uncommitted voters became more careful about casting their votes and the other opposition parties often made agreements not to split the anti-JCP vote on the Left.

The inability of the JCP to promote and become a member of a united front of all so-called progressive opposition parties is another factor in the party's weakness. Its failure has not come about for lack of trying, however. Indeed, at recent party congresses, considerable attention has been paid to the concept of a "progressive united front," especially with the Socialist party (JSP) and some future "democratic coalition government."

Yet another important factor in the JCP's electoral reverses has been the move of the Democratic Socialist party (DSP) and the Kōmeitō (Clean Government party, or CGP) to the Center, accompanied by a similar trend on the part of the Japanese voting public. (Public opinion polls for the past quarter century have consistently shown that larger and larger segments of the Japanese people consider themselves part of the middle class, with the figure falling around 90 percent.) This trend erodes the traditional support of the "progressive" parties, especially those—as with the JCP—perceived to be on the extreme Left.

Although the JCP's strident defense of democracy and freedom was largely a reaction to domestic developments and the growing "Communist allergy" of the Japanese public, it has fed suspicions about the party's motives. This "Communist allergy," coupled with attacks by the mass media in recent years, has forced the JCP to the defensive. In fact, its Fourteenth Congress in October 1977 concerned the "anti-Communist counteroffensive,"[22] and subsequently the JCP characterized the domestic situation as being the second worst for the party since the end of World War II.

Public opinion polls substantiate the low popularity of the JCP and the erosion of its support in the past decade and a half. A public opinion poll taken in October 1990 shows 1.6 percent support for the JCP, 1.9 percent for the DSP, 3.5 percent for the CGP, 17.1 percent for the JSP, and 47.9 percent for the LDP.[23]

It is probable that media attacks on the JCP have been effective in moving the Japanese electorate further away from the party. In 1976, attention centered on the validity of the party's commitment to democracy and on Miyamoto personally.[24] These points were underscored by the latest and potentially the most damaging party purge—the expulsion of Hakamada Satomi, vice-chairman of the Standing Committee of the Presidium as well as Miyamoto's prison mate and erstwhile right-hand man. Hakamada openly characterized Miyamoto's rule in the JCP as "despotic" and directly linked him to the "lynching" case, to which he was a witness.[25] Furthermore, even the JCP membership does not evaluate the leadership of the party very highly.[26]

Aside from launching a counteroffensive against anti-Communist forces, how did the party react to these electoral setbacks? One measure undertaken was the revamping of study texts for all levels of membership. For several years the party deemphasized the writings of Marx, Engels, and other Communist classics and stressed indigenous JCP documents. The Fourteenth JCP Congress in October 1977 went even further. Since then, the list for new members contains only JCP documents, and only the highest level contains a substantial number (about one-third) of non-Japanese materials.[27] Significantly, these materials omit the writings of Mao Zedong, Stalin, Tito, Castro, and even Togliatti. The JCP is stressing its Japanese heritage, but its borrowings betray its real policy of favoring Lenin over Togliatti. Two quotations, one from a Japanese and the other from a U.S. analyst of the JCP, sum up the matter: The JCP under Miyamoto can be characterized as following a "structural reform line without structural reform theory" and as pursuing "iron discipline" with a "smiling image."[28]

Recent Developments, 1980–1990

In the past ten years (1980–1990), the JCP held five congresses. A brief comparison of the circumstances, policies, and resolutions of these congresses will illuminate the present concerns and future direction of the party.

The Fifteenth Party Congress was held in February 1980, after the October 1979 House of Representatives election in which the JCP recouped its losses from 1976 and immediately after Miyamoto's trip to Moscow and the normalization of relations with the CPSU after fifteen years. The atmosphere at the congress was upbeat and, because of peace with the Soviets, was well attended by thirty foreign Communist party delegations.[29] Ironically, as the JCP broke out of isolation in the international Communist movement, it became more and more isolated on the Japanese political scene.

The Sixteenth Party Congress, which was held in July 1982, coincided with the celebration of the party's sixtieth anniversary;[30] it also followed the disastrous 1980 double election to both houses of the National Diet (in which the party lost heavily) and occurred in the midst of strained relations with the CPSU because of the events in Afghanistan and Poland and other matters. Yet, in spite of these problems and the worsening domestic isolation of the JCP, the party staged elaborate celebrations, including an International Symposium on Theory.

The Seventeenth Congress was held in November 1985 following the Miyamoto-Chernenko summit of December 1984 (devoted exclusively to the "abolition of nuclear weapons"—a public relations event) and elections to the Tokyo Metropolitan Assembly, where the party registered some gains (as will soon be discussed).[31]

The Eighteenth Party Congress was held in November 1987, over a year after the double election to the National Diet in which the JCP generally held its seats in spite of an LDP landslide. The Nineteenth Congress in July 1990 came four months after a disastrous election to the House of Representatives in which the party lost almost half of its parliamentary delegation in spite of only one percentage point drop in the popular vote. Of course, the election was held right after the collapse of communism in Eastern Europe, the disintegration of the external Soviet empire, and the retreat of ideology and centrally planned economy in favor of market reform in the Soviet Union.

Let us now look at the drafts, reports, discussions, and resolutions of these crucial party meetings. The leadership reports generally deal with the international situation, the domestic scene, and the party work at hand.

On the international level, at the Fifteenth Congress, Fuwa stressed the need to dissolve all military blocs including, of course, "the struggle to abolish the Japan-U.S. military alliance." At the Sixteenth Congress, the draft resolution stated that the plans for limited nuclear war are "threats to the peoples of the world" and spoke of the "harm done by Big Powerism" (code words for Soviet interventions in Afghanistan, Poland, and elsewhere, and especially their meddling in the affairs of the JCP itself), while the Seventeenth Congress addressed itself to the elimination of nuclear weapons, the defense of Nicaragua, and, more broadly, the right of nations to self-determination. The resolutions of the Eighteenth Congress stressed contradictions in the capitalist world and the importance of the antinuclear peace movement, though attendees hardly realized that two years later the contradictions in the socialist world would lead to the collapse of communism in all of Eastern Europe. The Nineteenth Congress took up not only this unhappy development for Communists everywhere, but also the demise of the world Communist movement. The JCP lashed out against Gorbachev's "new thinking" and stressed the correctness of Japanese "scientific socialism" and the need to continue the struggle against nuclear weapons, military blocs, and hegemonism and "Big Powerism."[32]

On the domestic front, at the Fifteenth Congress, Miyamoto described the situation as "Amidst Tense Counteroffensive JSP's Rightward Degeneration" and called for a Progressive United Front through the expansion of "Progressive Unity Forums." At the Sixteenth Congress, Fuwa predicted "the bankruptcy for the JSP-CGP agreement," while the Seventeenth Congress assailed the Nakasone cabinet and warned of the danger of revival of the "Imperial Rule Assistance Politics" (a reference to the prewar merger of all political parties except for the illegal JCP) and of "opening the way to Japanese-style fascism."[33] The resolutions at the Eighteenth Congress condemned the policies of the new Takeshita government as a continuation of the bad policies of its predecessor and deplored the ongoing "rightward fall" of the Socialists. The party also expressed concern over the rightward realignment of the Japanese labor movement and skyrocketing land prices. At the Nineteenth Congress, the party called for the breakup of the old political order, dominated by big capital and the LDP, and the Japanese-U.S. military alliance. On the defensive because of the developments in Eastern Europe, the party resorted to platitudes: "The Japanese people should truly share in the benefits of the world's second largest economy, democracy should flower, and the people should be masters of their own destiny."[34]

Regarding party work in particular, the Fifteenth Congress stressed the "Four Pillars" of mass activities, election struggle, party building, and party defense. The Sixteenth Congress, held after serious setbacks, set "Two Pillar" goals: (1) strengthening of study and education and the establishment of disciplined party life, and (2) preparation for elections and creating bases for electoral support. The Seventeenth Congress called for "building a strong party in numbers and quality . . . with intellectual awareness and vitality . . . and . . . closely linked with the masses."[35] The two most recent congresses stressed revitalizing primary party units, achieving political and ideological "self-awakening," promoting mass activities and mass movements, and working toward increasing party membership and readership of party organs. It is significant that the party pledged to overcome the "vast vacuum" of young people and students.[36]

Thus it would seem that in terms of membership and readership drives, the JCP, despite denials, is going after quantity instead of quality. Miyamoto and his disciples probably feel that the policies that produced rapid growth in the 1960s might also to some extent work in the 1990s. Time will tell if they are right, but they are in total command and there are no challengers.

Let us now examine just how Miyamoto's party is structured, led, and financed.

THE PARTY

Party Structure

The nerve center of the JCP is the national Party Headquarters in Tokyo. Like other Communist parties, the JCP is organized under the principle of

FIGURE 5.1
JCP organizational chart (as of Nineteenth Party Congress, July 1990)

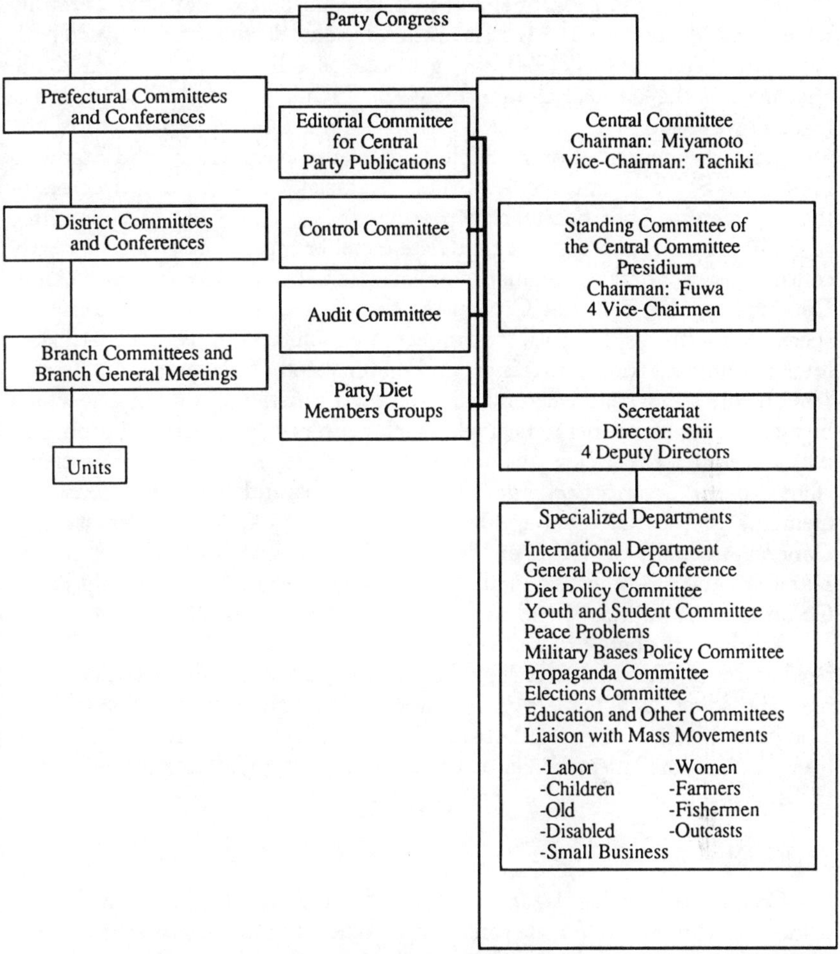

Sources: Sayoku Binran, p. 177; *Shiryo Tsushin*, (July 30, 1990).

"democratic centralism," maintaining the fiction that the Party Congress, consisting of "democratically" elected delegates from the party cells or branches, districts, and prefectures, is the party's highest authority. In practice, however, the JCP is run dictatorially by Miyamoto and his protégés, who freely co-opt members into the Presidium, the Secretariat, and the Central Committee and appoint the heads of all central party departments and national committees as well as prefectural and local party officials. Shown schematically in Figure 5.1 is the party organization, from the branches, through districts and prefectural committees, to the central party organization with its governing Presidium and subordinate agencies.

Leadership

The present top personnel of the party, most of whom were carefully selected by Miyamoto and his assistants and then "elected" at the Nineteenth Party Congress in July 1990, are grouped as follows:[37] Miyamoto Kenji, chairman of the Central Committee (CC); Tachiki Hiroshi, CC vice-chairman; Fuwa Tetsuzō, chairman of the Presidium; four vice-chairmen of the fifty-seven-member Presidium, including twenty members of the Standing Presidium; Shii Kazuo, director of the Secretariat;[38] four deputy directors of the fourteen-member Secretariat; the members of the Central Committee (150 full members and fifty-six candidate members); Nosaka Sanzō, the nearly century-old honorary chairman; the members of the Control and Audit Committees; the Editorial Committee for Central Party Publications; the specialized agencies, consisting of nineteen committees, fifteen departments, fourteen bureaus, one conference, and one institute; two campaign committees on educational and electoral matters; eight functional committees, which bring together personnel to deal with such matters as international problems, national and local policy, the united front, mass movements, educational affairs, party organization and discipline, propaganda, and elections; the members of the JCP Diet group guidance structure, which consists of a General Assembly of JCP Diet Members Groups, separate House of Representatives and House of Councillors Party Diet Members Groups and Policy Committees, and, finally, the Party Diet Members Group Secretariat.[39]

In addition, there are more than 1,000 party *apparatchiks* in the Tokyo headquarters, over 10,000 party officials in prefectural and district committees, and some 70,000 chiefs and members of branch leadership committees. The party headquarters regularly convenes conferences of prefectural chairmen, district chairmen, chiefs of prefectural party organ departments, and provincial activists.

The Gender Gap

Compared to other Japanese political parties, the JCP takes particular pride in the number of female candidates it officially endorses and the number of female members of the two houses of the National Diet elected under its auspices. In the House of Representatives election of December 1983, the JCP elected seven female parliamentarians compared to two for all of the other parties combined.[40]

The number of women in the party hierarchy overall, however, is quite another story. Although women constitute almost 40 percent of the party membership, they have accounted for only 17.6 percent of the delegates to the Nineteenth Party Congress and 18.9 percent of the 206-member Central Committee elected 1990.[41] There is only one woman in the twenty-member Standing Committee of the Presidium, including one vice-chairman, six in the fifty-seven-member Presidium, and a total of sixteen women out of almost two hundred top positions in the party.

Membership

As indicated in Figure 5.2, the growth of JCP membership following World War II has gone through five periods: (1) in 1945–1949 phenomenal growth occurred, from 1,000 to 84,000 members (an eightyfold increase); (2) in 1950–1958 the membership was reduced by half to 40,000, following the disastrous leftist course dictated by the Cominform and the CCP; (3) in 1958–1970 rapid growth occurred, amounting to a sevenfold increase in twelve years under Miyamoto's leadership, to roughly 300,000 members; (4) in 1970–1987 the growth was slow (65 percent in seventeen years), probably approaching the half-million mark; and (5) after 1987 came a slow decline. It thus seems that the JCP's goal of a half million members (and 4 million *Akahata* subscribers) discussed during the past decade and a half will not be reached. As the membership claims are party figures, Japanese government analysts tend to dispute them, pointing out that the party typically sets membership goals for its congresses and during the preparatory periods carries a lot of "sleepers," that is, members who either have been delinquent in their payment of party dues or have not participated in party activities for a period of one year and can thus be subject to expulsion (Article XII of the JCP constitution). (Party dues are 1 percent of a member's salary.) Figure 5.2 also indicates party strength minus the "sleepers," whose number reached 100,000 in September 1990, reducing effective party membership to around 360,000. Nevertheless, the JCP membership figure, however it is calculated, is greater than that of all other Japanese opposition parties combined and represents the third largest (after the Italian and French Communist parties) nonruling Communist party in the world. This dramatic growth of party membership is one measure of Miyamoto's organizing skill.

Party Affiliate Organizations and the Larger Network

An integral part of the Japanese Communist movement is its youth and women's affiliate organizations; its influence in certain labor unions, particularly those in which JCP members are in leadership positions and control the unions' affairs; and a whole range of front organizations focusing on such areas as peace, international friendship, the antinuclear movement, welfare, and livelihood protection. Several of these organizations are constituent members of international Communist front organizations, even though their membership is by no means exclusively Communist. Many of the organizations are also part of larger federations of organizations on the Left, some of which, especially those originally co-sponsored by the JCP and the JSP, have split into JCP and JSP groups. Most notable among these is the antinuclear movement of the early 1960s.

Some analysts have singled out the youth, women's, and small-business organizations as the party's "Three Great Families" (or *Gosanke*, an ironic reference to the three main branches of the Tokugawa family). More recently, three other organizations—namely, the associations of doctors, lawyers, and tax accountants—have been jokingly designated as the JCP's "New Three Great Families," in recognition not only of the importance the party attaches

FIGURE 5.2
JCP membership growth, 1945-1990

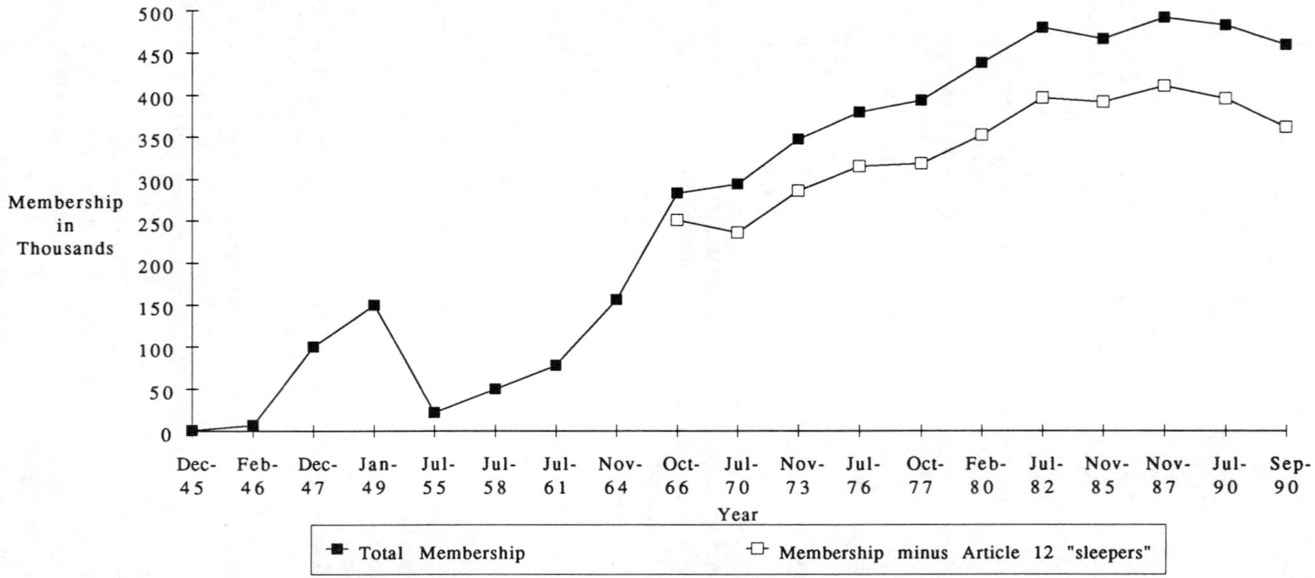

Source: JCP secret document from JCP Organization Bureau reproduced in *Sekai Nippō*, November 13, 1990.

to these professions but also of the significant role these organizations have played in projecting an image of the JCP as a party that is helping people in their daily lives.[42]

Publications

The JCP recognizes the power of propaganda and at the same time, surprisingly, is able to make a nice living from it. It maintains a truly profitable big-business publishing empire, so that the party has been facetiously called "The Yoyogi Newspaper Publishing Company, Limited." This publishing business, as we shall see in the next section, practically maintains the party by providing it with operating funds and makes it possible for the JCP to be independent of special interest groups. The most important party publication—its financial lifeline as well as a measure of its success in Japanese society—is the party organ *Akahata,* which comes out in a daily edition (and has since October 1945) and a weekly Sunday edition (since March 1959). *Akahata* has maintained permanent correspondents in several major Communist capitals as well as in Washington, London, Paris, Rome, Mexico City, Manila, and New Delhi. In Japan it has at its service some 13,000 correspondents, or stringers, as well as more than 50,000 unpaid delivery workers.

Combined circulation figures of the daily and Sunday editions of *Akahata* are used by the party as both a measure of its success and a perennial target. For some years now, the party's goals were to achieve an *Akahata* readership of 4 million. The figure reported by party leaders at the Fifteenth Party Congress in 1980 was 3.5 million, the highest number ever claimed by party authorities. Since then, as seen in Figure 5.3, the circulation is down by about one million (or almost a third), although there are artificial increases before each party congress when members try to sign up as many relatives, neighbors, coworkers, and friends as they can. Nonetheless, *Akahata* easily surpasses the circulation of a party newspaper of any other nonruling Communist party. In fact, Miyamoto bragged that his colleagues in the French and Italian Communist parties were astounded when they learned about *Akahata*'s readership of 3 million.[43]

In addition to *Akahata,* the party publishes *Zen'ei,* an authoritative theoretical monthly; *Sekai Seiji,* a semimonthly on international affairs; *Kurashi to Seiji,* a monthly report on parliamentary affairs; an illustrated monthly for potential party members; and a dozen other periodicals (weeklies to semiannuals) ranging in circulation from 4,000 to 280,000. Most of the latter publications are directed to the party's youth and to women's affiliates; others include agricultural, economics, science, and "thought" monthlies, a monthly for cadres in the labor union movement, weeklies for students and children, a general cultural monthly entitled *Bunka Hyoron,* and the organ of the Democratic Literary League, *Minshu Bungaku.* Total circulation figures for these publications, excluding the *Akahata,* are over 1.5 million copies.[44] In addition, the Central Committee Publishing Bureau puts out millions of pamphlets, especially during elections, as well as a wide range of books.[45]

FIGURE 5.3

Akahata subscribers, 1958-1990

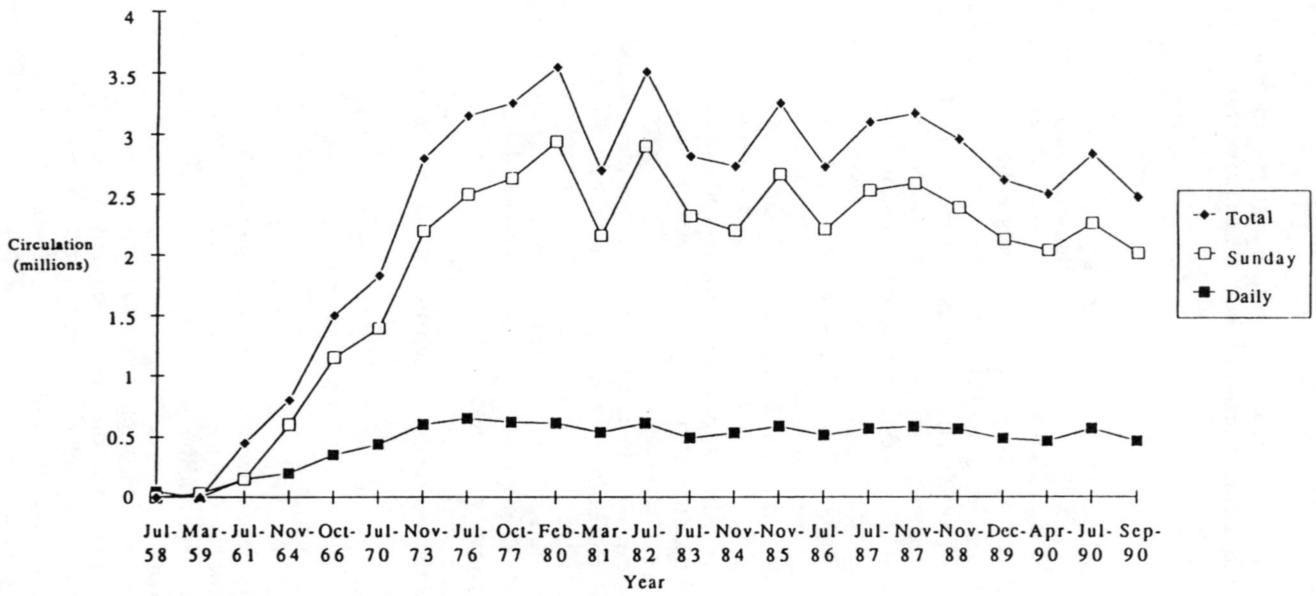

Source: *Sayoku Binran*, p. 217; *Sekai Nippō*, November 11, 1990.

TABLE 5.1
JCP income and expenditure, 1989 (in millions of yen)

Income	*Total*		*Percentage*
Party dues	1,260		4.2
Donations	382		1.0
Party Enterprises	27,626		92.4
Akahata		25,061	
Magazines and books		2,506	
Akahata festival and people's university		57	
Miscellaneous income	694		2.4
Total income	29,962		100.0
Carry-over from the previous year	2,658		
Grand total	32,620		
Expenditure	*Total*		*Percentage*
Administrative expenses	3,719		11.8
Personnel		2,853	
Utilities		27	
Equipment and office supplies		89	
Party offices		750	
Political activities	27,716		88.2
Organizational activities		340	
Election campaigns		1,013	
Enterprise expenses			
Publishing expenses		22,485	
Publicity		690	
Other business expenses		50	
Research and surveys		64	
Gifts and grants		3,068	
Other expenses		2	
Total expenditures	31,435		100.0

Note: Not all subcategories are included in the table.

Source: Adapted by author from *Rosei Jōhō*, no. 76 (October 15, 1990), p. 12.

Party Finances

During the immediate postwar period, the JCP unquestionably benefited from the funds secretly provided by the Soviet mission accredited to the Headquarters of the Supreme Commander for the Allied Powers. Somewhat later, moneys earned by visiting Soviet performers were conveniently laundered and made their way into the party coffers. There were also some instances of unlawful importation of prescription medications and heroin.[46] In the 1950s and early 1960s, trade contacts with the Soviet Union, mainland China, and other Communist countries were deliberately structured in a way to benefit left-wing causes, including the JCP. Communist China, for example, moved most of its trade with Japan through the so-called friendly firms. But following the breaks with the CPSU and the CCP in the mid-

1960s, the Japanese party was largely on its own, with the income from the sale of its publications constituting the predominant part of the budget, followed by "donations."

Although Japanese political parties have to report their income and expenditures to the government authorities, these figures must be handled with great caution, as they most probably reveal only a fraction of the actual income. Nonetheless, the figures are not without significance. For one thing, we can see the relative increases, as the reported party budget rose from $367,000 in 1958, to $1 million in 1961, to $3.6 million in 1965, $11.4 million in 1970, and $40 million in 1975.[47] From 1978 to 1989, the party's income almost doubled, from 16.7 billion yen to 29.9 billion yen. But because of the dramatic appreciation of the Japanese currency, the 1989 figure represents $200 million (see Table 5.1). Unfortunately, the expenditure figures also rose to 31.4 billion yen, or a deficit of 1.6 billion yen (over $10 million, which was more than offset by carryover funds from previous years of $20 million).[48] Over 90 percent of the income (but also 74 percent of the expenditures) was associated with party publications; dues constituted only about 4 percent. Party publications showed a healthy $40 million profit.

There are problems, however, in the distribution of the publications and the collection of subscription fees—and for dealing with these problems, the party has a special committee. The party also experiences liquidity problems—especially in election years, when extra funds are needed. It has been estimated that the party spent around $3 million on each election campaign during 1969–1971, $5 million to $8 million in 1974–1977, and some $13 million in the four years between 1980 and 1983. In 1979 the combined cost of local and House of Representatives elections (in the spring and fall, respectively) was as high as $18 million.[49] The cost of the 1989 House of Councillors election was about $8 million, whereas the deficit of some $20 million for 1986, the year of the double elections to both houses of the National Diet, was largely attributed by the JCP to election expenses.[50]

An amazing fact is that according to official reporting, the JCP is the richest political party in Japan. The LDP, of course, enjoys the generous support of big business, and political donations are more easily concealable than the JCP income from its publishing empire.[51] As indicated earlier, the reported JCP income for 1989 was 29.9 billion yen, followed by 24.6 billion for the LDP, 14.9 billion for Kōmeitō, 5.5 billion for the Socialists, and 4.2 billion for the DSP.[52] These figures are even more remarkable if we recall that the other opposition parties enjoy the financial support of large labor union federations and a religious organization. In other words, the JCP is not indebted to outside interest groups—an obvious advantage when one considers that the other parties get bad publicity because of "money politics" and conflicts of interest. Privately, LDP politicians have a grudging respect for the integrity of the JCP legislators, much as they despise the Socialists who are regularly being bought off by the government party.[53]

THE ELECTORAL RECORD

Since the establishment of democratic Japan by the U.S. Occupation, the JCP has participated fully in the electoral process at all levels: at the national level (for the House of Representatives and the House of Councillors—the latter in both the national and local constituencies), at the prefectural level (governors and prefectural assemblies), and at the local level (mayors and assemblies of cities and villages). Of course, the JCP's electoral record can be measured in different ways: by the number of seats won in the national, prefectural, and local legislative bodies; in terms of party participation in prefectural and local governments; by the number of votes cast for party candidates; and by the percentage of votes and seats at all levels. The latter figure can be further broken down into percentages of all eligible voters, of the total election vote, of the total opposition parties vote, and of the total vote of the parties on the Left. But, broadly speaking, the party's performance in the postwar electoral politics of Japan has undergone four phases: (1) 1945–1949: a period of growth; (2) 1950s and early 1960s: debacle and slow rebirth; (3) late 1960s to early 1970s: rapid growth; and (4) mid-1970s to the present (1991): stagnation, gain and loss, or slow growth (depending on the electoral level or electoral indicator).

House of Representatives

The most important elections in Japan are those for the current 512 seats in the House of Representatives, which is the lower but more powerful house of the National Diet. As can be seen in Table A.1, in 1946 and 1967 the party received a little more than 2 million votes, in 1949 and 1969 a little more than 3 million votes, and since 1972 some 5 million votes. This last figure seems to be the limit. The JCP usually outpolls the CGP and the DSP, but this is because the JCP puts up candidates in every electoral district (including some eighty districts in which the candidates have absolutely no chance of winning, but which give the JCP an additional 1.5 million votes). By contrast, the CGP and the DSP put up fewer candidates, coordinate their electoral tactics in some districts, and by agreement support each other's candidates. Very often a joint candidate will get elected, whereas two separate candidates would have split the vote and lost. This is good electoral strategy, but it does lower the total number of votes for these parties.

If we disregard the votes that the JCP gets without any chance of translating them into parliamentary seats, the party suffers from the inequities of the present electoral system, which greatly favors the ruling conservative party, the LDP. In many rural and semirural districts, far fewer votes are required to elect a member of the Diet than is the case in the urban areas, where the JCP votes are concentrated. Thus, the JCP's percentage of the total vote is much higher than the percentage of party seats in the Diet (8 percent versus 3 percent in February 1990; see also Chapter 2).

The 1972 vote represents the high point of the party's share of the total vote, which was almost 11 percent if one adds the votes of the two members who ran under the Progressive Unity party (Kakushin Kyōdotō) label. In the ensuing eighteen years the total vote for the party fluctuated between 5 and 6 million, but the percentage fell gradually to 8 percent.[54] (Of course, in some urban areas, such as Kyōto and Ōsaka, JCP candidates get around 20 percent of the vote, or more than double the national average.)

Although the total vote for the Communist party has been fairly steady (with a slight decline in the last decade), the number of Communist Diet members in the lower house has fluctuated wildly. As seen graphically in Table A.1, the figures for the past seven elections (from 1972 to 1990) are as follows (the figures in parentheses represent the party's contingent with the addition of candidates elected on the Progressive Unity party slate): 38 (40), 17 (19), 39 (41), 29 (29), 26 (27), 26 (27), and currently 16 (16). How can one account for these variations, which occurred in spite of the relative steadiness of the total electoral vote? One explanation is that in multiseat constituencies the difference between the last winner and the closest runner-up (*jiten*) is sometimes only a few thousand votes. Bad publicity can sway a number of votes and cost the party a few marginal seats. It can also be domestic, as in the Miyamoto "lynching" incident and the revelations of the purged vice-chairman, Hakamada Satomi, or it can be international, as in the Soviet invasion of Afghanistan, the repression in Poland, the shooting down of a Korean airliner (with many Japanese passengers on board) by a Soviet fighter plane, the assassination of South Korean cabinet ministers by North Korean agents in Burma in 1983, and the Tienanmen Square massacre in June 1989. All such incidents create an *imeiji daun* ("image down")—that is, a worsening in the Japanese perception of Communist countries and of communism, which therefore affects the JCP. The disintegration of Communist regimes in Eastern Europe in late 1989 must have also had an impact on the Japanese electorate in the February 1990 elections.

A second, and more important, explanation is that the JCP can more easily win a seat in a multiseat constituency if all the other opposition parties field candidates and split the non-Communist vote. But the JCP electoral successes in 1972 and 1979 taught the CGP and the DSP to enter into election agreements, not to run against each other's candidates in certain constituencies. In fact, in the December 1983 election, 59 joint candidates were put up in 58 electoral districts and 46 of them won, while in the February 1990 election 70 joint candidates were put up and 48 of them were elected.

Finally, are fluctuations in the number of JCP seats correlated with the number of JSP seats, or the total number of left or opposition seats? The only pattern of negative or positive correlation appears to be that associated with the JSP. It seems that in elections in which the JCP gains seats, the JSP loses them, and vice versa. This was certainly true in 1949, when the JCP's dramatic increase in seats occurred at the expense of the Socialists, and again in 1990 when the Socialists gained seats at the expense of the JCP as well as other parties.[55]

House of Councillors

Although elections to the upper house are less important than those to the House of Representatives, a similar trend is evident. As indicated in Table A.1, the party's popular vote in both the national and local constituencies grew from the 1959 election, when it was 1.6 million, until the 1974 election, when the JCP garnered 11.8 million votes (6.8 million, or 12.8 percent, in the local constituency and 4.9 million, or 9.4 percent, in the national) and had 20 members in the upper house. Similar to the trend in the House of Representatives voting, the party has yet to attain this number of votes and legislators. The JCP group in the House of Councillors has fluctuated from 12 to 18 members; the present (1991) figure is 14.

As a group, Communist parliamentarians in both houses of the National Diet are the youngest of any party and, after the LDP, the second most educated group.[56] They do their homework, so to speak, and, at least since the 1970s, have not engaged in opposition for opposition's sake.[57]

Local Elections

The JCP has also vigorously contested elections at the subnational level—that is, elections of prefectural governors and mayors of major urban centers, cities, towns, wards, and villages, and elections to prefectural, municipal, ward, and village assemblies.

Party history was made in 1967 when a Communist was elected mayor of Shiojiri in Nagano Prefecture.[58] In general, however, the JCP has participated in broad left-wing coalitions to elect "progressives" as governors or as mayors of major cities (the election of Governor Minobe of Tokyo in 1967 being the most important). In subsequent years, all six of the largest cities came under nonconservative control. But as the "progressives" became entrenched in city government, the united front of the opposition parties collapsed; some elections became three-cornered affairs with one conservative and two "progressive" candidates. Thus, in the past two decades, the JCP has backed some candidates in an election alliance with other opposition parties, and has run some candidates alone. In 1974 and 1975 it succeeded in electing the governors of Kyōto and Ōsaka against two other candidates in each case. In April 1978, however, the party lost the Kyōto and Yokohama elections, and in April 1979, it lost Tokyo and Ōsaka. In the April 1983 local elections, the JCP ran its own candidate for the governorship of Ōsaka, a joint candidate with the JSP in Tokyo and Fukuoka, and it officially endorsed other candidates. Only in Fukuoka did the JCP-JSP candidate win the governorship; most other winners were candidates endorsed by the LDP, CGP, and DSP. As of 1990 (prior to the 1991 local elections), Fukuoka was still run by a JSP/JCP-endorsed governor, and in Saitama Prefecture the governor was endorsed by the JCP, JSP, DSP, and two other minor parties. Considering the fact that at one time the JCP participated in the election of governors in Tokyo, Ōsaka, Kyōto, Okinawa, Okayama, Kanagawa, Shiga, and Kagawa, the tide has clearly turned against the JCP and the JSP.

If one looks at the JCP's record of electoral success at the prefectural and local assembly levels, it becomes clear that compared to 1958 the total number of JCP-elected assembly members rose sixfold from roughly 650 to 3,600 in 1980 (out of 70,000 seats). But during the 1980s, when the JCP was losing votes and seats at the national level, the party's contingent in the provincial and local assemblies continued to increase, reaching almost 4,000 legislators in 1990.

In the June 1985 elections to the Tokyo Metropolitan Assembly, the JCP increased its delegation from 16 to 19 members. However, the number of votes and the percentage of the total vote declined compared to the previous election.[59] The picture was also mixed in the 1989 election: Although the total Communist vote slightly increased (from roughly 695,000 to 713,000 votes), the JCP percentage of the total vote declined (from 15.5 percent to 13.9 percent), and so did the number of JCP assembly members (from 19 to 14).[60]

Another way to measure the electoral success of the JCP below the national level is to look at the number of local governments in which the JCP is the governing party or, more likely, a part of the governing coalition. The JCP's participation rose from 10 members in 1960 to over 200 by the mid-1970s. By 1989, this number declined to 129 members (in two prefectures discussed above, with the rest in cities and wards, and towns and villages). To place these figures in perspective, we must compare them with the total number of local self-governing bodies, which is 3,315. But even the number 129 is deceptive, because it includes coalitions with the JSP; moreover, in many instances, these coalitions embrace several parties including the LDP. Of the 127 cities, towns, and villages in which the JCP is part of the governing coalition, only six town mayors or village heads are of Communist persuasion—and only three are formally JCP members.[61]

CONCLUSIONS

This chapter began with the observation that poor, repressive, Imperial Japan was very inhospitable to the fledgling alien, radical Japanese Communist movement. Paradoxically, conditions in affluent and democratic postwar and post-Occupation Japan are, in effect, equally inhospitable to a "Eurocommunist"-type party, which is working hard to project an image of an indigenous Japanese party that is independent from both Moscow and Peking, accepts parliamentary democracy, and is prepared to play by the rules of a pluralist society in an open political system. Japan is, indeed, a postindustrial society with an ever-growing service sector of the economy.

One can argue, of course, that the ongoing shrinkage of the blue-collar working class will not affect the JCP much, as that class was never well represented in the party's membership and was virtually absent in the top leadership. Japan in the 1990s is on the road to being a welfare state with hardly any real proletariat, whose interests the JCP is supposed to uphold. Over 90 percent of the Japanese public consider themselves to be "middle class." Students and other young people in their twenties at one time voted

Communist in great numbers, but this group is becoming, if anything, more conservative, as is the case in Western Europe and the United States.

In fact, this shift could mean a weakened JCP for the future. Party leaders now admit that over 60 percent of the party membership is in their thirties and forties, another 20 percent in their fifties, but only 10 percent are in their twenties. Thus, the party baby-boomers from the 1960s and 1970s are now middle-aged, but no young replacements seem to be in sight. This pessimistic prognosis is further strengthened if we look at the party's youth affiliate, the Japan Democratic Youth League (Minsei Dōmei). The organization peaked in 1974, with 231,000 members. The membership dropped somewhat to 209,000 in 1984, then fell further to 171,000 in 1989. In the next two years came a precipitous decline in membership, with fewer than 120,000 members reported in October 1990. Because 25,000 of this number are also JCP members, it is clear that there will be no significant number of young people flowing into the party.[62]

Then, of course, there are the intellectuals who over the decades have provided sympathetic support and leadership to the party. But they, too, reflect the growing conservatism of Japanese society and their own disappointment, indeed dismay, over the ideological bankruptcy of the Soviet Union, with its repression of a humanist socialist regime in Czechoslovakia and a truly working-class movement in Poland, not to mention the recent collapse of communism in Eastern Europe and the unsettling aspects of Gorbachev's perestroika. All of this threatens the entire structure of the Soviet system and invalidates seventy years of claims to build a new, progressive, just, and prosperous society. Closer to Japan, there is the specter of China: It went through the horrors of the so-called Great Proletarian Cultural Revolution, only to begin, with the death of Mao Zedong, partially to dismantle socialism, to emulate certain key features of the capitalist system, and yet to engage in brutal repression in the Tienanmen Square massacre.

In spite of the JCP's protestations of commitment to nationalism, democracy, parliamentary pluralism, and independence from international centers of Communist power, the predominant image of the JCP among the Japanese public remains that of an alien political creature, espousing an ideology that is becoming less and less relevant to Japan and run dictatorially by a radical prewar leader not quite cleared of homicide charges. The JCP occupies that awkward middle ground in which it is not revolutionary enough for the radical fringe and not trustworthy enough for the adherents of democratic socialism. Above all, the Japanese economic miracle was accomplished by aggressive free enterprise (albeit guided by a conservative government) in the free world markets. But reality is often ignored, especially by ivory-tower intellectuals. The present author remembers, for example, hearing Japanese Marxist scholars talk about the pauperization of the Japanese farmer, at a time when a visit to the countryside just outside Tokyo would reveal a forest of television antennas and every conceivable type of electrical appliance and agricultural machinery. Perhaps there is a cumulative effect associated with Japan's economic growth and prosperity. Perhaps it has become difficult to accept the fact that Chinese Communist leaders were not only speaking warmly about the U.S.-Japan security ties but also encouraging the growth of the Japanese military establishment. Then there was always the northern neighbor refusing to budge from the Japanese northern islands, turning them into military outposts directed against Japan and, until very recently, relentlessly increasing its Pacific fleet, its nuclear-armed bomber force, and its strategic nuclear missiles. So it was not very reassuring to see the leader of the JCP attending summit meetings in Moscow, in spite of the party's rhetoric against Czechoslovakia, Afghanistan, Poland, or the shooting down of a Korean airliner.

Nonetheless, if prospects for the JCP are rather bleak, the party is still a formidable organization, at both the national and urban levels. It claims the loyalty of close to 100,000 dedicated cadres and probably another 100,000 faithful adherents, if not all true believers. Beyond party rolls, there are the youth and women's affiliates and the dozens of front organizations either directly controlled by the party or partially manipulated by party members in critical positions of power. Then there are the party cells in labor unions, the government agencies, the private enterprises, the universities, and the lower educational institutions. Japanese government analysts have been warning about the long-range effects on Japanese society of, for example, Communist teachers in elementary schools, labor union activists (particularly among governmental employees), and Communist lawyers who may advance in the judicial system perhaps all the way to the Supreme Court. Finally, there are over 5 million Communist voters in general elections. It is significant that even after the disintegration of communism in Eastern Europe, 5.25 million Japanese voted Communist, a drop of only 200,000 votes (a net loss of 1 percent of the total vote). Although the party's contingent in the House of Representatives dropped from 27 to 16, it is noteworthy that 16 of 19 Communist runners-up (*jiten*) lost by a *combined* total of less than 130,000 votes (or an average of only 8,000 votes per district). Unless there is a precipitous drop in the support of the JCP, it is quite likely that a number of these runners-up will be reelected, just as they periodically bounced back in the past. Clearly there is a reservoir of commitment to and sympathy for the Japanese Communist party, even though there must have been a certain number of protest voters disgusted at the sight of all major parties (except the Communists) sullied in the Recruit bribery scandal. The party tries to be attentive to the needs of local constituents, and its record in selected local areas is much better than at the national level, where many of the party's strongly held positions (e.g., against the U.S.-Japan Security Treaty or the Self-Defense Forces) run counter to public opinion polls.

On the positive side, the JCP helped diffuse the violence of the far Left and neo-anarchist elements, violence that was particularly ominous in the late 1960s and early 1970s. Here the party came out strongly and forthrightly against what Lenin called left-wing infantilism, and the party's youth affiliates, along with other organizations, certainly provided a counterpoint to the very visible and vocal ultra-Left fringe. Although no comparison can be made between the Japanese and Italian Communist parties in terms of the level of voter support nationally or active participation in local government, JCP legislators often play a constructive role in local assemblies, emulating the example set by the PCI. In the National Diet, the party contingent in both houses can be counted on to be vigilant with respect to LDP corruption and to support welfare, environmental, and consumer legislation. In contrast to the French and Italian Communist parties, the Japanese party does not enjoy the support of organized labor federations. But that makes the JCP the most independent of Japanese political parties in the sense that it can pursue its policies without regard to special interest groups. And that might pay dividends with the voting public.

At the moment, after fifteen years of stagnation, the JCP remains isolated, and its prospects for meaningful joint action with other opposition parties seem to have been checkmated by the unwillingness of the CGP and the DSP to cooperate. These two parties have visibly moved to the Center (even the JSP is taking some steps in that direction), and distance from the Communist party is helpful in promoting a centrist image.

In politics, long-term predictions are very hazardous. Nonetheless, since Miyamoto is eighty-three years old (as of 1991), his days at the top of the party are numbered. Indeed, he is no longer at the helm on a daily basis. His gradual retirement would be a blessing as it would remove one more reminder of the JCP's prewar alien and violent past, much as Miyamoto must be credited with building up the party from the nadir brought about by misguided Soviet and Chinese policies. The question remains whether his technocrat successors will be able to hold the party together, increase its strength quantitatively (and, more important, qualitatively), make inroads into the labor federations, reclaim the protest and the floating vote, and offer a program that is relevant to Japan in the last decade of the twentieth century and beyond. Can they do this and also change the structure of the party to one of internal democracy to conform to the Japanese political environment?[63] Fuwa, the physics graduate, seems to have a talent for commenting on Marxist-Leninist-Stalinist classics and engaging in sterile debates. He has yet to come up with a creative look at the present political, economic, and social reality in Japan. His brother Ueda and Shii, the latter the newly appointed head of the Secretariat, are better known for their organizational talents than for their ideas. Thus, prospects are not good for the JCP to overcome its history and ideology and to be able to present new, relevant, and attractive ideas.

An even more important problem is the very survival of communism in the world.[64] The ruling Communist parties in Eastern Europe tried to survive by dropping the word *Communist* and masquerading as socialists or social democrats. The voters' judgment in free elections was massive rejection, even though some former Communist leaders have hung on in a few East European countries by claiming to have been opponents of the ancien régime and promising to be reformers.

More relevant to the JCP is the position of the Italian Communist party which has moved from Eurocommunism to Euroleft, has sought to join the

Socialist International, and as part of the process has dropped the word *Communist* in its name.[65] Even Gorbachev has been making some noises about the Soviet Communist party's affiliation with the Socialist International. But why should the democratic Socialists forgive and embrace their former bitterest enemies? Moreover, the Japanese Communists have rejected Gorbachev's new political thinking and accuse him of betraying the most basic of Marxist dogmas by placing humanity's values over class values.[66] The JCP clings to the notion of the basic correctness of "scientific socialism."

Will the Japanese Communist party survive, whether under its present name or under a different name? At the moment, the Japanese Communists are not ready even to change the name of the party, even though they dropped Marxism-Leninism in favor of scientific socialism over fifteen years ago. A Nihon Kagaku Shakaishugi Tō? A Japan Scientific Socialist party? In the short term this seems unlikely, but the Italian Communist party has in the past served as a model for the JCP, without the Japanese Communists ever acknowledging their debt. Will the JCP again follow the PCI? And if so, what would be its relationships with the JSP and the DSP? With respect to Socialist collaboration with the Communists, the situation in Japan is even less favorable than in Europe. Both the orthodox Japanese Socialists and the moderate Democratic Socialists have given up on any united front or joint action with the Communists. In terms of any future cooperation, the JCP's present position of attacking perestroika, clinging to class struggle, and so on is clearly counterproductive. The JCP is isolated on the domestic political scene, Moscow and Peking have gone astray, and there is no world Communist movement to help. So what is the future of the Japanese Communist party?

When monarchies were falling right and left after the end of World War I, it was said that if there would remain one king, it would be the king of England. Should we paraphrase it and say that if there will remain but one nonruling Communist party in the world, it will be the JCP?

ACKNOWLEDGMENTS

I thank Paul Langer of the Rand Corporation for his careful reading of an earlier draft of this chapter and for his insightful suggstions; I also thank Minoru Koide and Bae Yeon Won for timely research assistance. Final responsibility is, of course, mine alone.

NOTES

1. There are several good English-language books on the Japanese Communist movement: Rodger Swearingen and Paul Langer, *Red Flag in Japan: International Communism in Action, 1919–1951* (Cambridge, Mass.: Harvard University Press, 1952); George M. Beckmann and Ōkubo Genji, *The Japanese Communist Party, 1922–1945* (Stanford, Calif.: Stanford University Press, 1969); Robert A. Scalapino, *The Japanese Communist Movement, 1920–1966* (Berkeley: University of California Press, 1967); and Paul F. Langer, *Communism in Japan: A Case of Political Naturalization* (Stanford,

Calif.: Hoover Institution, 1972). Also very useful are the section on Japan in the annual *Yearbook on International Communist Affairs* (Stanford: Hoover Institution, 1967–); the monthly *Kōan Jōhō*; handbooks periodically published by the Nihon Seiji Keizai Kenkyūjo, especially the 1983 edition entitled *Nikkyō, Minsei, Shakaishugi Kyōkai, Shin Sayoku: Kenkyū, Chōsa, Taisaku no Tebiki* (hereinafter cited as *Nikkyō . . . no Tebiki*), and the 1989 edition, *Sayoku Binran: Kenkyū, Chōsa, Taisaku no Tebiki* (hereinafter cited as *Sayoku Binran*), as well as the Institute's *Shiryō Tsūshin* [Research bulletin] and *Rōsei Jōhō*; and Shisō Undō Kenkyūjo, *Nihon Kyōsan Tō Jiten—Shiryō Hen* [An introduction to the Japan Communist party] (Tokyo: Zembōsha, 1978). Primary sources for the study of the JCP include its daily, *Akahata*, and the theoretical monthly, *Zen'ei*, as well as other publications of the party and its affiliated organizations. JCP headquarters also issues from time to time the English-language *Bulletin: Information for Abroad* (hereinafter cited as *Bulletin*), which contains translations of important party documents, statements, editorials, speeches, and the like. *Japan Press Weekly* is a 20–40 page press release that routinely provides material in English from *Akahata* and other party publications.

2. *The Russian Impact on Japan: Literature and Social Thought—Two Essays by Nobori Shomu and Akamatsu Katsumaro*, translated and edited and with an introduction by Peter Berton, Paul F. Langer, and George O. Totten (Los Angeles: University of Southern California Press, 1981).

3. "A Documentary History of the Japanese Communist Movement with Special Reference to Ties with Moscow and Peking" is under preparation by the author and his colleagues at the University of Southern California.

4. For a description of the prominent Japanese Communists, their roles in the party, the dates of Moscow links, and the fates of individual politicians, see Table 1 in Rodger Swearingen, *The Soviet Union and Postwar Japan: Escalating Challenge and Response* (Stanford, Calif.: Hoover Institution Press, 1978), pp. 56–57.

5. Tokuda Kyūichi and Shiga Yoshio, *Gokuchū Jūhachi Nen* (Tokyo: Jiji Tsūshinsha, 1947).

6. A charter member of the British Communist party, Nosaka spent many years in exile, first in Moscow, and then, since 1940, in Yenan with Mao Zedong trying to indoctrinate Japanese prisoners of war. See Nosaka Sanzō, *Bōmei Jūroku Nen* (Tokyo: Jiji Tsūshinsha, 1946).

7. See Omori Minoru, *Secret History of Postwar Japan*, vol. 4: *Akahata to GHQ* (Tokyo: Kōdansha, 1975), 350 pp.

8. For Soviet views, see I. I. Tamginskii, "Iz istorii bor'by Kommunisticheskoi Partii Iaponii protiv pravogo opportunizma, 1945–1950," *Narody Azii i Afriki*, no. 3 (1980), pp. 55–65; and I. I. Kovalenko, "Kommunisticheskaia Partiia Iaponii v bor'be protiv levogo ekstremizma, 1950–1955," *Narody Azii i Afriki*, no. 1 (1981), pp. 40–52.

9. See the biographical sketch of Tokuda by Tomita Nobuo in Uchida Kenzō et al., *Nihon Seiji no Jitsuryokushatachi* [Significant figures in Japanese politics], vol. 3 *Postwar* (Tokyo: Yūhikaku, 1981), pp. 75–112.

10. The "1951 Program" was written by Stalin himself and imposed upon the JCP. See Peter Berton, "The Soviet and Japanese Communist Parties: Policies, Tactics, Negotiating Behavior," *Studies in Comparative Communism* 15, no. 3 (Autumn 1982), pp. 273–275. See also the memoirs of the Soviet interpreter at the meeting, Nikolai Adykhayev, "Stalin's Meetings with Japanese Communists in the Summer of 1951," *Far Eastern Affairs*, no. 3 (1990), pp. 124–134.

11. This section updates some of the material appearing in Peter Berton, "Japan: Euro-Nippo-Communism," in V. Aspaturian et al., eds., *Eurocommunism Between East and West* (Bloomington: Indiana University Press, 1980), pp. 328–337.

12. For biographical sketches of approximately 160 JCP leaders, see Mizushima Tsuyoshi, *Shokugyō Kakumeika—Nikkyō Kambu 160 Mei no Rirekisho* (Tokyo: Zembōsha, 1970), 259 pp.

13. For a couple of years in the late 1980s, Fuwa was forced to relinquish the chairmanship of the Presidium because of health reasons and alleged differences with Miyamoto. During this interim period, he was designated as vice-chairman of the Central Committee under Miyamoto, while another party leader became chairman of the Presidium.

14. The polycentrism theory holds that the working class should move to accelerate capitalist reform, and the structural reform theory holds that quantitative reforms could lead to a qualitative change in the power structure.

15. *Asahi Shimbun* (July 7, 1970), p. 2.

16. *Akahata* Extra (June 7, 1976); *Bulletin*, no. 356 (July 1976), p. 31.

17. *Akahata* (January 8–9, 1976).

18. *Akahata* (April 27–May 8, 1976); *Bulletin*, no. 354 (July 1976), p. 74.

19. *Akahata* (July 31, 1976); *Bulletin*, no. 359 (October 1976), p. 17.

20. For a good discussion of these electoral reverses, see John F. Copper, "The Japanese Communist Party's Recent Electoral Defeats: A Signal of Decline?" *Asian Survey* 19, no. 4 (April 1979), pp. 353–365.

21. In a traditional interview at the beginning of a new year, Miyamoto said that the party has not only assisted in solving tax problems, installment-sale fraud, and housing loan swindles but has also helped in such personal matters as divorce and "finding a wife." See *Akahata* (January 8, 1977); *Bulletin*, no. 367 (April 1977), p. 15. For a discussion of JCP policies and activities in the Kyōto area, see Ellis S. Krauss, "The Urban Strategy and Policy of the Japan Communist Party: Kyoto," *Studies in Comparative Communism* 12, no. 4 (Winter 1979), pp. 322–350. For a description of party activities in both urban and rural settings, see George O. Totten, "The People's Parliamentary Path of the Japanese Communist Party, Part I: Agrarian Policies," *Pacific Affairs* 46, no. 2 (Summer 1973), pp. 193–217, and "Part II: Local Level Tactics," *Pacific Affairs* 46, no. 3 (Fall 1973), pp. 384–406.

22. *Akahata* (October 18, 1977).

23. *Yomiuri Shimbun* (October 25, 1990), p. 2.

24. The alleged "lynching" incident must have hurt Miyamoto substantially at the polls: He ranked forty-first in the fifty-member national constituency of the House of Councillors in July 1977.

25. It is interesting to note that Hakamada also accused Nosaka of being a U.S. agent. See Hakamada's articles in the weekly *Shūkan Shinchō* (January 12 and February 2, 1978). See also Hakamada, *Kinō no Dōshi Miyamoto Kenji e* [Miyamoto Kenji: A comrade of yesterday], (Tokyo: Shinchōsha, November 1978), 252 pp. For official and unofficial JCP statements on the expulsion of Hakamada and on Miyamoto's interview with a *Yomiuri* reporter, see *Akahata* (January 4 and 6, 1978); *Yomiuri Shimbun* (January 13, 1978); and *Bulletin*, no. 391 (January 1978) and no. 397 (May 1978).

26. In public opinion polls, when party supporters were asked why they supported the JCP, only 0.1 percent (the lowest category) said they did so because of party leadership, compared with almost seven times as many who listed ideology. *Jiji Seron Chōsa Tokuhō*, no. 538 (March 1, 1990), Tables, p. 2.

27. Of these latter materials, nine are by Marx and Engels, eight are by Lenin, and two are Comintern documents. See *Akahata* (January 1, 1978); *Bulletin*, no. 399 (June 1978). See also the party's basic reading, *Chi wo Chikara ni: Nihon Kyōsan Tō no Kihon Bunken wo Manabu* (Tokyo: Shin Nihon Shuppansha, 1988), 339 pp., and

a list of all three levels of the party's reading materials in *Sayoku Binran*, pp. 250–256.

28. Iizuka Shigetarō, *Miyamoto Kenji no Nihon Kyōsan Tō* (Tokyo: Ikkosha, 1973), p. 312.

29. For documentation of the Fifteenth Party Congress, see *Akahata* (February 27–March 9, 1980); *Bulletin*, nos. 431–434 (April 1980).

30. *Akahata* (June 11 and July 28–August 5, 1982); *Bulletin*, nos. 488-492 (June–September 1982).

31. "Draft Resolution of the 17th Congress of the Japanese Communist Party," *Akahata* (September 9, 1985); *Bulletin*, no. 552 (October 1985), pp. 2–9.

32. *Akahata* (November 26–28, 1987, and May 25, 1990). For a description and analysis of the JCP's reaction to Gorbachev's perestroika and new political thinking, see Peter Berton, "The Japanese Communist Party's View of Gorbachev's Perestroika," *Acta Slavica Iaponica* (Slavic Research Center, Hokkaido University, Sapporo, Japan), vol. 7 (1989), pp. 121–144.

33. *Bulletin*, no. 552 (October 1985), pp. 9–15.

34. *Akahata* (November 26–28, 1987, and May 25, 1990).

35. *Bulletin*, no. 552 (October 1985), pp. 23, 27, and 29.

36. *Akahata* (November 26–28, 1987, and May 25, 1990).

37. Nihon Seiji Keizai Kenkyūjo, "Nihon Kyōsan Tō Dai Jūkyū-kai Tō Taikai no Zenyō," *Shiryō Tsūshin* 34, no. 13/14 (July 30, 1990), pp. 37–56.

38. For an analysis of the JCP leadership and the groupings of the Presidium members, see Haruhiro Fukui, "The Japanese Communist Party," in M. Kaplan, ed., *The Many Faces of Communism* (New York: Free Press, 1978), pp. 287–298.

39. For brief descriptions of the functions of party agencies, see *Shimpan: Nihon Kyōsan Tō Shōkai* (Tokyo: Nihon Kyōsan Tō Chūō Iinkai Shuppan Kyoku, 1988), pp. 92–101.

40. *Asahi Shimbun* (December 20, 1983), p. 8. In subsequent elections, however, other opposition parties began to field more female candidats. In the 1986 election to the House of Representatives, the JCP again elected seven female parliamentarians, but other parties elected nine women. In February 1990 the JCP elected only two female parliamentarians compared to nine from the JSP and 1 from the CGP. See *Yomiuri Shimbun* (February 20, 1990), p. 1. This was primarily due to the popularity of Doi Takako, the female chairman of the Socialist party. In fact, the Japanese media called this phenomenon "the Madonna strategy." At the same time, it should be noted that it was the JCP that first championed female representation in the Japanese Diet.

41. *Shiryō Tsūshin* 34, no. 13/14 (July 30, 1990).

42. Shiso Undō Kenkyūjo, compiler, *1981—nemban Nihon Kyōsan Tōkei Dantai Yōran* (Tokyo: Zembōsha, 1981), Preface, pp. 2–3.

43. *Shūkan Asahi* (May 30, 1975), cited in the *Yearbook on International Communist Affairs* (1976), p. 304. The circulations of *L'Unita* and *l'Humanite* were about 1 million and .5 million, respectively.

44. Mizushima Tsuyoshi, *Kore ga Kyōsan Tō* (Tokyo: Zembōsha, 1977), pp. 94–105. See descriptions of party publications in *Shimpan: Nihon Kyōsan Tō Shōkai*, pp. 145–160. For a complete list of party-sponsored publications, see the table in Peter A. Berton, "Japanese Eurocommunists: Running in Place," *Problems of Communism* 35, no. 4 (July-August 1986), p. 10; and *Sayoku Binran*, p. 219.

45. Many books and journals are published under the imprint of Shin Nihon Shuppansha, a party affiliate organization.

46. J. P. Napier, *A Survey of the Japan Communist Party* (Tokyo: Nippon Times, 1952), p. 62.

47. Public Security Investigation Agency, *The Recent Aspects of the Japan Communist Party* (Tokyo, March 1959), pp. 10–11; see also the later editions in English and Japanese.

48. *Yomiuri Shimbun* (September 14, 1990), p. 2. For a detailed analysis of the 1988 and 1989 JCP income and expenditure, see "Nihon Kyōsan Tō no Zaisei no Jittai ni Tsuite," Nihon Seiji Keizai Kenkyūjo, *Rōsei Jōhō: Sayoku-kei Rosho no Shuyō Dōkō*, no. 76 (October 15, 1990), pp. 11–16. See also the official JCP discussion of its finances in *Shimpan: Nihon Kyōsan Tō Shōkai*, pp. 163–173. Reported party dues represent only the 15 percent of the total dues allocated to the party headquarters. Of the remainder, 25 percent goes to the prefectural committee, 40 percent to the district committee, and 20 percent to the primary party unit.

49. See Mizushima Tsuyoshi, *Watakushi no Yoyogi Tokuhain: Nihon Kyōsan Tō no Shindan* (Tokyo: Zembōsha, 1981), pp. 189–191; see also the note on party election financing in *Zembō Tokubetsu Tsūshin*, no. 788 (November 20, 1982), pp. 1–3.

50. *Rōsei Jōhō*, No. 76, p. 12, and *Shimpan: Nihon Kyōsan Tō Shōkai*, p. 168.

51. The LDP is, of course, structured in such a way that the finances of the various factions and support groups need not be reported by central party headquarters.

52. *Yomiuri Shimbun* (September 14, 1990), p. 2.

53. Communist legislators even refuse to accept souvenirs that fellow Diet members customarily bring back from their travels in foreign countries and distribute to their neighbors in the Diet office buildings.

54. *Sayoku Binran*, p. 223, and *Yomiuri Shimbun* (February 20, 1990), p. 1.

55. In the 1990 elections, the JCP lost eleven seats to the Socialists, two to the LDP, and one to the DSP. *Yomiuri Shimbun* (February 20, 1990), p. 1.

56. Taketsugu Tsurutani, *Political Change in Japan: Response to Postindustrial Challenge* (New York: Longman, 1980), pp. 143–144.

57. Hong N. Kim, "Deradicalization of the Japanese Communist Party Under Kenji Miyamoto," *World Politics* 28, no. 2 (January 1976), pp. 273–299—especially p. 299, Table V entitled "Voting Records of JCP Diet Members, 1967–1971."

58. For a first-hand look at Shiojiri and its Communist mayor and his policies, see George O. Totten, "Progressive Administration in a Rural Japanese City: The Case of the First Communist Mayor, Takasuna of Shiojiri, Nagano, 1967–1971," in Graciela de la Lama, ed., *Japan and Korea* 2, Proceedings of the 30th International Congress of Human Sciences in Asia and North Africa (Mexico City: El Colegio de Mexico, 1982), pp. 141–181.

59. *Yomiuri Shimbun* (July 8, 1985), evening edition, p. 1.

60. *Asahi Shimbun* (July 4, 1989), evening edition, p. 1.

61. In April 1989, the only Communist *city* mayor in Japan (in Ōsaka prefecture) was defeated by a candidate endorsed by the LDP, JSP, CGP, and DSP. *Sayoku Binran*, pp. 242–246.

62. Mizushima Tsuyoshi, "Chōraku ichijirushii Minsei Dōmei," *Sekai Nippō* (November 16, 1990).

63. In a study of the belief systems of the leaders of the JCP and the Socialist Association, which was the JSP's left wing, the Communists as a group were shown to be more totalitarian and authoritarian. See Shigeko N. Fukai, "Beliefs and Attitudes of the Japanese Left During the Early 1970s," *Asian Survey* 20, no. 12 (December 1980), pp. 1185–1209.

64. Zbigniew Brzezinski has already pronounced the demise of communism. See his latest book *The Grand Failure: The Birth and Death of Communism in the Twentieth Century* (New York: Scribner, 1989).

65. Joan Barth Urban, ed., *Gorbachev and the Global Left* (forthcoming from Cornell University Press).

66. Berton, "The Japanese Communist Party's View of Gorbachev's Perestroika."

PART THREE

The Parties of the Center

6

The Kōmeitō: Party of "Buddhist Democracy"

RONALD J. HREBENAR

In many respects the Kōmeitō, or Clean Government party (CGP), is the anomaly within the Japanese political party system. It is the only religious party in modern Japanese history, and it is the most disciplined party organization in Japanese politics. Feelings toward the Kōmeitō among the Japanese people are seldom neutral. They range from intense support to intense dislike. The reason for this intensity lies in the Kōmeitō's relationship with the giant Buddhist lay organization, the Sōka Gakkai. To understand the position of the Kōmeitō in Japanese society and politics, one must first have an understanding of its parent, the Sōka Gakkai.

THE SŌKA GAKKAI-KŌMEITŌ CONNECTION

At the Kōmeitō's eighteenth national convention held in early December 1970, party chairman Takeiri Yoshikatsu spoke to the party activists and stressed the separation of the Kōmeitō from its founding organization, the Sōka Gakkai. Subsequently, during the decade of the 1970s, the Kōmeitō leadership went to great lengths to establish an image of the separateness of the two powerful organizations. As the Sōka Gakkai and the Kōmeitō were and are so totally intertwined, an awareness of the nature of the parent organization is of crucial importance to an understanding of its creation.

The Rise of the Sōka Gakkai

The Sōka Gakkai is clearly the largest and most successful of all the "new religions" (*shinkō shūkyō*) that came to prominence in the post–World War II years. By the time its third president, Ikeda Daisaku, had resigned in April 1979, the Buddhist lay organization had grown to a claimed membership of 10 million. The Sōka Gakkai, whose name literally means "value-creating academic society," is a religious movement of lay believers who are attached to a traditionally nationalistic Buddhist sect, the Nichiren Shōshū (Orthodox Nichiren Sect).[1] The Nichiren Shōshū is a very popular Buddhist sect in Japan that traces its beliefs back to the Buddhist monk Nichiren (1222–1282), who sought to establish what he believed was the one correct sect of Buddhism in Japan (and whose teachings reflected this belief). Nichiren condemned all other religions for heresy and taught that all its precepts are absolute.[2] The Nichiren Shōshū is just one of the many sects within the Nichiren school of Japanese Buddhism, and the Sōka Gakkai is a lay organization charged with the "world-wide propagation of Nichiren Shōshū's doctrines and the creation of social programs which will enable the sect's religious ideals to be transferred into social reality."[3]

The Sōka Gakkai was created on November 18, 1930, by Makiguchi Tsunesaburō, a school teacher in Tokyo, who sought to reform the nature of Japanese society by restructuring the nation's education system. After seven years of failure, Makiguchi switched to advocating a religious revival based on a belief in Nichiren Shōshū to set the stage for his goal of educational reform. Both Makiguchi and his successor, Toda Josei, were imprisoned by the Japanese military during World War II for failure to support the war effort. Makiguchi died in prison, but Toda survived and immediately after the war began to transform the organization into a "religious movement dedicated to the creation of a Buddhist society in Japan."[4]

At the core of this reconstructed religious movement, the Sōka Gakkai's central objective is the improvement of Japanese society in particular and the world in general through the reformation of human character. The movement continues to be true to Nichiren's intolerance of other "false sects," and its adherents still believe that Nichiren is the true Buddha and that Shakyamunu was a transitory Buddha. The truth of this true Buddha and his religion is to be communicated to all so that mankind can become enlightened and thus construct a far better life and society. Consequently, each member of the Sōka Gakkai must actively participate in proselytizing the unconverted into the organization. This aggressive conversion process (called *shakubuku*, meaning literally "to break and subdue" or "to vanish evil aggressively") occasionally involved continual pressure on a prospective convert until the Sōka Gakkai members had achieved their purpose[5]—one aspect of the organization that contributes to the group's strongly negative image among many Japanese.

More than any of the other postwar "new religions," the Sōka Gakkai melds the religious and secular worlds into a single world. Political ideas are a natural product of this religion. The "Buddhist Democracy" sought by the Sōka Gakkai is defined as a combination of "social welfare and individual happiness."[6] Such a Buddhist Democracy (*Obutsu Myogo*) would occur when *all* realize the truth of Nichiren Buddhism and are thus converted to the true faith.

Hence the Sōka Gakkai conceives of this democracy as a form of socialism or neosocialism that anticipates an important role for governmental institutions. Accordingly, it was quite logical for the Sōka Gakkai to branch out into politics during the 1950s and to form its own political party in 1964. In an unprecedented action (within the context of modern Japanese history), the Kōmeitō was invented with a view toward using politics to convert the nation.[7] Or, as one political scientist has put it: "It was the transition from Sōka Gakkai religious politicking to Kōmeitō political religioneering." In short, the party was formed to mold the environment toward acceptance of its religious objectives.[8]

In defense of their creation of the Kōmeitō, Sōka Gakkai leaders point to the Christian-Democratic parties of Western Europe as being analogous to their Buddhist party in Japan. In addition, they have repeatedly tried to reassure the Japanese public that they have no intention of forcing Nichiren Shōshū on an unwilling nation. Statements to support that position include a promise not to make Nichiren Shōshū the state religion in defiance of the constitution. Former President Ikeda has commented on this problem by saying: "A religion which tries to impose itself on people by the use of state power proves by that it is impotent."[9] Despite such statements, however, many knowledgeable Japanese fear that the promises of the Kōmeitō and the JCP to protect freedom of religion, freedom of speech, and democracy may not be kept if total power is won by those parties.

Generally speaking, the Japanese have not been considered a very religious people. Many of them profess to support one or more religions, but few seem to take these religions seriously except as institutions within which special ceremonies (e.g., weddings, funerals) are performed. In this nation of approximately 120 million people, about 98 million profess to be followers of Shinto, another 88 million follow Buddhism, and still another million are Christians. Of course, these figures imply almost two religions per person—quite a feat in a nation that is not very religious! Such a situation can exist only in a society where such affiliations are lightly held.

James White has noted that the Sōka Gakkai differs in some important respects from the rest of the new religions of postwar Japan. Whereas the new religions, in general, were considered tolerant, eclectic, and attentive to everyday life, and were characterized by a belief in faith cures, the Sōka Gakkai was considered intolerant, exclusive, and characterized by a strong group orientation.[10]

As noted, the Sōka Gakkai and the Kōmeitō generate strong negative feelings among many Japanese. In a Nippon television (NTV) survey conducted in the spring of 1964, 42 percent of the 1,500 respondents chose the word *fanatical* to describe the Sōka Gakkai.[11] James Dator's poll of non-Sōka Gakkai respondents discovered that 4 percent liked the Gakkai, 57 percent disliked it, 16 percent were neutral, and 23 percent had no answer.[12] Other students of the Gakkai noted that it was described by many Japanese as "militaristic," "fascistic," "sacrilegious," "dangerous," and "ultranationalistic."[13] The U.S. magazine *Newsweek* noted that "the Sōka Gakkai looks like an Oriental blend of Christian Science and the John Birch Society."[14] These negative feelings toward the Sōka Gakkai have also been attached to the Kōmeitō to a certain degree. However, the Kōmeitō has gradually managed to earn a certain respect after being seen as extremist in its early years. Clearly, its professionalism and zeal are respected by many Japanese.[15]

The major characteristics of the Sōka Gakkai include a complex organizational structure, an intensity of commitment on the part of its members, and a vigorous and wide range of activities. Its organization comprises two hierarchies. The first of these is a religious guidance and membership indoctrination structure based on the religious conversion process, in which a new member becomes a disciple of the member who converted him. The basic unit (or cell) is composed of approximately ten families who meet daily for discussion meetings. Still larger units are made up of groups (50–100 families) and districts (500–1,000 families).[16] Districts are combined to form chapters, general chapters, local headquarters, and general headquarters. In all, the Sōka Gakkai encompasses tens of thousands of cells.

The second hierarchy, also geographically based, utilizes the *buroku* (block) system, which was developed to facilitate the entry of the Sōka Gakkai into the world of politics. The blocks are carefully combined and directed to concentrate the organization's political power within the appropriate political subdivisions being contested.[17] Prior to 1983, the system was apparently flexible enough to concentrate a combination blocks for a town- or village-level election and to combine membership in several prefectures for a House of Councillors national constituency election.[18]

On April 24, 1979, Sōka Gakkai President Ikeda Daisaku unexpectedly resigned, sending a shock wave through both the parent and the offspring organizations. Ikeda, without doubt, has been the most influential and charismatic of the four Sōka Gakkai leaders. Under his leadership the organization grew tremendously, from approximately 1 million families in 1959—the year prior to Ikeda's rise to the presidency—to 7 million families only a decade later.[19] By the time of Ikeda's resignation, 7,880,000 families were claimed by the Sōka Gakkai. Ikeda's personality, intensity, and commitment to the Sōka Gakkai all combined to give him an unprecedented amount of power in such an organization structured on authoritarian principles. His abrupt resignation was viewed by many as having been forced by unhappy leadership in the Nichiren Shōshū sect, which objected to the worship of Ikeda as a godlike figure by many members of the Sōka Gakkai. Some of the members even believed Ikeda to be the "true Buddha."

What further increased tensions was Ikeda's policy of constructing Sōka Gakkai assembly halls, which tended to separate the lay organization even more from the Nichiren Shōshū. Despite the series of apologies directed to the Nichiren Shōshū, tensions rose to the point that Ikeda was forced to tender his resignation not only as president of the Sōka Gakkai but also as worldwide leader of all the Nichiren Shōshū lay associations. As has often happened in Japan, Ikeda was given the position of honorary president and will remain president of Sōka Gakkai International. Moreover, many speculate that Ikeda remains firmly in control of the apparatus of the Sōka Gakkai despite his resignation.

Ikeda twice demonstrated the enormous financial potential of his organization. In 1965, approximately 35.5 billion yen was raised in only four days to construct a hall of worship. According to Harashima Takashi, the former chief of the Doctrine Study Department of the Sōka Gakkai, many members gave all the money they had saved for marriages, canceled their insurance policies, and took out personal loans. A second sum of 67 billion yen was collected between 1964 and 1977 for assembly hall construction.[20]

Such sums seem enormous, given the basic nature of the Sōka Gakkai's membership. Many of the members are recruited from the underclass of Japanese society—those who were affected by the demoralizing nature of Japan's defeat in World War II and by the alienating aspects of the rapid urbanization and increased complexity of modern life. As Arvin Palmer has argued, the most important reason behind the tremendous growth in the Sōka Gakkai has been the basic breakdown of the traditional social structure and value system, which has forced many to seek purpose, identity, and a sense of belonging.[21] The organization responds to these needs and offers a relief from misery as well as a sense of belonging and a hope of economic prosperity. In short, Sōka Gakkai propaganda is clearly "an appeal to the down and out, the economically deprived and the socially disoriented."[22]

Several surveys of Sōka Gakkai members were conducted in the early and mid-1960s. James Dator summarized the findings of those Japanese research projects by noting that Sōka Gakkai members are below average in income and have a lower-than-average standard of living. They also exhibit less formal education than the average Japanese. It should be emphasized, however, that while many Sōka Gakkai members are below average in income, they do not represent the lowest rung in the national income ladder.[23] The surveys do indicate that many join because of the problems they were having prior to their affiliation. One survey, for instance, found nearly 60 percent gave negative reasons for joining the Sōka Gakkai. These reasons included poor health (26 percent), economic distress (3 percent), poor human relations (7 percent), and other troubles (23 percent).[24] Azumi Koya, in his study of 386 members, found that 97 joined for reasons of ill health, 38 because of loss of success in work, 27 because of family frictions, and 34 because of "undisciplined lives."[25] And a Tokyo University study in 1962 discovered that 81 percent of the Sōka Gakkai members surveyed related some problem as the reason they joined.[26] Dator saw members of the Sōka Gakkai as a somewhat less satisfied and more friendless group whose members generally had no religious affiliation before joining.[27] Finally, Azumi concluded that these members tend to be no more or less apathetic politically than the general Japanese population but also that their turnout at elections is nearly 100 percent once they have joined the Sōka Gakkai.[28]

Sōka Gakkai members were seen as consistent, but critical, supporters of the LDP during the years prior to the formation of Kōmeitō.[29] One study of Gakkai members' voting habits during this period indicated that 51 percent supported the Right (LDP) and 37 percent supported the Left, with 31 percent supporting the JSP and 3 percent the JCP. The remaining 12 percent supported one side or the other depending on the situation.[30]

Voters' surveys, as expected, show very similar demographic patterns for Kōmeitō supporters. Generally, they are more likely to be women than men (59 percent versus 41 percent, respectively), younger more likely than older, workers in small or medium-sized business, or manual laborers, and less educated. In short, Kōmeitō supporters come from the lower middle class and the middle class in Japan. This generalization is supported by the voting pattern for the Kōmeitō in that the party performs best in districts characterized by low income and low levels of education.[31]

Recognizing these membership characteristics and the psychological attitudes associated with them, the Sōka Gakkai has structured itself to appeal to the needs of the people involved. It has constructed an entire educational system including its own university, Sōka Daigaku. Several million young men and women are organized by men, women, and student departments. Other major departments emphasize athletic, musical dance, and drama skill development.

Accurate numbers regarding Sōka Gakkai membership are difficult to obtain. One set of figures suggests the presence of about 2,000 members in the organization in 1943, when Makiguchi Tsunesaburō was imprisoned. After the war, Toda Josei built the organization from about 5,000 families to 750,000 during his lifetime. By 1982, the Sōka Gakkai claimed a membership of about 4 million persons, whereas 7,910,000 had embraced the Nichiren Shōshū faith.[32] Another source states that when Ikeda became president in 1960, the organization consisted of 172,000 families. This total grew to 500,000 families five years later and totaled 800,000 families in 1981. In the first six months of 1981, the Sōka Gakkai claimed an increase of 100,000 members—mostly from the Tokyo and Ōsaka areas.[33]

In recent years, then, the Sōka Gakkai's rate of growth has dramatically slowed, a decline that has obviously hurt the Kōmeitō. Various explanations have been advanced to explain this decline. Perhaps the continued prosperity of postwar Japan was responsible; or the recruiting efforts of the Sōka Gakkai may have been undermined by the constant scandals of the late 1970s. In any case, Akiya Einosuke, now Sōka Gakkai president, said in a 1980 newspaper interview: "We are now in a period of stabilization after an era of very rapid growth. Our organization has become so huge and has problems that need adjustment."[34]

The Sōka Gakkai Becomes a Political Party

The history of the Sōka Gakkai's direct involvement in electoral politics dates back to November 1954—a full decade prior to the founding of the Kōmeitō. In that month, a department of cultural affairs was established within the Sōka Gakkai organization to promote a variety of activities in political, economic, cultural, and educational fields. Such a department was based on the organization's belief in the necessity of creating a cultural state founded on Buddhism. In the April 1955 local elections, 51 Sōka Gakkai members running as independents were elected to mark the first Gakkai effort in the world of politics. The following year, 3 out of 6 Gakkai candidates won election to the House of Councillors.

A major reason underlying the desire of this religious group to embark upon a course of political activities was the avowed goal to establish a national ordination hall (*kokuritsu kaidan*). Such a hall would be a state-sponsored temple for the ordination and confirmation of the followers of Nichiren Shoshu. A 1954 editorial in the Sōka Gakkai's official newspaper, *Seikyō Shimbun,* indicated the high priority of the project: "We must work to have this message [a Diet order for the construction of a national ordination hall] issued. Because a majority of the members of the House of Representatives will have to agree to its issue, our activities to propagate the true faith must acquire a new dimension."[35]

In August 1957, Sōka Gakkai President Toda wrote a series of articles on the theory of Obutsu Myogo, which postulated the combination of secular government and Buddhism into a single entity of "Buddhist Democracy." At the 1959 annual meeting of Sōka Gakkai leadership, the new president, Ikeda Daisaku, stated that "the Sōka Gakkai is participating in elections because it must overcome the obstacles to the construction of a national ordination hall, obeying the supreme order of our great Saint Nichiren."[36]

By late 1959, Ikeda had concluded that it was time to upgrade the organization of the Sōka Gakkei's political arm. In May 1961, the Cultural Affairs Department was upgraded to a bureau, and a separate Political Affairs Department was established. A new organization of the religion's politicians, the Kōmei Political League (Kōmei Seiji Renmei), was created in November 1961. At its founding, it had 9 House of Councillors members; 7 prefectural assembly members; and 268 municipal and ward assembly members.[37] The league's charter and platform indicated the reliance of the group on the "Great Saint," and among the four points in the platform was a strong opposition to nuclear weapons. In fact, this antinuclear stance has long been a policy of the Sōka Gakkai. In 1982, Ikeda led a Sōka Gakkai delegation to the United Nations to give a speech opposing nuclear weapons.

Following the successes scored in the 1962 House of Councillors elections (15 seats won by Gakkai members), the organization decided to create a regular political party to facilitate the Gakkai's advance into the House of Representatives. Thus on November 17, 1964, the Kōmeitō was formed by the Sōka Gakkai. The party platform indicated that the goals of the Kōmeitō were to be as follows: world peace, humanitarian socialism, a mass party formed on Buddhist democracy, and the eradication of corrupt politics.[38] Immediately following the party's victory in the next general elections held in 1967 (25 new seats in the House of Representatives), Takeiri Yoshikatsu and Yano Jun'ya were named chairman and secretary-general, respectively, of the new party. Each remained in these offices from 1967 to the late 1980s, thus giving the Kōmeitō extraordinary stability in terms of the party's leadership. No other party in Japan has been so stable in terms of its leadership.

In those early days, it was clear that the Kōmeitō was merely a political arm of the Sōka Gakkai. Ikeda has been quoted as saying that the "Kōmeitō cannot exist without the Sōka Gakkai" and that these two organizations are "one and indivisible."[39] All of the Kōmeitō leaders and Diet members held highly visible leadership positions in the parent Sōka Gakkai. Kōmeitō Chairman Takeiri Yoshikatsu was an executive director of the Sōka Gakkai, and Yano Jun'ya, the secretary-general, was also a vice-chairman of the Sōka Gakkai national board of directors.[40] In addition, all of the party's candidates for public office were drawn from the ranks of the parent body. This pattern continued through the rest of the 1960s until the so-called Fujiwara Affair, which occurred in late 1969 and early 1970.

Fujiwara Hirotatsu is a political scientist whose book *I Denounce Sōka Gakkai [Sōka Gakkai o Kiru]* criticized the Kōmeitō for its attempts to make Nichiren Shōshū the Japanese state religion.[41] The Sōka Gakkai exerted considerable pressure in order to suppress criticism of the organization during this time period. It urged journalists not to write articles unfriendly to the religion and threatened to boycott newspapers that planned to carry any such articles. Initially, the Sōka Gakkai tried to prevent Fujiwara's book from being published; failing that attempt, it then sought to halt its distribution and subsequent sale. Apparently, the services of then LDP Secretary-General and, later, Prime Minister Tanaka Kakuei were requested by the Kōmeitō chairman to try and halt publication of the Fujiwara book. Fujiwara fought back, and, with the assistance of *Mainichi Shimbun* reporter Naito Kunio (who later lost his job at the newspaper), the book became a best-seller and the center of political debate during early 1970. Later, during the Diet debate on this issue, the JCP, JSP, and DSP tried unsuccessfully to exploit the "suppression of free speech" issue but were blocked in these attempts by the LDP leadership. Ultimately, the criticism of the actions of the Sōka Gakkai became so loud that the organization was forced to withdraw formally from politics. On May 3, 1970, the Sōka Gakkai officially separated from the Kōmeitō and all party references to the goal of establishing a national ordination hall were dropped. All Kōmeitō leaders and officeholders had to give up their leadership posts in the Sōka Gakkai, and the Kōmeitō made a considerable effort to recruit non–Sōka Gakkai members and candidates. At the 1970 annual meeting of the Sōka Gakkai, President Ikeda announced that the planned ordination hall need not be maintained by the state; that it would no longer be referred to as a "national hall"; and that "no Diet resolution would be sought for such a hall." Finally, he announced that a new set of rules and policies would be established for the Kōmeitō in 1970 (to be examined later in this chapter).[42]

One result of this scandal and others that rocked the Sōka Gakkai during the 1970s has been a decrease in the number of new conversions to the religion and a small exodus of former believers. Moreover, as the media seem to be less intimidated by the religion issue, the scandals that came to light in the late 1970s were very well covered in the national press and news magazines.[43]

Nevertheless, in everything the Kōmeitō does, it must be aware of its subordinate position vis-à-vis the Sōka Gakkai. As Akiya Einosuke, then a vice-president of the Sōka Gakkai, warned in 1980: "If the Kōmeitō goes beyond the limit of acceptability from our point of view, we will indicate our concern to the party."[44] Such a concern might revolve around the question of state recognition of the Yasukuni Shrine or around the defense issue in general.

The Sōka Gakkai Scandals

The Sōka Gakkai suffered through a period of particular strain at the end of the 1970s and the beginning of the 1980s as a series of scandals rocked the Kōmeitō's parent organization. These scandals may have contributed to the party's terrible showing in the 1980 House of Representatives elections; they certainly received a great deal of public attention and were gleefully reported and commented upon by nearly every facet of the nation's mass media.

The Yamazaki Affair centered on the person of Yamazaki Masatomo, who was a lawyer and adviser to the Sōka Gakkai. Yamazaki apparently participated in many of the organization's most secret and sensitive activities during the 1970s. When he allegedly threatened to divulge these secrets to the media, the Sōka Gakkai paid him 300 million yen to keep quiet. It was only after Yamazaki allegedly made a second demand for an additional 500 million yen that the Sōka Gakkai turned the case over to the police. The organization's leadership defended the initial payoff by arguing that Yamazaki was intimately involved in the negotiations between the Nichiren Shōshū and the Sōka Gakkai, and claimed that if those sensitive talks failed, the possibility existed for "10 million members of the Sōka Gakkai being excommunicated." As Miyakawa Kiyohiko, chief of the Youth Department of the Sōka Gakkai, has noted, "The fact that we paid it shows the importance of ties with the sect for us."[45]

In a different but related case, Yamazaki was charged with the wiretapping of JCP Chairman Miyamoto's home from June to July 1975. Yamazaki, in Tokyo District Court hearings, said that he and others committed this act on orders from Hōjō Hiroshi, then vice-president and later president of the Sōka Gakkai.[46]

When he resigned, Harashima Takashi was the chief of the Sōka Gakkai's doctrinal study office late in 1979; in the spring of 1980 he began to criticize his old employers, for which he was subsequently expelled in August 1980. Harashima's central attack was directed against the role played by former President Ikeda. He charged Ikeda with "reigning over it [the Sōka Gakkai] as an absolute dictator and behaving toward the members as if he were the reincarnation of Nichiren." Harashima blamed Ikeda for many of the problems the organization has had with the leadership of the Nichiren Shōshū sect, and noted that the "antagonism grew strong among the Nichiren Shōshū priests, particularly the younger ones. As a result, the Sōka Gakkai has repeatedly had to beg the sect's pardon. Eventually, Mr. Ikeda found it necessary to resign as president of the organization."[47]

Finally, Ikeda was involved in a well-publicized libel suit against an editor of a monthly magazine. The magazine published a pair of stories in 1976 alleging that Ikeda had had extramarital affairs with two female Sōka Gakkai members who later became Kōmeitō Diet members.[48] This case was also given a great deal of attention by the media during 1982 and 1983. Such negative press attention cannot help but have a weakening effect on the Sōka Gakkai and, of course, on its offspring, the Kōmeitō.

October 1982 was an especially bad month for Sōka Gakkai leader Ikeda Daisaku, who appeared in court three times to deny having affairs with Kōmeitō Diet members, to testify in the Yamazaki blackmail case, and to acknowledge that Sōka Gakkai members had wiretapped the house of JCP leader Miyamoto Kenji.

The Sōka Gakkai–JCP Accord

On July 27, 1975, an Agreement of Reconciliation was announced by the leadership of the Sōka Gakkai and the Japan Communist party. It provided for the coexistence of the two organizations aiming at the common goal of world peace. Both parties recognized the need for noninterference between them in their respective political stands, as well as for the JCP's acceptance of the freedom of religious propaganda and the espousal of faith. In return, the Sōka Gakkai promised not to view communism with hostility. It was also agreed that both sides would take action to help prevent nuclear war and to banish nuclear weapons. Finally, both the JCP and the Sōka Gakkai promised to refrain from name calling and to settle disputes by mutual negotiation.[49]

Later in 1975, the *Mainichi Shimbun* brought together both Ikeda and JCP Chairman Miyamoto for a series of dialogues, which were given extensive publicity.[50] Meanwhile, Ikeda argued in a journal article that the agreement could be the basis of coexistence with the Communists in order to secure fundamental stability in Japan during the next twenty to thirty years.[51]

Many political analysts in Japan have speculated on the actual motivations behind this agreement. Some believe that Ikeda sought an understanding with the JCP in order to facilitate the Sōka Gakkai's future expansion into Communist countries. Indeed, it could be argued that given President Ikeda's visits to the People's Republic of China and the Soviet Union, he may have wanted to establish the idea that both Sōka Gakkai and socialism have doctrines in common.

The Kōmeitō's leadership and general membership reacted with shock to the announcement of the accord. Takeiri and Yano had apparently fought against the agreement prior to its announcement, but they lost that battle. The July announcement precipitated a series of meetings by the top leaders of the Kōmeitō as they tried to devise a plan to react to this bombshell from their parent organization. Ever since its founding in 1964, the Kōmeitō has taken a firm anticommunist line as one of its fundamental principles, and its anticommunism can be found in nearly every part of its range of activities. It takes every opportunity to highlight any JCP missteps in its publications, and its campaigners have frequently clashed in the streets during election campaigns with those workers of the JCP.[52] Its antagonism toward the JCP seems to be based on two factors: a conflict between the philosophies of Marxist-Leninism and Nichiren Buddhism, and a national competition between the two organizations for membership, with both drawing their support largely from the same lower-class urban voters (especially those in the large cities of Tokyo, Ōsaka, and Nagoya).

The Kōmeitō's reaction was to reject the implications of the accord and to continue the same anticommunist line it had taken before the accord. Takeiri stated that the basic policies of his party would not be affected by the agreement, which definitely did not imply any type of "joint struggle" or "united front" with the JCP. Ikeda later restated his adherence to this position and also reaffirmed that the support relationship between the Sōka Gakkai and the Kōmeitō had not changed in the slightest degree.[53]

Kōmeitō officials frequently voiced their suspicions concerning the motives of the JCP. Secretary-General Yano was noted in the press as maintaining that the JCP had three basic political objectives to be achieved by the agreement—namely, that it sought to change the Kōmeitō's course in the JCP's direction, to alienate the Sōka Gakkai from the Kōmeitō while drawing Sōka Gakkai members toward the JCP, and to have Kōmeitō Chairman Takeiri replaced.[54] In short, the Kōmeitō's leaders saw the accord as nothing less than a full-scale attack on the party's very existence. They could not help but notice that Miyamoto had called for "a people's unified opposition front without the participation of political parties."[55]

Continuing its strongly anticommunist posture, Takeiri warned of the JCP's objectives of violent revolution. On the other hand, the JCP and its daily newspaper *Akahata* escalated its attacks on the Kōmeitō as an ally of the LDP and as being unworthy of the name of a "progressive political party."[56] By the end of the decade, the JCP was repeatedly attacking the Sōka Gakkai for killing the accords. The December 29, 1979, issue of *Akahata* carried a two-page special supplement that proclaimed the death of the accords, and the Sōka Gakkai was severely criticized for reverting to its original hostile stance toward "scientific socialism" and communism.[57] It is interesting to note that the JCP seemed to refrain from directly attacking the Sōka Gakkai until Ikeda had resigned as its leader in April 1979.[58] Finally, in an *Akahata* editorial in February 1980, the Sōka Gakkai position of endorsing a coalition of the Kōmeitō, the DSP, and the JSP was described as an act of treachery.[59]

The Kōmeitō survived the "accord crisis" largely because it was able to ignore the implications of the parent body's agreement with its arch-opponent and to successfully argue that such an intellectual agreement had little relevance to the world of politics. When the Kōmeitō put together its coalition agreements for the 1980 elections, the one issue it would not compromise on was its demand for the exclusion of the JCP from any future coalition government. The two bitterest enemies in Japanese politics are still the JCP and the Kōmeitō. The "accords" also provide some evidence as to the types of situations in which the Kōmeitō can pursue a line independent from the Sōka Gakkai.

The Organizational Strength of the Kōmeitō

Of all the political parties currently operating in Japan, the Kōmeitō probably has the strongest organizational structure. Its only close competitor in this connection would be its archrival, the Japanese Communist party. The Kōmeitō's strength is almost totally dependent on the extensive organization of the Sōka Gakkai. Each Sōka Gakkai member is expected, at the very least, to support Kōmeitō-recommended candidates at the polls. In addition, the Kōmeitō has an army of volunteer workers of a quantity much greater than that of any other Japanese political party. This is the great advantage that the Kōmeitō has over its opponents in elections. Jooinn Lee noted the case during the 1965 Fukuoka prefectural elections in which a large group of Sōka Gakkai members, estimated at between 10,000 to 20,000 in number, moved from the neighboring prefectures of Kumamoto and Saga to help elect Kōmeitō candidates. Many of these Sōka Gakkai members who had made this move were day workers with few ties to any given area, but the discipline and obedience they displayed were indeed impressive.[60]

As the Kōmeitō is based on the multimillion-member organization of the Sōka Gakkai, it is somewhat surprising that the Kōmeitō claimed a party membership of only 157,000 as of mid-1981. The Kōmeitō has never released any details regarding the geographical distribution of this membership base, nor has the Sōka Gakkai released any numbers regarding its membership other than gross totals of the estimated number of families enrolled in the organization. Still, the Kōmeitō membership total easily makes the party the third largest in Japan. Most experts estimate that about 10 percent of the membership is composed of non–Sōka Gakkai individuals.[61]

This Kōmeitō membership base is a dedicated, hardworking core of party activists. By relying on such a base, the Kōmeitō does not have to pay campaigners to distribute literature and to perform other campaign activities (as other parties, except the JCP, must do). As mentioned earlier, the Kōmeitō keeps the details of its membership an internal secret. When Azumi submitted a survey questionnaire to the Tokyo Kōmeitō leadership in 1966, a question concerning whether or not Sōka Gakkai members always voted for a Kōmeitō candidate was deleted as "quite unnecessary since they were absolutely certain that 100 percent of the members would answer in the affirmative."[62] However, when a 1979 *Asahi Shimbun* poll asked Kōmeitō supporters if they always voted for the candidates of the same party in general elections, the supporters replied in the affirmative 76 percent of the time. This was the highest such support rate in Japan.[63] The gap between the Kōmeitō estimate of 100 percent support rate and the 76 percent discovered by the *Asahi Shimbun* may be partly explained by the fact that many Kōmeitō supporters may not have Kōmeitō candidates to vote for in their home districts; in addition, they may be urged by the party to vote for other party candidates in recent elections in which the Kōmeitō has cooperated with other parties.

The structure of the Kōmeitō party organization appears to be very similar to that of the LDP and the Socialist parties. Its central party headquarters in Tokyo is situated in Minamoto-cho, Shinjuku—a location somewhat removed from most of the other party headquarters, which are clustered around the Diet building near the Nagatocho area. (The JCP is another exception, given that its national headquarters are located in a working-class section of Tokyo in Yoyogi.) Kōmeitō's offices are situated in a modern building that communicates a sense of professionalism and organizational competence to visitors. The national headquarters had a staff of some 300 persons in 1981. Approximately half of those persons perform party work for the general affairs bureau, and the other 150 work for the publications bureau, which turns out the many polished publications of the party.[64]

Imazu has argued that the Kōmeitō organization is basically a copy of the Sōka Gakkai organization, which on every level of Japanese politics serves as a base for Kōmeitō activities. He has also noted that the *shakubuku* (evangelical conversion campaign) of the Sōka Gakkai is a form of election campaigning for the Kōmeitō.[65] Others have indicated that Kōmeitō campaigns serve as a proselytizing effort to bring new converts to the Sōka Gakkai. Whichever way it may be, and it certainly could be either or both, the two organizations are very closely tied together in almost all respects. As Arvin Palmer concluded, the "Kōmeitō is a subsystem of the Sōka Gakkai and integrated at every level with the main organization." He also noted that for the Kōmeitō, "any but the most limited autonomy is prevented."[66]

The resignation of Ikeda from the presidency of the Sōka Gakkai inevitably affected the operations of the Kōmeitō. Initially, the event shocked many Kōmeitō members. As Chairman Takeiri said at a press conference on April 24, 1979: "I believe that the announcement was a big shock to most of the party members, Kōmeitō Diet members, and the personnel of the party headquarters."[67]

The new Sōka Gakkai president, Hōjō Hiroshi, was quick to declare that "Sōka Gakkai's attitude toward the Kōmeitō will not change." The JCP immediately observed that Ikeda's resignation would result in the Kōmeitō's movement toward the LDP and, more generally, in the adoption of a more conservative posture—a conclusion derived from the transfer of power from Ikeda, who approved the accord with the JCP, to Hōjō, who seemed to be less interested in such ties during his tenure in office. However, after only a short time in office, Hōjō died and was replaced by the then vice-president, Akiya Einosuke.

The current leadership of the Kōmeitō was reelected at the party's national convention held in November 1990. CGP Chairman Ishida Koshirō and Secretary-General Ichikawa Yuichi represent second-generation leadership; founders Takeiri Yoshikatsu and Yano Jun'ya ran the party from 1967 to the late 1980s.[68] Initially, Takeiri and Yano were handpicked by Sōka Gakkai President Ikeda, as were all the other top-level Kōmeitō executives and candidates. Of the two leaders, Yano is perhaps the more interesting to study. He was a registered Communist during his years as a student at the elite Kyōto University, and his political debut as a Kōmeitō man in the Ōsaka Prefectural Assembly reportedly astonished many of his former classmates.[69] Takeiri, on the other hand, came from Nagano prefecture, became a Japanese National Railway employee in 1948, and then won a seat in one of the Tokyo ward assemblies in 1949. In 1963 he was elected to the Tokyo Assembly, and in 1967 he was elected for the first time to the national House of Representatives, along with Yano.

Relatively little is known about the nature of the subnational units of the Kōmeitō's organization. Following the formal separation from the Sōka Gakkai in 1970, an effort was made to create a distinctly separate party organization. However, as with some of the other parties in Japan, most of the Kōmeitō organization seems to be operating out of the offices of Diet members and prefectural or local-level assembly members. Perhaps the best description of local-level party organizations in Japan can be found in the research performed by James J. Foster in Hyōgo prefecture. Foster found that the Kōmeitō, like all the other major parties, maintained a full-time office in the prefectural capital, Kōbe. The party also established a set of intermediary organizational units called *so-shibu*. Each of the five Kōmeitō *so-shibu* was located in cities in which the party had a large local assembly delegation; however, in late 1979, none of these units had offices or staff members. The lowest level of organization in Hyōgo is the *shibu,* and all 63 Kōmeitō *shibu* were connected with the Sōka Gakkai organization. As Foster has noted, prior to 1970 the Kōmeitō operated only through the existing Sōka Gakkai organization, and only after 1970 did it open up its prefectural level office in Kōbe. Kōmeitō campaigns in Hyōgo are run by Sōka Gakkai members who belong to personal support groups (*kōenkai*) organized by Kōmeitō candidates; the official party offices seem for the most part to be left out of this important activity. The Kōmeitō Hyōgo chapter has claimed about 7,000 members consistently throughout the 1970s, and this membership base is almost entirely composed of Sōka Gakkai members. Foster discovered that the Kōmeitō had the smallest income and weakest party organization among the major parties in Hyōgo. Kōmeitō, he concluded, simply relied on the activities of its elected officeholders and the Sōka Gakkai organization to turn out its large vote in elections.[70]

Although some parties are most active on the national level (e.g., the DSP), the Kōmeitō is an extremely active party on all levels of Japanese politics. It is known among Japanese experts of politics as a party that works hard on the local and prefectural levels on so-called bread-and-butter issues. Cecil Brett gives a picture different from that of Foster of the Kōmeitō organization in Okayama. In particular, Brett discovered that the party had a prefectural office in Okayama, four or five regional offices in smaller cities, and more than fifty branch offices scattered around the prefecture.[71] He did not, however, note how active these offices were or if they were separate from the Sōka Gakkai offices.

The range of Kōmeitō activities is nearly impossible to fathom. In October 1982, for example, Chairman Takeiri journeyed to a suburb of Peking, the capital of the People's Republic of China, to help open a chicken farm at the Sino-Japanese Friendship People's Commune. This modern farm, capable of raising 120,000 chickens at a time, was built with the technical and financial assistance provided by the Kōmeitō and Japanese private companies.[72]

Takahashi Harashima, the former head of the Doctrine Study Department of the Sōka Gakkai, commented in 1980 that the financial burden on Gakkai members of supporting the Kōmeitō is considerable: "In every election, they are asked to make more contributions to the Kōmeitō."[73] Dues-paying members of the Kōmeitō pay a minimum of 1,000 yen per year, but they are asked for much more during campaigns.

A significant number of the Kōmeitō's activities revolve around the party's string of "consulting centers," which constitute part of the organization's strategy of "working for the people." These centers numbered around 7,300 units in 1969 and recorded hundreds of thousands of consultations a year in the late 1960s. By 1980, the number of "people's consultations" had risen to 1.3 million a year. Over 10 million cases were accepted between 1964 and 1980.[74] About half of the cases dealt with citizen complaints concerning housing, welfare, education, and sanitation. In other words, the Kōmeitō has for a long time been operating a private "ombudsman" system to help citizens deal with the Japanese governmental bureaucracy. (Incidentally, the JCP offers very similar services in competition with the Kōmeitō.) The casework tends to revolve around local-level Kōmeitō assembly members and is available to all constituents. The image of the Kōmeitō as a party of action, protecting the common people from harmful governmental intrusions, has been a crucial element of the party's attempt to earn respect in Japan. In a 1976 *Asahi Shimbun* poll, Japanese respondents were asked whether a political party existed that one could consult. Affirmative answers were very low among supporters of the JSP (14 percent), the LDP (18 percent), the DSP (19 percent), and even the JCP (23 percent). Only a large percentage of Kōmeitō supporters (60 percent) answered in the affirmative.[75]

The Sōka Gakkai offers a very extensive internal program of self-improvement, education, and entertainment; the Kōmeitō does not. Perhaps the Kōmeitō feels that such a party education program would be redundant given the Sōka Gakkai's youth, athletic, music, drama, and school system (including Sōka Daigaku, the organization's own university).

The Kōmeitō makes extensive use of the various media to communicate with its supporters and to reach potential supporters. Its daily mass circulation newspaper, the *Kōmei Shimbun,* has one of Japan's largest circulations, with weekday sales of 860,000 copies and sales of the Sunday edition at the 1.4 million level.[76] Of the major parties, only the Kōmeitō and the JCP (*Akahata*) publish their own daily newspapers. The Kōmeitō also publishes a wide range of magazines. To these must be added the various publications of the Sōka Gakkai, including its daily newspaper, the *Seikyō Shimbun;* the theoretical journal, *Dai Byaku Renge;* and a picture magazine, *Seikyō Graphic.*

Japanese labor unions have not been a fruitful recruiting area for the Kōmeitō. Most labor federations (e.g., Sōhyō and Dōmei) have been hostile and difficult to move toward support of the Kōmeitō.[77] When the Kōmeitō and the SDF cooperated in the 1979 elections, the Kōmeitō opened communication channels with several labor unions including Zentai (Japan Postal Workers Union), Zendentsu (All Japan Telecommunication Workers Union), and Kokurō (National Railway Workers Union).[78]

Finally, in contrast to most of the other Japanese parties, there is no strong pattern of factional politics to be found inside the Kōmeitō organization. Some indications of internal conflict within the Sōka Gakkai do exist, however—and this conflict could adversely affect the loyalty of Gakkai members toward the Kōmeitō. As Lee has noted, there may be at least four factions in the Sōka Gakkai, and some of the organization's youth groups, such as the 120,000-member Shingakudo (Student League), have adopted some very militant, leftist policy positions.[79] However, these factions are neither clear to the outsider nor an identifiable part of Kōmeitō politics. In the early 1990s it appeared that the major factional divisions within the CGP revolved around whether the party should move closer to the LDP during the 1990s or maintain the 1980s strategy of cooperating with the JSP and DSP in overthrowing LDP rule on the national level.

Kōmeitō Support as Measured in Elections and Public Opinion Polls

There are many ways to measure the popular support of a political party such as the Kōmeitō. The most obvious procedure would be a close examination of the vote totals of the party in the various constituencies within which it operates. A second obvious way to study popular support would involve an examination of the public opinion support patterns. It is this latter method that we will turn to initially; then we will conclude with a look at voting patterns.

Public opinion polls conducted by Japan's major newspapers have discovered that Kōmeitō support has remained remarkably stable for the last decade. The *Mainichi Shimbun* polls observed a 6 percent support level in 1969 and a 5 percent level a decade later.[80] In recent years, the party has ranged between 4 to 5 percent in popular support according to the *Asahi Shimbun's* polls. In one such poll conducted in March 1982, the Kōmeitō secured the support of 4 percent of the population and had no "leaners" at all. This is an interesting characteristic of the Kōmeitō polling pattern: It has almost no visible support from those citizens who call themselves "nonparty supporters" and then later "lean toward one party or another." The JSP, for example, in 1982 received the support of 12 percent of the population plus an additional 5 percent from "leaners."[81] There is a strong feeling among some Japanese political experts that the newspaper polls consistently underestimate the Kōmeitō's public support levels. Why then, they ask, does the party get voting percentages of 10 percent or more in recent elections? Clearly, some Japanese may be reluctant to say to pollsters that they support the Kōmeitō, but it is also true that the Kōmeitō's supporters

TABLE 6.1
Kōmeitō support levels (in percentages)

Support level	*Kōmeitō*	*All parties*
Supported very strongly	34.7	12.9
Supported somewhat strongly	56.9	47.3
Supported not strongly	6.9	38.4
No answer	1.4	1.5

Source: Compiled by author from Kōmeitō sources.

vote at very high turnout levels and that the party seems to attract some protest votes as well.

It is worth noting that the Kōmeitō's public opinion support is relatively intense when compared to the other parties. Table 6.1 indicates the Kōmeitō support pattern revealed by a *Yomiuri Shimbun* poll conducted in October 1982. As one would expect from its largely Sōka Gakkai base, Kōmeitō supporters strongly identify with and support their party. On the other hand, the party receives very little support from the 35 percent of the population that does not support a given political party. Although 22.7 percent of this latter group is favorably inclined toward the LDP, only 1.4 percent is inclined toward the Kōmeitō.[82]

With respect to the personal characteristics of Kōmeitō supporters, an *Asahi Shimbun* poll uncovered the following pattern:

Occupation	
Industrial workers	25.4%
Small-business employees	21.4
Clerical workers	17.4
Self-employed people	15.8
Administrative employees	7.1
Agricultural workers	6.3
Education	
Junior high school or less	62.7
High school–educated	31.7
College-educated	5.5

Imazu Hiroshi concluded, after analyzing these numbers, that the average Kōmeitō supporter runs a small business, is an employee of a very small union enterprise, or is an industrial worker.[83] Perhaps the most distinctive characteristic of the typical Kōmeitō supporter is a low level of formal education.

Candidates for the House of Representatives, whether officially supported or recommended by the Kōmeitō, tend more likely to come from professional backgrounds than do candidates from other parties. Yet, as is appropriate for a party with its particular support base, the Kōmeitō among the major parties tends to have the lowest percentage of candidates who are university graduates. If a party is known by its candidates, then the Kōmeitō is characterized by a strong local flavor because it has the largest number of candidates who can claim local government experience.[84] These candidates also tend to be younger than those of the other parties. Prior to 1972, Kōmeitō candidates were selected by the national-level Sōka Gakkai leadership, although there is now some reason to believe that more local decision-making is involved in the candidate-selection process.[85] Only in the late 1970s did the party try to run non–Sōka Gakkai candidates in order to broaden the image and appeal of the party. In the 1980 double elections in Aichi prefecture, two non–Sōka Gakkai Kōmeitō candidates won seats—one in each of the twin chambers of the Diet. In the 1983 House of Councillors national constituency, the top five Kōmeitō candidates in the proportional representation (PR) contest were not members of the party. All were elected on the Kōmeitō ticket.

Since the Kōmeitō entered into the House of Representatives arena in 1967, it has managed to stabilize its seat totals near 50 in recent elections. Its seat totals since winning 25 seats in 1967 have been in the high forties or fifties in every election since 1976 except for the double elections of 1980.

The only party to be badly hurt by the double elections in 1980 was the Kōmeitō. Its HR seats fell from 58 to 33, whereas its vote increased over 1979 totals by 47,000 votes. The large increase in total voter turnout in 1980 had the effect of raising the minimum number of votes needed to win an HR seat above the vote-gathering capacity of many of the previously successful Kōmeitō Diet members. The average vote total per Kōmeitō candidate actually increased in 1980 over 1979 from 82,542 to 83,280 votes. But the increase of 47,000 votes for all of the Kōmeitō candidates was the smallest increase in votes of any major Japanese party in 1980. The DSP, in contrast, increased its average vote per candidate in 1980 by almost 9,000.

Because of the inelasticity of the Kōmeitō vote (i.e., the failure to capture a significant portion of the so-called floating vote), high turnouts have reduced the Kōmeitō's chances of winning marginal seats. The *Mainichi Shumbun* estimated that the high turnout recorded in 1980 cost the Kōmeitō 16 seats (and the JCP 5 seats), which would have been captured if the cutoff line had been the same as in the 1979 elections.[86] Equally significant, Kōmeitō's record-high number of seats won in the 1981 Tokyo Metropolitan Assembly elections were won in the election marked by the lowest voter turnout (54.2 percent) in the history of the assembly.

Some Kōmeitō leaders viewed the 1980 electoral disaster as an opportunity to rebuild the party during the 1980s. The chairman of the Kōmeitō Diet Policy Committee, Ōkubo Naohiko, commented that 27 Kōmeitō House candidates finished as runners-up in their districts in 1980. Included in the total were many of the most promising young Kōmeitō Diet members. Ōkubo noted that after the party's defeat in the 1972 elections, it modernized itself and became a truly national political party.[87] In 1990, the Kōmeitō won 8 seats in Tokyo, 7 in Ōsaka (one in every district), 4 in Fukuoka, and 4 in

Kanagawa. Thus, although 21 percent of the nation's HR seats are in these four metropolitan prefectures, the Kōmeitō won 42 percent of its seats there in 1990.

After running candidates (either official or recommended) in 64 of the nation's 130 HR districts in 1979, the Kōmeitō decided to run the same number in the 1980 elections. Between 1976 and 1979, 42 Kōmeitō candidates experienced vote declines, including the party's secretary-general. Some political analysts have attributed these declines to the series of crises besetting the Sōka Gakkai. However, the Kōmeitō leadership has argued that the reduction of candidates and the cooperation strategy with the other centrist parties, especially the DSP, resulted in just such a decline in the party's vote total in 1979. Actually, they have claimed that it was not so much a decline as a shift in strategy resulting in a transfer of Kōmeitō voters to DSP candidates as part of the "joint efforts" of the 1980 campaigns.[88]

As the Kōmeitō and the JCP seem to be battling for the same general constituency, one might guess that if the Kōmeitō decided to run fewer candidates in HR elections, the JCP might significantly increase its vote. However, the statistics show that the LDP and DSP gained 5 percent and 4 percent respectively in these constituencies. With respect to seat transfers between the Kōmeitō and other Japanese parties, it is worthy of note that almost none of the 24 seats the Kōmeitō lost in 1980 went to its archrival, the JCP. Although the Kōmeitō won 1 seat from the LDP, it lost 14 to that party, 5 to the JSP, 4 to the NLC, and 1 each to an independent and the JCP.[89]

Kōmeitō's policy of cooperation with other centrist parties produced a mixed bag of results in 1980. All 4 of the CGP-JSP candidates won, but of the 34 joint CGP-DSP and other party candidates, only 14 won. This poor performance compared very unfavorably with the results in 1979, when the CGP-DSP cooperation was successful in 17 of 24 districts. Of the 21 "joint-effort" winners in 1980, only 7 were Kōmeitō members. In terms of the House of Councillors local constituencies, the Kōmeitō cooperated on 25 candidates in 22 constituencies; 10 won in this case, but only one was a Kōmeitō candidate. There was a strong feeling among many Kōmeitō members that these "joint efforts" produced too one-sided a result.[90]

In the 1983 HR elections, the Kōmeitō cooperated with the DSP in 28 constituencies, electing 14 out of 15 CGP candidates and 11 of 13 DSP candidates. In the Kōmeitō cooperations with the JSP, 5 out of 6 candidates were elected (3 JSP members and 2 CGP members). Thus, of the 34 candidates the Kōmeitō ran or supported in other parties, 30 won. Cooperation was a great success in 1983.

However, cooperation agreements in 1990 proved to be difficult to establish with both the JSP and DSP. Few joint efforts were made, and one outcome was the large number of Kōmeitō (11) and DSP (18) candidates who finished as runners-up in their districts. The CGP runners-up needed only an average of 9,500 additional votes to have won seats in the HR. By running only 61 candidates in 1986 and 59 in 1990, the CGP continued its election

TABLE 6.2
Kōmeitō vote-getting strength in metropolitan and rural prefectures
(1986 and 1989 House of Councillors national constituency vote by prefectures)

Type	*Prefectures*	*1986 CGP Vote Percentage*	*1989 CGP Vote Percentage*
Shikoku Island	Tokushima	14.7	11.8
	Kagawa	14.1	10.0
	Ehime	13.3	10.9
	Kochi	14.3	11.7
Metropolitan	Tokyo	15.4	13.0
	Ōsaka	18.9	16.8
	Fukuoka	15.3	13.6
National Average		13.0	10.9

Source: Compiled by author.

strategy of putting its resources into sure and almost-sure winning situations. It had 46 winners and 12 runners-up in 1990; only one CGP candidate failed to finish as a runner-up, and that candidate lost by only 8,000 votes.[91]

As the Kōmeitō (like the DSP) runs in fewer than half of the nation's 130 House constituencies, the best way to ascertain the Kōmeitō national vote is to examine the party's vote in the House of Councillors national constituency. In recent elections it has ranged between 6.0 million and 7.4 million votes. In this measurement the Kōmeitō often is nearly the equal of Japan's number-two party, the JSP, which in 1983 captured only 275,000 more votes than the Kōmeitō. It is very interesting to note how the Kōmeitō collects its votes across Japan's 47 prefectures. Its lowest prefectural percentage in 1989 was 5.3 percent in rural Toyama, and its highest was 16.8 percent in Ōsaka. These were also the low and high percentages in the 1986 HC elections. In the most congested prefectures (Tokyo, Ōsaka, and Nagoya) and their "bedroom" prefectures, the CGP scored its highest vote percentages—in Tokyo, 13.0 percent; Kanagawa, 11.0 percent; and Saitama and Chiba, 11.4 percent. The only exception to this pattern of big-city voting support was the CGP's strength on the rural island of Shikoku, where it also won vote percentages in double digits. The CGP has been unable to convert this voting support into a comparable number of seats either in the House of Representatives or in prefectural assemblies. On Shikoku Island, for example, Kōmeitō members in 1990 held only a handful of prefectural assembly seats and only 2 of the 25 HR seats in the Diet (Table 6.2).

Another way to measure a party's real strength is by looking at its seat-winning success at the grass-roots levels of politics. In the 1983 unified local-level elections, Kōmeitō candidates won 182 seats in the 44 prefectures holding elections that year—an increase of 16 seats over its previous peak in 1975. With approximately 200 seats in prefectural assemblies (about 7 percent of the total number of seats), the Kōmeitō showed a significant improvement over its 1971 figure of 4.4 percent of the seats. And as Japanese voters tend to select area representation over ideological representation on the local levels of politics, the tendency toward rejection of ideological representation would work in favor of the conservatives, who win the vast majority of local- and prefectural-level seats. As of 1990, the CGP held 5 percent of Japan's 67,278 prefectural, city, and village council seats. Included in this total are 217 prefectural assembly seats, 1,924 city council seats, 1,132 village council seats, and 203 of the 1,051 council seats found within the political subunits of Tokyo. At the various levels of local government, the Kōmeitō is strongest in Tokyo city government with almost 20 percent of the seats, but wins only about 7.5 percent of the prefectural assemblies. Traditionally, it has been strongest in the urban prefectural assemblies of Tokyo and Ōsaka and relatively well represented in others, such as Hyōgo, Kanagawa, and Fukuoka. Many rural prefectures, on the other hand, have only one or two Kōmeitō members, and frequently there are none.

Until the 1983 elections, zone voting was one of the distinctive characteristics of the Kōmeitō organization, especially in the national constituency of the House of Councillors. The phenomenon of zone voting illustrates both the strong discipline imposed by the Kōmeitō leadership on its supporters and the total electoral strength of the party. In 1980, the Kōmeitō ran 9 candidates in the national constituency and all 9 were elected. Their vote totals ranged from 689,042 to 814,950, and they ranked between 27 and 45 out of the 50 winners that year. Since the bottom-ranked winner needed over 627,272 votes, even the last-place Kōmeitō candidate seemed safe. It was the zone voting that made such an impressive showing. Each of the nine CGP candidates was assigned a geographical group of CGP supporters. Outside of each candidate's zone these candidates collected few votes, but they received massive vote totals in their respective zones. Shown in Table 6.3 are each of the candidate's vote totals in Tokyo and the rural prefecture of Fukushima, for an interesting comparison.

THE KŌMEITŌ'S POLICY POSITIONS

As one might expect, the policy positions of the Kōmeitō have been well grounded in the philosophies of the Sōka Gakkai and the Nichiren Shōshū. When the Kōmeitō's predecessor, the Kōmei Political League, was created in 1962, its charter and platform stated that "our political ideal is the spirit of the Great Saint Nichiren's teaching that national security be realized through true Buddhism; on the basis of the supreme philosophy and compassion of the Great Saint, we will conduct activities as a modern and most democratic organization."[92]

The original declaration of the founding of the Kōmeitō issued in November 1964 was characterized by frequent Buddhist references to Nichiren (i.e., to the ideal of *Obutsu Myogo*). Yet, from the beginning, the Kōmeitō emphasized the goals of world peace, humanitarian socialism, Buddhist democracy, and the eradication of corrupt politics. The 1964 action policy of the party included specific opposition to harmful amendments to the constitution, support for global disarmament, an independent foreign policy, and a strong commitment to the welfare of the masses.

TABLE 6.3
Kōmeitō candidates' vote totals by zones (national constituency of 1980, House of Councillors)

Kōmeitō Candidate	*Total Vote*	*Rank*	*Zone*	*Zone Vote*	*Zone Vote as Percentage of Total Vote*	*Tokyo Vote*	*Fukushima Vote*
Suzuki	814,950	27	Kanagawa Saitama Tochigi	693,130	85.0	26,757	6,105
Mineyama	787,124	30	Ōsaka Nara, Hyōgo Wakayama	737,948	93.8	3,190	598
Okawa	770,333	33	Tokyo Yamanashi	639,294	83.0	602,596	4,481
Ninomiya	748,751	37	Ōsaka Hyōgo, Shikoku Okinawa	668,516	89.3	10,441	1,374
Ota	727,811	39	Mie, Aichi Shizuoka, Gifu	645,436	88.7	12,966	1,374
Shiode	712,619	40	Chūgoku (5) Shiga, Kyōto Fukui	646,869	91.2	4,243	290
Fujiwara	709,698	41	Hokkaidō Ishikawa Toyama Tōhoku (6)	665,863	93.8	6,574	91,689
Tsuruoka	709,044	42	Ibaraki Gunma, Chiba Shizuoka Nagano	632,722	89.2	12,786	2,386
Nakano	689,042	45	Kyūshū	649,802	94.3	4,685	297

Regions in Zones:

Shikoku:	Kagawa, Tokushima, Kōchi, Ehime.
Chūgoku:	Tottori, Okayama, Hiroshima, Shimane, Yamaguchi.
Tōhoku:	Aomori, Akita, Iwate, Yamagata, Miyagi, Fukushima
Kyūshū:	Fukuoka, Saga, Ōita, Nagasaki, Miyazaki, Kagoshima.

Source: Compiled by author.

As Matsumoto Shiro has noted, an action policy based on the establishment of a Buddhist orientation hall and the concept of *Obutsu Myogo* was not a sufficient policy foundation for a modern political party: "The party began with a clean policy slate . . . and gradually the Kōmeitō's policies on welfare, national security, Japan-China relations, and other issues took shape."[93] Again, according to Matsumoto, Kōmeitō chairman Takeiri reportedly followed newspaper reporters' advice to adopt a reformist line in opposition to the LDP and to continue its successful tactic of pressing for reform of the corrupt style of politics that has tended to characterize the image of the LDP. Yet, beyond the long-term goal of "clean government," the Kōmeitō followed an ad hoc approach to practical policymaking and thus tended to switch policy positions on given issues repeatedly throughout its history.

After 1970, the Kōmeitō officially dropped its goal of a national ordination hall and began to concentrate on more mundane policy areas such as pollution and defense. At its Eighth Annual Convention held in 1970, the Kōmeitō dropped its references to *Obutsu Myogo* and Buddhist democracy, and began to use such contemporary Kōmeitō policy terms as *humanitarian socialism* and *middle-of-the-road reformism.*

In addition, the party runs on a pacifist and democratic platform. The four basic principles of the 1982 Kōmeitō platform are presented, as follows, in the party's own words:

Party Platform

1. The Party shall maintain its stand as a political party based on middle-of-the-road reformism, whose purpose is to promote the welfare of all people in this nation. Holding highest respect for human dignity, it shall pursue its goals together with the people, with zeal for reform and sincere practice of its principles.

2. Founded on a new concept of "humanitarian socialism," the Party values the dignity of human life above all else, and it aims to establish an economic system which will guarantee free and responsible economic activity with fair distribution of the fruits thereof, and to construct a welfare society which will permit the realization of social prosperity and individual happiness.

3. Firm in the belief that all peoples of all races and nationalities are equal citizens of one world, the Party shall endeavor to bring about permanent peace and prosperity for all people through independent and peaceful diplomacy formulated on the principles of equality, reciprocity and non-interference in the internal affairs of other peoples or nations.

4. Upholding the Constitution of Japan and respecting the dignity of human life, liberty and equality, the Party shall protect the fundamental rights of freedom of religion, assembly and expression, and shall endeavor to establish fundamental social rights and create a firmer foundation for parliamentary democracy, eliminating all forms of violence.[94]

Middle-of-the-Road Reformism

"Middle-of-the-road reformism" is generally discussed by the Kōmeitō within the context of the crisis that engulfs current politics in Japan. The world is described as being affected by an extreme form of social anomie and a change in basic values. The only way to solve the crisis is to reestablish the primacy of values over politics. The Kōmeitō believes it offers a very special type of reformism, one that differs greatly from that practiced in Western democracies. As Chairman Takeiri has stated: "The essence of reformism lies in the will and practice to pursue reform in every reality around you without being submerged in and complacent with daily life."[95] This concept is then coupled with "images of moderation, steadiness, and harmony" as well as with the image of constant struggle for change. The sense of militancy derived from the parent Sōka Gakkai is evident in the party statement: "A political philosophy without a fighting spirit is only a degraded slogan."[96] And the "fighting spirit" of the party is best articulated in the official party slogan: "Talk with the people, fight with the people and die among the people." Such a slogan may seem to many Westerners to be more appropriate to the more radical Socialist or Communist parties than to the pacifist Buddhist party of Japan.

The Kōmeitō characterizes its middle-of-the-road reformism in terms of the concepts of humanism, holism, gradualism, and pacifism. Humanism places "ultimate value on man as he exists" and argues that "everything exists in order for man to be able to lead a better life." Within this context, people must strive for freedom and equality. Holism is a method of seeing the individual and the totality of society. Consequently, politics must be viewed as an integral part of the larger Japanese society and treated accordingly. All reforms must be accomplished gradually and peacefully: "Kōmeitō clearly rejects any kind of violence, and it supports the establishment of parliamentary democracy." Not only physical violence but "mental violence" and the "violence of numbers, speech, and negligence" are opposed as well. Gradual changes in the Japanese democracy, such as the correction of the Diet malapportionment and the liberalizing of election campaign laws, must be pursued. "Pacifism," as one Kōmeitō leader has claimed, "is definitely the most outstanding feature of our party platform. There are no good or bad wars"; hence the Kōmeitō claims to be the first party to make the peace constitution a part of its platform.

Humanitarian Socialism

Many who have come into casual contact with the Kōmeitō since its founding in 1964 are surprised to discover that it considers itself a Socialist party. The Kōmeitō rejects both the Marxist and Fabian Socialist paths: "As long as private interest remains the dehumanizing principle of the economy, it will be impossible to overcome the shortcomings of any kind of capitalist system."[97] Human rights and dignity would be damaged, and the "dehumanizing evils of capitalism—pollution, inflation, and the growth of the industrial-military complex—would remain to proliferate." Indeed, Socialist systems suffer from hardened institutions and an ignoring of the human rights of freedom of religion, assembly, and speech: "Kōmeitō's political and economic beliefs are socialist, but with a major difference: they are based on respect for human dignity. Our socialism is, therefore, progressive and democratic, totally pacifist; it is rooted in Japan's economic and political realities, and at the same time universal in its outlook on the world and the future."[98]

Such a Socialist world as envisaged by the Kōmeitō's leadership would be achieved very gradually and very incrementally:

> We are rejecting radicalism as a means of achieving our goals. We shall instead attempt to carry through reform step-by-step in vigorous daily efforts, in a spurt of innovation and hope. We are convinced that if we keep up our fight against the daily worries, taxes, housing shortages, traffic accidents, and the long-term problems of inflation and pollution, among others, and if we press relentlessly to ease the problems of the rural poor and the struggling small businesses, we will have opened up the way for effective and permanent economic reforms.[99]

In keeping with this spirit of gradual socialism, the Kōmeitō calls for the gradual nationalization of key manufacturing and energy industries, the utilization of progressive real estate and inheritance taxes, and a reduction of the inequalities in the distribution of wealth.

The Kōmeitō's domestic policy, developed in the 1960s—fighting inflation, housing shortages, traffic congestion, pollution, and public hazards, as well as seeking lower taxes—continued to be central to the party's public image in the 1980s. An examination of Kōmeitō news releases and news films will disclose not only a survey of the nuclear power issue in Japan but also a summary of the activities of Kōmeitō assembly women in local assemblies "striving to solve the various problems of city suburbs"; there are stories detailing, for instance, the struggle of a female Kōmeitō municipal assembly member to establish a welfare center for old people, and of Kōmeitō members "going all out to aid the victims of a typhoon."[100]

Toward a Coalition Government

In its 1982 brochure, the Kōmeitō gave top priority to an explanation of its coalition policies:

> On December 6, 1979, Kōmeitō and the Democratic Socialist Party (DSP) agreed on a plan for a middle-of-the-road coalition government. Our party also reached a similar agreement with the Japan Socialist Party (JSP) on January 10, 1980. The common features of the two coalition plans are, first, that they spell out realistic, political principles and goals that can be applied to international and domestic situations expected to emerge in the first half of the new decade. Second, the three parties have agreed that the Japan Communist Party will be excluded from the projected coalition. Although there may be some fine differences in nuance between the two plans, they are nevertheless identical in substance, especially as they concern actions for the first half of the 1980s.
>
> The LDP won by a substantial margin in the June 1980 elections for both houses of the Diet, but as far as we are concerned, it was only a temporary aberration. We still believe that our concept of coalition government is basically sound and provides a valid formula for the age of transformation. We must renew our determination to unite and advance forward to seize a golden opportunity for the opposition parties to form a coalition government for the first time in three decades.[101]

Asserting that the opposition parties can only grow from the experience of the 1980 electoral defeats, Kōmeitō leaders have argued that the "concept of coalition government will regain strength . . . and the 1980s will indeed emerge as an era of coalition government."[102] One of the key aspects of the 1980 coalition agreements for the Kōmeitō was the exclusion of the JCP from any future coalition government. The Kōmeitō's reasons were that the JCP cannot guarantee freedom and democracy, that its policies were too far from the other parties to form a partnership, and that "anticommunism" has been an important part of Kōmeitō's policy orientation.[103] A glance at the Kōmeitō's list of Japanese-language publications, for instance, would reveal the following titles translated into English: *Criticism of the JCP; Dictatorship Problems of the JCP and Its Declaration of Freedom; An Expose of the Deception of the JCP in Its Proletarian Dictatorship Problem and Freedom Declaration;* and *The JCP's Inability to Reply on the Issue of the Constitution and Its Contradictory Principles.*

In the party's draft action program for 1983, special emphasis was placed on the recouping of its Diet strength in elections anticipated in 1983 to pre-1980 levels—*prior* to any full-scale continuation of electoral cooperation with other centrist parties. It thus established a two-step process toward an eventual coalition government: First, each party's seat totals in the Diet would be built up; then, a plan of full-scale cooperation would be created to form a limited front for a coalition government. The Kōmeitō reaffirmed its desire to seek such a coalition government with the JSP, DSP, and the NLC-SDF.[104] By winning 58 seats in the December 1983 House elections, it raised its seat totals to the highest level in the Diet.

Kōmeitō Shifts on Security and Defense Questions (1978–1989)

Kōmeitō's security and defense positions appear to have undergone considerable change since the founding of the party in the early 1960s. The early Kōmeitō positions were ones of strong opposition to the Japan-U.S. Security Treaty and the Japanese Self-Defense Forces (*Jietai*). However, by the mid-1970s, it had become clear to the Kōmeitō leadership that some modification of the party's security policies would be necessary if political power was to be attained on the national level in coalition with either the LDP or the centrist parties.

At the Fifteenth Annual Kōmeitō Convention (January 1978), the party officially shifted its security policies. Chairman Takeiri stated that "Our party recognizes the 'right of self defense. . . .' [The existence of the Self-Defense Forces] is an established fact. Therefore, I believe that we should no longer relegate them to an ambiguous status."[105] Still the Kōmeitō's official position regarding the SDF held that the Self-Defense Forces had to be reorganized into a "National Guard . . . equipped with the minimum arms necessary to protect our territory from invasion and maintain neutrality."[106]

With regard to the Japan-U.S. Security Treaty, the early position of the Kōmeitō called for an "abrogation of the Japan-U.S. security setup by gradual stages." In 1973, it called for "immediate abrogation" of the treaty; and by the early 1980s, the Kōmeitō, as a result of the coalition agreements it had concluded with the DSP, had adopted a very moderate stand on the treaty: "Since immediate abolition of the Japan-U.S. Security Treaty would bring about rapid change in the international situation and might intensify tension in Japan and Asia, we therefore support the continuation of the Japan-U.S. Security Treaty for the time being, while endeavoring to create an international environment conducive to the discontinuation of the Japan-U.S. arrangement."[107]

This new Kōmeitō security position was justified and approved at the December 1981 convention after being drafted by the party's enlarged Central Executive Committee meeting held in October 1981. Fundamental to this new position was a set of new perceptions of a series of international events. The end of the Vietnam War, the Soviet invasion of Afghanistan, the Polish situation, and the Soviet military buildup in the formerly Japanese, now Soviet-occupied Northern Islands were all influential in setting the mood for a policy shift by the Kōmeitō. Yano and Takeiri had led delegations to Europe, the United States, and South Korea, and the resulting discussions had helped to broaden the perspectives of the leadership. Clearly, Takeiri and other leaders had concluded that the party needed to adopt defense and security policies closer to those of the LDP in order to be perceived by the electorate as a reasonable alternative governing party.[108]

Kōmeitō Policy Debates in the 1990s

Increasingly in 1990 Kōmeitō leaders debated the wisdom of continuing the policies and strategies of the 1980s. Prior to the November 1990 Kōmeitō national convention, party leaders called for a reexamination of the party platform, which had been adopted in 1970. At the convention, Chairman Ishida indicated that the Kōmeitō had decided to abandon its long-term strategy of being a part of a JSP-based coalition government and to begin a study of the prospects of joining the LDP in a coalition government during the 1990s.[109]

Kōmeitō leaders had lost patience with the JSP's inability to convert the Socialists' 1989 HC victory into a lower house victory in 1990. Kōmeitō criticized the JSP for its inability to develop realistic policies in the defense and security sectors as well as in a number of foreign policy areas such as Korea.[110] The last part of 1990 was dominated by the policy debate in the Diet and the country over the Kaifu government's request for permission to send members of the Self-Defense Forces to support the U.S. military coalition in Saudi Arabia. The DSP and CGP agreed to support the LDP-backed bill, but JSP and JCP opposition managed to kill it. Thus, the continuing inability of the opposition parties to come to a joint policy position on military security threatened to split the five parties further and reduce their chances of securing control of the Japanese Diet without the participation of the LDP.

CGP leadership has also called for the careful review of central parts of the party platform, such as "humanistic socialism" and "centrism." With the destruction of socialism in Eastern Europe in 1990, the utility of the concept of socialism is being questioned by some, and others are demanding that the party sharpen some of its other symbols and concepts to make it more attractive to voters. Clearly, the Kōmeitō appears to be on the verge of a long-delayed self-evaluation that may perhaps set it on a new political course in the 1990s.

The Role of the Kōmeitō in Japanese Politics

The Kōmeitō occupies a very sensitive and significant role in contemporary Japanese politics. As the number-three party in a six-party system, the Kōmeitō, along with the DSP, anchors the moderate position within the five-member opposition camp. Without the Kōmeitō, the moderate opposition (DSP, SDF, and right-wing JSP) would have no chance of creating the viable moderate alternative necessary to break the LDP-JSP dominance. The problem is that many members of these other opposition parties are very suspicious of the Kōmeitō and the sometimes "authoritarian" nature of the Buddhist party. Overall, in fact, the big dilemma of Japanese politics is that without the Kōmeitō, the Japanese party system would have only a very small prospect for a power pattern reversal; still, it seems nearly impossible for the Kōmeitō to become an acceptable part of the new coalition.

Although the Kōmeitō has been welcomed into Japanese politics as "a worthy opposition party with a moderately reformist platform" and as a "political party with a solid support basis . . . [and] an asset to our democracy," there is still a great deal of concern about its authoritarian tendencies and the policies it would enact if it gained national political power.[111]

Despite the efforts of the Kōmeitō leadership, there is little indication that the party has broadened its appeal signficantly beyond its Sōka Gakkai base. As only 10 percent of its members are unaffiliated with the Sōka Gakkai and are apparently unable to consistently capture more than a small share of the floating vote, the prospects of significant growth appear to be relatively small in the foreseeable future.

One can say that the Kōmeitō has drastically changed the nature of Japanese politics. Its formation in 1964 siphoned off an important part of the LDP religious constituency and changed a two-party system into the multiparty system currently in existence. By cutting into LDP support, it hastened the decline of that party during the 1960s and 1970s. In addition, the Kōmeitō functions as the bridge between the two Socialist parties (the JSP and DSP), which, although they do not get along very well together, often cooperate when they come together with the Kōmeitō in "joint struggles"—hence Palmer's reference to the Kōmeitō as the "equilibrator for the Japanese political system."[112] If we analyze the Kōmeitō using some of the functional labels applied to parties and groups in other political systems, additional functions become obvious. The party serves both as an articulator and as a broker in representing the 10 to 15 million people who are Sōka Gakkai members. The party's natural constituency is one that does not automatically obtain representation elsewhere in society. Moreover, these people are socialized into the larger political system and encouraged to participate politically as voters and candidates of the Kōmeitō. Innovative ideas have been advanced by the Kōmeitō in its role as part of the governing coalition in many of Japan's larger cities. Finally, the Kōmeitō as the Clean Government party continues to function as a "watchdog" that focuses on excesses committed by Japanese politicians, especially those of the LDP and JCP.[113] In particular, the Kōmeitō has been a leader in exposing LDP corruption (though relatively silent on the Tanaka scandals—Tanaka being an old ally of the party) and has supported its conservative version of the welfare state on all levels of Japanese politics.

It is very difficult, however, to place the Kōmeitō on a Left-Right scale of Japanese politics. It claims to be a militant Socialist party, but many argue that the Kōmeitō constituency is basically conservative and that its rhetoric is not matched by its day-to-day deeds.[114] As Lee has suggested, the Kōmeitō takes a slightly leftist policy position in the Diet, but on the local level it has often adopted right-of-center positions.[115] In addition, the Kōmeitō leaders themselves have argued that the party is outside the Left-Right continuum altogether in that the party represents *all* the people inasmuch as it rises above class and other cleavages in society.[116]

From the perspective of the Sōka Gakkai leadership, the original objectives behind the creation of the Kōmeitō have been more than fulfilled. As Imazu has noted, the pressure from the LDP and other religious groups on Sōka Gakkai members has been relieved, and the values of the Sōka Gakkai have been projected into Japanese politics.[117] Perhaps more significantly, the Kōmeitō has helped to legitimize and moderate the image of the Sōka Gakkai for the general Japanese public. But the most significant aspect of the Kōmeitō lies in its stability as a continuing, stable force in national and local politics. As its Diet contingent is usually double the contingent of the next largest moderate opposition party (i.e., the DSP), any future non-LDP government must include the Kōmeitō as an essential component. One must also keep in mind that the Kōmeitō is also a prime prospect to join the LDP in a coalition government if the conservatives ever drop below a majority in the Diet.[118]

NOTES

1. J. W. White, *The Sōka Gakkai and Mass Society* (Palo Alto, Calif.: Stanford University Press, 1970), p. 1.
2. Arvin Palmer, *Buddhist Politics: Japan's Clean Government Party* (The Hague: Nijhoff, 1971), p. 54.
3. Daniel A. Metraux, "The Last Word: Japan's Sōka Gakkai," *Asian Mail* (November 1977), p. 23.
4. Ibid.
5. *Japan Times* (May 8, 1979).
6. Palmer, *Buddhist Politics,* p. 58.
7. Kiyoaki Murata, *Japan's New Buddhism* (New York: Walker-Weatherhill, 1969). The critical works in Japanese on both organizations include Naito Kunio, *Kōmeitō No Sugata* (Tokyo: Ierv, 1969); Murakami, *Sōkagakkai-Kōmeitō* (Tokyo: Aoki, 1967); and Sawaki Toshio and Nakagawa, eds., *Kōmeitō Sōka Gakkai Hihan* (Tokyo: Shin Nippon Shuppan, 1970).
8. Jooinn Lee, "Kōmeitō: Sōka Gakkai-ism in Japanese Politics," *Asian Survey* 10, no. 6 (June 1970).
9. *Japan Times* (January 15, 1967), p. 8.
10. White, *The Sōka Gakkai,* pp. 21–22.

11. James A. Dator, *Sōka Gakkai: Builders of the Third Civilization* (Seattle: University of Washington Press, 1969), pp. 79–80.
12. Ibid., p. 81.
13. Lee, "Kōmeitō," p. 502.
14. *Newsweek* 67 (March 7, 1966), p. 86.
15. See generally Palmer's *Buddhist Politics* for a positive treatment of this group.
16. Ibid., p. 39. In 1969 there were 57 general headquarters; 195 local headquarters; 718 general chapters; 3,818 chapters; 17,453 districts; tens of thousands of groups; and hundreds of thousands of cells in Japan.
17. Nishijima Hisashi, *Kōmeitō* (Tokyo: Sekkasha, 1968), p. 65.
18. See White, *The Sōka Gakkai,* pp. 310–311.
19. Ibid., p. 303. (It should be noted that units other than families are referred to in some sources, so that organization numbers may seem to vary.)
20. *Mainichi Daily News* (December 15, 1980).
21. Palmer, *Buddhist Politics,* pp. 34–35.
22. Ibid., p. 32.
23. Dator, *Sōka Gakkai,* pp. 63–70.
24. Ibid., p. 79.
25. Azumi Koya, "Political Functions of Sōka Gakkai Membership," *Asian Survey* 11, no. 9 (September 1971), p. 929.
26. Dator, *Sōka Gakkai,* p. 79.
27. Ibid., p. 93.
28. Azumi, "Political Functions," p. 928.
29. Nishijima, *Kōmeitō,* pp. 128–134.
30. Azumi, "Political Functions," p. 928.
31. Roger Benjamin and Kan Ori, *Tradition and Change in Post-Industrial Japan: The Role of the Political Parties* (New York: Praeger Publishers, 1981), p. 45. The control the Gakkai exerts over its members is the greatest advantage of the Kōmeitō in terms of facilitating the formation of the party's electoral strategies. Apparently, when the Sōka Gakkai leaders speak to their followers on political matters, such pronouncements are considered to be religious commandments that must be followed. See Kashihara, *Politics in Japan* (Tokyo: Japan Echo, 1982), pp. 44–45.
32. Kiyohiko Miyakawa, Chief of the Sōka Gakkai Youth Department, *Mainichi Daily News* (December 12, 1980).
33. *Japan Quarterly* 28, no. 2 (April-June, 1981).
34. *Japan Times* (November 29, 1980).
35. *Seikyō Shimbun* (January 1, 1954).
36. Quoted in Shiro Matsumoto, "Twists and Turns of Kōmeitō," *Japan Echo* 9, no. 1 (1982), p. 61. Originally published in *Sekai* (December 1981), pp. 36–44.
37. Shiro, "Twists and Turns," p. 61.
38. Ibid., p. 62.
39. Ibid.
40. Benjamin and Ori, *Tradition and Change,* pp. 146–150.
41. Fujiwara Hirotatsu, *Sōka Gakkai O Kiru* (Tokyo: Nisshin Hodo, 1970).
42. Azumi, "Political Functions," p. 921.
43. *Japan Echo* 9, no. 1 (1982), p. 107.
44. *Japan Times* (November 29, 1980).
45. "Sōka Gakkai Controversy: Part 5," *Mainichi Daily News* (December 13, 1980).
46. "Sōka Gakkai Vice President Speaks Out," *Japan Times* (November 29, 1980).
47. Interview with Harashima Takashi, *Mainichi Daily News* (December 4, 1980).

48. *Japan Times* (October 16, 1982).
49. *Japan Times* (July 28, 1975).
50. Miyamoto Kenji and Ikeda Daisaku, "In Quest of Civilized Coexistence," *Bengei Shunjū* (October 1975).
51. Miyamoto Kenji, "At a Historical Turning Point," *Bungei Shunjū* (October 1975).
52. See Naito Kunio, "History of Antagonism Between the JCP and the Sōka Gakkai," *Gakkai Shokan* (October 1975). See also *Mainichi Daily News* (December 26, 1975).
53. "Ikeda Speech," *Asahi Evening News* (August 2, 1975).
54. "Nagatacho Doings," *Mainichi Daily News* (September 10, 1975).
55. *Mainichi Daily News* (July 17, 1975).
56. *Japan Times* (October 2, 1975).
57. *Akahata* (December 29, 1979).
58. *Asahi Evening News* (December 31, 1979).
59. *Akahata* (February 8, 1980).
60. Lee, "Kōmeitō," p. 513.
61. *Japan Quarterly* 20, no. 2 (April-June 1981), p. 155.
62. Azumi, "Political Functions," p. 924.
63. *Asahi Shimbun* poll (September 10, 1979).
64. Letter from Kōmeitō headquarters to author dated August 29, 1981.
65. Hiroshi Imazu, "The Opposition Parties: Organization and Policies," *Japan Quarterly* 24, no. 2 (April-June 1977).
66. Palmer, *Buddhist Politics*, p. 67.
67. "Nagatacho Doings," *Mainichi Daily News* (May 2, 1979).
68. Yano was forced to resign from the party leadership because of his involvement in the Recruit Cosmos stock scandal of 1989–1990. Yano rose to the chairman position when Takeiri resigned in December 1986.
69. *Mainichi Daily News* (September 26, 1975).
70. James J. Foster, "Ghost Hunting: Local Party Organization in Japan," *Asian Survey* 22, no. 9 (September 1982), pp. 846–847.
71. Cecil C. Brett, "The Kōmeitō and Local Japanese Politics," *Asian Survey* 19, no. 4 (April 1979), p. 373.
72. *Daily Yomiuri* (August 25, 1982).
73. *Mainichi Daily News* (December 5, 1980).
74. Kōmeitō press release (September 18, 1980).
75. *Asahi Evening News* (April 5, 1976).
76. See the party publication entitled *Kōmeitō* (Tokyo: Kōmeitō, 1980).
77. Lee, "Kōmeitō," p. 512.
78. "Nagatacho Doings," *Mainichi Daily News* (October 13, 1979).
79. Lee, "Kōmeitō," pp. 514, 503.
80. *Mainichi Shimbun* (October 3, 1979).
81. *Asahi Shimbun* (March 17, 1982).
82. *Yomiuri Shimbun* (November 3, 1982).
83. Imazu, "The Opposition Parties," pp. 166–169.
84. Jung-suk Youn, in John Campbell, ed., "Candidates and Party Images: Recruitment to the Japanese House of Representatives," *Parties, Candidates and Voters in Japan* (Ann Arbor: Center for Japanese Studies, University of Michigan, 1980), pp. 106–109. Kōmeitō lower house members were better educated in 1990 than were their CGP predecessors in previous decades. Of the 45 CGP candidates elected to the House of Representatives in February 1990, 32 had college degrees and another

7 had some college education. In terms of identifiable occupations prior to being elected to the Diet, 13 were prefectural or local assembly members; 19 were Kōmeitō party workers; 7 were lawyers; and 4 came from educational positions.

85. Ibid., p. 113.

86. *Mainichi Shimbun* (June 24, 1980).

87. *Asahi Evening News* (October 4, 1980).

88. Tawara Kotaro, *Look Japan* (March 10, 1980), p. 3.

89. *Asahi Shimbun* (June 24, 1980).

90. *Tokyo Shimbun* (June 24, 1980).

91. Kōmeitō was forced to fight the 1990 HR elections from a weakened position after its long-term party leader Yano was implicated in the Recruit Cosmos stock market scandal and a top aide of Ikeda Daisaku was also involved in a money scandal.

92. Matsumoto, "Twists and Turns," pp. 61–62.

93. Ibid., p. 63.

94. *Kōmeitō* (Tokyo: Kōmeitō International Bureau, 1982).

95. *Kōmeitō Shimbun,* (September 30, 1969).

96. *Kōmeitō,* p. 12. (The remaining quotations in this section are also attributed to this party publication.)

97. Ibid., p. 16.

98. Ibid., p. 16.

99. Ibid., pp. 16–17.

100. Kōmeitō press release, no. 42 (November 21, 1978).

101. *Kōmeitō,* p. 3.

102. Ibid., p. 7.

103. Ibid., p. 37.

104. *Japan Times* (October 19, 1982).

105. "Kōmeitō's 15th Annual Convention Summary" (January 1978).

106. Kōmeitō press release, no. 58 (November 30, 1981).

107. Kōmeitō, p. 29.

108. "Tilting Toward the Right: Sweeping Changes in Kōmeitō Defense Policy," *Japan Quarterly* 29, no. 1 (January-March 1982), pp. 1–5.

109. At the convention, the CGP formally decided to establish a panel to discuss cooperation with the LDP after the CGP breaks with the JSP and DSP. The CGP justified this shift by arguing it would give ordinary citizens a better chance of voicing their views in politics. Kōmeitō Secretary-General Ichikawa gave three criteria for cooperation with the LDP: that both parties observe the constitution, seek clean politics, and champion ordinary citizens. *Yomiuri Shimbun* (November 29, 1990).

110. "Komeito Action Plan Draft," *Asahi Shimbun* (March 31, 1990).

111. *Japan Times,* Editorial (May 8, 1979).

112. Palmer, *Buddhist Politics,* p. 78.

113. Ibid., p. 2.

114. Some have suggested that the Kōmeitō is really a conservative party. See, for example, Murokami Shigeyoshi, *Kōmeitō* (Tokyo: Shin Nippon Shuppan, 1969), pp. 174–182.

115. Lee, "Kōmeitō," p. 512.

116. Azumi, "Political Functions," p. 918.

117. Imazu, "The Opposition Parties."

118. For more information on the Sōka Gakkai and the Kōmeitō, see Noah S. Brannen, *Sōka Gakkai: Japan's Militant Buddhists* (Richmond, Va.: John Knox Press, 1964); James Allen Dator, "The Sōka Gakka: A Socio-Political Interpretation," *Contemporary Religion in Japan* 6 (1965), pp. 205–292; Dator, "The Sōka Gakkai in

Japanese Politics," *Journal of Church and State* 9 (Spring 1967), p. 223; H. Neill McFarland, *The Rush House of the Gods* (New York: Macmillan; 1967); Felix Moos, "Religion and Politics in Japan: The Case of the Sōka Gakkai," *Asian Survey* 3 (March 1963), pp. 36–42; Robert Ramseyer, "The Sōka Gakkai and the Japanese Local Election of 1963," *Contemporary Religions in Japan* 4 (December 1963), pp. 287–303; Charles Seldon, "Religion and Politics in Japan: The Sōka Gakkai," *Pacific Affairs* 33 (December 1960), pp. 382–386; and James White, "Mass Movements and Democracy: The Sōka Gakkai in Japanese Politics," *American Political Science Review* 61 (September 1967), pp. 744–750.

7

The Democratic Socialist Party: Enigma of the Center

RONALD J. HREBENAR

Of all the parties currently operating within the Japanese political system, the Democratic Socialist party (DSP) may be the most difficult to describe accurately. If there is a party in Japan with an identity crisis, it must be the DSP. One reason for this problem is found in the confusion over its raison d'être. Is it really a Socialist party? A Democratic Socialist party? Does it really want to change Japan into a European-style social democracy? As the 1980s began, Tsuneo Fuji, a DSP member of the House of Councillors and the chairman of the party's Election Policy Committee, noted: "I don't think it would be a bad idea if we changed the party's name."[1] Fuji's comment underlies the basic concern of many within the party regarding its reception by the Japanese public since its birth in 1960. As Fuji further noted in his analysis, many Japanese think the DSP must approve of socialism or communism: "Those without a party affiliation end up voting for the LDP because they don't want to change the economic and social systems of the conservatives." Among the suggestions Fuji made for a new name for the DSP were "Labor Party" or "Democratic Party."[2]

It is somewhat ironic that in a world in which so many industrialized nations are or have been ruled by Democratic Socialist parties, the DSP has never been able to establish itself as a reasonable alternative to the conservative rule of the LDP. Many reasons could be advanced to explain the failure of the DSP to legitimize social democracy in Japan, but the most fundamental is the inability of the party to convince the Japanese voters that, amidst the growing prosperity they have enjoyed under LDP rule since 1955, they should abandon the existing system and turn to some vague alternative. The concept of social democracy simply has not been considered a viable economic and political system for the postwar Japanese society. Given the DSP's failure to sell its basic idea, then, what should be the future course of the party?

To answer this question, we must first explore the DSP's past. Accordingly, this chapter will begin with the circumstances surrounding the birth of the DSP during some of the most traumatic events experienced by Japan in the postwar political experience.

FROM FACTION TO FRACTION: THE BIRTH OF THE DSP

Like the New Liberal Club and the Social Democratic Federation, the Democratic Socialist party is a splinter from one of the two largest parties operating in post-1945 Japan. Its "mother party," the Japanese Socialist party, has been torn by internal conflict over ideological orientations throughout its long history. During the prewar years, the Right tended to dominate the organization of the socialist movement, but after the war, the Left gradually established its domination. After the Katayama coalition cabinet fell in March 1948, the JSP continued its pattern of intraparty ideological struggles. It split and merged several times during the 1950s. The first Left-Right split occurred in January 1950, but the party reunited after seventy-five days. A more serious split over the party's position on the San Francisco Peace Treaty and the Japan-U.S. Security Treaty began in October 1951. The two wings of the Socialist party ran separate slates of candidates during the next three general elections. The Right wing came to victory over the Left in the October 1952 election by securing 57 seats. Yet this election was actually a leftist victory in that the Left increased its seat totals from the mid-teens to over 50. In the April 1953 elections the Right increased its seat totals to 66, but the Left won 72. Finally, in February 1955, the Right won 67 seats, whereas the Left captured 89 seats. Soon after the last election in this series, the two wings merged into a reunited Socialist party. The reunification was initiated by the moderate Right.

Although the Right was ultimately willing to rejoin the Socialist party, basic questions of ideology were clearly not settled. Signs of internal warfare emerged during the May 1958 general election campaign. The debate concerned the nature of the Socialist party and its future. The most visible leader of the Right wing was Nishio Suehirō, who later focused the party's attention on the question of the Japan-U.S. Security Treaty revision negotiations. The differences between the two wings went well beyond this one issue, which nevertheless came to symbolize the deeper conflict for many of the participants. Nishio advocated that the JSP should adopt a pragmatic approach to the Security Treaty and, rather than pursuing a position of complete and total opposition to the treaty's existence, that it should concentrate on a small number of specific changes. He also recommended that the party focus on such issues as the duration of the new treaty and the nature of abrogation procedures.[3] However, the Left wing would settle for nothing less than the termination of the treaty. It looked on Nishio's position as a threat to party unity and was determined to punish him for his acts. At the JSP convention held in September 1959, the leftist-controlled party voted to censure Nishio for breaking party unity. Nishio and his followers, representing the JSP faction that had come from the moderate Right wing of the prewar socialist movement (the Shamin, or Socialist People's party), bolted the party. Later that year, part of the old Nichirō faction (from the Japan Labor Peasant party, a more middle-of-the-road Socialist party of the prewar period) also split with the JSP and joined Nishio. The two groups in January 1960 established the Democratic Socialist party (Minshu Shakaitō). Nishio was elected chairman of the new party, which had a total of 40 Diet members at the time of its formation. However, the next election was a disaster, inasmuch as only 17 seats were captured, and the party since then has not won even as many as 40 seats in the House of Representatives. During the 1980s the DSP won 32 seats in 1980 HR elections, 38 in 1983, and only 26 in 1986. It plummeted to a mere 14 seats in 1990.

The Political Arm of Dōmei

The DSP is often viewed by many Japanese as the political arm of Dōmei, the All Japan Labor Federation (Zen Nihon Rōdō Sōdōmei). Accordingly, before we turn to a discussion of the relationship between the DSP and Dōmei, a brief examination of the state of organized labor in postwar Japan is necessary. Dōmei can trace its history back to a labor organization, Yūaikai, which began in 1912 but was disbanded during World War II. It was divided after the war into the Sōdōmei (General Federation of Trade Unions of Japan) and the Kaiin Kumiai (All Japan Seaman's Union). In 1950 Sōhyō (General Council of Trade Unions of Japan) was formed, and within two years its leftist political tilt had become a concern to the moderates within Sōhyō. Sōdōmei left Sōhyō and in 1954, along with three other moderate industrial unions (textiles, seamen, and cinema workers), organized a rival trade union confederation, Zenrō (Japanese Trade Union Congress). Other organizations joined Zenrō, and its membership expanded from 800,000 to 1.4 million members. In a related development, Zenkankō (National Council of Government and Public Corporation Workers' Unions) was organized in 1959. Three years later, in January 1962, Zenrō, Sōdōmei, and Zenkankō reached an agreement on a unification policy, and in April 1962 Dōmeikaigi was formed as a transitionary group. On November 12, 1964, the constitution of Zen Nihon Rōdō Sōdōmei was approved.[4]

Organized labor in Japan for the most part formed around four central organizations, or national centers, that are the most influential among the 308 nationwide joint labor organizations. These four were Sōhyō, Dōmei, Shinsanbetsu (National Federation of Industrial Organizations), and Chūritsurōren (Federation of Independent Unions). Sōhyō was the largest and Dōmei the second largest of these national centers. Sōhyō, a confederation of fifty national organizations—including national unions, industrial federations, and joint councils—is leftist in its political orientation and has been a strong supporter of the JSP since the 1950s. Chūritsurōren and Shinsanbetsu are much smaller organizations, with ten and four affiliated organizations, respectively.

At the beginning of the 1990s, there were approximately 45 million workers in Japan. Slightly over 12 million are labor union members, with 78 percent of that number belonging to private-sector unions and 22 percent to public-sector unions. Only 25.2 percent of Japanese workers are unionized. This percentage has been constantly declining and represents a record low percentage since labor union membership surveys began in 1953. The 12 million unionized Japanese workers belong to over 30,000 individual labor unions organized on a company-by-company basis.[5]

Prior to 1989, private-sector unions were primarily represented by the Dōmei labor confederation. Dōmei was until 1989 a confederation of Japanese trade unions that principally represents the private sector. As of 1981, it included within its ranks a total of thirty-one unions and federations representing a membership of 2.1 million workers.[6] The largest constituent Dōmei-affiliated trade unions were Zensen Dōmei (494,896 members: textiles), Zenkin Dōmei (313,612: metal workers), and Zōsenjuki Rōren (220,697: shipbuilding and heavy machinery workers). The geographical distribution of Dōmei membership was heavily concentrated in the urban industrial prefectures. Tokyo (231,885 Dōmei members), Kanagawa (169,212), Ōsaka (238,013), Hyōgo (141,169), and Aichi (148,450) prefectures represented the real Dōmei strongholds, whereas Tottori (8,371), Kōchi (9,786), Yamanashi (5,368), and Nara (6,095) prefectures represent rural sectors of almost negligible Dōmei power.[7]

Just as the Right wing of the Sōhyō was eventually forced out of that labor confederation to form Dōmei, the Right wing of the Japan Socialist party was forced out during the 1959-1960 period and formed the Democratic Socialist party. This split in the JSP in 1960 was accomplished with a great deal of encouragement by the Sōhyō defectors. In fact, there are many who argue that without the support of Dōmei, the DSP would not have become a reality in 1960. Very quickly after its formation, the DSP established firm ties with Dōmei and the two have remained political partners ever since.

The DSP's reliance on Dōmei as its main supporting organization (as well as on Chūritsurōren) has been both a help and a hindrance for the DSP. Dōmei control of its membership was weak; indeed, the party encouraged only 1.3 percent (38,000 members) of its total membership to formally join. Of the thirty-one Dōmei unions, fifteen were listed as official supporters of the DSP, while the remaining sixteen provided less formal support for the party. Dōmei officials estimated that about 30 percent of the labor federation supported DSP candidates at the polls. Among the constituent Dōmei unions, the auto workers gave the DSP about 70 percent of their votes and the textile workers, about half.[8]

According to a May 1977 survey conducted by the Labor Research Institute (Rōdō Chōsa Kekyū-jo), of the 14,510 members of eighteen labor unions in the Kansai area, the DSP was supported by 11.3 percent. The union members supported the JSP at a 27.8 percent level, whereas 5.6 percent supported the LDP, 3.1 percent the NLC, 2.9 percent the Kōmeitō, and 2.5 percent the JCP (45.1 percent expressed no political party preference).[9] Labor union members have demonstrated a growing sense of alienation and lack of confidence in the political actors of the nation. According to a 1979 survey of 4,500 members of six labor unions, the educational center of Sōhyō reported that only 1 to 1.8 percent had confidence in either conservative or reformist politicians. Conservative politicians came in dead last in the poll, trailing even fortune tellers.[10]

In recent years, the political attitudes of Japanese workers have changed as well. According to the polls released by the Prime Minister's Office, 89 percent of all Japanese see themselves as members of the middle class. With the rise in general affluence in Japan, there has also been a significant decline in the number of labor union respondents opting for socialism as a desired political system in Japan as well as a sharp increase in the number choosing some form of a welfare state.[11] All of these attitude changes bode ill for a party trying to sell "socialism" in a capitalist, middle-class political economy.

On a year-to-year basis and before the formation of Rengō, Dōmei as an organization contributed about 100 million yen to the DSP. In addition, each Dōmei member was expected to make a contribution of 200–300 yen to an election fund that mounted to as much as 500–600 million yen overall. During election campaigns, local Dōmei headquarters were mobilized for campaign support activities. Many individual workers took holidays paid by the union in order to work for DSP candidates. Some companies encouraged their workers to participate in election campaigns and to give financial support, especially when candidates came from their companies. Each supporting Dōmei union also collected money for the party. Some unions contributed regularly to the DSP by multiplying the number of supporting members by a fixed number of yen per month. The Electrical Workers Union, having 100,000 registered DSP supporters each contributing 5 yen per month, made a total monthly contribution to the DSP of 500,000 yen.[12] Dōmei thus estimated that in recent general elections, the union's contribution to the DSP totaled between 500 million and 600 million yen in direct financial assistance.

The DSP-Dōmei relationship was an interesting one. Clearly, the DSP could not survive without the organizational and financial support of Dōmei. On the other hand, the appeal of the DSP was limited by its identification as Dōmei's political party. In this respect, it shared many of the same problems as the JSP (Sōhyō) and the Kōmeitō (Sōkka Gakkai). The organizational limitations of the DSP to Dōmei's collection of moderate, private-sector labor unions boded ill for the future growth of the party. The 1980 Ministry of Labor report on the state of organized labor in Japan pointed out one of the serious weaknesses of Dōmei. When 1979 is compared to 1978 in terms of the percentage of workers who belonged to labor unions, a decrease of 1 percent is noted. Most of this decline took place in the private sector in general and in large businesses in particular. These were areas of strength for the Dōmei. Public-sector employees accounted for about 11 percent of the total regular work force in Japan. Of these 3.4 million public-sector workers, 87 percent were members of Sōhyō. In fact, public-sector workers made up approximately two-thirds of Sōhyō's total membership. The failure of Dōmei to make inroads into this important group of workers severely limited the ability of the DSP to expand its electoral strength and to run campaigns in all parts of the nation. In the section on electoral strategies, we will examine the implications of this failure in more detail.

The Dōmei led the movement in the 1980s to reunify the organized labor world. In September 1980 Dōmei and Sōhyō, along with Chūritsurōren and Shinsanbetsu, agreed that "our basic stance will be the attempt to unify all labor organizations beginning with those representing workers in the private sector and progressing to include those in the public sector." In the same month, a "council to promote labor-front unification" was also established. The six-member council contained many of the major supporters of both Dōmei and Sōhyō and their respective parties. Tamura Yuzo interprets these moves toward unification both as a possible acceptance of the moderate policy positions of the DSP and Dōmei by Sōhyō and, perhaps, as an opening for a radical restructuring not only of labor but of the Socialist parties in Japan as well.[13]

In 1988 and 1989 the pieces were put together for the establishment of Rengō (Nihon Rōdō Kumiai Sōrengōkai) under the leadership of Yamagishi Akira. Rengō was formed by merging 17 unions from Sōhyō and 21 unions from Dōmei for a combined total membership of over 7.6 million. As of 1990, the Japanese labor world consisted of the new Rengō; the Zenrōren (Zenkoku Rōdō Kumiai Sōrengō), with 835,000 members and politically supporting the JCP; and the Zenrokyo (Zenkoku Rōdō Kumiai Renraku Kyogikai), with 290,000 members primarily from the Tokyo Metropolitan Government Workers Union and close to the Left wing of the JSP.

A revolution has occurred in the Japanese world of organized labor with the merger of Sōhyō and Dōmei into Rengō. What is not clear at all is what this means in terms of politics and political parties, for as we will see later in this chapter, the early impact of Rengō has been very mixed.

The studies of Alan Cole, Robert Scalapino, and Haruhiro Fukui reveal a good deal of information concerning the organizational nature of the JSP, the JCP, and the LDP, respectively. Western students of Japanese political parties have little access, however, to information on the internal organization of the newer moderate parties such as the DSP.[14]

As is the case with most Democratic Socialist parties around the world, the key organizational unit of the party is the branch. Each branch, which can be formed by as few as five party members, serves as a communications link between the leadership and the membership. In late 1979 the DSP had approximately 1,200 branches. Two branches constitute a general branch office, which serves an administrative support function. Branches can be formed on either a geographical or an occupational site.

DSP membership in 1981 stood at 50,000. Although the number of members has fluctuated throughout the last two decades, it appears that about 30,000 members make up the "hard core" party base. Party leaders consider a 300,000 membership with a hard core of about 30 percent to be an ideal target. But such an aspiration is unlikely to be achieved in the foreseeable future.

Recent increases in the DSP general membership are explained by the party leaders in four ways. First, they note that their competition within the opposition parties has been declining in the public's favor and that the DSP, which has been climbing in the polls, has been the beneficiary of these attitude changes. Second, they argue that the recent oil-related recessions have increased workers' political awareness and encouraged them to join moderate, effective parties. Third, the DSP major sponsor-supporter, the former Dōmei, continues to support the DSP even while Dōmei has merged with Rengō. Finally, the DSP has intensified its internal party educational programs as well as its recruitment efforts among special targeted groups such as youths.

Regarding the geographical distribution of DSP membership, the party is largely a mirror reflection of Dōmei membership patterns. Where large concentrations of Dōmei-associated labor unions exist, there will be an active DSP organizational effort. Currently, the prefectures in which DSP membership is relatively strong include Tokyo, Ōsaka, Aichi, Kanagawa, and Hyōgo. Conversely, the party is quite weak in rural areas such as Tōhoku, Shikoku, Sanin (Shamine and Tottori), and Hokuriku. The efforts made to penetrate into these and other rural areas have thus far been relatively futile. The recent phenomenon whereby 80 percent of farmers are "dual-employed" (i.e., on farms and in factories) has encouraged DSP leadership, but the rural voters' historically strong agricultural ties to the LDP have proven stronger than the farmers' identity as workers.

In addition to its Dōmei support, the DSP has significant support among religious organizations.[15] One such group, Sekai Kyūsei Kyō (World Salvation), claims nearly 800,000 adherents and endorses all DSP candidates. Five other religious organizations collectively totaling almost 14 million followers frequently support both DSP and LDP candidates. Other DSP-support organizations include the steel workers' union from the former Sōhyō, the Electric Independent Workers' Union, a small farmers' union, a 5,0000-member Democratic Socialist (DS) Women's Organization, and the DS Medium and Small Enterprise Association with 35,000 members.

The DSP has formal organizations in about 80 of the 130 electoral districts to support lower house candidates and to guide the lower levels of party organizations on the city and branch levels. It also has prefectural federations in each of the forty-seven prefectures used to support Diet election campaigns, to seek out future candidates, and to campaign for the local assembly members. These prefectural offices frequently overlap the offices of the incumbent DSP Diet members.

Every year the party holds an annual national convention. Delegates are chosen according to the criterion of 1 percent of membership (about 460 delegates in 1980). The qualifications for becoming a delegate are quite simple: payment of the average monthly party fee of 1,000 yen (300 yen to headquarters and 700 yen to lower levels). These delegates are selected by the respective prefectural executive party committees. National conventions are usually held in February, but the timing can be affected by the political situation. The 1980 convention, for instance, was scheduled for April because of the projected House of Councillors elections in June. Decisions are made by the national convention on such questions as party action policy, budgets, and candidate selections for Diet elections. DSP conventions usually are tame affairs in which the decisions of the party leadership are rather calmly ratified.

The organizational structure of the DSP is not complicated. Four top party officials are selected by the national convention: the chairman, two vice-chairmen, and a secretary-general. An Executive Committee of twenty-seven members (not including the four party leaders) is elected for two-year terms. The secretary-general runs both the party secretariat and a party headquarters in Tokyo, which employs about seventy-five persons. The DSP publishes a weekly newspaper, *Shūkan Minsha,* and a monthly magazine, *Kakushin* (which means "progressive") with circulations of 130,000 and 20,000, respectively.

The Executive Committee meets monthly to make the important decisions of the party. It is also charged with the implementation of decisions made by the party national convention and makes recommendations for those convention decisions. One step below the Executive Committee is the 170-member Central Committee, which performs an advisory function of less importance than that of the Executive Committee.

It is interesting to note that the DSP leadership claimed there was almost no evidence prior to 1985 of internal strife, ideological conflict, or LDP-style factions within the party. As one DSP official ironically observed, "We are too small a party to afford the luxury of factions." As the DSP runs a maximum of one candidate per house district, there is little chance that the type of intraparty factionalism found in the LDP will arise. Before 1985, whatever factionalism the party did have seemed to center around the policy preferences of two of the party's main support bases, Dōmei and small business, which tended to support one or the other of the party's top leaders. In the early 1980s, the former DSP chairman, Sasaki Ryōsaku, was viewed as more union oriented; his predecessor DSP chairman, Kasuga Ikkō, came from the conservative business-oriented part of the party. DSP Diet members are either labor union members or professional politicians with ties to conservative business and religious associates. One result of these different orientations can be seen in the DSP policy battles over the years. The union-oriented Diet members seem to be more socialistic in their policy preferences, whereas the professional career politicians are much more conservative.

After the 1989 and 1990 election defeats, some DSP factionalism based on support for different electoral strategies was noted in the Japanese press. A Right-leaning group centering around a former chairman, Tsukamoto Saburō, and the chairman in 1990, Ōuchi Keigo, suggested that the DSP should change its name to the Japan Democratic (versus Socialist) party as it moves closer to the LDP and a possible coalition government. This group appeared to have as supporters a majority of DSP Diet members, whereas the former Dōmei union activists have been more supportive of the second group (symbolized by former Chairman Nagasue Eiichi and Secretary-General Yonezawa Takashi), which argues that the DSP should continue to support the JSP and CGP in an effort to promote the opposition into the government without the LDP. Concerns over both these courses threatens to split the small party as it attempts to survive the first half of the 1990s.[16]

The leadership of the DSP was in the hands of a small group of men from 1960 to 1985. The first party chairman, Nishio Suehirō, was symbolic of the party during his seven years as party leader between 1960 and 1967 in that he came to the DSP as a trade union leader and Diet member in the prewar period and served as secretary-general in the Katayama cabinet and vice-prime minister in the Ashida cabinet in the late 1940s. Considered an enemy by the Marxists of the JSP, he became the primary target of their attacks on the party's Right wing and was largely responsible for the decisions that led to the founding of the DSP. Nishio brought to the new party a power base largely concentrated in his Ōsaka home area.[17] After his retirement from parliamentary politics, the DSP lost all six of its Ōsaka house seats in the December 1972 general elections.

Nishio's successor, Nishimura Eiichi, a former insurance company manager, had served only four years in office when he died in 1971. Kasuga Ikkō, a writer and long-time party leader, was selected as party chairman in 1971 and kept the position until he suddenly and unexpectedly resigned in November 1977. Then, at the party's extraordinary convention held on November 28, 1977, the party's secretary-general, Sasaki Ryōsaku, was selected as chairman. Sasaki came from the position of secretary-general of the electrical workers' union and from a series of high-level DSP leadership positions. Kasuga was given the post of "permanent counselor," a position from which he continued to exercise great power in the party through his representative, Sasaki.

Kasuga is often mentioned in the Japanese vernacular press as having very close ties to some of the major LDP factions, especially those of Tanaka Kakuei and Fukuda Takeo, two former prime ministers. He is also referred to as being very close to the Kōmeitō leadership. Distinguished by his very strong opposition to the JCP and its leadership, Kasuga was the Diet member who broke the story on the prewar violence of the JCP chairman, Miyamoto Kenji. Much of Kasuga's anticommunism can be detected among the other leaders of the party. During the vote counting in the 1980 "double elections," newspaper reporters noted that the DSP leaders often showed more interest in the defeat of JCP candidates than in the fate of their own candidates.[18]

When four-term (eight-year) DSP chairman Sasaki decided to resign early in 1985, pressure for a restructuring of the party leadership was felt from the midlevel Diet members. Sasaki had indicated that he wanted a fifth term when he spoke at a party meeting held at a Tokyo hotel on January 25, but his statement met with a negative reaction from his opponents, who expected to hear his intention to resign.

Among the major reasons for the attacks on Sasaki was his unsuccessful part in the "Nikaidō coup" in the fall of 1984. DSP Diet members felt that he should have consulted them about the scheme and that he had been "used by Takeiri," the Kōmeitō chairman. Sasaki was apparently driven by his ambition to lead the DSP into a coalition government, and his desire to hold onto the party chairmanship fit into this unfulfilled ambition. Kasuga moved to force Sasaki out of the chairmanship as partial payment for Sasaki's failure to consult with the elder Kasuga prior to his commitment of the DSP to the Nikaidō scheme.

After it became apparent that Sasaki could not retain his post, he quickly installed two of his loyal lieutenants into key party posts. The late "boss" of the DSP, former party Chairman Kasuga, and Sasaki endorsed a leadership slate of Chairman Tsukamoto Saburō, Vice-Chairman Nagasue Eiichi, and Secretary-General Ōuchi Keigo. Nagasue, despite his advanced age of 67, came to be a spokesman for the rebellious middle-aged Diet members in their battle with the so-called Elders Group. The Elders Group was composed of Kasuga, Sasaki, and party Vice-Chairmen Kodaira Tadashi and Nakamura Masao. Tsukamoto was Kasuga's closest aide in the DSP, and Ōuchi has also been closely associated with Kasuga. Kasuga's critics have charged him with the selection of party leaders who are clearly subordinate to him and have suggested that if a coalition opportunity were to arise in the next two years, Kasuga would then move in to take control of "his party" and lead it into the government.

The selection of the new, young leadership was seen by some as the kind of personnel change the DSP needed to prepare itself for the late 1980s. Tsukamoto (57) and Ōuchi (55) were the first Shōwa era politicians to rise to the top three party posts. Ōuchi's selection was the one that drew the most serious opposition from the Nagasue critics. As Ōuchi was the youngest of the three, one would have expected him to be the most acceptable to the anti-Elders group. However, many within the DSP resent Ōuchi's personal style and, perhaps, even the fact that he is quite good-looking. The form of the anti-Ōuchi sentiment represented a protest against the way the nomination had been forced upon the party by the Elders. Ōuchi came out of the party ranks as a headquarters staff member specializing in political theory. As he had been elected to the Diet only four times, many felt that there were others with much more seniority who deserved the prestigious position of party secretary-general before Ōuchi. Whatever the precise reasons, there was considerable opposition to the Ōuchi nomination.

This opposition rallied around the person of Nagasue Eiichi, chairman of the Diet Policy Committee. Nagasue, at 67, strongly desired to be selected as party chairman himself and perhaps assumed that this was his last chance, especially given the nomination of such young men as Tsukamoto and Ōuchi. Among Nagasue's supporters were Kawamura Katsu (70), the deputy secretary-general; Nishida Hachirō (63), the vice-chairman of the Diet Policy Committee; and Yoshida Yukihisa (57), head of the Education and Propaganda Bureau. This group of senior leaders, having been elected to the Diet between six and eight times, eventually rallied a majority of junior- to middle-level Diet members (i.e., those elected three or four times to the Diet) who were the most unhappy with the role of Kasuga in the naming of the new leadership. These younger Diet members were also very critical of Sasaki's tendency not to deal with the junior members on a personal basis—a very serious complaint in Japanese political circles. They claimed that there was virtually no communication between Sasaki and themselves. The criticism reached crucial levels after Sasaki's mentor, Kasuga, advised the Nakasone cabinet to reshuffle and include DSP cabinet members. Supporters of this idea moved against Sasaki, who had backed Nikaidō in the ill-fated coup attempt of December 1984. They reasoned that as long as Sasaki led the DSP, Nakasone would avoid dealing with the DSP and thus abandon the proposed construction of a coalition government. Apparently, among these junior Diet members, there is near unanimous agreement that the future of the DSP lies in the breaking of the 1955 system through its joining with the LDP rather than through establishment of an opposition government based on the JSP-CGP and DSP. Sasaki had long been viewed as the primary sponsor of the Middle Party Coalition plan, and his replacement would facilitate the formal switch to the LDP-oriented line.

Sasaki complicated the confrontation by declaring in an angry moment that those who opposed his nominations would be expelled from the party and that DSP politicians born in the early Taishō era would be forced to retire from party leadership positions. One interesting characteristic of the DSP Diet membership was its aging nature. The DSP was clearly becoming an elderly party. Of the thirty-eight DSP Diet members holding office in the early summer of 1985, two were born during the reign of Emperor Meiji, seventeen in the Taishō era (1912–1925); and nineteen in the current Shōwa era. Sasaki's angry statements ran contrary to the placid history of the DSP and the general Japanese deference to seniority as important criteria for selection to leadership posts. Ultimately, Kasuga and Sasaki lobbied the junior Diet members on a one-on-one basis and reminded them of the favors and support they had received in the past from these party leaders.

In April, Tsukamoto and Nagasue met to fill out the key national party-appointed positions. Tsukamoto recommended that Ozawa Teiko be selected as the DSP Diet Policy Committee chairman, whereas Nagasue nominated Yoshida Yukihisa, the former Education and Propaganda Bureau chairman. Tsukamoto prevailed on this decision, and Watanabe Ryo was selected the head of the International Affairs Bureau.

Tsukamoto's career has been closely linked with his sponsor Kasuga. Both came from Nagoya, and Tsukamoto had served as secretary-general for eleven years under both Kasuga and Sasaki. Nagasue, on the other hand, came from Kyōto, and most of his supporters came from western Japan—hence the talk among Japanese politicians of the "western bloc" versus the "eastern bloc."

In late June another party elder, 71-year-old former Vice-Chairman Nakamura Masao, organized a party to honor the role played by Kasuga in the DSP. Only 31 of the 51 DSP Diet members were invited, and of that number 29 attended. The group decided to formalize itself by scheduling regular monthly meetings and by identifying itself as a "policy study group" similar to those found in the LDP. According to some accounts, the attending members were given 300,000 yen apiece as a special allowance.

A major characteristic of this "Kasuga faction" seems to be its loyalty to Kasuga. The policy implications of such budding factions are directly related to the question of whether the DSP should actively pursue a coalition with the LDP. Kasuga and his supporters continue to be eager to join the LDP in a coalition government—even if the LDP has a pure majority in the House of Representatives; Nagasue and his supporters, on the other hand, tend to be more reluctant to join the LDP in a coalition—especially if the LDP continues to maintain an absolute majority in the lower house.

Usami Tadanobu, the president of Dōmei, voiced his concern over this development at his group's regular meeting with DSP leadership in the second week of July 1986. Usami argued that the DSP must unite itself prior to the next general elections or face the prospect of electoral disaster.

By early 1985, the DSP began to reexamine its basic identity in an effort to come to grips with the possibility of joining the LDP in a coalition government. This effort included a reviewed study of the DSP platform and the basic premises behind the party and its democratic socialism. Some members of the DSP have wondered whether the party could ever grow to the size necessary to win control of the national government by advocating democratic socialism. These critics suggest that the word *socialist* should be dropped from the DSP name and platform, and insist on acknowledgment of the fact that the party was once basically conservative in nature, with a welfare and antinuclear weapons orientation. The party decided in late March 1985 that nothing dramatic would be done for the moment, but that intraparty discussions would be held in order to determine if a new party Action Policy was necessary.

The DSP had more rapid turnover in party leadership in the late 1980s than ever before in its history. Tsukamoto was a casualty of the Recruit Cosmos scandal in 1989 and was replaced as DSP chairman by Nagasue Eiichi. Nagasue had an interesting history as a former Imperial Navy paymaster who served with former Prime Minister Nakasone during World War II and survived the sinkings of several of the ships to which he was assigned. His Diet offices are decorated with ship models and navy mementos. However, when the DSP suffered a significant defeat in the February 1990 HR elections, there was a strong call for Nagasue to resign. He opened talks with two former DSP chairmen, Sasaki Ryōsaku and Tsukamoto Saburō, regarding his successor as party chairman. Nagasue supported his follower, DSP Secretary-General Yonezawa Takashi, while Tsukamoto touted his loyal supporter, former party Secretary General Ōuchi Keigo. Nagasue and Yonezawa were closely identified with the pro-JSP coalition electoral strategy, whereas Tsukamoto and Ōuchi believed the DSP should move closer to the LDP and seek a place in a future LDP government.[19]

After the talks were completed, the three leaders offered the party chairmanship to Yonezawa, who declined to accept, saying that he could not unify the party. Ōuchi was then selected as chairman; he came from the junior tier of DSP Diet members, having been elected only five times to the lower house. In fact, Ōuchi was out of the Diet between 1986 and 1990 when he failed to win his seat in his Tokyo Second constituency in the 1986 elections. During this time, he served as DSP secretary-general despite not having a seat in the Diet. Ōuchi is often referred to as a "star" by the Japanese media. He is youthful in appearance, often eloquent as a speaker, and a graduate of the prestigious Waseda University School of Law. Yonezawa is considered the probable next party leader if Ōuchi is forced to step down.[20]

Because of the DSP's weak organization and regional nature, its national headquarters exerts very little centralized control over its prefectural components. Closer in style to the JSP and LDP, the real power structures in the party seem to be based on the personal organizations of the party politicians. Thus, the DSP is characterized more by a "politics of personality" than by a "politics of faction." Regardless of who leads the DSP, the party chairperson is not an all-powerful force in the party organization.

In 1989, the DSP collected a total of 8.1 billion yen in political funds—about one-fifth of the total formally reported by the LDP (not counting the LDP factional fund-raising) and approximately two-thirds of the JSP fund-raising. The DSP's largest contributors continued to be its old Dōmei labor union supporters, who channel money through an organization called Yūai Kaigi.

Other than the LDP, the DSP is the only party to be heavily supported by "corporated Japan." The DSP fund-raising organization, Seiwa Kyōkai, raised over 800 million yen, largely from business, in 1989. Of the 11 associations that donated 50 million yen or more, 9 gave money to the DSP; included in this group was the Tokyo Stock Exchange Regular Members Association, which donated 33.2 million yen. Nineteen of the top 20 corporate political funds donors gave money to the DSP, usually in relatively small amounts of less than 7 million yen. This pattern of corporate support has existed since the birth of the party, according to DSP leaders.[21]

ELECTORAL FORTUNES AND CAMPAIGN STRATEGIES

After its formation, the DSP was the third largest party in the Japanese Diet, with 40 seats in the House of Representatives and 17 in the House of Councillors. During the next twenty years, the DSP was never able to regain these record seat totals. In fact, it had trouble surviving even the first general election campaign held in November 1960. Only 17 of the party's 40 incumbent Diet members survived the election, and not a single nonincumbent was elected. The party subsequently began a slow climb back toward its original levels. This DSP disaster was explained by party leadership as being a result of the electorate's sympathy for the JSP following the assassination of JSP Chairman Asanuma Inejirō. The weak DSP party organization was also blamed for the dismal showing in which only 17 of 105 candidates were elected.

In the 1963 general elections, the DSP leadership changed its strategy and sharply reduced to 59 the number of its candidates running in targeted districts. Twenty-three were elected in 1963; 30 and 31 DSP candidates were victorious in 1967 and 1969, respectively. However, the 1972 general election proved to be another disaster for the DSP: Only 19 of 65 DSP candidates were elected. This election saw the Japanese Communist party increase its seats by 271 percent to a new total of 38. Many of these JCP gains were won at the expense of the DSP, which was a victim of the JCP's organizational superiority and strategic campaign attacks. An additional factor compounded the 1972 losses: The party founder, Nishio, retired and his Ōsaka stronghold votes shifted to other parties. Four years later the DSP responded to the JCP challenge directly, reduced its selected candidates to only 51, and won 29 seats. (The JCP, incidentally, slumped to 17 seats in the 1976 elections.) The pair of elections that closed out the 1970s and opened the 1980s confirmed the ability of the DSP to hold 30 or more seats (35 seats in October 1979 and 32 in June 1980).[22] In 1983 the DSP won 38 seats, thereby nearly returning to its pre-1960 level. This gradual rise in the number of DSP House of Representatives seats was accomplished on a very steady proportion of the total vote. The DSP total vote percentage in the House of Representatives elections peaked in 1960 (its first contested election), reached a later but lower peak in 1969, and remained at around 6.5 percent throughout the 1970s. In 1986 the DSP won 8.78 percent of the vote, but fell to only 4.84 percent in the 1990 House of Representatives elections.

In terms of absolute vote totals the DSP has stayed in the 3 to 4 million vote range in election after election. One partial explanation for its failure to attract an increasing percentage or absolute number of votes stems from the conservative strategy of the party limiting the number of candidates it offers the electorate. In most constituencies, Japanese voters simply do not have a DSP candidate to vote for—even when they want to vote for the DSP. The JCP, on the other hand, has followed the strategy of running a candidate in every one of the 130 lower house constituencies, thus picking up many protest votes nationwide but diluting the organization's resources in many futile races. In 1983 the JCP won nearly 1.2 million more votes than the DSP, but twelve fewer seats.

A second reason for the DSP consistency in vote totals has to do with the agreements it has forged with the Kōmeitō and other parties to jointly support candidates in constituencies when it is advantageous to do so. This policy of cooperation with the Kōmeitō began formally in 1979 and was renewed through the 1990 elections. It actually began on an informal level in unannounced decisions on the prefectural level in the 1976 general elections. During the 1979 campaign, the DSP and the Kōmeitō cooperated in 28 constituencies, with each party running 14 candidates. The results were 19 wins (DSP 8 and Kōmeitō 11) and 9 losses (DSP 6 and Kōmeitō 3). The Minshatō leadership reportedly believed that the cooperation produced three additional seats for the party. Cooperation agreements were struck with the Kōmeitō and other parties for the 1980 House of Councillors elections but were greatly complicated by the surprise simultaneous upper and lower house elections held in June 1980. In these elections, the various opposition parties cooperated in 43 constituencies involving 44 candidates, half of whom were successful. Of the 22 winning candidates receiving joint party support in 1980, 7 were DSP incumbents. In 1983 there was cooperation in 34 constituencies, and 11 DSP candidates were victorious. In 1986 and 1990 cooperation strategies proved to be relatively unsuccessful for the DSP, as it won only 26 and 14 seats, respectively.

The upper house of the Japanese Diet has proved to be a difficult area for the DSP. In the ten House of Councillors elections held between 1962 and 1989 (inclusive), the DSP won 7 seats twice and 6 seats three times. In the national constituency of the House of Councillors, all 4 DSP candidates won in 1983; indeed, the party had won 4 seats in that constituency in each of the five previous elections. The DSP strategy has been to allocate its four candidates their supporting Dōmei labor unions. Given the fact that the national constituency candidates in 1983 polled only 3.8 million votes and the last successful candidate needed 832,775 votes, it is unlikely that another DSP candidate could have been elected.

The four successful 1983 DSP House of Councillors national constituency PR candidates won a total of 3,888,429 votes. Totaling the votes won by these four in Tokyo, Kanagawa, Aichi, and Ōsaka, we find that the party won just about the same number of votes in each of these prefectures—that is, between 262,000 (Kanagawa), and 380,000 (Ōsaka). The four winners finished 8th, 19th, 30th, and 43rd, respectively, among the 50 successful candidates. Under this election system, the DSP appeared to be running the perfect number of candidates given its national vote-drawing performances.

However, in the 1986 and 1989 HC national constituency elections, the DSP's seat-winning abilities declined sharply. In 1986 the DSP candidates slipped to 3 seats in the national constituency and then dropped to only 2 seats in 1989. Between the 1983 and the 1989 elections, DSP national constituency vote totals declined by 1.1 million votes down to 2.7 million votes. The DSP's unsuccessful third-ranked candidate fell more than 70,000 votes behind the 50th and last successful candidate from the JSP.

The local constituency of the House of Councillors represents an even more disadvantageous arena for DSP candidates. Only once in its history (1968) has the DSP been able to capture 3 seats in the HC local constituency. In 1986 the DSP won only two seats and only a single seat in 1989 (Nagoya).

A summary of the electoral data in this section is as follows: The DSP has been able to win about 5 percent of the seats in both the House of Representatives and the House of Councillors, a percentage roughly proportional to the party's share of the total vote cast. The DSP also continues to be relatively weak in terms of seats it wins on the subnational level in city, town, and prefectural assemblies. As of 1990, the DSP had 909 subnational seats, a decline of approximately 50 from its total in the mid-1980s. In comparison, seat totals for the other opposition parties were CGP, 3,476; JCP, 3,941; and JSP, 3,354.[23] As lower-level assembly seats often form the base of a political party in a city or a prefecture, it can be seen that the DSP's extremely weak base contributes to its weakness as a national party as well.

Frequently the DSP has joined in a coalition with the LDP to elect prefectural governors. In 1990, 31 of the 47 prefectural governors were jointly supported by the LDP, DSP, and other opposition parties.

The most important political change in the last decade in terms of a short-term negative impact on the DSP has been the rise of Rengō (Japan Trade Union Confederation), formed in the late 1980s by a merger of the Dōmei and the Sōhyō labor confederations. As noted previously, Dōmei had been the foundation of the DSP since the latter's founding in 1960, and Sōhyō played the same role for the JSP during this time.

The merger of these two longtime labor rivals caused some confusion regarding the nature of the appropriate campaign support for the two Socialist parties. Rengō focused initially on the details of establishing a huge new consolidated labor confederation formed by the joining of two powerful rivals. Other considerations, such as preference of political parties to support in elections, were tabled until the structural details were settled. Consequently, Rengō decided to run its own candidates in the 1989 upper house elections and postpone the tough political decisions on which of the two Socialist parties it would choose. Of the 12 Rengō candidates who ran in the HC prefectural districts in the July 1989 elections, 11 were successful and largely contributed to the inflicting of the first national-level election defeat on the LDP in those elections. Following this unexpected victory, Rengō talked about running candidates in as many as 47 districts in the 1990 HR elections. However, only 4 Rengō candidates were run in Ōsaka, Hyōgo, and Gunma prefectures. The two Ōsaka candidates were also supported by the JSP, DSP, and SDF, but fell an average of 3,500 votes short of winning seats. In contrast with the 1989 HC results, only one of the Rengō candidates (Hyōgo 5th) was successful in 1990.[24]

Not only was Rengō unable to elect its own candidates to the HR, but it was unable to support many of the DSP candidates the Dōmei had helped to elect in so many previous elections. The LDP reacted to its 1989 HC loss by pressuring Japanese businesses into forcing their labor unions to support LDP candidates in the 1990 elections. This was a successful strategy, for two major Rengō unions—JR Sōren (General Federation of Japan Railroad Unions) and Shōgyō Rōren (Federation of Commercial Labor Unions)—openly supported the LDP.[25] The automobile workers' unions, which had been strong DSP supporters since the 1960s, were placed under impressive pressure by Japan's automobile companies to support individual LDP candidates. DSP candidates from various parts of Japan reported that they were not receiving the same support from automobile unions and companies that they had enjoyed in previous elections. Both Nissan and Toyota, along with several hundred other corporations, were strongly asked to support the LDP, and they issued appeals to all their branches, plants, and sales networks throughout the nation to support LDP candidates.[26] As a result of this successful

LDP strategy and the Rengō confusion, 18 of the DSP's candidates finished as runners-up in their districts. Twenty-one DSP candidates lost by an average of over 18,000 votes behind the final seat winners. Only 6 DSP candidates lost by 5,000 votes or less. With only 14 DSP HR winners in 1990 and its losing candidates so weak, clearly a great deal of work remained to be accomplished to return the DSP to the rank of the fourth largest party in the Diet.

Rengō was still trying to establish its own political identity in late 1990, leaving the DSP's future very uncertain. Rengō's president, Yamagishi Akira, admitted that the labor confederation had not been ready for a lower house election in 1990. He estimated that only about half of its political potential was used in the 1990 elections due to a lack of regional and local organizations throughout Japan and a failure to establish a clear political stance. After the February elections, Rengō appointed a special political committee to study the questions of which political party or parties it should support and how it should be involved in elections in the future. Until these questions are clearly resolved, the DSP's future cannot be predicted. For example, it is not impossible that Rengō may decide to support only one opposition party and force the DSP to reunite with the JSP. Corporate Japan did this in 1955 and set the stage for the next thirty-five years of Japanese politics. Perhaps the newly reunified labor world will try to accomplish the same thing in the 1990s.

POPULAR SUPPORT FOR THE DSP

There are several ways to measure popular support for a political party in a democratic society. First and most obviously, the vote-drawing power of the party can be clearly seen in the vote totals it accumulates in the various electoral arenas. Second, the various responses to public opinion poll questions can be used to probe into the motivations and reasons for support of a party. Both of these methods will be discussed in the following section in relation to the reasons for which the DSP has never been able to fulfill its potential in Japanese politics.

We have already examined certain electoral data in the preceding section. In terms of aggregate totals of votes received in national elections, the DSP has been remarkably consistent. In election after election (1990 excepted), it has won about 3.5 to 4 million votes nationally and collected about 5 to 7 percent of the total vote. These totals are somewhat misleading, however—especially when compared with the party's archrival, the JCP. It has long been the policy for the JCP to run candidates in each of the 130 constituencies for propaganda purposes. Most of these candidates have no chance to win, and many lose their election deposits because they draw so few votes. But in every district they win some protest votes and some votes from their regular supporters. The DSP has a policy of running candidates only in those districts in which the leadership has determined that a reasonable chance for victory exists. Thus, many DSP supporters never have a chance to cast a House of Representatives ballot for their party's candidate. Accordingly, one might be led to speculate that if the party ran more candidates, its voting percentage might increase by at least 2 or 3 percent. That seems a reasonable argument, but there is one area of politics in which all the nation's voters have a chance to cast a vote for a DSP national-level politician—the national constituency of the House of Councillors. When the DSP House of Representatives vote totals are compared to the DSP House of Councillors vote totals, an interesting pattern emerges. For instance, the DSP won a maximum of 3.9 million votes nationwide in the 1986 House of Councillors national constituency elections—that is, about 6.9 percent of the total votes cast in these races. Hence the DSP won about the same percentage of the vote in both types of races. One explanation for this pattern is that the candidates the DSP runs in the national constituency are selected primarily as labor union candidates and allocated to groups of DSP supporter unions. The appeal of these candidates is thus not very great to average voters, who usually vote for much more attractive candidates running as independents in affiliation with other parties, even if those voters are DSP supporters.

In 1983 the DSP won 39 seats in lower house races. Thirty-eight of those seats came under the DSP label and one (Aichi Fifth) was an independent-DSP candidate. Aichi prefecture is especially important to the DSP because it is the home of many of the companies whose unions are supporters of the party. Five of the party's 39 HR seats and one-third of its upper house local constituency seats are found in Aichi (Nagoya) prefecture. The DSP earned 18.8 percent of the total vote in the prefecture in 1983—the highest DSP percentage in the nation. The 1986 and 1990 HR elections were disasters for the DSP in this Aichi stronghold. DSP seats in Aichi prefecture dropped to 4 in 1986 and sank to only 2 in 1990. In Aichi First and Second constituencies where DSP candidates won in 1986, they were losers in 1990 by 15,000 and 9,000 votes, respectively. In Aichi Third, the 1986 DSP runner-up fell 11,000 votes short of winning a seat in the HR in 1990. Clearly, the DSP must act to shore up its labor union support in Aichi or face the prospect of the disappearance of its electoral foundation.

Strangely, the DSP is at its best seat-winning power in the highly congested metropolitan constituencies, but it is also stronger than all of the other opposition parties, except the JSP, in the semirural districts. The DSP is the number-five party in the metropolitan areas, trailing the LDP, CGP, JCP, and JSP, but it is the third most successful party in the semirural district, trailing only the "big two" parties. As with all of the other opposition parties (except the JSP), it has very little success in the real Japanese countryside, but even there it does four times better than any of the other "middle-ground" parties.

According to newspaper public opinion polls, about 4 to 5 percent of the Japanese public support the DSP. These figures would correspond almost perfectly to the vote percentages won by the party in national-level elections. However, one must indeed be careful when reading the different newspaper polls regarding public support for parties because each newspaper has a different method of aggregating the responses. The *Yomiuri Shimbun* polls, for example, showed the DSP receiving only about 3 percent public support in early 1982, but the poll also found that of the 32 percent who did not support a party, 5.4 percent selected the DSP as the party toward which they were favorably inclined.[27] Thus, the total of DSP supporters (though their levels of support varied) was about 8.5 percent. The *Yomiuri* poll, as well, revealed the segments of the population among which the DSP was particularly weak: women, youth (20–30 years old), and elderly citizens (70 years plus). About 10 percent of the DSP supporters supported the party "very strongly," and another 56.1 percent supported it "somewhat strongly." Yet another 33 percent supported it "not strongly"—a category that may be similar to the *Asahi* poll's "leaners," who were noted earlier. These subtotals for the intensity of support for the DSP are remarkably similar to those recorded by the entire sample for all the parties collectively.

In the *Mainichi Shimbun* poll, the DSP support levels remained at about 3 percent during most of the 1970s until just after the October 1979 elections. Between September and December 1979, DSP support doubled from 3 percent to 6 percent. What accounted for this rise in support? First, the October 1979 elections, which resulted in a near dead heat between the LDP and the opposition parties in the lower house, caused the voters to become concerned about the prospects of a coalition government in the near future. The DSP apparently picked up the support of many who had been in the "no party" category and then decided to support the moderate DSP. Among those people who have become alienated from the LDP over the years are intellectuals and self-employed persons in the fishing or forestry professions who had occasionally voted for the JCP as a protest vote in the past but, when the LDP-opposition balance became a reality in 1979, began to look for a moderate alternative. An *Asahi Shimbun* poll in October 1976 found that only 17.6 percent of DSP supporters were industrial workers. In fact, more industrial workers supported the LDP, JSP, and Kōmeitō than the DSP. Clerical workers (36 percent) constituted the largest DSP support group; self-employed businessmen (19.1 percent) made up the second largest group.

The *Mainichi* poll released on June 12, 1980, just before the "double election," reveals both the problems and the potential of the DSP.[28] See Table 7.1 for the responses to the two interesting questions asked. It is interesting to note that one question revolves around what became of the missing 5 to 6 percent who supported the DSP and then did not plan to vote for it. The answer seems to lie in the combination of two facts: (1) the DSP's decision not to run candidates in most of the House of Representatives districts and to run some in only four House of Councillors (local) districts, and (2) the lack of attractive candidates running under the DSP label in the national constituency. In addition, many voters in HR races, though they might have been DSP supporters, may not have found their DSP candidate an attractive choice.

DSP Policy Positions

Upon examining the original DSP platform of January 24, 1960, one would discover a very moderate set of principles and policy positions. While

TABLE 7.1
Public opinion preferences regarding parties' electoral success

1.	The advance of which political party do you think will be desirable in connection with the elections for both houses?	
	Responses:	
	LDP	40%
	JSP	20%
	DSP	10%
	CGP	6%
	JCP	5%
	NLC	3%
	SDF	2%
	Other	5%
2.	In the elections, which party do you intend to vote for?	
	DSP Responses:	
	House of Representatives	5%
	Councillors (Prefectural)	4%
	Councillors (National)	5%

Source: Adapted from *Mainichi Shimbun,* (June 12, 1980).

professing a belief in "democratic socialism" and a triumph over both capitalism and communism, the DSP from its very birth has been a moderate party relative to the Japanese political spectrum. Among its list of basic principles are a stress on the dignity of the individual, the maximum expansion of civil liberties, the realization of a socialist society within the context of parliamentary democracy, and the rejection of "revolution by violence and . . . dictatorship, either of the left or of the right." The socialism sought by the DSP is a welfare socialism of a "minimum level of living for the people from the cradle to the grave."[29]

In terms of current domestic policies, the DSP shares very similar positions with the other opposition parties and the LDP. As one senior DSP leader said in an interview, the policy similarities among the parties are like a single bottle of wine that is marketed under seven different labels.[30] The parties differ most over the issue of atomic energy for electric power generation and the issue of election law reform. On the one hand, the DSP supports greater utilization of atomic energy in Japan than does the Kōmeitō; on the other, although the Kōmeitō wants to eliminate corporate contributions to political parties, the DSP, heavily supported by corporate Japan, opposes such a reform.[31] The major policy differences between the DSP and JSP center on the latter party's willingness to cooperate with the JCP and on its opposition to nuclear power and to the Japan-U.S. Security Treaty.

Following the October 1979 general elections, the DSP began to negotiate with the Kōmeitō for a possible "coalition government" agreement. The DSP's draft of its policy proposals provides an excellent outline of its major policy objectives. The following are paraphrased excerpts from that DSP draft:

1. Break down the money-is-everything corrupt politics and open the realization of politics to the people. Promote the thorough-going

publication of political funds, the expansion of public management of elections, the correction of the imbalance in the fixed number of seats for election districts, the enactment of a law for the publication of information, and the strengthening of the right to investigate the national administration.

2. Thoroughly reform the administration and finances aiming at "simplification, service, and fairness." Reform the structure of the central government, merge and abolish the branch offices, special corporations, councils, etc., and re-scrutinize the subsidies, the reduction of the number of public service personnel, and their relocation. Decentralize power to local districts.
3. Realize the five-year plan for the improvement of welfare and a basic annuity system. Expand the construction of public housing, secure the political neutrality of education, and establish a lifelong education system.
4. Construct nuclear power plants, with the agreement of the local inhabitants. Maintain the Japan-U.S. Security Treaty. Strictly limit the Self-Defense Forces to defense under strengthened civilian control.[32]

The major policy shift performed by the DSP leadership has occurred in the area of defense policy. The initial party position on the Self-Defense Forces (SDF) and the Japan-U.S. Security Treaty was that "minimum measures to defend our country with our own strength should be taken until a complete disarmament agreement is concluded." By 1977 the DSP had shifted to firmer support of the SDF. Its "action policy for 1977" stated that "We shall *build up* a military set-up exclusively for defense on the basis of a national consensus. At the same time, the Japan-U.S. mutual security arrangement will be made supplementary to this defense force."[33]

By 1980 the DSP leadership had become almost hawkish on the defense issue. In October of that year, the DSP Policy Study Council declared that Japan defense expenditures should no longer be limited to 1 percent of the GNP, and in 1982 party Secretary-General Tsukamoto Saburō urged a sharp increase in the 1982 defense budget. Another indication of the DSP shift on the defense issue can be seen in the selection of Kurisu Hiromi, the former chairman of the Joint Staff of the Self-Defense Forces and the nation's highest-ranking uniformed defense official, to be the party's candidate for the Tokyo constituency in the 1980 House of Councillors elections.

At the party's 1982 national convention, the "activity policy" adopted for 1982 supported closer Japan-U.S. cooperation in defense areas as well as a mutual sharing of the defense burden. When the Defense Agency issued its 1982 White Paper on defense, which strongly supported increased Japanese commitments in defense, the DSP was the only opposition party that supported its conclusions. The DSP's commitment to building up Japanese military forces has become so strong that the *Japan Times* was prompted to comment editorially that the "present DSP leadership often sounds more insistent on the need for a major defense buildup than even the LDP right wingers."[34]

What accounts for this change in DSP leadership attitudes on the defense issue from one of a grudging acceptance of a minimum defense force to one of enthusiastic support of a major Japanese military buildup? DSP leaders have stressed several points in their explanation of the party's stronger support of the SDF. First, they noted that the fear many Japanese had of becoming accidentally involved in some U.S. war largely disappeared with the ending of the Vietnam War. Second, they noted that the Soviet Union and the People's Republic of China (PRC) have not really criticized the current Japan-U.S. Security Treaty, and that the threat from these two nations is more significant than any possible deterioration in relations with these nations that could result from such a buildup.[35] In addition, former party Chairman Sasaki Ryōsaku has suggested that the party is using as its model the Social Democratic party of West Germany, which successfully rose to political power by supporting German rearmament in 1959. As the Japanese public opinion seems to be moving toward stronger support for the SDF, the DSP believes it can profit politically from such a position.

In any case, we must realize that the DSP leadership is strongly anticommunist and that a gradual acceptance of such a commitment to join with the United States to defend the northwest Pacific from the Soviet Union is a natural tendency for such a party orientation. Some Japanese political analysts point out that the DSP's leaders have been hawks on defense issues since the party's birth but found the political climate unfavorable to such positions in the 1960s. Clearly, these leaders believe that support for defense is an issue whose time has come.

DSP support for a strong Japanese defense appears to have survived the disintegration of the communist bloc in the early 1990s. When the Persian Gulf crisis erupted in late 1990, Prime Minister Kaifu asked the Diet to support a bill to permit Japanese Self-Defense Forces to be deployed to Saudi Arabia in support of the U.S.-led military deployment to force Iraq out of Kuwait. The bill eventually died in late 1990 due to JSP and JCP opposition, but the DSP indicated to the LDP that it was sympathetic on that question.

DSP POLICY POSITIONS AND THE PROSPECTS OF AN LDP-DSP COALITION

Following the dismal showing of the LDP in the October 1979 general elections, there was a great deal of speculation in the Japanese press regarding possible coalition partners for the conservatives if in the following election they failed to secure a simple majority in the lower house after independents joined the LDP. Some political analysts began to study the possible areas of conflict between the LDP and its most likely coalitional partner, the DSP.

In late 1979 and early 1980, the DSP began to formulate a list of its demands to be presented to the LDP if the latter party was in need of a coalition partner. Of course, the precise nature of such a coalition would depend on the unique political situation existing following such an election. The major demands contemplated by the DSP during this time were as follows: First, the DSP would demand that the LDP institute a reform of the electoral laws, especially in the area of political finance. Included in this political reform would be a freedom-of-information act and changes in the election laws to allow increased media advertising in campaigns. Second, the DSP would demand administrative reforms on the local-government level as well as a reduction in the number of public officials, including public corporations. Third, the LDP would have to support an annual plan of welfare in the "Japanese style." Such a plan would be a combination of public and private (family and corporate) support programs for the nation's needy.[36]

Historically, the major difference between the DSP and the LDP centered on the Japan-U.S. Security Treaty issue. Originally, the DSP was in favor of a gradual abolishment of the security treaty; but when it sensed a greater chance of attaining power, it modified its stand on the treaty. The DSP now supports the continuation of the treaty. As a result of this policy shift, there were no longer any major policy obstacles to a DSP-LDP coalition government.

Upon surveying the public regarding what form of government is desired in the future, the major Japanese newspapers have found that most respondents indicate a strong desire to experience some form of moderate to conservative coalition government. According to a *Sankei Shimbun* poll published just prior to the 1990 HR elections, only 19 percent of the Japanese public supported a one-party LDP government. Fifty-four percent wanted an LDP–opposition parties coalition government; only 14 percent wanted a coalition of opposition parties.[37]

With the disappearance of the NLC, the most logical pairing for a conservative-moderate coalition would appear to be the LDP and the DSP. The polls also indicate that the other opposition parties have serious problems of negative public images. The Kōmeitō, for instance, is afflicted with the negative image of the Sōka Gakkai, whereas the JSP is considered too ideological to participate in the effective government of the country. With the JSP absolutely eliminated as an LDP coalition party and the NLC gone the only logical choice is the DSP. The June 1980 elections indicated that as the political situation edged closer either to opposition party control of the Diet or a coalition government, the voters tended to return to the LDP. The DSP was not invited into a coalition with the LDP in 1983, but it is still ready and eager to join if the opportunity presents itself in future elections.

If, however, the DSP cannot join the LDP in a coalition government (its best and most realistic chance for future political power), then its normal fall-back public position has been one of seeking to form a middle-of-the-road party coalition with the Kōmeitō and SDF. The JSP's participation is assumed, as well, as such participation is dictated by the sheer numbers necessary to form a government. The moderate party coalition idea was first proposed by then DSP Chairman Nishimura Eiichi in June 1970, when he called on all opposition parties except the JCP to work toward the establishment of a coalition government. Chairman Sasaki Ryōsaku became the prime mover behind the same idea during the October 1979–June 1980 interelection period, when the LDP had a bare majority in the House of

Representatives.[38] The DSP, in its 1982 national convention, reaffirmed as the party's central strategy (at least for the public consumption) the seeking of a close alliance with the moderate-center parties. Many DSP members publicly criticized such a policy line, however. Some objected to such close cooperation with the Kōmeitō; others pointed to the failure of such an alliance in recent Diet sessions.

Such a plan for a middle-of-the-road coalition government is unrealistic in terms of the reality of the Diet membership of the parties involved. As of this writing (1991), the three moderate parties (DSP, CGP, and SDF) have only 81 seats in the lower house. Because they need 256 seats to form a government without LDP help, the task of these small parties is clearly hopeless in almost any possible future scenario. They simply have no realistic chance of gaining power by themselves. Consequently, when the DSP talks about the opposition parties forming a coalition government in the future, one should interpret that to mean either coalition with the LDP if that ruling party loses its pure majority or coalition with a significant part of the LDP if that party splits in the future.

Indeed, in April 1990 the DSP leadership made a strategic decision of potentially great significance. It decided to pull out of discussions to form a coalition government with the JSP, CGP, and SDF and to begin internal discussions on moving toward a coalition government with the LDP. The new DSP leadership argued that there was little prospect that the JSP would adopt sufficiently realistic defense and security policies in the foreseeable future. Additionally, the DSP admitted that it had little in common with the religious political party, the CGP. At least for the short term, the Ōuchi leadership was committing the DSP to moving closer to the LDP and the abandoning of the policy line that had dominated the DSP during the 1970s and 1980s.

THE DSP: PARTY OF THE FUTURE OR OF THE PAST?

The crucial question regarding the DSP is whether it peaked in power the year it was formed or whether its brightest days are still ahead of it in terms of a future role in governing Japan, in coalition either with the LDP or with other opposition parties. When the DSP celebrated the twentieth anniversary of its founding in 1980, the *Mainichi Shimbun* began to wonder about the future of a party that had undergone "more downs than ups in the past two decades." The newspaper also recalled the statement of the party's founder, Nishio Suehirō, in which he noted that a "political party incapable of seizing power is like a cat which cannot catch a mouse."[39] In this respect, the DSP has been hungry for over thirty years and cannot reasonably expect to be fed in the foreseeable future.

If, as Nishio said, the purpose of political parties is to capture public offices and government, the DSP has been largely unsuccessful.[40] However, if one attributes other purposes or functions to a party in performance under a given political system, then that party can be seen as making very significant contributions to that system. Clearly, the DSP performs some very significant functions in Japan. First, it offers the potential for moderate rule if the LDP fails to secure a majority in the Diet in some future election. Many voters have become unhappy with the LDP leadership as a result of the party's long series of scandals; the removal of complete power from the LDP while retaining conservative policies, then, may seem an attractive option to many voters in a given election. The DSP stands ready to offer such a continuation of conservative policies. Given an opposition dominated by a religious party (Kōmeitō), a Communist party, a party generally thought to be an irresponsible Socialist party (JSP), and a splinter party of insignificant size, the strategic value of having a moderate opposition party ready to join a ruling coalition is a positive feature of any parliamentary system.

The DSP also serves the role of criticizing the errors of the LDP leadership. In this sense, it functions as the "loyal opposition" in the constructive sense of the idea. It has followed the tradition of approving of what is good in the LDP policies and opposing what is felt to be not good. It is often said that the number-one opposition party, the JSP, follows a policy of opposing any policy advocated by the LDP merely because it is the main opposition party—and, indeed, it has so defined its role.

Yet to many Japanese, the image of the DSP is a blurry one. To some, it is just a "second LDP"; to others it represents the moderate wing of the progressive camp and, hence, an alternative to the conservative rule of the LDP. A major problem of the DSP is that the Japanese people do not really understand what "democratic socialism" means in a Japanese context. The DSP is not a major force in Japanese politics at present. It has usually been ranked as the number-four party in terms of Diet seats, and its numbers have not been crucial in national-level politics since its formation in 1960. If the party is to become a major force on its own, it must begin to act like a major party. In other words, it must expand beyond its former Dōmei base, build an organization throughout the nation, and run candidates in more than the current 50 of the nation's 130 House districts. Fuji Tsuneo, the chairman of the party's Election Policy Committee in 1980, concluded that the party had the resources to run candidates in at least 80 districts. Fuji also noted that the DSP had the attitude of a businessperson: "We need to shift our attitude from that of a medium or small company to that of a large one."[41]

Many media commentators on politics and parties refer to the DSP as the opposition party with the most potential. Gary Allinson, for example, in his 1972 study of organized labor in Japan, appears to have concluded that the DSP has a great future inasmuch as Japanese labor moderated its political views in the 1970s.[42] But the more common evaluation is one similar to that of Nishihira Sigeki, who wrote in 1977 that "looking at the activity of the DSP, it is apparent that unless some revolutionary change occurs, the party cannot expect to make the jump to major party status."[43] That, indeed, is where the DSP stands in the early 1990s: as a party with potential but unable, because of its own limitations and given the circumstances of Japanese politics, to bring that potential to reality.

The immediate goal of the DSP must be the survival of the party after the disaster of the 1990 HR elections. Its mere 14 seats placed it in the same power position as the NLC faced a decade earlier, and the DSP should reflect upon the fact that the NLC dissolved in 1986. To become a significant actor in the Japanese national level of politics, the DSP must return its HR seat totals to the high 20s or 30s. To achieve this, it is essential for the party to win the political support of Rengō. If this cannot be achieved, the DSP's likely fate would be a merger with either the LDP or a return to the JSP.

NOTES

1. See the *Asahi Shimbun* series on rising young politicians in Japan, reprinted in the *Asahi Evening News* (October 18, 1980).
2. Ibid.
3. Koichi Kishimoto, *Politics in Modern Japan* (Tokyo: Japan Echo, 1982), p. 96.
4. "This Is Dōmei" (booklet provided by Dōmei, December 1979).
5. *Asahi Shimbun* (November 21 and 27, 1989).
6. Ministry of Labor, "Labor Union Survey" (June 30, 1981).
7. See "This Is Dōmei."
8. Interview at Dōmei headquarters (December 14, 1979).
9. Nobuo Tomita et al., "Japanese Politics at a Crossroads," *Bulletin of the Institute of Social Sciences* (Meiji University) 1, no. 3 (1978), p. 17.
10. *Japan Times* (November 4, 1979).
11. Bando Satoshi, "Undo no Shitsu Teki Tenkan Semaru Rodosha no Ishiki Henka" [Qualitative changes in political orientations of Japanese labor], *Shūkan Tōyō Keizai* (October 25, 1981), pp. 51–55.
12. Interview at Dōmei headquarters (December 14, 1979).
13. Tamura Yuzō, "Dakyo kara Ukeika e'" [From conciliations to consideration], *Sekai* (December 1981), pp. 45–52.
14. Much of the material for this and other sections of the chapter on the DSP came from a series of interviews at the DSP headquarters in Tokyo, the offices of various DSP Diet members, and the headquarters of Dōmei. Although the LDP receives many foreign visitors and scholars, the DSP has very little experience with foreign scholars. No one at the DSP headquarters could recall having seen a foreign scholar interested in the everyday operation of the party. The author wishes to thank the DSP officials who gave me their valuable time in answering my long series of questions. My sincere appreciation also goes to the officials at the Dōmei headquarters. Any errors of interpretation are the sole responsibility of the author. For summaries of the activities of the DSP, see Imazu Hiroshi, "The Democratic Socialist Party," *Japan Quarterly* 24, no. 2 (April-June 1977), pp. 163–166; and Kishimoto, *Politics in Modern Japan*, pp. 115–120.
15. Among the major religious organizations that have supported the DSP in recent elections are the following: Rissho Kōseikai (4.7 million members), Seicho no Ie (3.1 million), Reiyukai (2.7 million), "Perfect Liberty" (2.6 million), and Myochikai (680,000). Sekai Kyūsei Kyō supported all DSP local candidates and national-level independents recommended by the DSP, together with two LDP national-level candidates, in the 1977 House of Councillors elections (see *Asahi Shimbun* [January 8,

1980]). It has been estimated that the first three of the above-mentioned organizations have a total of between 2 and 2.5 million voters within their membership ranks.

16. *Nihon Keizai Shimbun* (March 26, 1990), and *Tokyo Report* (May 2, 1990).

17. When Nishio Suehirō died in October 1981, newspaper obituaries used the term *unlucky politician* to describe him in relation to his career. For an interesting summary of the life of this important Japanese political figure, see Yuzō, "Dayko kara 'ukeika e.'"

18. *Asahi Shimbun* (June 24, 1980).

19. *Nihon Keizai Shimbun* (March 26, 1990).

20. *Tokyo Shimbun* (April 2, 1990).

21. Political Funds Control Law, Annual Report for FY 1989.

22. MacDougall, "Asukata Ichio," pp. 54, 64.

23. *A Handbook of Local Autonomies* (Tokyo: Ministry of Home Affairs, 1990).

24. *Japan Times* (February 6, 1990).

25. *Sankei Shimbun* (April 12, 1990).

26. *Mainichi Shimbun* (April 11, 1990).

27. *Yomiuri Shimbun* (February 28, 1982).

28. *Mainichi Shimbun* (June 12, 1980).

29. *This Is Minshatō* (Tokyo: DSP International Department, 1977), p. 28.

30. Interview with Umezawa-san of the DSP (December 6, 1979).

31. The differences expressed over the development of atomic energy in Japan between the Kōmeitō and the DSP are just a matter of degree: The DSP would have liked to see more electricity generated by atomic energy by now than the Kōmeitō would have.

32. *Yomiuri Shimbun* (December 2, 1979).

33. *This Is Minshatō*, p. 28.

34. *Japan Times* (February 24, 1982).

35. DSP interview, DSP Headquarters (Tokyo staff), n.d.

36. Ibid.

37. *Sankei Shimbun* (February 6, 1990).

38. See Yuzō, "Dakyo kara 'ukeika e.'"

39. *Mainichi Daily News* (January 21, 1980).

40. Gerald Curtis claims the DSP was formed too early to obtain broad support from the Japanese electorate. In 1960, when the DSP began, Japan was still divided between conservative and progressive camps and the DSP did not fit well into either camp. The DSP, continues Curtis, was too weak and captured by the Dōmei to exploit new opportunities in the 1970s and 1980s. Gerald Curtis, *The Japanese Way of Politics* (New York: Columbia University Press, 1988), pp. 23–24.

41. *Asahi Evening News* (October 18, 1980).

42. See Gary Allinson, *Japanese Urbanism* (Berkeley: University of California Press, 1985). See also Allinson, "The Moderation of Organized Labor in Post War Japan," *Journal of Japanese Studies* 1, no. 2 (Spring 1975), pp. 409–436.

43. Nishihira Sigeki, "76 senkyo o kaibo suru" [To analyze the 1976 election], *Keizai Orai* (February 1977), as well as *Asahi Shimbun* series on "rising young politicians," reprinted in the *Asahi Evening News* (October 17, 1980). The graph curve of the DSP Diet membership following the 1980 election was gourd-shaped if viewed in terms of age groups. Sixty percent of the DSP Diet members had served three terms or fewer, and six were less than 40 years old. The *Asahi* writer then concluded that the DSP was the opposition party with the most potential for playing an important role in Japan's future.

8

Political Party Proliferation: The New Liberal Club and the Mini-Parties

RONALD J. HREBENAR

The appearance of new political parties in any political system is an exciting event for political scientists who study voting behavior, parties, or elections. With the advent of a new party comes the prospect that the fundamental nature of a system's politics could be radically altered. A once-dominant party could be severely weakened or even destroyed by the new challenger, or a delicate shift in voting support patterns could eventually force a realignment of great signficance. Many new parties have been established throughout the world since 1945. Despite the great proliferation of these new parties, relatively little has been written about the conditions necessary for the emergence of new parties and almost none on the reasons for the failure of the vast majority of these parties to achieve power in their respective societies.[1]

Minor parties perform important functions in modern Western democracies. Historically, they have acted as systemic "safety valves" by providing more radical voting alternatives for citizens dissatisfied with the candidates and policies of the major parties. In this way, disgruntled citizens are provided an opportunity to participate in the political process in a peaceful manner, and possible violent behavior is avoided. A second function served by minor parties has been the articulation of alternative ideas on policy positions. In this function, such parties may actually operate as de facto interest groups. At times, the issues or policies in question may be "stolen" by the major parties if the issue positions are attractive to large numbers of people.

Minor parties can also serve both as alternative nomination vehicles for candidates who have lost the nomination of major parties and as temporary havens for dissatisfied groups that have broken away from a major party and are moving toward a possible new affiliation.[2] In parliamentary systems, moreover, minor parties can play the crucial role of potential coalition partner willing to join a larger party or parties in the establishment of a parliamentary majority for the construction of a government.

Charles Hauss and David Rayside, in their examination of twenty-three cases of new parties formed in Western democracies after 1945, focused on two sets of facilitators: institutional factors (i.e., those involving the electoral focus of the new party, electoral system, and degree of centralization of the party system) and political factors (involving the reactions of the existing parties, the nature of mass commitments to the existing parties, the nature of the new party leadership, and the organizational power of the new party). In these cases, the basic reason behind the emergence of new parties had to do with the issue cleavages or "strains" in the political system that the existing parties were unable to alleviate. Hauss and Rayside concluded that "institutional factors have only a marginal bearing on the formation of new parties.[3] In the Japanese experience, however, institutional factors seem to be of paramount importance in explaining why so many new parties have appeared since 1960.

First of all, almost everyone who studies Japanese parties acknowledges that the unique electoral system has promoted the emergence and maintenance of new Japanese parties. The medium-sized districts represented in the House of Representatives (3 to 6 seats per district, with each voter having 1 vote) and the national constituency of the House of Councillors have both operated to produce forms of proportional representation without a minimum percentage requirement. Computer studies have indicated that if a small district system were introduced into House of Representatives elections, nearly all of the seats held by the four minor parties (CGP, DSP, JCP, and SDF) would be absorbed by the two giants, the LDP and the JSP. Second, as Japan has a purely parliamentary system, its legislative focus facilitates multiple parties because the various interests do not have to coalesce to elect a president. Finally, Japan, as a very centralized state, does not facilitate the growth of regional parties based on regional interests. One should also realize that the religious, language, racial, and ethnic forces behind many of the European parties are almost completely absent in largely homogeneous Japan. Consequently, electoral system facilitators may be more important in Japan than in other nations because many of the other facilitating forces such as federalism, race, and language are not significant in Japanese politics. Rather, most of the new Japanese parties seem to be parties of opportunity facilitated by favorable election laws.

It is interesting to note that the new Japanese parties created since 1976 do not easily fit into the categories proposed by Hauss and Rayside—namely, orthodox socialist revival parties, radical new left parties, new right parties appealing to the less fortunate in society, and ethnic and language parties (see Table 8.1). Of the Japanese parties, only one (the Japan Labor party) fits into any of the above four categories—namely, the one comprising the less fortunate. Four of the remaining Japanese parties are classified as moderate socialist or leftist, one as a moderate conservative party, six as special interest parties, and five as personal election vehicles.

TABLE 8.1
Status and types of selected new Japanese minor parties, 1974-1990

Year	*Party*	*Status as of 1990*	*Party Type*
1974	Japan Labor Party (JLP)	Active	5
1976	New Liberal Club (NLC)	Inactive	2
1977	Japan Women's Party (JWP)	Inactive	4
1977	Socialist Citizens League (SCL)	Inactive	1
1977	United Progressive Liberals Party (UPL)	Inactive	1
1977	Liberal Reformist Union (LRU)	Active	1
1977	Wheelchair Party (WP)	Inactive	4
1978	Social Democratic Federation (SDF)	Active	1
1982	"No Party Club" (Mutōha)	Inactive	4
1983	Welfare Party (Fukushito)	Active	6
1983	Salaried Man Party (SP)	Active	4
1983	Second Chamber Club (SCC)	Active	6
1983	Non-Partisan Citizens League (NPCC)	Active	6
1986	Tax Reduction Party	Active	4
1986	Salaryman Party	Active	4
1989	Peace Through Sports Party	Active	6
1990	Progressive Party	Active	6

Note: Party type: 1=more moderate socialist, 2=more moderate conservative, 3=religious party, 4=special interest party, 5=more left socialist, and 6=personal election vehicle.

Source: Compiled by author.

The political facilitators identified by Hauss and Rayside concern such matters as voter commitments, leadership in existing and new parties, and the nature of the organization developed by the new parties. The Japanese refer to many of the same points in their traditional analysis of the ingredients crucial to a party's success. Three such ingredients are *jiban*, *kanban*, and *kaban*—the "three *ban*," which, literally translated, mean "supporting ground," "billboard," and "attaché case," respectively. More specifically, *jiban* refers to the personal support organization of a candidate; *kanban* means facade or image; and *kaban* refers to money. These concepts will be evaluated along with the major points of the Hauss and Rayside model.

Presented in the following section is an analysis of the rise and fall of the most successful of the post-1976 new parties, the NLC. A series of sketches of the other Japanese minor parties is also provided.[4] Finally, we will return to the central question of this chapter: why minor parties fail in Japan.

THE NEW LIBERAL CLUB

Defection occurred within the ranks of the LDP in the summer of 1976. Although minor in terms of absolute numbers, it was significant in its impact on the proliferation of new parties. Kōno Yōhei, a young LDP Diet member, led 5 other Diet members out of the LDP, set up a new Diet-level party, and named it the New Liberal Club (NLC). From this humble start of only a few seats, it increased to 18 seats in the December 1976 election, thereby touching off a Kōno and NLC "boom" in the Japanese media. This boom subsequently encouraged the establishment of other new parties in the 1977, 1979, 1980, and 1983 general elections. The 1983 House of Councillors elections had twelve new mini-parties (mini-*seitō*) on the ballot that cumulatively captured over 15 percent of the vote and won 5 seats (10 percent) in the upper house. Two of these parties—the NLC and the Social Democratic Federation—will be examined in some detail in this chapter because of their continuing impact upon Japanese politics; others—such as the Japanese Women's party—will be mentioned only briefly because of their lack of impact. The most important of the new parties, the New Liberal Club, will provide the first context for our discussion of the problems encountered by minor parties in contemporary Japan.

On June 14, 1976, Kōno Yōhei led five followers out of the Liberal Democratic party and set in motion plans for a new political party that threatened to revolutionize Japanese party politics. The splinter group left the LDP during the dark days of the Lockheed scandal, and many conservative politicians feared that its six members represented the vanguard of a mass exodus to a new second conservative party. Despite the abruptness of the public announcement of the split in the LDP ranks, such a division had long been anticipated by the LDP leadership, who represented a group of small mini-parties that had coalesced within the framework of the LDP. The glue that has kept the LDP together during the three decades since its inception has been the taste of power generated by continued successes in achieving absolute majorities in the national Diet. Kōno Yōhei, a young conservative politician from Kanagawa prefecture, was in many respects a logical choice to lead such a secession. He is the son of the late Kōno Ichirō, a one-time LDP factional boss who in the mid-1960s led a group of followers out of the LDP, only to return to the fold after acknowledging that the time was not right for the establishment of a second conservative party. Kōno Yōhei's uncle, the late Kōno Kenzō, was a member of the House of Councillors from Kanagawa, and in 1976 Kenzō was president of the chamber.

Kōno Yōhei himself became a professional politician in 1967 at the age of thirty, winning a Diet seat from his family's Kanagawa stronghold. He quickly established himself as one of the rising young conservatives in the nation and was frequently mentioned as a member of the small group most likely to capture the party presidency and prime ministership in the future. However, he soon criticized his faction-plagued and scandal-ridden party. As a member of the Nakasone faction, he led a revolt of young LDP Diet members in late 1971 and demanded the resignation of then Prime Minister Satō. And in December 1971, Kōno and eleven other LDP Diet members resisted party pressures and boycotted a vote-of-confidence motion against then Foreign Minister Fukuda Takeo. The group included three of the original six members of the NLC. Three years later Kōno and his supporters demanded the resignation of all involved members of the Tanaka administration following revelations of financial improprieties. The group planned to support Kōno as LDP president to replace Tanaka, but party Vice-President Shiina Etsusaburō's appointment of Miki Takeo thwarted them.

Following these events Kōno set up a new organization of young LDP members that cut across factional lines in an attempt to reform the party procedures involving election of party president—a process long considered to be the root of many of the LDP's problems. By mid-1976 the group had concluded that the LDP leaders were less than serious in their attempts to reform the party, even after the Lockheed revelations. Some of Kōno's critics have pointed out that despite his substantial support by the media, he had been losing ground in the race for party leadership to a rising generation of conservative Diet members, such as Abe Shintarō, Miyazawa Kiichi, and Kosaka Tokusaburō. But these critics have also alleged that the alternatives facing Kōno were few: He could stay in the party and see his prospects for the party presidency—a goal long sought and never achieved by his father—ebb slowly away, or he could make a bold maneuver to establish his claim to conservative leadership, perhaps by establishing a second conservative party. Whether Kōno's true motives were political or idealistic, he has managed to force the LDP into a series of reforms while rocketing himself to the status of one of the most important politicians in Japan.[5]

In order to create a long-term, successful impact on Japanese politics, the NLC had to build a strong party organization. This it attempted to do in the prefectures of the original six NLC Diet members and in those selected prefectures that seemed responsive to its reformed conservative call. The major initial success in party building occurred in Kanagawa prefecture (consisting of Yokohama and its suburbs) at the home of Kōno Yōhei and his cousin, Tagawa Seiichi. The NLC very quickly became the most powerful party in several of the key cities of that prefecture. Major young politicians defected from the LDP in Tokyo and Ōsaka during 1976 and 1977. But in most of Japan's forty-seven prefectures, the NLC could claim no Diet members, no prefectural assembly members, no organization, and no core of party activists.

However weak the NLC's organization had been in late 1976, the party was lucky. In the December 1976 House of Representatives elections, it surged from 5 seats to 17 and ignited a "Kōno boom" in the media. Of the 25 official candidates it ran in 1976, 19 candidates (including 2 recommended candidates) won, and 12 of the 17 came in first in their multimember districts. These candidates are of interest in that the anticipated second wave of LDP defectors to the NLC never occurred on the national level; in addition, the NLC discovered that a group of former LDP Diet members seeking to regain their HR seats had been co-opted by the LDP as well. Moreover, many of the best "new face" conservatives had been promised LDP endorsements since the previous year. Thus, the 25 NLC candidates were a mixed bag consisting of the original 5 (one in the House of Councillors did not run in 1976), some friends of the Kōno family, some former LDP "losers," and some who could not even secure LDP nominations. Seventeen of this group won seats in a shocking challenge to the LDP.

The NLC, riding the "Kōno boom," expected to do well in the House of Councillors elections scheduled for July 1977. Eleven candidates—four in the national constituency and seven in the prefectural contests—were officially endorsed. These candidates, as a result of the 1976 victory, were considerably more prestigious than the 1976 group. Okita Saburō, a leading economist, was one such candidate. The party leaders expected at least seven winners out of the eleven campaigns but were crushed when the party captured only three seats—one in the national constituency and one prefectural seat each in Tokyo and Saitama. Clearly the boom had collapsed, and the major reason was a weak party organization.

Actually the NLC had become the third most popular party in Japan by the summer of 1977, but it did not have the capability of converting its popularity in votes and seats. The *Kyōdo* news poll reported a 6.5 percent support level for the NLC on July 7, 1977. Other newspaper polls indicated a 10 percent level during 1977. But by 1981 the NLC had crashed to 1 to 2 percent support levels.[6]

Yet, despite its initial successes, the NLC remained a party deeply divided over the proper future course it should follow. Many of its Diet members were of the opinion that it should operate to reform the LDP and thus have as its eventual goal a reunion with its parent and the creation of a new reformed LDP. The major leader of this group of Diet members was Nishioka Takeo, one of the original six defectors from the LDP and the NLC's secretary-general in 1979. Tagawa Seiichi was later to remark that Nishioka "troubled us most among the six at the time of the split. Nishioka hesitated about leaving the LDP until the last moment."[7] The party's other group centered on Kōno Yōhei and his advocacy of the creation of a new middle party to be formed from the union of the NLC, DSP, and SDF. Most of the members of this second group were Diet members from the metropolitan prefectures such as Tokyo and Kanagawa, whereas most of the pro-LDP Diet members represented suburbs or more rural areas.

The conflict between Nishioka and Kōno came to a head in 1979 after the central issue had been debated repeatedly by the pair throughout the preceding year. When the 1979 NLC Action Policy was drafted, Nishioka was quite clear about his lack of support to the idea of an opposition parties coalition. Nishioka's view was that the LDP was the only competent party capable of leading Japanese politics. In his book entitled *The Development of the New Liberal Club*, he had written that in order to reconstruct conservatism, the NLC would have to "hijack" the LDP. Kōno, on the other hand, insisted that the primary task of the NLC was the destruction of the LDP's stranglehold on national government, and that the best way to accomplish that goal was to cooperate with other moderate opposition parties to destroy the status quo. Nishioka feared that such cooperation with other opposition parties would force the NLC to lose its image as a conservative party.[8]

Thus, by 1979 it made sense to talk about two major factions in the NLC, the Kōno and Nishioka factions, which were fundamentally divided over their attitudes toward the LDP. In that year the DSP began serious efforts to seek a merger with the NLC, thus bringing the Kōno-Nishioka dispute to a crisis point. In June, Kōno met with Nishioka in one such all-night effort at the Tokyo Hilton Hotel concerning the future of the party. An attempt was made on June 2 by the senior NLC Diet member, Arita Kazutoshi, to reconcile this dispute without damaging the party; but in late June, Kōno reportedly asked Nishioka to resign his post as NLC secretary-general and then asked Yamaguchi Toshio to resign as chairman of the NLC Diet Policy Committee after the latter tried to keep Nishioka in his leadership post. Kōno wanted to replace them with Tagawa (Kōno's cousin) and Kobayashi Masami, the strongly anti-Nishioka chairman of the party's Information Committee.[9]

Nishioka responded to Kōno's actions by resigning from the NLC on July 16, 1979, and taking with him four other Diet members from his "faction." Another Nishioka supporter, Yamaguchi Toshio from Saitama prefecture, became the crucial factor in the survival of the NLC. Kōno offered Yamaguchi the post of secretary-general, but he refused and suggested that Tagawa be named to the office. Yamaguchi was a very significant political leader in his own right in Saitama, and his loss would have crushed the viability of the NLC. After a period of uncertainty, both Yamaguchi and Arita agreed to stay in the party after Kōno agreed to respect their views in future party decisionmaking sessions. Yamaguchi sharply criticized Kōno's leadership at a July 13 press conference: After noting Kōno's charismatic personality, he commented that Kōno's "political behavior contains elements that are like the fictional and dreamy 'Milky Way 999 train'" (a children's cartoon television series).[10]

The Nishioka defections rocked the NLC to its very foundations. Some of the local prefectural chapters were dissolved when the defecting Diet members departed. Miyagi prefecture's (Sendai) NLC dissolved when Kikuchi Fukujiro left with Nishioka to join the LDP, and no new NLC organization later emerged in this most important city in northern Honshū. Other chapters were dissolved in Gifu and Mie prefectures, and budding NLC movements were severely hurt in many parts of Japan by the party split.[11] The nation's mass circulation newspapers gave considerable attention to the split and questioned whether the NLC could possibly survive such a disaster just prior to the national elections anticipated for later in 1979.

Tagawa, the new party secretary-general in 1979, announced his determination to purge other pro-LDP members from the party: "The New Liberal Club created a new conservatism. Nishioka did not fully understand the spirit. We will sift out any member who cannot join hands earnestly in our battle against the LDP."[12]

Despite Tagawa's declaration, the problem of the NLC's future was not resolved in 1979 but, rather, continued to be a central concern for many of the NLC leaders. In early 1983 *Sentaku,* in an article entitled "Internal Trouble in the NLC over Its Action Policy," reported that there was substantial conflict between Secretary-General Yamaguchi and party Representative Tagawa. Yamaguchi wanted a new party to be formed from the NLC, DSP, and SDF, whereas Tagawa wanted to combine the NLC, DSP, and SDF, and parts of the JSP and LDP, into a new coalition. Tagawa had come to the conclusion that as a new party consisting of middle parties was impossible to form, the NLC should act as a catalyst to assist the LDP in fragmenting and then combining with a part of the LDP.[13] Tagawa's plan was to attack Tanaka's role in the LDP as Tanaka's Lockheed bribery trial moved toward its climax in late 1983. By attacking Tanaka, Tagawa hoped to force some of the anti-Tanaka factions (e.g., the Fukuda and Miki factions) out of the LDP. There was general agreement among many in the moderate opposition parties that power could be gained only through the combination of a new moderate party and part of the LDP. The major difficulties toward this end involved a widespread dislike for the Kōmeitō and a disagreement over which part of the LDP it should seek to join.

Throughout 1979 Japanese political leaders had been preparing for House of Representatives elections. Although they finally occurred in October 1979, the NLC was in a shambles in terms of both its internal organization and its public image. The Nishioka defection (and his supporting Diet members and their supporters) had deprived the NLC of a significant part of its organizational base and its major fund-raiser (Nishioka). It had insufficient time to begin to rebuild these lost organizations or to select attractive replacement candidates. Worst of all, the media depicted the NLC as a once-promising party that had lost both its purpose and its appeal. Clearly, the NLC media boom had ended.

From its peak of 18 seats just after the 1976 general elections, the NLC sank to only 4 seats in the October 1979 elections. Only Kōno, Yamaguchi, Tagawa, and a Tokyo newcomer, Tajima Mamoru, managed to win seats for the party. The first three were very secure politicians with powerful personal supporter organizations (*kōenkai*). All of the other "boom winners" from 1976 had either lost their seats as NLC incumbents or defected to the LDP. Even with only 4 HR seats, the NLC was split into two factions: Kōno and Tagawa on the one hand, and Yamaguchi and his friend Tajima on the other.

On October 7, 1979, an election day, a powerful typhoon struck much of the Japanese archipelago. Voting rates declined all over Japan, but especially in the large metropolitan areas such as Tokyo and Kanagawa. Parties with a dedicated corps of supporters, such as the Kōmeitō and the JCP, performed well in such a situation, but any party without a real organization—one that relied on the so-called floating vote—could only have been devastated when such low-interest voters decided to stay home in the bad weather. Indeed, in district after district, the NLC "new face" winners in 1976 (most of whom had come in first in total votes in their districts) finished only as runners-up in 1979. The reduced turnout, the shattered party organization, and the negative media image that resulted all set the stage for the October defeat.

Aside from the reduction of the NLC to a handful of HR seats, an interesting feature of the 1979 election was the loss of a working majority by the LDP. The LDP won only 248 seats in the election and reached a working majority only by recognizing several conservative independent winners after the election. Nonmainstream factions attacked LDP President Ōhira for the defeat and demanded that he resign from the prime ministership.

When the Diet convened in late October to select the government, the LDP had two candidates for prime minister, Ōhira and Fukuda, and the fight over each vote was a bitter battle. Both Ōhira and Fukuda came to the NLC, with its 4 votes, looking for support. Kōno Yōhei, seeking a way to turn his devastated party into a major force in the now evenly balanced House, hit upon the idea of offering the NLC's 4 votes to one of the LDP's candidates for the prime ministership.[14] Tanaka Rokusuke, Ōhira's chief cabinet secretary, apparently approached the NLC seeking an agreement; later, Kōno and Ōhira met privately to hammer out a personal deal. Again, there was the crucial problem of deciding which part of the LDP the NLC would cooperate with. The Ōhira faction's policies were closer to those of the NLC in many respects, but Ōhira was also the candidate of the Tanaka faction, which had become the symbol of the corrupt politics the NLC opposed. Fukuda, on the other hand, was considered by many NLC members to be too hawkish on security issues. Kōno eventually negotiated a deal with Ōhira to exchange the 4 NLC votes for the fulfillment by Ōhira of 5 promises:[15] First, Ōhira promised that a cabinet ministry would be given to an NLC Diet member and, hence, that a coalition government would be the result. (Ōhira was originally thought by some to have suggested Tagawa as his justice minister, but later published accounts reported that an NLC member had become education minister in the new Ōhira cabinet.) Ōhira also promised to support national-level administrative reforms, political finance reforms, a review of education and cultural policies, and efforts to strengthen Diet discipline.

The coalition offer was headlined in the Japanese press, but it received less than enthusiastic reviews in both the LDP and NLC. Nonmainstream (anti-Ōhira) factions strongly attacked the plan to the point where Ōhira himself had to temporarily take the education ministership he had reportedly planned to give to the NLC. In the NLC, many grass-roots activists attacked Kōno for his plan to cooperate with the LDP in such a government. Many NLC members noted that Kōno had sharply attacked Ōhira during the previous campaign. Kōno called Ōhira "a power drunk man without fear for God" and a "wicked politician."[16] Although many NLC members were understanding about the loss of NLC Diet seats in the October 1979 elections, they could neither understand nor accept the trade of the NLC's 4 votes for the coalition offer.

Ultimately, Ōhira failed to appoint any NLC members to the cabinet, and Kōno Yōhei was forced by internal NLC pressures to resign his leadership post, which was turned over to Tagawa.[17] The *Mainichi Shimbun* observed that the NLC was on "the verge of collapse" and that "we have the impression the NLC has been outwitted by Ōhira's skill."[18] Kōno defended his decision by arguing that as there were "only four of us, we were trying to create the opportunity for destroying the long-term, one-party rule which is the cause of all evils."[19] In mid-November, Miruyama Masaya, an NLC member of the House of Councillors who had been a friend of Kōno for thirty years, left the NLC as a result of the Kōno decision to support Ōhira.[20] When the NLC voted for Ōhira, the *Asahi Shimbun* referred to the decision as a "dangerous gamble." In retrospect, it is clear that the gamble failed.[21]

When the House of Representatives was dissolved in May 1980 and double elections (both House of Representatives and House of Councillors) were held simultaneously for the first time, the prospects for the NLC were not favorable. The double-election format prevented effective cooperation among the opposition parties, and the death of Ōhira during the short campaign created a wave of sympathy for the LDP.[22] The two big surprises of the June 1980 elections were the big wins for both conservative parties, the LDP and NLC. The four 1979 NLC winners repeated their victories, and four of the 1976 winners who had lost their seats in 1979 regained their seats. Finally, four new NLC members were elected in Tokyo and Tōhoku. By tripling their seat totals in the HR, the NLC was "born again" as a factor in Japanese politics. However, the problem of defections had not been solved, as two of the new winners soon defected to the LDP, leaving the NLC with a total of 10 House of Representatives seats.

In 1985 the NLC held on to 6 of the 8 seats in the Tokyo Municipal Assembly elections and appeared to have established a presence in Tokyo and its Saitama-Kanagawa suburban ring. Nine of the 12 NLC Diet members elected in 1980 came from this Tokyo area. The same regional bias can be seen in the delegate list for the 1981 NLC National Convention, which had 67 of 89 elected representatives and 93 of 123 observers from Tokyo, Kanagawa, and Saitama prefectures.

The NLC fought the 1983 House of Councillors elections in an alliance with the SDF called Jikuren. The alliance, which had 4 seats to defend, lost 2 of them. It collected 2.5 percent of the total national PR vote (1 seat) and won only a single seat in the local constituencies (Saitama) with 1.2 percent of the total vote.

On December 26, 1983, the LDP joined hands with its small conservative splinter, the NLC, to form Japan's first coalition government since 1947 and only the third such government in the postwar era. When Prime Minister Nakasone Yasuhiro's LDP won only 250 seats of 511 total in the House of Representatives, it had to scramble to recruit nine independent conservative Diet members to join the LDP to construct a simple majority in the lower house of the Diet. However, to have a "working majority," it needed additional votes. These it obtained by convincing the NLC, which won 8 seats in the 1983 general election, to enter into a joint parliamentary association with the LDP called the "LDP-NLC National Union."

The NLC had some very serious concerns after viewing the results of the December 1983 elections. It could see that the LDP would be able to secure sufficient independent votes to have a pure majority, thus denying the moderate opposition parties any chance of somehow patching together a governing majority. It also feared that the LDP might raid its successful Diet members to enlarge the LDP majority. This had happened in 1979 and 1980, when NLC members were enticed to rejoin the LDP. When Tanaka Rokusuke of the LDP Suzuki faction approached the NLC leadership with a coalition offer, as he had done in 1980, the NLC was again interested. In exchange for 8 NLC votes, the LDP would make NLC Representative Tagawa the

Home Affairs minister, select an NLC Diet member to fill a parliamentary vice-minister position, and promise to work on several political reforms sponsored by the NLC.

When the NLC held its Seventh National Delegates Convention (Regular Party Convention) in February 1985, it had much to celebrate. First, it had just embarked upon its second cabinet coalition with the LDP and could now count among its members two who had held cabinet ministries and two others who had performed as parliamentary vice-ministers. Home Minister Tagawa Seiichi spoke to the convention and declared the significance of the NLC-LDP: "In some opposition parties, self-reflection on their being 'perpetual opposition parties' in the past, and enthusiasm to take part in the government are quickly mounting." Tagawa then declared that the age of coalition had arrived: "The age of a coalition and alliance is about to open its curtain. We are making a challenge for carrying out a precious experiment, riding in the van of that trend."[23]

Tagawa went on to explain why the NLC had embraced the LDP in 1983: "We established the coalition in order to materialize, in a clearer way, pluses to be brought about by the situation where the conservatives and renovationist forces are about equal in strength, which situation the people hoped for." He also declared that as a result of the NLC participation in the government, the cabinet ministers' assets were publicly disclosed and a Political Ethics Council was actually established.[24] Central to the unfinished tasks on the NLC agenda was the issue of political ethics. The NLC was still strongly opposed to the continuation of the dominance of Tanaka Kakuei in the LDP and the Nakasone cabinet.

Some leadership changes were enacted at the 1985 NLC convention. Tagawa was reelected as party representative and Yamaguchi as secretary-general. Kōno Yōhei was brought back into the spotlight for the first time since 1979 and filled the newly created post of acting representative. NLC Diet members were pleased about their coalition with the LDP. The NLC received three cabinet ministries during the three years of the coalition (1983–1986), in addition to three vice-minister positions and a great deal of media attention. Despite these positive aspects, NLC leaders were unsure about how the Japanese public would react to the coalition in the next parliamentary elections. The party survived the 1985 Tokyo Assembly elections with just a small loss of seats and votes, but it worried about returning to its 1979 base of 4 or 5 seats in the next HR elections.

The NLC's "last hurrah" was in the 1986 double elections, in which it won 6 seats in the House of Representatives and a single seat in the national constituency of the House of Councillors. Its vote totals in the lower house fell to an all-time party low of about 1.1 million votes. Four of its winners came from Kanagawa; one winner each came from Tokyo and Saitama prefectures.

Immediately following the elections, Yamaguchi wanted the NLC to ally with the LDP in the Diet, though to remain a separate party, but Kōno wanted the NLC to be completely separate from the LDP. After Yamaguchi threatened to leave the NLC if Kōno refused to agree to his demands, Kōno unilaterally decided to dissolve the NLC and negotiated for its members to enter the LDP. Prime Minister Nakasone welcomed all six NLC lower house members back into the LDP, and all but Tagawa accepted the offer. He decided to remain in the Diet as an independent, but later formed the Progressive party (Shimpotō) to support his demands for political reforms. Of the remaining five NLC members, three (including Kōno) joined the Miyazawa faction, while two (including Yamaguchi) joined the Nakasone faction.

Curtis suggests that the major political function performed by the NLC during its ten years in the Diet was to save the LDP from political losses resulting from the Lockheed and Tanaka scandals.[25] LDP seat and vote losses following these scandals were almost exactly the same as the NLC gains. Thus, a "safe" protest outlet for unhappy conservative voters was created, and the true opposition parties were denied opportunities to increase their seat totals. One could also argue that there were some corollary benefits resulting from the existence of the NLC: It forced the LDP into being slightly more responsive to demands for political reforms, and it contributed to a more modern, U.S. style of election campaigning.

Thus, of all the parties created since the mid-1970s, the NLC was the most successful. It survived five lower house elections while winning a total of 47 seats and positioned itself to become a coalition partner for Nakasone between 1983 and 1986. In the final analysis, the NLC proved to be a party based on several media stars (Kōno, Yamaguchi, Nishioka, and Tagawa) who would have been elected regardless of their party label. The NLC had no supporting organization and no financial base of sufficient size to allow it to expand its Diet seats to a level that would overcome the label "splinter party." The party began with a sense of great excitement and potential and ended amid a feeling of a return to normal conservative politics.

THE OTHER JAPANESE MINOR PARTIES

The NLC's successful debut in 1976 encouraged an explosion of other minor parties. The most successful of those parties formed in the wake of the NLC 1976 successes was the Social Democratic Federation (Shaminren), sometimes also called the United Social Democrats by the press. The first leader of the SDF was a member of the House of Councillors, Den Hideo, but the party traces back to its actual founder, Eda Saburō, a long-time faction leader and former vice-chairman of the JSP. Eda left the JSP in March 1977 after a long battle against the JSP leftists—particularly those of the Socialist Association (Shakaishugi Kyōkai). As he was preparing to form the Socialist Citizens League (SCL) as a vehicle to run in the 1977 elections, he died suddenly in May 1977 and left the new party leaderless. His son, Eda Satsuki, the leader of the party since 1985, carried on his father's candidacy and won a seat in the national constituency of the House of Councillors with the second highest vote total (1,392,477) in 1977. In 1983, Eda won a seat in the House of Representatives from Okayama.

The SCL was formed officially after the election. However, it soon became clear that the loss of the senior Eda would sharply limit the future of the new party. Eda Saburō had expected the defection of hundreds of JSP prefectural and city assembly members—in addition to many new members from the JSP chapters in Kyōto, Tokyo, Ōsaka, Aichi, and Okayama prefectures—to the new party after the 1977 elections. But defections of this magnitude never occurred—Eda's death had eliminated the catalyst for the new party. Den Hideo and two other Diet members left the JSP in the autumn of 1977 in another protest against the leftist domination of the Socialist party and formed the "Den group" while beginning negotiations to join together with the Eda SCL. On March 26, 1978, the merged party officially began its existence under the name of the Social Democratic Federation (SDF).

The SDF entered the 1980 double elections hoping for a "Den boom" similar to that of Kōno Yōhei of the NLC in 1976. Although the SDF did not experience a "boom," it was also not destroyed as some had predicted would happen. Three seats were won in the House of Representatives with incumbents returned in Fukuoka and Yamagata, and 33-year-old Kan Naoto, a one-time campaigner for Ichikawa Fusae, won in Tokyo. Another 3 seats were held in the national constituency of the upper house. In 1983, the SDF took 3 seats in the House of Councillors.

Some Japanese critics as well as the leadership of the SDF saw the new party as "glue for a future coalition,"[26] whereas the party's early policy position (1978–1980) saw the party as part of a coalition with the JSP, Kōmeitō, and DSP. This latter goal fell into disfavor among the SDF leadership after the 1980 elections. Consequently, at the SDF's first convention held on November 17, 1980, party Representative Den announced that the new party policy was to seek an alliance with the "reformist and conservative" parties and to begin such an effort by merging with the NLC. This new policy was strongly opposed by many of the SDF's membership, and one leader, Hata Yutaka, the deputy secretary-general, a former newscaster and one of the original "Den group," resigned in protest. The opponents argued that the party should not abandon its socialist cause merely to move closer to political power. As such opposition was clearly evident at the convention, the new policy was not voted upon but, rather, was "approved by the applause" of a majority. Subsequently, during the Diet session of 1982, the SDF and NLC Councillors formed a joint party, Shinjiren, to coordinate their activities and were no longer listed on the party summaries as members of their respective parties. When the NLC joined the LDP in coalition government, its coalition with the SDF was terminated.

The SDF organization is structured much like the other Japanese political parties. It has a party representative (Eda Satsuki), a pair of deputy representatives, a secretary-general, and the regular range of party committees (including, among others, those dealing with policy affairs, theory, finance, public information, youth, women, fishermen, and farmers). Twelve local chapters (each of which is established when there are more than 100 members) were created early in 1978. By the end of June 1978, the SDF claimed 600 local assembly members, including 7 on the prefectural level. Supporters of the late Eda Saburō constituted most of the SDF's membership, and by 1985 the party had a total of approximately 10,000 members.

The SDF has been consistent in its seat totals in the Diet. It consistently ran 4 to 6 candidates for the lower house in the 1986–1990 period, increasing its HR members from 2 in 1979 to 3 in 1983 to 4 in 1986 and 1990. As one would expect, the SDF has only a small base of officeholders on the local level of Japanese politics. In 1990 it numbered among its officeholders 5 members in prefectural assemblies, 12 in city councils, 1 in a village/town council, and 3 in Tokyo city councils.

Like many of the new parties, the SDF has not had a great deal of success in political fund-raising. It was the bottom-ranked party in terms of funds raised during 1989 with about 65 million yen raised and expended that year. Compared with the NLC, the SDF is able to raise only about one-tenth the funds the NLC raised when it was in existence.

The SDF appears likely to continue on as it did during the 1980s. Its Diet members are secure enough in their own districts that they will continue to be elected, but the SDF has clearly not caught the fancy of the Japanese electorate to the degree that the party will emerge from its "minor party" status of 2 to 4 lower house seats. On the other hand, the SDF remains the only minor party to win multiple seats in the lower house. It can continue its present course with little effect on overall Japanese politics, or it may decide eventually to disband and return to the JSP or merge with the DSP.

THE MINI-PARTIES

Of the number of "mini-parties" that appeared in the Japanese national level of politics during the 1970s and 1980s, few have won more than a single seat in the Diet. Others have not won even a single seat, but are interesting because of the causes they support and how the parties represent those causes in Japanese politics. In certain respects, some of these parties are really interest groups promoting their cause as a political party because of the attention they can receive during an election campaign. The following is a selection of some of these new mini-parties.

The Japan Women's Party

The 1977 House of Councillors elections set the stage for the unveiling of the Japan Women's party (JWP). The JWP was created by Enoki Misako, who was the former leader of Chūpiren, an organization that opposed Japan's anti-abortion law and supported legislation favoring the use of birth-control pills. The members of Chūpiren (otherwise known as the Women's Liberation League Against the Abortion Law and for the Pill) gained fame in Japan as the "pink-helmeted" women who demonstrated outside the offices of men who allegedly treated women badly—and who continued to demonstrate until corrective action was promised. When the new party was announced in March 1977, Enoki stated that the JWP would be the world's first political party for women only. Its avowed aim was the rebuilding of Japanese society in favor of women. Included in its platform were demands for

- a revision of the Civil Code such that married women could keep their maiden names if they so desired and be entitled to receive 50 percent of the assets if divorced;
- exemption of women wage earners from taxation when their annual income is less than 10 million yen; and
- passage of a law designed to promote women's employment (such a law would offer tax exemptions for corporations with equal numbers of male and female management personnel).

This platform seemed rather moderate when compared to the statements made by Enoki. "I am serious," she said; "I want to establish a women's dictatorial society."[27] Later in the campaign, she elaborated that the JWP was seeking not equality with men but women's superiority over men. Then, in late May, she announced that the members and candidates of the JWP would undergo extensive karate training to prepare for fights with male members of the Diet: "If they are elected and feel a disadvantage in getting laws unbeneficial to women revised, then they can resort to physical action and knock down male lawmakers."[28]

This women's liberation party had a unique financial base. Enoki borrowed 17 million yen from her husband, a 36-year-old physician who exacted a promise in return for the loan. That is, Enoki promised to repay the loan by July (after the election); but if she failed to do so, she promised either to give up her feminist activities or to divorce him.

Ten unknown feminist candidates were recruited for the JWP—the minimum number necessary to qualify as a political party in Japan. The original plan had been to hold a primary election to select these women, but potential candidates were few in number. Later during the campaign, five of the ten either gave up their candidacies or left the party to form a new group when disagreements arose over campaign practices.

Ultimately, the JWP failed as a political party. Its candidates won 161,692 votes in the national constituency (.3%) and only 45,328 (.09%) in the local constituencies. As one might expect, these vote totals failed to elect any JWP candidates. Two weeks after the election, Enoki disbanded both Chūpiren and the Japan Women's party. She and the Japanese women's liberation movement disappeared from the Japanese political scene. Yet the existence and experience of such a militant women's liberation party, as well as the nature of its demise, tell us a great deal about Japanese society as a whole—at both the political and the social levels.

The United Progressive Liberals Party

A group of about 100 intellectuals formed the United Progressive Liberals party (UPL) and ran candidates in the 1977 upper house elections. The UPL leadership was composed largely of popular novelists, philosophers, university scholars, critics, movie directors, cartoonists, and even a jazz musician. Its three representatives were Yazaki Yasuhisa, a magazine editor; Baba Kōichi, a broadcast journalist; and Nakayama Chinatsu, a female television personality. The UPL based its campaign on an open distrust of the existing parties and hoped to establish a nonprofessional style of politics. It also hoped to attract as many apathetic citizens as possible with its slate of interesting candidates. The UPL ran 10 candidates—5 in the national constituency and 5 in the local constituencies—but only one was successful. That candidate was Yokoyama Nokku, a comedian and former member of the House of Councillors, but he later left the party. The UPL refused corporate, union, and religious contributions, seeking instead to appeal to the "ordinary voters" by extolling the virtue of its members' amateurism.

The Liberal Reformist Union

A spinoff of the UPL (which died organizationally in 1977) was the Liberal Reformist Union (Kakushin Jiyū Rengō), which ran several candidates in the 1980 upper house elections. Nakayama Chinatsu (former representative of UPL) won a seat in the House of Councillors with the fifth highest vote total (1,580,899) in the national constituency. Nakayama, a 31-year-old television talent, spoke of "taking politics from the dirty hands of professionals and giving it to the clean hands of amateurs." She spent a total of about 4.7 million yen, an extraordinarily small amount of money for a national campaign.

The Niin Club

The Niin Club is one of the several quasi-parties that periodically operate in the House of Councillors. This organization of "conscientious independents," when founded in 1962, had more than ten members; but by 1982 it had declined to four: Ichikawa Fusae, Kiyan Shinei, Yamada Isama, and Aoshima Yukio. When Ichikawa died at the age of 87 years, the Niin Club lost its symbol of her opposition to major parties and the big-money style of Japanese politics. Such organizations as the Niin Club and the Liberal Reformist Union may or may not call themselves political parties, but they function in much the same way: Their purpose is not so much to organizationally assist the candidate in election campaigns as to give their candidate an identity and frame of reference once he or she is in the Diet.

The "No-Party Club" and the Non-Partisan Citizens League

The 1982 revision in the election rules for the national constituency of the House of Councillors resulted in the birth of eleven new parties for the 1983 upper house elections. Since 1983 the 50 seats in the national constituency have been elected on a proportional representation basis, using party lists. Voters, therefore, no longer cast votes for a specific candidate but vote instead for an entire party. Since its inception the House of Councillors has seen a number of independent candidates win seats by capitalizing on their personal popularity. In 1980, seven such independents won seats. In December 1981, these independents and some members of small political groups such as the Niin Club announced their plans to form a "No-Party Club" (Mutōha) in order to run in the reformed 1983 elections. If such a party is to get on the ballot, it must have either five incumbent House of Councillors members or more than ten candidates for the national constituency. The "No-Party Club" agreed that it would not align with any of the big parties and that it would do without party rules, a platform, and a party leader. The party featured several television personalities such as Aoshima Yukio, Yokoyama "Knoc," former TV newsman Hata Yutaka, Nakayama Chinatsu, and the former governor of Tokyo, 80-plus-year-old Minobe Ryōkichi.

In 1983 the "No-Party Club" merged with a citizens' group to form the Non-Partisan Citizens League (NPCL). Of the incumbent upper house Diet members, only one, Eita Yashiro, another former television personality, was up for reelection in 1983. The new party split in May 1983 after Minobe, Hata, and Aoshima claimed that the group's operations were undemocratic. Attempts were made to seek a sufficient number of Diet members to qualify it for the 1983 ballot, but the negative publicity had taken its toll. Eita later left the party and formed his own party, the Welfare party, and successfully retained his seat, whereas the NPCL failed to win any new seats.

The New Salaryman Party

Another new party formed in January 1983 in order to run in the 1983 House of Councillor elections was the New Salaryman party, whose major target was the reformation of a tax system that the party representative argued was unfair to wage earners. The party leader, Aoki Shigeru, a professor at Otsuma Women's University, told the media that his group would launch a nationwide campaign in March, select its candidates in April, and hold its party founding convention on May 3, 1983. The Salaryman party proved to be the surprise party of 1983 when it captured a pair of seats with 4.3 percent of the vote. As many Japanese political commentators noted, its name may have rung a bell of sympathy in the minds of many of Japan's salaried men and women.

The Japan Labor Party

The Japan Labor party runs candidates in several constituencies around the nation but manages to collect only a handful of protest votes in each election. In 1979 it collected zero seats on a total of 56,892 (.11 percent) votes by running 25 candidates in 19 of 47 prefectures. A Maoist-oriented party that claims some 5,000 members, most of whom are apparently former student radicals, the Japan Labor party was formed by its chairman, Osumi Tetsuji, in 1974. It survives but has little or no impact on the system. Ironically, it is better financed than the more successful SDF.

The Wheelchair Party and the UFO Party

Periodically, as in the United States, minor parties are formed in Japan that quickly disappear without any substantial impact on the political system. The Wheelchair party, for instance, was established in 1977 by physically handicapped persons. When one of its candidates won a seat in the House of Councillors, the presence of a wheelchair in the Diet building caused some physical changes in the operating of the building. In 1983 the Wheelchair party's incumbent, Eita Yashiro, ran under the Welfare party's banner and secured another six-year term in the Diet. One should not, however, place too many hopes on the future of the UFO party, which was announced by nine UFO enthusiasts in May 1982. Its platform of "opening up the Earth to other planets and make an interplanetary society" is unlikely to strongly affect Japanese society (barring unforeseen events of great magnitude!).

The Progressive Party

After Tagawa Seiichi of the NLC refused to reenter the LDP in 1986, he eventually formed his own party (Shimpotō) to carry on his crusade for political reform in Japanese politics. Tagawa easily won reelection to the lower house in 1990 under the Progressive party banner, but no other Progressive candidates were successful. Tagawa had to survive some ethical questions himself in mid-1990 as he and the former deputy leader of the Progressive party, Aoki Katsuji, argued about whether Tagawa had taken 240 million yen from Aoki illegally. Tagawa admitted that the party had received the money from Aoki as a political donation and had not reported it as such. Aoki was placed at the top of the party's PR list in the national constituency in the 1989 HC elections, but the party did not win enough votes to elect even one candidate to the HC. Tagawa claimed the money was used in the 1989 campaign, but Aoki questioned whether the money had been used for Tagawa's personal use instead.

Tagawa decided to focus on the 1991 local elections to win a base upon which to build the party's fortunes. At the Progressive party's fourth convention held on May 1, 1990, the party adopted a resolution calling for environmental protection, control of the high price of land, and laws to limit corruption in politics. In terms of its Diet identity, the Progressive party has allied itself with the SDF; they had a combined lower house total of 5 seats in 1991.

The Green Party

Finally, following the example of the successful "Greens" of West Germany, Japan's first Green party was founded in Kōchi (Shikoku) prefecture on October 27, 1982. Additional such parties will likely be formed in other prefectures. The objective of this party is to promote solutions for environmental problems. Its leader is Yamazaki Keiji, the head of the National Nature Preservation Federation. The party planned to run candidates in Kochi city and prefectural assembly elections.

TABLE 8.2
Mini-party results in House of Councillors elections, 1983-1989

	Mini-parties	*Constituency*	*Votes*	*Percent*	*Seats*
1983	Salaryman Party	N	1,999,244	4.3	2
	Welfare Party	N	1,577,630	3.4	1
	Niin Club	N	1,142,349	2.45	1
1986	Salaryman Party	N	1,759,484	3.07	1
	Niin Club	N	1,455,532	2.54	1
1989	Niin Club	N	1,250,022	2.23	1
	Tax Reduction Party	N	1,179,939	2.10	1
	Tax Reduction Party	L	889,633	1.56	1
	Peace Through Sports Party	N	993,989	1.77	1
	Rengō	L	3,878,783	6.82	11

Source: Compiled by author.

Of the new parties mentioned here, only the two "splinter" parties, the NLC and SDF, have managed to compete effectively in the lower house elections. When the HR seats of these two parties are combined for the last six elections (1976–1990), they account for 64 of 3,068 seats, or 2 percent of the total. The only other minor party seat in the lower house was Tagawa's Progressive party seat won in the 1990 elections. There were 64 additional minor parties' candidates in those elections; combined, they drew only 53,631 votes—a number insufficient to elect even one of these to the House of Representatives.

The House of Councillors, on the other hand, was a much friendlier arena for minor or mini-parties during the 1980s. As Table 8.2 indicates, the splinter minor parties have not enjoyed as much success as the new mini-parties. The NLC-SDF joint effort in the 1983 HC elections won only 1 seat in the new PR national constituency, whereas the twelve mini-parties won a total of 4 seats. Clearly, the success of these minor parties can be directly traced to the adoption of proportional representation in 1983 rather than to a particular popular issue being articulated by newly formed parties.

In the same HC PR constituency in 1986 and 1989, the mini-parties continued to score surprising victories. Generally, these mini-parties have won up to 15 percent of the total vote. Three mini-parties won seats in the 1986 elections: the Tax Reduction party, the Salaryman party, and the Niin Club. In 1989 a record 36 mini-parties were on the ballot, including the Movement for Peace and Democracy, the UFO party, the Education party, the Renew Japan party, and other parties that dealt with AIDS, gay rights, and chemical-free vegetables. But in that year's upper house elections, perhaps the most interesting new mini-party was the Peace Through Sports party of professional wrestler Inoki "Antonio," which ran a slate of professional wrestlers and sports figures advocating a platform stated in the party's name. Antonio, placed first on the PR list, won election easily as the 48th-place candidate out of 50 winners. Subsequently, he allied with the DSP in the upper house. In 1989 the NLC had disappeared and the Salaryman party failed to win a seat, but the Tax Reduction party won 1 seat each on both the local and national levels, bringing its upper house seat total to 4.

Despite these isolated mini-party victories, the 1989 upper house local constituencies produced the greatest victory ever for new parties when the 11 winners of Rengō helped wrench control of the House of Councillors away from the LDP. Given Rengō's lack of success in the 1990 lower house elections, however, it is not clear whether Rengō will be able to duplicate its 1989 success again.

FROM JAPANESE CONVENTIONAL WISDOM TO WESTERN MODELS: EXPLANATIONS FOR THE APPEARANCE AND FAILURE OF JAPANESE MINOR PARTIES

Introduced earlier were the three elements of Japanese conventional wisdom pertaining to the establishment of minor parties—namely, *jiban*, *kanban*, and *kaban*. *Jiban*, as noted, refers to the personal support organization of a candidate. Established politicians call such organizations *kōenkai*. Of all the parties in Japan, the LDP and SDF rely the most on such personal organizations, whereas the Kōmeitō relies on the Sōka Gakkai, the JSP and DSP rely on the former Sōhyō and Dōmei organizations, and the JCP relies on the party faithful to provide the organizational support needed for electoral victory.

Actually one could argue that no party in Japan other than the JCP has a party organization of any significance. Of the new parties, the NLC and SDF were built around a core of established politicians (four in the case of the NLC) who could expect to be reelected on the power of their own efforts; and there is little or no organizational power behind the rest of the other party candidates, who are at the mercy of the whims of the so-called floating vote.

Kanban, which means facade or image, represents a problem for all new Japanese parties. It is in this connection that the importance of a famous name or charismatic leader can be seen. The initial success of the NLC and the survival of the SDF in its first four elections, for instance, can largely be attributed to the personalities of the respective leaders, Kōno Yōhei and Den Hideo. As young men (by Japanese political standards), they set the image of their parties in the voters' minds. Kōno was far more successful than Den in this respect, but he had the advantage of coming to the role earlier. In fact, he was so closely identified with the NLC that many political commentators referred to it as "Kōno's Private Company." The NLC was able to establish its image through the media as clean, fresh, and young—a winning combination in the 1976 elections, which were held in the shadow of the Lockheed scandal perpetrated by former Prime Minister Tanaka. Neither the SDF nor any of the other post-1970 parties (except the NLC) was ever really able to catch the public's attention.

The third factor, *kaban* (meaning attaché case), refers to money. Many conservative politicians used attaché cases to collect and distribute millions of dollars worth of yen for political expenses. One source estimated that a new party in 1976 needed a minimum of 5 billion yen ($20 million) to become established in Japanese national-level politics.[29] Most of the new Japanese parties foundered as a result of financial problems. Only the NLC had enough money, whereas the SDF is just barely surviving.

According to the Home Affairs Ministry, which released the totals for political funds collected and expended in 1984, the NLC recorded a total of 420 million yen—down from its record-high political funding of almost 700 million yen in the double-election year of 1980.[30] As each Diet member receives 600,000 yen a month for legislative research, this money is usually donated to the party headquarters and helps to pay the costs of operating party offices and paying the salaries of party staff. When the NLC had only 8 Diet members in 1979, the monthly income from this source was only 4.8 million yen, as compared to the NLC's peak year of 1978, with 23 Diet members and a monthly research income of 13.8 million yen. Given the NLC's 24 full- and part-time employees, the 1979 figure, 4.8 million yen, was not enough to pay even the basic salaries. The NLC victories in the 1980 elections again boosted this monthly governmental subsidy to a substantial total.

Several aspects of the NLC budget are of interest. First, in the 1984 budget, the NLC expected to collect from party members a total of 44 million yen (3,000 yen per year) in dues. Another 70 million yen in individual contributions and 100 million yen in the above-mentioned research income, combined with 130 million yen in "business income," were expected to form the central core of the party's income. In terms of expenditures, office and staff costs came to about 30 million yen, 70 million yen were to be spent on party activities, 150 million yen on election activities, 30 million yen on advertising, 20 million yen for research, and 70 million yen for debt payments, subsidies, and other expenses.[31]

Each of the other five major parties has a financial godfather who picks up most of the bills of the party. The LDP, for instance, is financed by corporations and businesses. But the corporate funding of politics was one of the major complaints of the NLC founders. As they prepared to face their first election, Kōno and the other leaders made efforts to disassociate their fledgling party from the evils of corporate political funding. Of primary interest in the area of fund collection was the unique attempt at grass-roots support of a party made by the nation's citizens. "Political participation for the cost of a cup of coffee a month" was the NLC's appeal to the citizenry. Supporters would contribute from 250 to 1,000 yen per month, some by ordering their banks to transfer such amounts monthly to NLC headquarters. "If our attempt to raise funds from private donations turns out to be successful, and if we can support ourselves with money collected in this way alone, it will be epoch-making," argued Kōno Yōhei soon after he founded his club.

Despite some initial successes (in 1976 and 1977) involving individual contributors, the NLC leadership soon realized that, like the LDP, it would have to rely mostly on corporate funds and money collected from political fund-raising parties. As most of the money collected at these large parties was corporate money, the NLC essentially abandoned its original hopes to avoid corporate funding. By 1979, individual contributions had dropped to only 1.2 percent of the party's total income, whereas corporate contributions had mounted to account for 33 percent of its income.[32] A glance at the list of corporations giving money to the NLC in a given year would indicate that many of the largest corporations and banks contributed 1 million yen or more to the splinter conservative party. Of the top thirty-five contributors to parties, twenty-six gave money to the NLC, including 23 million yen from Sumitomo Bank.[33]

In 1979, the *Yomiuri Shimbun* commented on the four factors indispensable to the survival of a political party in Japan. Three of these factors—*shikken*, or political funds; *soshiki*, or organization; and *imeigi*, or image—have already been discussed; the fourth is *seisoku*, or policy.[34] Regarding this last factor, many criticized the NLC for being a pale copy of the LDP except in the areas of political ethics and education policy. Other minor Japanese parties may have greater policy emphasis, but their appeal is usually to a narrow sector of the overall society. Domestic policy differences have seldom been important in differentiating among Japanese parties; moreover, they appear to be much less signficant than those encountered in the U.S. party system. Upon adding policy distinctiveness or attractiveness to the aforementioned three crucial factors of party success (political funds, organization, and image), then, we find that the most successful new party, the NLC, had difficulties in all four categories, and the other minor parties have fared even worse.

Still other factors appear to have facilitated the rise of these parties. For instance, much of the political support for the NLC (now disbanded) and the SDF came from the approximately 30 percent of the electorate that refuses to identify with any political party. In the *Mainichi Shimbun* poll of November 11, 1982, 35 percent of the sample responded that they were not supporting any party.[35] It is this group of "floating voters" that largely sustained the NLC and SDF and offers hope to all of the other new parties. The Japanese electorate is not completely committed to the old established parties, but something special is required to move this largely uncommitted group to consistent political support of a new party.

CONCLUSION

In sum, none of the post-1970 new parties have a supporting "godfather" who can give them an instant organizational base for communications, political activities, fund-raising, and electoral campaigning. This is in contrast to the strong external organizations that support the new parties of the 1960s: the former DSP (Dōmei Labor Confederation) and the Kōmeitō (the Sōka Gakkai Buddhist sect). Needless to say, the other new parties have no external supporting organization. The NLC was able to prosper in the 1976 election by riding the crest of its media "boom," but its organizational weakness was clear in the election defeats of 1977 (House of Councillors), 1979 (House of Representatives), and 1980 (House of Councillors). The SDF, unable to benefit from a media boom, never experienced a great initial success and has remained small throughout its political life—for the most part limited by its organizational weaknesses.

It is important to realize that in many ways the future success of the new parties is largely beyond the control of their leadership. The appeal of the reformist image of the NLC was largely undercut by the LDP's adoption of reforms while selecting its president. The runoff or primary elections that constitute these reforms were held twice in the period after the NLC split. In the case of the SDF, its defection from the JSP was largely in protest of the extreme leftist influence in control of the JSP. Its reason for existence has been discounted by the JSP's apparent shift to more moderate policies and the selection of more moderate members into the party leadership group between 1982 and 1990.

Certain scholars of Japanese politics, such as Bradley Richardson and Scott Flanagan,[36] held the opinion that the NLC and SDF may be the prototypes for the major parties of a future party system in Japan. They viewed the NLC as a party that advocated the self-reliant individual, free enterprise, and a libertarian political philosophy while focusing on such issues as education reform and quality of life. On the opposition side of Japanese politics, the SDF is characterized as a Socialist party without Marxism—or perhaps even without socialism. In other words, the former NLC and the SDF appear to be the moderate, modern manifestations of the LDP and the JSP. It is toward the policies of these that the two mainstays of Japanese politics appear to be heading, though somewhat slowly and fitfully. It was just this moderation and reform on the part of the JSP and LDP that caused the demise of the NLC and the failure of the SDF to become a major party.

This chapter has focused on the question as to why all of the new post-1975 Japanese parties have not developed into major parties. Most significant among the inhibiting factors have been problems of image, problems of factionalism, weak organizational bases, the lack of powerful supporting organizations, the inability of the parties to raise large sums of political funds, the lack of charismatic leadership, and the countermoves made by the established parties either to reduce the attractiveness of the new parties or to weaken them by causing new party members to once again return to the parent parties. Indeed, these factors all help to answer the question: "Why do new parties fail to develop into major political institutions in Japan?"

NOTES

1. Charles Hauss and David Rayside, "The Development of New Parties in Western Democracies Since 1945," in L. Maisel and J. Coopes, eds., *Political Parties: Development and Decoy* (Beverly Hills, Calif.: Sage, 1978), pp. 31–57.

2. Ruth K. Scott and Ronald J. Hrebenar, *Parties in Crisis: Party Politics in America* (New York: Wiley & Sons, 1984), pp. 51–54.

3. Hauss and Rayside, "The Development of New Parties."

4. Much of the data produced for this chapter come from a series of interviews with Kōno Yōhei and other NLC and minor party leaders conducted in 1977, 1979, and 1983.

5. See Ronald J. Hrebenar, "Kōno Yōhei and the Future of the Shin-jiyu Club," *Japan Interpreter* 12 no. 1 (Spring 1978), pp. 223–233. See also Susan J. Parr, "Liberal Democrats in Disarray: Intergenerational Conflict in the Conservative Camp," in Terry E. MacDougall, ed., *Political Leadership in Contemporary Japan* (Ann Arbor, Mich.: Center for Japanese Studies, 1982).

6. *Kyōdo* news poll (July 7, 1977); *Tokyo Shimbun* poll (April 24, 1977).

7. *Asahi Shimbun* (September 20, 1979).

8. Kōno Yōhei, "My Determination to Challenge Political Innovation" [Seiji-Sasshin ni Chosensuru Watashi-no Ketsui], *Gekkan Shinjiyu Club* (September 1979), pp. 15–17.

9. *Japan Times* (June 20, 1979).

10. *Mainichi Daily News* (July 25, 1979).

11. *Mainichi Daily News* (July 22, 1979).

12. *Mainichi Daily News* (August 14, 1979).

13. "Internal Trouble in NLC over Its Action Policy," *Sentaku* (January 1983), p. 42.

14. *Asahi Evening News* (November 7, 1979, and November 27, 1979).

15. *Nihon Keizai* (November 7, 1979).

16. *Asahi Shimbun*, editorial (November 27, 1979).

17. *Yomiuri Shimbun*, editorial (November 27, 1979).

18. *Mainichi Shimbun*, editorials (December 1, 1979, and November 22, 1979).

19. Tagawa Seiichi, quoted in the *Asahi Evening News* (November 27, 1979).

20. *Yomiuri Shimbun* (November 27, 1979).

21. *Asahi Evening News* (November 7, 1979).

22. See Hans H. Baerwald, "Japan's Double Elections," *Asian Survey* 20, no. 12 (December 1980), pp. 1169–1184.

23. *Nihon Keizai* (February 18, 1985).

24. *Nihon Keizai* (February 19, 1985).

25. Gerald L. Curtis, *The Japanese Way of Politics* (New York: Columbia University Press, 1988), pp. 34–35.

26. *Asahi Shimbun* (June 24, 1980).

27. *Japan Times* (April 8, 1977).

28. *Japan Times* (May 25, 1977).

29. Shimizu Minoru, *Japan Times* (June 24, 1976).

30. *Asahi Shimbun* (September 9, 1982).

31. *Gekkan Shin Jiyu Club* (March 1980), p. 19.

32. Ibid. (February-March 1979), p. 75.

33. *Kampo*, Political Fund Report (1985).

34. *Yomiuri Shimbun* (March 8, 1979). A more modern variant of the "three ban" is the "three ki": *soshiki* (organization) in place of *jiban; ninki* (popularity) in place of *kanban;* and *rieki* (interest or group support) in place of *kaban.* It is now said the "three ban" are necessary for winning in a traditional rural district, whereas the "three ki" are needed to win in the more modern urban districts.

35. *Mainichi Shimbun Poll* (November 11, 1982).

36. Bradley M. Richardson and Scott C. Flanagan, *Politics in Japan* (Boston: Little, Brown, 1984), p. 257.

PART FOUR

The Ruling Party of Japan and Its Future

9

The Liberal Democratic Party: The Ruling Party of Japan

NOBUO TOMITA
AKIRA NAKAMURA
RONALD J. HREBENAR

Among the political systems of nonsocialist developed nations, Japan is unique in that except for a short period after World War II, when a Socialist-centered coalition government ruled Japan in 1947–1948, conservative forces have continuously held power on the national level. In 1955, when two conservative parties merged to form the Liberal Democratic party (LDP), conservative rule was concentrated within that single organization and has maintained its reign as the governing party for more than thirty-five years. During this time, the various opposition parties have been effectively excluded from real power in the national-level government of Japan.

Only on limited occasions have the opponents gained a substantial number of Diet seats in elections and come close to taking control of government. Most recently this happened in the July 1989 election for the House of Councillors, a contest held against the background of four detrimental developments to the LDP's political fortune.

First was a series of political scandals generally referred to as the "Rikuruto" (Recruit) affairs. The Recruit Cosmos Company distributed large amounts of its stock to a list of Diet members, including such conservative leaders as Nakasone and Takeshita. By cashing them in later, these politicians made handsome, tax-free capital gains. Second, the insider trading by the Diet members naturally outraged the Japanese electorate, particularly because the conservatives instituted a new indirect tax despite strong opposition from many sectors of the society. From April 1, 1989, the Japanese began to pay a 3 percent consumer tax for all items across the board, even for daily food, child bearing, and funeral expenses. Third, as if these would not be enough, the Liberal Democrats drove their traditional supporters into a fury in yet another way. Prime Minister Uno Sōsuke, who ascended to the post after Takeshita stepped down in the wake of the Recruit scandal, was publicly exposed to have a mistress. Although womanizing had not been unusual among Japanese politicians, and historically such personal behavior had been considered irrelevant to political affairs even among Japanese mass media, clearly the rules had changed in 1989. Uno's sex scandal was followed by similar exposés of other LDP members. These affairs gradually became a significant political liability for the conservative party. Finally, the eroding relationship with the United States over trade issues tended to place many in the LDP in a precarious position. To alleviate the imbalance, the Japanese government needed to accede to the U.S. demands and pledge to open its market for major agricultural commodities by April 1992. Rural voters, the bedrock of the conservative governance, were naturally unhappy with this decision and were not reluctant to show their discontent.[1]

There was an important harbinger of the disastrous upper house elections of July 23, 1989. Twenty-two days previously, on July 2, the Tokyo Metropolitan Assembly held elections to choose its members. As in many other prefectural and local polities in Japan, the LDP had, up to this election, dominated the Tokyo assembly. Prior to this contest, the total membership of the body had been 127, of which the LDP had held a commanding 63 seats, whereas the Socialists had remained in fourth place with only 12 seats. This was all, however, radically altered in the July 2 election. Although the Tokyo Metropolitan Assembly had little to do with the four national events previously noted, Tokyo voters nonetheless availed themselves of the occasion and sent their stern message of displeasure over the scandals as well as other policies to the governing Liberal Democratic party. In the election, the LDP marked a substantial defeat, losing 20 of its 63 seats; the Socialists tripled their membership by capturing a total of 36 seats. The Democratic Socialists also advanced their share by 2, to a total of 5 members. However, other parties could not take advantage of the situation; the Japan Communist party and the Kōmeitō secured only 14 and 26 seats, respectively. Thus, the Japan Socialist party became the second largest party in the Tokyo assembly.

In the House of Councillors election, the LDP "bashing" continued. In the 1989 election, 50 seats were at stake in the PR district. Both the LDP and the Socialists listed 25 candidates. In these lists, the conservatives were mindful of the fact that the Socialists were led by a female, Doi Takako, and that women voters appeared unhappy about the consumer tax and the scandals. As a way to appease this electorate, the LDP thus ranked a female at the top of its candidate list.

However, the political ploy was not successful. A number of past surveys have demonstrated that not only is the Japanese electorate rather passive, but it is also indifferent to national problems. Generally, Japanese voters are so concerned about local issues that they often show reverence to those Diet members from their own district. Many claim that this is one of the major reasons why so many Diet members who have been involved in various scandals are often left unpunished in the general election and remain active and powerful in the national legislature. To be sure, such trends continue especially in rural districts; however, the 1989 elections appeared different from past contests. National issues seemed to become the key determinant of voting behavior for large numbers of the Japanese electorate.

In the local districts, 50 conservative members were up for reelection, while in the PR district, 19 LDP seats were at stake. For the Socialists, 20 seats were up for reelection: 13 for the local and 7 for the PR districts.[2] When the results came in, the conservatives won only a total of 37 seats, whereas the Socialists overtook the conservatives by winning a total of 52. When these numbers were added to the seats not up for election, the new totals for the LDP were 110 seats, down by 32 from the previous share of 142. Socialist seats were increased from the old strength of 43 to a stunning 74 members. Other than the Socialists, the newly formed Japan Trade Union Confederation (Nihon Rōdō Kumiai Sōrengōkai, or Rengō) also performed extremely well. The group scored 11 wins, mostly in several single-member districts, and advanced its strength to a total of 12 seats. Interestingly, except for the Socialists and Rengō, other parties did not do well. The Kōmeitō, Japan Communist party, and Democratic Socialists reduced their share by 2 or 3 seats in the upper house.

The 1989 House of Councillors election thus brought a new political landscape to Japan. The contest left the Liberal Democrats 17 seats short of the majority in the upper house. If the Japan Socialist party cooperates with other groups, these forces could become a major stumbling block to the conservative domination of Diet politics. The chairwoman of the Japan Socialist party, Doi Takako, observed that "the mountain has moved," thus indicating that Japanese politics had entered a new era.

However, one should not underestimate the political resilience of the conservative party. The conservatives have been highly sensitive to the public mood and quick to adopt aspects of it in their political agenda. When, for instance, the public outcry for welfare programs became rampant, as in 1972, the LDP (then headed by Tanaka) took the issue and announced its intention to increase expenditures for the handicapped and the elderly. Again, during the Miki administration, as the Lockheed scandal caught the attention of the public, the conservatives responded by announcing their determination to entrench political ethics in the party and its policies.

In the February 1990 election for the House of Representatives, the first contest after the electoral debacle of summer 1989, the LDP once again took a highly pragmatic approach to ease the growing discontent among its regular supporters. In this campaign, the LDP was not reluctant to use openly whatever leverages it could command. The 1989 supplementary budget, which was compiled by the government approximately a month prior to the 1990 election, was one of the best examples of this LDP effort. For two consecutive years, the size of the supplementary budget grew, reaching nearly 6 trillion yen. The inflationary trend of this budget was clearly the result of the conservatives becoming highly sensitive to political attitudes of a large number of annoyed voters. By parceling out the public fund to different groups, the governing party tried to buy favors of these disgruntled electorates.

When the LDP encountered trouble with rural voters during the 1990 HR elections, a special extra grant of 50 billion yen was provided for traditional supporters of the LDP in the rural constituencies under the title of the Promotional Fund for the Development of Agricultural and Fishing Industries (Nōson Gyoson Shinkō Kikin). Likewise, another 50-billion-yen subsidy was also prepared for those urban voters who owned small- and medium-sized industries. The endowment was made available for these proprietors to improve operation of their firms and factories.[3] In addition, by the end of 1989, the Liberal Democrats once again had to recognize the need to placate Japan's farming interests. They decided to put off enactment of a measure to reduce arable land for rice growing, despite the recommendations of a nonpartisan advisory commission. Similarly, elderly voters also were targeted by the conservative campaign. In December 1989, the LDP called off a plan to increase a number of medical charges of the national health program for the aged. Taking the coming election into account, the governing party felt the need to keep the elderly voters in check and kept such individual expenses under this program, at least for the time being.[4] Not until December 1990 were individual medical charges in the national health program for the aged finally increased to 1,000 yen a month for out-patient services and 500 yen a day for in-patient services.

The conservatives' efforts apparently worked to their advantage. In the lower house election on February 18, 1990, the Liberal Democrats succeeded in halting further erosion of their electoral fortune. In spite of a large number of preelection projections pointing to another major defeat of the LDP, the governing party gained a total of 286 seats, including 11 members who were elected as independents but who later joined the LDP. Not only did the LDP muster a majority of the 512 lower house seats, but it also surmounted one of the major political crises in its party history.

Interestingly, the Japan Socialist party also advanced its share of seats in the lower chamber, increasing to 141 from its previous 83 seats. However, other opposition parties declined: The Clean Government party (Kōmeitō), for example, lost 9 seats for a total of 46, the Communists reduced their share by 11 to a total of 16 seats, and the Democratic Socialists declined to a mere 14 seats from the preelection total of 26.[5]

Many other examples of the LDP's pragmatic political style could be cited. It is likely, moreover, that the LDP will continue such a pragmatic approach in the future, and if this is the case, the conservatives will be able to consolidate their leading position in Japanese politics. It is from this perspective that we will analyze the LDP and its role within the overall context of contemporary Japanese politics.

Any discussion of postwar Japanese politics must start off with an explanation of the particular importance of the year 1955. It was in November of that year that the two major conservative political parties, the Liberals and the Democrats, joined to create the Liberal Democratic party. Further-

TABLE 9.1
Major issues in Japanese politics and LDP policy responses

Year	Major Issue	Cabinet	Party Platform
1958		Kishi	Increase defense expenditures Clean and fair politics
1960	Following revision of the U.S.-Japan Security Treaty and after turmoils have subsided	Ikeda	Open and consensual parliamentary politics Implementation of revised Security Treaty
1963	Rapid economic growth	Ikeda	Income-doubling policy Making a New Japan
1967	Black Mist scandal	Satō	Rectification of politics Stabilized consumer prices
1969	Okinawa reversion	Satō	Returning Okinawa Non-nuclear policies
1972	Sino-Japanese peace accord	Tanaka	Remaking the Japanese economy Increase welfare policies
1976	Lockheed affair	Miki	Clean politics Factions dissolved
1979		Ōhira	Consolidation of national finances Secure energy sources
1980	Double elections	Ōhira	Stabilize consumer prices Increase defense power
1983	Tanaka's trial	Nakasone	Administrative and financial reforms Entrenching political ethics
1988	Recruit Cosmos affair	Takeshita	Political ethics
1989	Consumption tax	Uno	Reform tax base
1990	Trade conflict	Kaifu	Political reform Trade concession packages

Source: Adapted from the *Asahi Shimbun* (November 12, 1985), p. 2. Updated by authors.

more, it was just shortly before the birth of the LDP that, in October 1955, the formerly divided Right and Left factions of the Socialist party merged to form a regenerated Japan Socialist party (JSP). Thus, by late 1955, the plethora of parties that had appeared during the period of confusion following World War II had essentially consolidated, at least for a period of time, into a two-party system.

In view of these significant developments, the Japanese mass media, as well as many academics, tended at that time to become sanguine about the political future of Japan. Not only did they regard Japanese politics as having finally emerged from the disorderly postwar period, but they were also inclined to consider the appearance of the two-party system as a quite favorable step toward the construction of a mature democracy. These enthusiastic responses were attested by the fact that the situation was labeled by academics and journalists alike as "the political system of 1955" (*gojū-gonen taisei*).[6]

The decision of the conservatives to merge was expedited by two external forces: pressures from "corporate Japan"—what is called the financial world, or *zaikai*—and the reunification of the progressive or Socialist parties and their strengthened challenge to the conservatives. Historically, there have been extremely close ties between conservative parties and corporate Japan. This tight relationship has led some to refer cynically to the cooperative efforts of the government and the *zaikai* as "Japan Incorporated." It is also attested by the fact that the major income of the LDP has been and still is drawn almost completely from the contributions of the giant corporations. At the end of every August, the contributions reported to the Ministry of Home Affairs are made public. In 1989 the record showed that the LDP generated over 24.6 billion yen as political funds, an increase of 10.5 percent from the previous year. Of those amazing volumes, 54.1 percent came as political contributions mainly from major enterprises, while 18.3 percent and 6.0 percent were party fees and incomes from various activities, respectively. Party fees and other miscellaneous incomes as a share of total party funds were declining, however. Instead, the Liberal Democrats depended heavily on borrowings from different sources. Private loans, primarily from financial institutions, increased to 20.3 percent of the total. Three quarters of the total political funds of the conservative party, in other words, came from either contributions or borrowings from private firms, reflecting the extent to which the LDP relied on corporate Japan for its funding.

In addition to these monies, additional political contributions would usually go directly to leading party members or major factions of the LDP. With respect to factions, the leading Takeshita group alone collected a total of 1,053 million yen, an increase of 26.4 percent from the previous year. The rival Abe faction, likewise, generated more than 1,387 million yen, although this was a decline of 23.0 percent. Comparable to these groups in reference to political funds was the Nakasone faction (currently the Watanabe group), which accumulated more than 1,196 million yen in 1989. When these figures were added to the funds amassed by two other groups, Miyazawa and Kōmoto, the five major factions in the LDP together acquired the staggering sum of 5,492 million yen from various sources in the 1989 reporting period.

The donors of these funds revealed an interesting pattern. In 1989 the number of business organizations that contributed more than 20 million yen a year reached 148. These enterprises provided a total of 6.8 billion yen for political purposes. Naturally, the lion's share went to the conservative forces, though a meager sum was also offered to the moderate Democratic Socialists. Of the different types of businesses, banking and financial institutions were the top contributors. Eleven leading banks, including Fuji, Daiichi Kangyō, Sumitomo, Sanwa, and Nihon Kōgyō were ranked at the top of those 148 major enterprise donors. The contributions by banking and financial organizations accounted for more than 29.1 percent of the total political donations in 1989. Aside from them, real estate and construction industries were the second largest donors of political funds. With contributions of more than 6.8 billion yen, these land-related firms contributed over 15.2 percent of the total political funds. A number of academics argued that this large contribution had been one of the major reasons why the conservative government, responsive to the interests of these land-related firms, had eased land price controls and allowed the value of land to spiral out of sight.[7]

The reason the business world, and especially the banking community, has supported the LDP more than the other parties lies in the fact that the conservatives constitute the party that has helped provide the most favorable environment for rapid economic expansion. Japanese economic development has been marked by heavy investments in plants, facilities, and equipment on the part of the various levels of government and especially by the private sector. To invest in modern equipment and factories, corporations had to borrow money from banks and other financial institutions. With these financial means available, Japanese industries have been able to scrap archaic facilities and build new and sophisticated plants, often equipped with the most modern robots. By means of such heavy borrowing, Japanese companies have been able to produce reliable products that have been very competitive in the international market. However, this pattern of heavy borrowing has naturally put almost all Japanese firms into perennial debt; indeed, the debts owed to the various banks by the average major Japanese enterprise account for roughly 80 percent of its entire capital. If this situation occurred in the United States, the company in question would have declared bankruptcy. But this is not the case in Japan for several reasons. First, the major stockholders of the big businesses are, with few exceptions, banks and lending institutions, which prefer to keep lending money to the corporations and to generate profits on the loans. Second, as long as the company is a leading one, the government would be likely to rescue it if for any reason it is in danger of bankruptcy—particularly if the government fears serious repercussions for other sectors of the economy. It follows that the banking institutions are by and large failure-proof, thanks to the government policy of promoting the economy by means of capital investment. And it is therefore not surprising that the leading banks are one of the major contributors to the LDP's treasury.

The political influence of the *zaikai* during the 1950s was perhaps even more pronounced than it is today. The Japanese economy was still in a period of recovery, and business leaders were strongly united in their objective of attaining high economic growth. In implementing this goal, business first sought to establish political stability as an essential condition for maintaining economic growth. Such stability was of particular concern given that the conservative politicians were divided into two rival parties and had engaged in a pattern of serious power rifts. From the viewpoint of corporate Japan, that political situation was detrimental to the achievement of economic goals and had to be rectified by nearly any means. Fortunately for Japanese business interests, they had sufficient leverage to correct the situation and were not reluctant to utilize their power.[8]

Even though the conservatives had separated into the Liberal and Democratic parties before the unification of 1955, the two parties were similar in that both had depended heavily upon the *zaikai* for their political funding. The *zaikai* was then, and still is today, the only reliable source of political funds for the conservatives. Especially during the 1950s, when the conservatives had no alternative but to build their campaigns upon corporate funding. Business, wanting its needs in Japanese politics to be articulated by a single powerful political party, forced the conservatives to resolve their differences.

Four major business organizations constitute what is commonly referred to as the *zaikai*: the Federation of Economic Organizations (Keizai Dantai Rengōkai), the Japan Federation of Employers' Association (Nihon Keieisha Dantai Renmei), the Committee for Economic Development (Keizai Dōyūkai), and the Japanese Chamber of Commerce and Industry (Nihon Shōkō Kaigisho). These four groups had called for the merging of the conservatives as early as 1952. As a result of their pressure, two conservative groups were forced to reconcile and from January 1955, the *zaikai* began to channel the flow of their political contributions through a single organization, thereby establishing the Economic Reconstruction Forum (ERF, or Keizai Saiken Kondankai). The purpose of this organization was to administer political contributions from the business world, which had previously flowed directly from each company to its preferred party or parties. The conservative politicians eventually knuckled under to the *zaikai*'s financial pressures and moved to form the LDP in November 1955. Responding to this positive act by the politicians, the Economic Reconstruction Forum made periodic political contributions of 20 million yen to the LDP between 1955 and 1961, when the ERF was dissolved—for a total of approximately 3.8 billion yen.[9]

The second factor promoting the merger of the conservatives was the advance of the progressive political forces within Japan. The Peace Treaty, which brought Japan back into the international society of nations, was signed by forty-eight nations including the United States in September 1951. This brought an end to the Occupation of Japan by the Allied powers and officially ended World War II for the Japanese. Consequently, Japan regained its status as an independent nation, and a new era of domestic politics began to emerge. Concomitant with the signing of the Peace Treaty, Japan signed a Security Treaty with the United States that encouraged Japan to play an increasingly vital role in the U.S. world strategic plan against the Soviet Union. The conservative and progressive camps conflicted head-on over these treaties, but the progressives were sharply divided among themselves as well. A deep division within the Socialist movement made the split between the Left and the Right even more serious. The Left opposed both treaties, whereas the Right approved of the Peace Treaty but opposed the Security Treaty with the United States. The difference of opinion was so intense that it could not be easily reconciled by either faction. The two Socialist factions eventually recognized that they could not resolve the conflict at the time, and thus the party was split into two parts in 1951.[10]

Despite the split, the strength of both the Left and Right Socialist parties continued to grow. In the lower house election of 1952, the first such election after the split in the party, the Left captured 54 seats and the Right won 57 seats. This brought the total number of seats held by Socialists to 111, or 23.8 percent, of the 466 seats in the chamber. Although both the Right and the Left made gains in the next lower house elections, the Left began to increase its seat totals from 54 to 72, and the Right increased its share by 9 to a total of 66. The total number of seats held by Socialists, both Right and Left, thus increased to 138 (29.6 percent of the total) in 1953. Adding the seats held by other small minor opposition parties to the Socialists' totals, we find that the anticonservative forces held nearly one-third of the House seats. In the February 1955 HR elections, the opposition, composed of the Right and Left Socialists, the Farmer-Labor party, and the Communist party, made still more gains. The Left Socialist party alone surged to 89 seats, and the progressives as a whole took 162 seats, or over 34 percent of the total seats.[11]

Partly because of this series of electoral triumphs, the Socialists believed that control of the national government would soon be theirs. Under the leadership of the Left, the Socialists moved to suspend their factional differences and reunited the party in October 1955. In the eyes of both the conservatives and the Japanese business community, this reunification of the Socialist party undoubtedly posed an alarming threat to the future stability of Japan. Grave concern was voiced for the new Socialist party, and its string of electoral victories appeared to represent the first realistic step toward the realization of a Socialist Japan. Conservative politicians began to discuss methods to combat the threat. Miki Bukichi, in particular, a conservative leader who had participated in conservative politics since prewar times, was a leader in these discussions. Miki and other such "Old Guard" leaders were highly dissatisfied with the division within the conservative camp—a division they felt was largely based around personal conflicts to the detriment of conservative policies. From their point of view, if such a state of affairs continued, the Socialists would sooner or later overwhelm the conservative forces. As a means to prevent such a disaster, Miki Bukichi proposed that the conservatives be unified. In this manner, only one month after the unification of the Socialist party, the Liberals and the Democrats merged on November 15, 1955. Japan had a two-party system for the first time in the postwar period, and a new era had begun.[12]

THE DEVELOPMENT OF THE 1955 POLITICAL SYSTEM AND ITS SUBSEQUENT DECLINE

The promising appearance of a party system dominated by two large parties after 1955 has not endured. In retrospect, it seems that the "system of 1955" did not have a solid enough substance to be accurately termed a party system. A deviant pattern from the original 1955 two-party system has instead evolved, with the continuation of the LDP in a status of permanent power being its central characteristic.

The major change in the "system of 1955" was the fragmentation of the opposition into a number of parties from the single-party opposition of the

TABLE 9.2
Lower house election results of 1990: The case of the third district of Gunma Prefecture

	Number of seats to be elected = 4	
Candidate	*Party Affiliation*	*Number of Votes*
Fukuda Yasuo	Liberal Democrat	88,445
Yamaguchi Tsuruo	Socialist	87,758
Nakasone Yasuhiro	Independent (Ex-LDP)	86,552
Obuchi Keizō	Liberal Democrat	76,832

Source: Adapted from *Political Handbook*, 1990, p. 217.

Socialists (plus the nearly invisible JCP) in 1955. The explosion of opposition parties began in 1960 with the splintering of the DSP from the JSP and then accelerated in 1964 with the formation of the Kōmeitō.[13] Many reasons account for the rise of the opposition parties, but a major one has been the existence of an election law that is supportive of minor parties. For a more detailed examination of this Japanese electoral system, please consult Chapter 2 of this book; for the purposes of our present examination of the LDP, however, we make the following observations.

The Impact of Electoral Law on the LDP

The medium-sized constituency system used for the House of Representatives has had a profound impact on the nature of the LDP. The distinctive feature of this election system is that each voter casts but a single vote for one candidate, yet in each district multiple members of the HR are elected. Of the total of 130 election districts, one constituency, that of the Anami Islands, elects a single member, while four districts return two. And only one, the first district of Hokkaidō, has six winners. These districts under the current system are the exceptions, however. The most popular patterns are the constituencies returning from 3 to 5 members for the House of Representatives; there are 42 districts with 3 members, 39 constituencies with 4 members, and 43 districts with 5 members.

Under the current system, a strong party can run multiple candidates in the same district. The LDP often does this, usually electing two or three party members in its strong constituencies. A rather good example of this pattern can be seen in the third constituency of Gunma Prefecture, which has a total of four seats—and three of them (counting the seat held by Nakasone, though he has become independent as a result of his implication in the recent Recruit scandal) are held by the LDP (see Table 9.2). It is important to understand that the political situation in such multimember constituencies differs significantly from that found in single-seat districts in many Euro-American-style democracies. In particular, as evidenced in the case of the third Gunma district, a situation may develop in which the bitterest competition is often between members of the same political party rather than between rival parties. The five big LDP factions will often recruit a factional candidate to run in a given district and then give him significant support in his race to defeat candidates supported by other rival LDP factions in the same district. The real contest in a district, then, may be between a

Takeshita candidate and a Miyazawa candidate but not between the LDP and the JCP or JSP.

In the final analysis, the year 1955 is important for a number of different reasons. Beginning in that year, the LDP took on its role as Japan's seemingly permanent governing party (on the national level) and eventually proved that it could work with those interested in maintaining a policy of high economic growth—a growth that would enable Japan to become an economic giant by the 1970s. The year 1955 also marks the beginning of the collapse of the expectation of those who believed Japan was about to embark upon a path of a stable two-party system such as that of the United States. Eventually, however, there developed a party system characterized by the LDP at its center and surrounded by a host of opposition parties unable to gather enough strength to seriously challenge the LDP's political supremacy. Even though this one-time rather neat arrangement was modified somewhat by the upper house election in 1989, the simple fact is that the conservatives continue to run Japan on the national level, and that pattern appears to have sufficient strength to persist for the foreseeable future.

LDP Electoral Support: A Trend Analysis from a Historical Perspective

The fact that the LDP has ruled Japan since 1955 does not necessarily suggest that the base of conservative support has remained unchanged. As we have already indicated, significant changes have occurred in the LDP's base of support during the last nearly four decades.

The first election following the formation of the LDP was held in 1958. In this election, the LDP and the Japan Socialist party together shared 90.7 percent of the total vote, while they also took 97.0 percent of the seats. This outcome proved to be the beginning of—and the peak for—the LDP-JSP system of 1955, as both parties have since experienced a decline in vote percentages. In terms of the number of seats, the Socialists have never been able to surpass the conservative share, leaving Japan's party system as a one-and-a-half rather than a genuine two-party system. It ought also to be pointed out that the 1955 system soon began to disintegrate, because several moderate parties gradually came to play a significant role in Japanese politics in the 1960s and 1970s. First, two moderate factions in the JSP left the party and formed the Democratic Socialist party in 1960. This was followed by the formation of the Kōmeitō (Clean Government party) as a political arm of the religious organization, Sōka Gakkai, in 1964. In the 1970s, as an open expression of protest against money politics, Kōno Yōhei split away from the LDP and formed the New Liberal Club in June 1974.

Ever since the beginning of 1960, these moderate parties in general and the Kōmeitō in particular increased their political strength and developed into forces to be reckoned with in the Japanese political environment. It is primarily because of this rise in the power of the moderate parties that the LDP's vote-getting ability declined below the 50 percent mark for the first time in 1967 (to 48.8 percent), while its share of the seats also fell under 50 percent (to 48.7 percent) in 1976. In view of the continuing erosion of its base of conservative support, the LDP tried to lure independent Diet members to its camp and barely remained in power by adding them as new members to its ranks. Particularly from 1976 to 1983, the competition and rivalry between the conservative party and these moderate forces became so fierce that it literally put an end to the nascent two-party system in Japan.

Historically, the LDP has been said to be strong in rural communities and weak in urban constituencies. We have tried to probe the reasons behind this conventional knowledge in Japan by analyzing both 1972 and 1977 electoral outcomes. We attempted to see if there would be any positive correlation between the number of votes each party gained and variables associated with voters' living conditions. These included (1) whether or not the voters were living in the same communities in which they were born; (2) how long they had lived in these communities; and (3) whether or not they owned their houses in these districts. We found that in terms of these three indices, the electorates in rural communities scored much higher than those in urban districts. In other words, those who lived in rural Japan tended to reside in the communities of their birth, and they also remained in the same districts. At the same time, chances were good that these rural voters owned houses in their respective areas of residence. Our investigation found that the positive scores on these variables were positively associated with increases in voter turnout. This is because the rural voters living in the place of their birth for a long period of time in their own homes were generally inclined to have a strong sense of "community consciousness" and strong concern for their home districts. We might add that a large number of the LDP candidates also shared the same characteristics and concerns with the rural electorates, and they had a better chance of establishing a rapport with these rural voters than did other party candidates. In the eyes of a large number of the rural Japanese, the conservatives appeared to be highly conscious of and eager to look after the well-being of their communities. In contrast, our investigation demonstrated that urban communities with large populations living in densely populated districts and with large numbers of the labor force in tertiary industries reflected an inverse relationship with respect to voter support of the conservatives. These seemed the major reasons for the general decline of the LDP's popularity in the late 1960s and beyond.[14]

This downward trend in the LDP's fortunes was clearly foreseen by some even within the conservative camp. For instance, Ishida Hirohide predicted in an article published in 1963 that electoral support for the LDP would drop to 46.6 percent by 1968, that the JSP's support would increase to 47 percent, and that the two parties' positions would be reversed by the end of the decade. Ishida's calculations were based on the assumption of a change in the employment structure that would result from continued vigorous growth of the economy. He further estimated that the proportion of persons employed in the primary sector (farming, fishing, and lumber) would decrease to 24 percent in the 1970s, or half its percentage of only a decade earlier. On the other hand, he foresaw that 32 percent of the labor force would be employed in the secondary sector and 44 percent in the tertiary sector. He felt that these latter two increases would result in an increase in the ranks of organized labor and thus lead directly to gains for the JSP. Ishida therefore encouraged the LDP to quickly reform itself in order to be able to compete in the coming social order.[15]

The Ishida article produced a great response because it had been authored by an important member of the LDP. Those within the conservative camp seriously considered the central arguments of the article, and "the crisis of the conservative party" became a major point of discussion in Japanese politics. Ishida's predictions proved to be too conservative, however—at least in terms of the assumed changes in the occupational structure of Japan. By 1970 the percentage of workers in the primary sector had declined to 19.3 percent, while those in the secondary and tertiary sectors had risen to 34.1 percent and 46.5 percent, respectively. Following Ishida's logic, the transformation of the structure of the economy during the 1960s should have worked against the interests of the LDP and, in the worst possible case, could have led to a reversal of the positions of the LDP and the JSP.

However, it is crucial to remember that, given the nature of the Japanese electoral system, the decline in the LDP vote share did not necessarily mean a reduction in its number of seats in the HR. In the elections of the 1960s, the LDP won 296 seats in 1960, 283 in 1963, 277 in 1967, and 288 in 1969. In terms of percentages of seats captured, the LDP ranged from 57 percent in 1967 to 63 percent in 1960 and finished the decade with almost 60 percent in the 1969 elections. In the LDP's case, then, the percentage of seats it captures has always been higher than its voting percentage—a fact that helps to explain how it has managed to hold on to power for so long at the national level of Japanese politics.

It also must be noted that the bias in the LDP's favor is a most important result of one aspect of Japanese electoral law—namely, the malapportionment of the electoral districts. The apportionment of the lower house was originally based on the census of 1946. A very large rural population existed at that time as a result of the marked decline in the population of the great urban centers such as Tokyo, which in turn resulted from such war-related factors as persons leaving for military service, civilian evacuations, and the Allied bombings. However, the reindustrialization of the urban areas in the years immediately after the war led to a mass migration to the cities.[16] Despite the enormous increase in urban population, the apportionment of HR seats has not been adjusted, except for minor changes including small additions in 1964 and 1975, when few seats were added to some urban constituencies.[17] Also, another minor alteration was implemented in 1986. Seven seats were taken from rural districts and distributed to urban constituencies, and eight new seats were assigned to urban districts, making the total size of the lower house now 512 seats.

The decline of the conservative support tapered off somewhat by the mid-1970s despite a number of significant demographic changes occurring

FIGURE 9.1
Lower house election results, 1958-1990

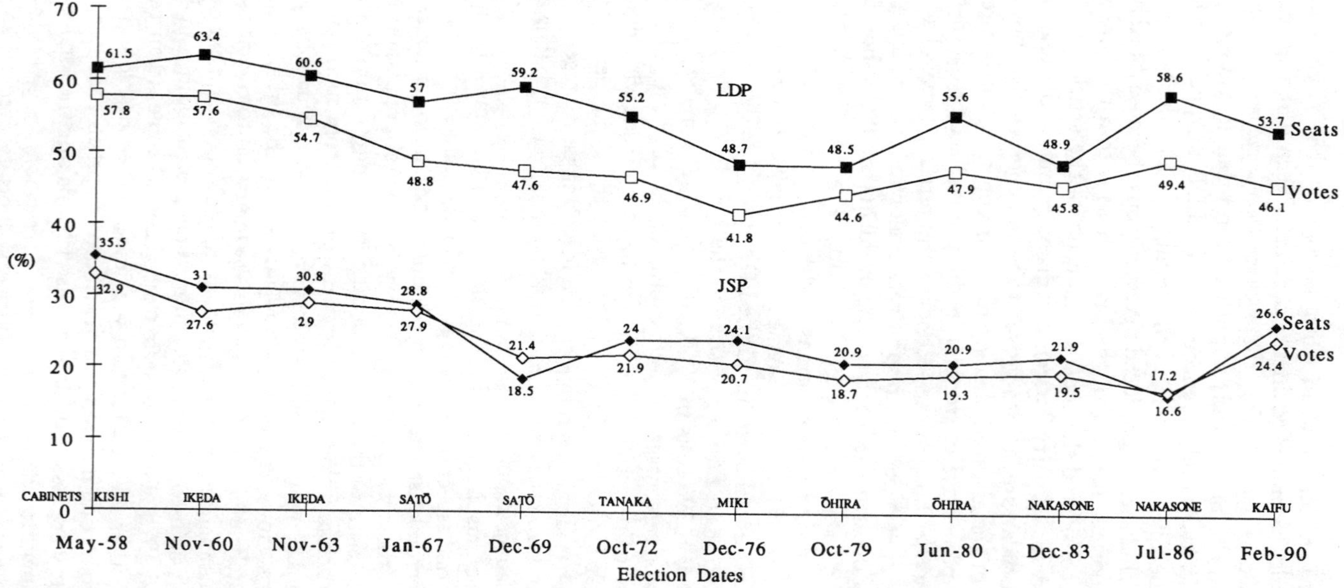

Source: Compiled by authors.

TABLE 9.3
Possessions of durable goods in Japan, by region (1980), in percent

Items	*Rural Households*	*Urban Households*
Refrigerators	99.2	99.1
Vacuum Cleaners	93.5	96.2
Washing Machines	99.3	98.7
Color TV	97.6	98.3
Automobiles	74.5	54.2
Air Conditioners	17.4	42.9
Oil Stoves	96.4	90.7
Water Heaters	68.9	77.3

Source: Adapted from *Asahi Nenkan* (1981), p. 358.

that were inimical to the LDP's political fortunes. The reason for this reduced decline ought to be found in the fact that the LDP has been strong in the rural sector of the country, and rural Japan benefited the most from the rapid economic growth of the 1970s. Certainly, urban residents benefited from the Japanese economic expansion, but they also had to cope with many of the side effects of that economic growth (e.g., pollution and urban congestion). Urban residents have often expressed their doubts about the LDP's high economic growth policies by supporting opposition parties in national and local elections. In marked contrast, rural residents tend to be largely untouched by the ill effects of economic development. They can enjoy the fruits of the expanding economy to the extent that the traditional image of rural Japan has become obsolete. By 1980, 99.1 percent of all Japanese families owned refrigerators, 95.8 percent had vacuum cleaners, and 98.8 percent possessed washing machines. It is indeed interesting to note that rural Japanese have more of these modern conveniences than do their urban counterparts (see Table 9.3). Given this remarkable change in rural fortunes, it is understandable that the party that made it all possible has retained its voting loyalties.

As the 1980s opened, the LDP appeared to begin to restore its popularity among voters. Except for the election in 1983, the conservatives won more than 50 percent of the vote in the 1980, 1986, and 1990 elections. This growth of the LDP's support is generally attributed to a rise of neoconservatism among the Japanese electorates. As Japanese economic expansion has progressed since the 1960s, a large number of people have come to identify themselves as a part of the middle class. In fact, every public poll indicates that more than 90 percent of Japanese usually believe that they belong to this middle-class social strata. By the 1980s, the majority of Japanese voters thus came to possess something important in the form of either property, savings, or durable expensive goods. Becoming members of the "have" group, these voters tended naturally to act and think more conservatively than was previously the case.

In addition, once many Japanese became materially satisfied, they also demonstrated a tendency to seek nonmaterial values. One good example of this change is a growing public concern over "amenities," even though

TABLE 9.4
LDP factional patterns as of February 1990

Faction *(Name of Organ.)*	*House of Representatives*	*House of Councillors*	*Total in Faction (Diet)*
Takeshita (Keisei Kai)	69	36	105
Abe (Seiwa Kai)	63	24	87
Miyazawa (Kochi Kai)	63	21	84
Watanabe (Seisaku Kagaku Ken.)	50	17	67
Kōmoto (Shin Seisaku Ken.)	25	7	32
Independents	15	5	20
Totals	285	110	395

Source: Adapted from the *Political Handbook,* 1990. p. 194.

Japanese does not have an equivalent concept or expression. In this regard, the fact that the LDP is a party without any solid ideologies seems to have worked to the conservatives' advantage. Without ideological restraints, the LDP can be highly attentive of the public's demands and formulate various programs to cater to popular needs. It is perhaps against this background that Prime Minister Ōhira announced the development of garden cities, while Takeshita also enunciated a program of home town construction. These policies seem an echo of the growing interests in nonmaterial values on the part of Japanese voters.

THE POLITICS OF FACTIONALISM IN THE LDP

It is impossible to discuss the LDP and its dynamics without a thorough examination of its factional nature. Essentially, the LDP is an alliance of factions in which the greater part of the party's affairs is conducted by the factions. Most important, the factions play a crucial role in the resolution of party personnel matters: the selection of the party president (who also serves as the nation's prime minister), the appointment of cabinet ministers, and the naming of important party officials. Opportunities to acquire important governmental and party posts differ greatly depending on the party faction in which a given Diet member may hold membership. In the face of the factional nature of the LDP, the abilities of individuals, no matter how capable they may be, have little if any influence over whether they will receive key political positions. To this degree, the factions of the LDP form a "system" and become inextricable from LDP politics. Each faction maintains its own offices and holds meetings at regular intervals. These factions are, in essence, parties within a party, hence the LDP must be viewed as a party composed of several parties (see Table 9.4).[18]

Currently, there are five major factions within the LDP. The largest and most powerful is the Takeshita faction led by former Prime Minister Takeshita

Noboru. This group was originally led by Tanaka Kakuei, who was arrested in 1976 on suspicion of having accepted bribes from the Lockheed Corporation. Tanaka is currently being tried in the upper courts on this charge, even though the District Court in Tokyo issued a guilty verdict in October 1983, and this eventually forced him to retire from the main stage of conservative politics.

After Tanaka suffered a stroke, a mutiny occurred within his huge faction. One of Tanaka's closest confidants, Takeshita Noboru, planned to organize his own faction, the Future Creative Society (Sōsei-kai), within the Tanaka faction. By so doing, Takeshita was taking the first step toward his objective of gaining the LDP presidency and the prime ministership after Nakasone. Takeshita's challenge to the faction boss angered Tanaka, who ordered several measures to torpedo Takeshita's plans. Tanaka was obviously worried that Takeshita's plan to form his own faction within the larger Tanaka factions would force the elder leader into political oblivion. It was about this time that Tanaka suffered his stroke. Takeshita subsequently took over the Tanaka faction and later became the prime minister of the country after Nakasone.

Another group of importance within the LDP is the Miyazawa faction. This group, led by Miyazawa Kiichi, is an heir to the faction spearheaded by Ikeda Hayato, who directed Japan's period of high growth during the 1960s. After Ikeda's death, the faction was temporarily taken over by Maeo Shigesaburō and then by Ōhira Masayoshi. Prime Minister Ōhira died suddenly during the campaign of the double elections of 1980.

Suzuki Zenko, Ōhira's loyal assistant, then took over the faction and became LDP president and prime minister with the strong support of the Tanaka faction. However, he decided to step down from the premiership in 1982 and relinquished his government to Nakasone. Subsequently he also transferred his factional leadership to Miyazawa.

While he was the prime minister from 1982 to 1987, Nakasone Yasuhiro led his own faction, which had about 67 members. With a small-sized faction such as this, Nakasone was unable to run either the party or the affairs of government by himself. He simply could never have become party president or head of the government without the support of the Tanaka and Suzuki factions. Indeed, the very existence of the Nakasone government depended on its leader's ability to sustain its cooperation with these two powerful factions. In effect, the two supporting factions had a near veto power factions. In effect, the two supporting factions had a near veto power over policies advanced by Nakasone. The Nakasone cabinet's lack of independence regarding policy matters was strongly criticized by some who called the government the "Tanaka-Sone Government."

However, once Nakasone scored substantial victories in the 1986 double elections (so named because the elections for both houses were held simultaneously), he began to assume a much more independent political posture vis-à-vis his rival factions than was previously the case. This was testified by the fact that he initiated and undertook a number of critical measures, including administrative reforms and an introduction of consumption tax, regardless of the desires of the Takeshita and other factions. And yet as it turned out, Nakasone's reign of power could not last long. When he was implicated in the Recruit scandal, Nakasone was forced to leave the conservative party and reluctantly transfer his factional leadership to Watanabe Michio.

To use the parlance of Japanese politics, these factions sustain the incumbent government, dominate the LDP, and are called the "mainstream factions" (*shuryū-ha*). Factions that are actively opposed to the mainstream factions are termed antimainstream (*han-shuryū-ha*) or nonmainstream (*hi-shuryū-ha*). The mainstream and nonmainstream factions fluctuate somewhat. In the past, the Abe faction and its predecessor, the Fukuda group, as often as not, played an antimainstream role, even though both factions also collaborated from time to time with other leading cliques in order to stabilize the conservative party government. The Abe faction, led by Abe Shintarō until his death in April 1991, traces its lineage to the group led by two former prime ministers, Kishi Nobusuke and Fukuda Takeo. It currently has 87 members.

It was assumed by many that Abe would be the successor to Kaifu as prime minister in 1991. However, with Abe's death, the faction was thrown into disarray and its very survival is in doubt. A collective leadership of Mitsuzuka Hiroshi (the faction's secretary-general), Mori Yoshirō (former education minister), Shiokawa Masajurō (former chief cabinet secretary), and Katō Mutsuki (chairman of the LDP Policy Research Council) will probably try to keep the faction together until a new leader can be selected. Mitsuzuka and Katō aspire to the faction's leadership and are longtime rivals. Without Abe, the faction has no candidate for the LDP's presidency and thus the prime ministership. Mitsuzuka became Abe's successor in early summer 1991.

The last remaining and smallest faction within the LDP is the Kōmoto faction, led by Kōmoto Toshio. Among the LDP factions, it enjoys a "liberal" image and, more often than not, gives an impression of being relatively free from money politics. It is for this reason that although Kōmoto himself has never assumed the prime ministership, his favorite son, Kaifu Toshiki, could take control of the government in the summer of 1989 amid the Recruit political scandals. It was also in the middle of the Lockheed affair that Kaifu's mentor, Miki Takeo, was chosen as a "clean" prime minister despite the fact that Miki, Kōmoto's predecessor, commanded the fewest followers among the rival LDP factions. When Miki was selected, he thus remarked that it was the unlikeliest and least expected event in his life. To that degree, Miki's power was tenuous within the context of conservative politics. Miki was eventually deposed from power, however, when he ordered the minister of justice to arrest Tanaka. From the viewpoint of other powerful factions, this was an outrageous act, and they decided to withdraw their support of the Miki government. Incumbent Prime Minister Kaifu may encounter a similar fate, for his tenure in office is contingent upon Takeshita's backing. If the Takeshita faction, for one reason or another, decides to remove its support, the Kaifu administration may face a serious political crisis.

FIGURE 9.2
Lineage of the factional development of the LDP, 1956-1991

April 1956	*March 1957*	*July 1962*	*October 1970*	*June 1980*	*January 1986*	*March 1991*
ex-Ogata	Ishi	Ishi	Ishi			
ex-Yoshida	Ikeda	Ikeda	Maeo	Ōhira .... Ōhira	Suzuki	Miyazawa
	Satō	Satō	Satō	Tanaka .. Tanaka	Tanaka	Takeshita
				Hori		
Kishi	Kishi	Kawashima	Kawashima	Shiina		
		Fukuda	Fukuda	Fukuda	Fukuda	Abe
		Fujiyama				
Ōno	Ōno	Ōno	Funada	Funada		
			Murakami	Mizuta		
Hatoyama	Ishibashi					
Kōno	Kōno	Kōno	Mori	Sonoda		
			Nakasone	Nakasone	Nakasone	Watanabe
Miki	Miki	Miki	Miki	Kōmoto ... Kōmoto	Kōmoto	Kōmoto
	Matsumura					

Source: Adapted from Watanabe Tsuneo, ed., *Shin Seiji no Jyōshiki* [New common knowledge of politics], (Tokyo: Kōdansha, 1977), p. 92. Updated by authors.

As can be seen from the preceding discussion, the LDP factions are not always divided by differences in ideology or policies. Rather, they are exclusively the instruments by which struggles for political power are carried out, and the major reasons for their existence are the need to form personal ties to advance the careers of both leadership and followers, the need to raise large amounts of money for political activities, and the need to provide organizational support for Japan's frequent election campaigns. In any faction, individuals of ability who have been prime ministers or held important posts in the government or the party tend to assume leadership positions in the factions as well. These people usually possess charismatic qualities that assist them in their rise to power.

Underlying the rise of factions is the role played by presidential elections. But why do they play such a significant role within Japanese conservative politics? Why have they become semi-institutionalized and resistant to all efforts to eliminate them over the years? Some analysts have linked the factions to broader patterns found within Japanese political culture, especially the tendency toward groupism.

Within almost any group of Japanese there is a value placed on hierarchical order and the identity of the group. It is thus possible to argue that the existence of factions within the LDP is nothing more than the political manifestation of a cultural pattern prevalent throughout Japanese society.

While this may be true, there are more important reasons behind the emergence and maintenance of factions. One of the most important is the fact that they arise chiefly in connection with the struggle to attain control both of party leadership positions and of the Japanese government. More precisely, they have come about primarily because of the regular battles held to select a LDP president. Indeed, according to many analysts, the presidential battles are the source of many detrimental forces operating against the conservatives. It is conventional wisdom that each time the LDP selects a new president, several billion yen are spent to accumulate sufficient votes to win the office. In addition, the need to have organizational support in order to secure the party's endorsement to run for a Diet seat has pushed the factional battles out into the prefectures. One should not forget that these political activities cost a great deal of money and that, as a result, the factions have established a close relationship with corporate Japan and "money politics" has become a major characteristic of parties. This situation can be explained in great part by the nature of LDP presidential elections and the enormous amounts of money required for these contests. For these and other reasons, it is not inaccurate to state that the presidential elections are a root cause for the various negative aspects of conservative politics.[19]

It was in 1956 that the LDP first began to elect its party presidents, who had always served as prime minister as well. Based on the bylaws of the party, an election was held in that year to select a successor to the party's first president, Hatoyama Ichirō. According to the bylaws, those eligible to cast ballots in this election were all the Diet members belonging to the LDP and the representatives of the local prefectural chapters of the party.

In general, the candidate who captured a majority of votes from this electorate was declared the winner and party president. In the event that no candidate was able to muster a majority on the first ballot, a runoff election was held between the top two vote-getters. These methods were in use until 1978, when a reform set of rules were enacted. However, it is not at all unusual for the LDP to ignore its own rules and to fill the office by some other procedure that better fits the special circumstances of the particular situation. In 1987, for instance, three contenders sought to succeed Nakasone: Takeshita, Miyazawa, and Abe. Because none of them seemed to command a decisive majority, they held a series of marathon bilateral conferences in hotel suites and teahouses in downtown Tokyo. However, because each insisted that he should be named president, the discussions confirmed the deadlock. To break the impasse, the three candidates agreed to ask Nakasone to pick one of them as his successor. Consequently, he sought the seclusion of his resort villa to ponder his choice and in late October called on Takeshita to assume the leadership of the party and the country. Once this decision was made, Miyazawa and Abe openly promised to support the new Takeshita administration.[20]

As LDP politicians prepared for the 1956 presidential election, some became active in the establishment of formal factions to support candidates for that office. These activities revolved around two factors. One found its origin in the government of Yoshida Shigeru, the man who led Japanese politics during the confused postwar era. The other is related to the fact that the LDP was originally formed by the amalgamation of two separate parties—the Liberal party and the Democratic party. From the outset, therefore, the party had a significant potential for factionalism.

Let us note how this potential was realized. Hatoyama Ichirō took part in the reconstruction of political parties in the aftermath of World War II and became the founding father and first president of the Liberal party in 1945. In the following year, the Liberal party won the general election and Hatoyama was expected to become the new prime minister. Before he could assume the office, however, he was purged by the Occupation forces and Yoshida Shigeru assumed the prime ministership. Yoshida's government commenced in May 1946 and, aside from two brief periods during which a Socialist alliance controlled the government, lasted until late 1954. This period, known as the "Yoshida era," was also characterized by Yoshida's encouragement of many young bureaucrats to enter the political arena under the banner of the LDP. Yoshida himself was known as a man with a strong sense of elitism and a knack for conducting affairs in secret, and as a former bureaucrat in the Foreign Ministry. However, his favoritism for politician-bureaucrats was not merely a result of personal idiosyncrasy. These former bureaucrats were, in effect, the only group not drastically affected by the postwar purges. Other significant groups such as the *zaibatsu* and military cliques were dissolved, and most of the prewar conservative politicians were purged and barred from political offices. Among those purged beginning in January 1946 were such prominent politicians as Hatoyama Ichirō (a prewar cabinet minister and the first president of the LDP) and Kōno Ichirō (a politician who would recover from the purge to become an important figure in the LDP).[21]

These young bureaucrats, encouraged by Yoshida, entered the political world and stepped in to fill the void left as a result of the purge of the majority of the prewar conservative leaders. It should be noted that future Prime Ministers Ikeda Hayato and Satō Eisaku made their first appearances on the party scene as Yoshida's subordinates at the time of the 1949 lower house elections. As Yoshida immediately placed such men of obvious talent in important governmental positions, the Yoshida era is often remembered as a period during which freshmen Diet members were appointed to cabinet posts upon their election. Of the twelve such cases, seven were former bureaucrats who had had no previous political experience.[22]

In the summer of 1951, the purge was ended and a wave of prewar politicians returned to the political scene, thus causing an additional strain in the conservative political world. Although the center of conservative politics had shifted to Yoshida and his former bureaucrats, the returning politicians found no room for them to reenter into such an alignment.

When they attempted to make their reentry during the period prior to the founding of the LDP, the conflict between these new and old politicians developed into the factional conflict between the Yoshida and Hatoyama factions. As the two antagonists engaged in a number of heated struggles, the Hatoyama faction eventually broke off from the Liberal party and formed the Democratic party. The latter was established through an integration of such anti-Yoshida forces as the group led by the de-purged Kishi Nobusuke and the group composed of former members of the old Progressive party. In time, the Democratic party under the leadership of its president, Hatoyama Ichirō, triumphed in its rivalry with the Liberal party and took control of the national-level government.

The conflict between the Yoshida and Hatoyama groups subsequently reemerged in a somewhat different form—namely, as the LDP presidential election of 1956. By this time eight factions had formed in the LDP, and their lineages were very complex. Four had derived from the Liberal party: the Ikeda, Satō, Ōno, and Ishii factions; and the other four can be traced back to the Democratic party: the Kishi, Kōno, Matsumura-Miki, and Ishibashi factions. Another grouping is also possible, however: The Kishi, Satō, and Ikeda factions are "bureaucratic factions" in that they once held large numbers of former public officials within their ranks.[23] The remaining factions, which were largely dominated by traditional party politicians, are called *tōjin-ha*.

The most important factor in determining the course of conservative politics, up until at least 1965, were the LDP factions formed prior to the LDP presidential elections of 1956. Eventually, the eight factions were reorganized into five factions, which have endured to the present time. Thus the party election of 1956 can be seen as having given birth to the LDP pattern of factions. The three major candidates during this party contest were Kishi Nobusuke, Ishibashi Tanzan, and Ishii Mitsujiro. Supporting Kishi were the Kōno and Satō factions; the Matsumura-Miki and Ōno factions stood behind the Ishibashi candidacy; and the Ikeda faction supported Ishii. When the ballots of the initial round of voting were tabulated, Kishi led with 223 votes, Ishibashi followed with 151 votes, and Ishii captured 137 votes. Given that no candidate had a majority, a run-off between the top two candidates was in order, but some of the factions had already come to agreements as to what they would do in a second round of voting. For instance, Ishii had agreed to support Ishibashi on the second round—and, indeed, Ishibashi won 258 votes, beating Kishi by only 7 votes in the run-off.[24] Ishibashi held the prime ministership for only about two months because he fell ill and was forced to relinquish the position to Kishi.

This election of 1956 was more than just the prototype for future LDP elections. It set the pattern for the flow of immense amounts of money in presidential contests. It has been estimated that the Kishi faction spent 300 million yen for his election bid, that the Ishibashi faction spent 150 million yen, and that the Ishii faction spent 80 million yen. These totals, representing huge sums for that time period, were passed from the candidates to the heads of factions. Not surprisingly, then, the LDP presidential elections became known as "money politics."[25]

The factional pattern of LDP politics, revolving as it did around the eight major groups, came to be firmly implanted by the transfer of power from Ishibashi to Kishi. The factions became even more firmly established during the Ikeda era. The mainstream factions during the Kishi period were the Kishi, Satō, Kōno, and Ōno factions, whereas the nonmainstream factions consisted of the Ikeda, Ishii, Matsumura-Miki, and the Ishibashi factions. Then, near the end of the Kishi cabinet's term, the Kōno and Ōno factions broke from the mainstream over Kishi's high-handedness and lack of tact in his manner of dealing with the revision of the Japan-U.S. Security Treaty. This split resulted in the collapse of the Kishi government in 1960.[26]

The Ikeda era, following that of Kishi, was characterized by the start of an economic spurt that grew at a phenomenal rate during this period. Throughout this Ikeda era and the Satō period that followed it, the LDP enjoyed what could be called a "golden age." However, the factional conflict not only continued but intensified as the initial Ikeda government was formed by an alliance of the Ikeda, Satō, and Kishi factions. Because the nonmainstream factions were not well coordinated, Ikeda continued to serve as party president for a second term. However, as Ikeda began to move toward a third term, differences began to weaken the Ikeda camp. The party politicians of the Kōno, Ōno, Miki, and Kawashima factions supported Ikeda's bid for a third term. In opposition were the Satō faction and a newly rising bureaucratic group led by Fukuda Takeo, who had inherited the Kishi faction. This election of July 1964 became famous not so much for the third Ikeda victory as for the substantial amounts of money spent in the campaign. Some LDP Diet members took money from both supporters and opponents of Ikeda. Many felt that the campaign had been an appalling pattern of bribes and expensive entertaining.

Ikeda overcame Satō's challenge and won his third term with just four votes more than a majority.[27] But Ikeda was tragically stricken by cancer at this time and offered his resignation in October 1964. The elders of the party met, agreed to avoid another costly presidential election, and made Satō Eisaku his successor. The Satō government was launched in November 1964 and lasted until July 1972—the longest-running government in the postwar history of Japan. The ability of the Satō government to survive for nearly seven years was closely tied to factional affairs. The period immediately before and after the birth of the Satō administration was marked by a chain of deaths of rival faction leaders. Ōno Banboku, an archenemy of Satō, died in May 1964; then, in July 1965 Kōno Ichirō passed away. Only a month later, Ikeda died as well. The net result of these deaths was that there were no longer any serious rivals to Satō's power. Some of the leaderless factions even began to subdivide, and some members moved into the Satō faction. During this period Fukuda and Tanaka began to become prominent as potential successors to Satō, but Satō was so skillful in his manipulation of party members that he successfully played them off against each other and thus reduced their threat to his continuation in power.[28]

New Regulations for LDP Presidential Elections and the Intensification of Factional Politics

Satō eventually stepped down from the prime ministership in 1972, by which time the reorganization of the factions had been completed. As noted earlier, the eight former factions were replaced by the five factions led by Tanaka (currently Takeshita), Fukuda (later Abe and now Mitsuzuka), Ōhira (later Suzuku and now Miyazawa), Nakasone (presently Watanabe), and Miki (now Kōmoto). Factional politics, which had somewhat abated during the Satō period, reentered a period of intense activity during the 1970s. Supporting evidence for this position was the pattern of rapid changes of government throughout the decade following the end of Satō's administration. The reins of power passed from Tanaka to Miki, from Miki to Fukuda, then to Ōhira, Suzuki, and finally, to Nakasone.

These changes in LDP leadership could be attributed to the conduct of Tanaka and his faction, and to his style of money politics. Tanaka Kakuei became president of the party after defeating Fukuda in a runoff election in July 1972. It is common knowledge that the force behind Tanaka's victory was the overwhelming use of political money to bribe the neutral factions to support his candidacy. Prior to the showdown of 1972, the intense rivalry between Tanaka and Fukuda had been brewing since at least 1966. The two rivals had often collided head-on over such events as cabinet reshuffles and appointments to key LDP posts. As each tried to establish his respective political base in an attempt to succeed Satō as prime minister, the number and intensity of their fights increased. In the namecalling that ensued, Fukuda was labeled as Satō's offshoot who was trying to perpetuate political rule by former high-ranking bureaucrats. Abhorrence of such bureaucrats and of their predominance in the postwar political scene was high even among LDP Diet members. But Tanaka had a great appeal for the younger LDP Diet members, and he spent a great deal of money courting them. In fact, there were other recent Japanese national-level elections conducted during Tanaka's term as prime minister that earned a reputation as big-money Tanaka-style elections. This was especially true of the July 1974 lower house elections. The financial excesses in this contest were such that even those within the party criticized the flagrant use of business support organizations and the vast amounts of money spent. Tanaka has long had a reputation for being very generous with his supporters; but this pattern, of course, is not too dissimilar from that found in the United States, where machine politics and powerful political organizations (such as that in New York's Tammany Hall) were active in the late 1800s.[29]

After the Tanaka faction had been in office for several years, various aspects of its corruption were exposed in a popular journal, *Bungei Shunjū*. The criticism that was generated catalyzed an explosion of additional complaints against Tanaka, from both inside and outside the party. Approximately a year and a half later, during the administration of Miki, the Lockheed scandal came to light, and events led rapidly to Tanaka's arrest. Since then, the factional struggles have remained intense—particularly those being fought over which faction controls the presidency and such key party positions as the post of secretary-general.

In this connection, we should note that a new method for the election of the party president was initiated in 1978. The voting electorate for this post was expanded from LDP Diet members and representatives to include all party members and "party friends" (*tōyū*)—a scheme that largely corresponded with the theme of party modernization that had been urged by Miki Takeo for some time. The new election plan actually materialized during the Fukuda administration as a result of factional maneuvering, which led to the downfall of the Miki government. Fukuda's reason for putting the new plan into effect was to respond to the criticism that had arisen following the Tanaka Lockheed scandal. Such a radical reform as a mass-participation primary election would be the first step toward the modernization of the party. Fukuda, however, did not foresee that the reform would lead to the termination of his tenure as prime minister, or that it would cause the expansion of the factional struggle to the levels of the local districts as each faction built its cadre of primary voters in anticipation of the next primary election.

These unforeseen repercussions sparked factional conflicts to unprecedented levels of intensity. Under the new rules, the election of party president is carried out in two stages. First, general party members and "party friends" participate in a primary election. Prior to this primary, points are allotted to each of the 47 Japanese prefectures at the ratio of one point for every 1,000 eligible voters (a total of 1,525 points in 1978). The top two vote-getters in each prefecture share the number of points granted to that prefecture based upon the proportion of votes that they each managed to obtain. The top two vote-getters nationwide then advance to the second stage, in which the LDP Diet members elect the president by a majority vote. In the 1978 presidential selection process, there were four candidates: Fukuda, Ōhira, Nakasone, and Kōmoto, the new head of the Miki faction. It was crucial for the candidates to survive the primary, finish in the top two categories nationwide, and then go on to the Diet members' vote. Therefore, all four candidates worked hard to increase the general party membership by adding their own supporters to the ranks of the party. Their efforts centered on the electoral districts of the Diet members of the various factions. Membership in the LDP grew dramatically from 500,000 to 1,500,000 members (including 170,000 "party friends").

This tripling of the party membership had a number of important side effects, however. First, because most of the new members were brought into the party by factional representatives, these new members often viewed themselves as factional members on the local level. Thus, the problem of factions, once largely confined to the national level of politics, spread across the nation. Second, there were many cases in which the party membership fees of the alleged new members were paid by the factions. Despite the fact that a million new members joined the party, it is very difficult to estimate how many of these new members are members in the true sense of the word. This type of campaign expenditure also contributed to the high costs of a presidential campaign. A third effect was the enrichment of the local party chapters of the LDP and the relative satisfaction of the general membership's demands to be included in the leadership-selection process. Both of these latter two effects have perhaps contributed to the performance of the LDP in recent elections.

The results of the presidential election of 1978, on the other hand, were a shock to the supporters of Prime Minister Fukuda. Ōhira, the challenger, gained 748 points, while Fukuda secured only 638 points. Nakasone and Kōmoto followed with 93 and 46 points, respectively. Thus, according to the party bylaws, Ōhira and Fukuda should have been involved in the second-stage voting by LDP Diet members. However, Fukuda acknowledged his defeat after the primary and Ōhira became party president without that second-stage vote. Fukuda's defeat was a result of his overconfidence as the incumbent and a lack of information stemming from his failure to secure a list of party members. Fukuda had also grown complacent as a result of the mass media's polls and estimates that had placed Fukuda far ahead of Ōhira. Ōhira, by contrast, had vigorously campaigned for votes on the local level and, more important, had established an alliance with the Tanaka faction. To be sure, the victory of the Ōhira-Tanaka factions over the Fukuda faction left the LDP with an unpleasant feeling. Ōhira's government was constantly defending itself against attacks from the Fukuda faction. Obviously, this continued conflict caused Ōhira many anxieties, which may ultimately have contributed to his death in May 1980. In that month, the Socialist party presented in the House of Representatives a no-confidence motion against the Ōhira cabinet. Such motions are fairly routine and ritualistic but rarely successful. Strangely, it was at this time that the Fukuda and Kōmoto factions, along with a majority of the small Nakagawa faction (all of whom had for some time been unhappy with Ōhira's strong connections with the Tanaka faction and various tax policies of the government), left the chamber and did not participate in the vote of no-confidence. Much to the surprise of the Socialists, the motion carried. Ōhira quickly decided to dissolve the House of Representatives and hold an election. It was during this campaign that Ōhira died.[30]

Although the factional conflicts intensify from time to time, it is also true that the separate factions share the common aim of avoiding a splintering of the LDP. The party has been nearly fragmented several times during its existence. That it has avoided self-destruction can be attributed to its fear that if the conservatives should break up, they would not be a match for the opposition. It has also learned an important lesson through past experience—that there has never been a case in which a faction has broken off from a main conservative party and succeeded in becoming a large independent organization. The history of such breaks or attempted breaks has largely involved the Kōno family: Kōno Ichirō, who abandoned his plan to break off from the party after he decided it could not succeed; and Kōno Yōhei, his son, who led his followers out of the party in 1976 to form the New Liberal Club, ultimately to return to the LDP after finding that his mini-party would not increase beyond eighteen members of the Diet seats at any given time.

Therefore, after Ōhira's death, Fukuda, sharing the party mood of calling for the closing of the LDP's ranks in times of trouble, shifted to the side of those who supported the selection of Suzuki Zenkō, Ōhira's successor as leader of the Ōhira faction, for the party presidency. In other words, there is a limit to the extent of factional rivalry. This limit can be seen from a different perspective, as well. It is customary for the LDP, when forming a new cabinet, to select several cabinet members from the rival factions. This practice has remained true to this date, even though factional politics has been abated somewhat ever since the beginning of the 1980s. For example, in the case of the second Kaifu administration, which was formed in February 1990, six of the twenty cabinet posts were allotted to the Takeshita faction and four each to the Miyazawa, Abe, and Watanabe factions, respectively, while only two were reserved for the Kōmoto faction, to which Kaifu belonged. The fact that the important cabinet posts were allocated to such factions as Takeshita and Watanabe was an expression of gratitude for their invaluable support of the Kaifu administration. By appointing members of the rival factions to government posts, Prime Minister Kaifu hoped that discontentment or open antagonism on the part of the other major LDP factions against his governance would be mitigated. Cabinet appointments are thus an important leverage for an incumbent leader by which to seek party harmony and unity.

The Functions and Limitations of LDP Factions

As should now be evident, the LDP factions serve as instruments in the struggle for political power, which has as its ultimate prize the acquisition of the post of party president and thus, automatically, the prime ministership as well. In this struggle, the unity and relative size of the factions are of great importance. The name of the Tanaka faction—the "Tanaka Corps"—once attested to its great strength, which was derived partly from its huge numbers and party from its history (at least until 1985) of cohesion. Other factions have different resources, however. The range of such resources will be considered in the following pages.

Japanese elections require immense sums of money. This is especially true for new conservative candidates, who must spend enormous amounts of money for advertisements and personal organization. Such campaigns may cost as much as 200 million yen (roughly $800,000). For that matter, the average cost of election campaigns for experienced LDP Diet members is about 150 million yen ($600,000). As there are few candidates who can supply such sums of money on their own, some establish personal support organizations (*kōenkai*), which collect funds from businesses and individuals. Prime Minister Kaifu, for instance, has three separate support organizations: the Kaifu Toshiki Seisaku Kenkyūkai, the Seiyūkai, and the Shin Seiji Keizai Kenkyūkai. Through these organizations, Kaifu collected a total of 333 million yen in 1988 and 229 million yen in 1989, while his rival, Finance Minister Hashimoto, gathered a sum of 420 million yen from his network of organizations in the 1989 reporting period. As these examples indicate, the support organizations function as a money-generating machine, and with these finances, they also work as a vote-getting institution. The *Kōenkai* frequently use up large amounts of money on theater and outings to which supporters are invited.[31]

It is in this problem area of political funding that belonging to a faction has both advantages and disadvantages. Although the details are never clear, at the time of every election campaign the faction leader assists his members with a considerable amount of money. According to one survey, approximately 10 percent of conservative campaign funds comes from the purses of leaders. With the tightening of political campaign finance laws in recent years, many "dinner-plate parties" (similar to those in the United States) are held to raise money. In Japan, however, success in collecting funds by this method is contingent upon membership in a faction, given that only a faction would have the big-business connections sufficient to draw crowds of people to such a dinner. The faction's connections with big business are extremely valuable. The attendance of factional bosses at these parties is of utmost importance. Tanaka Kakuei, for instance, was used in much the same way that a panda bear attracts children in Japan: His mere appearance at a party for a Diet member of his faction ensured the success of the gathering.

A faction dispenses funds to its Diet members in order to increase their loyalty and their sense of identification with the group. The various factions normally set up dummy organizations to collect these monies. These dummy organizations usually carry names indicating that they are political research or policy research institutes, but, in actuality, their primary function is simply to collect as much political money as possible from corporate Japan. Despite the fact that laws regulating the collection of political funds have been tightened in recent years, the actual patterns are very difficult to decipher because they have been manipulated by extremely complicated accounting methods. The Nakasone (now Watanabe) faction, for example, maintained the Modern Political Research Association (Kindai Seiji Kenkyūkai), the New Political Survey Association (Shin Seiji Chōsakai), and the Policy Study Research Institute (Seisaku Kagaku Kenkyūjo). In 1980 these three institutions together collected nearly 1 billion yen. The New Political Survey Association in particular raised 655 million yen, but the greater portion of this total was recorded as donations from a variety of other political research groups—a procedure that makes it difficult to ascertain the names of the actual contributing corporations or individuals. Those factions without such "political research institutes" have other organizations for collecting funds. Yet in these cases, too, the identities of the actual contributors are extremely unclear.[32]

It is a well-known fact that the separate factions in Japan have their own sponsoring corporations. Ties between corporations and factions often begin as personal links between the factional leaders and the corporation presidents. In Japan, connections that have nothing to do with politics, such as those among alumni of the same college, or among people from the same region, are often of great significance. Regular meetings between factional leaders and business leaders are commonplace, but those with groups of labor leaders or women's groups are not reported. The morning newspapers, which carry daily articles on the prime minister's activities, are primarily concerned with indicating who met with the nation's top politician on that particular day. A regular reading of these articles reveals an astonishing frequency of comings and goings of people with corporate connections to and from the prime minister's official residence. On a randomly selected date, August 24, 1983,

Prime Minister Nakasone's schedule was the following: In the morning, Nakasone met with Hyūga Hōsai, chairman of Sumitomo Metals and president of the Kansai Economic Federation, accompanied by the governors of Ōsaka, Kyōto, and Nara, who came to lobby for the construction of a Cultural Science Research City. At four in the afternoon, Yahiro Toshikuni, president of Mitsui International Trading, and Nakauchi Isao, president of Daiei Supermarkets, called on the prime minister to report that they would be visiting the United States in order to investigate the methods by which to make the Japanese political and economic positions better understood by the Americans. Then at six that evening, Nakasone dined with an executive of one of Japan's leading computer firms.[33]

It is precisely because of *zaikai* functions as the guardian for the LDP's finances that the party leaders allot time from their busy schedules for the purpose of meeting members of the corporate world. Of course, the *zaikai* guards not only the LDP's fortunes but also those of the separate factions. Only a portion of *zaikai* contributions to the LDP factions and politicians is reported to the Ministry of Home Affairs. The details of these backdoor political funds do not come to light (except when a major scandal occurs). The fund-raising abilities of Takeshita and Abe were growing fast in 1984. With an anticipation to succeed Nakasone, Takeshita and his associates collected approximately 890 million yen—300 million yen more than Tanaka himself had collected in 1984. Clearly, many of Takeshita's financial supporters were betting that he would become the next prime minister, and he eventually did in 1987.

The LDP factions are deeply involved in a wide array of governmental and party personnel matters. They use the personnel matters in particular as a lever for the expansion of their power and to strengthen factional unity. One such opportunity revolves around the endorsement of LDP candidates. In order for an LDP member to become a candidate for the Diet, he or she must belong to a faction. New candidates choose a faction that does not have prior candidates in their particular election district. It is a general rule that a faction will not endorse more than one candidate in a given district—specifically in order to avoid intrafactional conflicts. Whether or not a candidate can secure the endorsement of the party has major implications for the candidate's chances in the election. Especially in the case of new candidates, the party endorsement is a sine qua non, because it is rare for a candidate to be successful without having received the support of the party. Such an endorsement would be made by the party's central committee; moreover, the process tends to be an additional support for the existence of factions given that, in recent years, the factions have become more deeply enmeshed than ever in the party's endorsements.[34]

Another form of leverage held by the LDP factions bears more on personnel matters. The awarding of key posts within the LDP is determined by the political balance among the factions. Powerful factions have a much greater opportunity to capture the most important posts of the party. Yet as a function of the Japanese political tradition, the rival factions also receive party and governmental posts—not in the same proportion or importance as those awarded the most powerful factions, of course, but they are not ignored either. LDP Diet members who aspire to become cabinet ministers or party executives must therefore attach themselves to powerful factions, continue to work hard, and remain loyal party members in order to gain the same recognition.

Within each faction, the question of who will become a cabinet minister is settled by an established unwritten code. In order to obtain an important cabinet post, it is necessary, in addition to having an affiliation with a faction, to be a multiple-time winner in Diet elections. For the House of Representatives, one is required to be a six-time winner or more, on the average. Without such "experience," one does not have the credentials for becoming a cabinet minister. Some exceptional cases have occurred in which Diet members with less experience were selected for the cabinet, but these cases involved politicians with unique personal histories or special political circumstances. Recently, even the attainment of nine election victories has not ensured a cabinet position because there have been more senior-level Diet members than cabinet positions. Two or three positions in the cabinet are usually reserved for LDP members of the House of Councillors. These are usually less prestigious posts; in addition, because the term in office in the upper chamber is six years, a Councillor with two election victories usually has a good chance to secure a cabinet position. For members from both chambers, there is an informal rule that they should have served a term as a parliamentary vice-minister (*seimu jikan*), or as a minor party official, before becoming a cabinet member.[35]

In this fashion, cabinet members are selected by "illogical" criteria that have no direct relation to the individual abilities of the politicians themselves. As a result, individuals selected for cabinet positions represent very dubious choices. One candidate within recent memory, the director of the Science and Technology Agency, admitted publicly, without reluctance that she had no scientific knowledge whatsoever. From the perspective of the bureaucrats, however, the best sort of minister is one who says and does very little while securing a large budget for the agency.

One other problem must be noted. The ability to be elected to the Diet in six or more elections increases when a candidate's district is stable and the base of support is firm. Candidates from the metropolitan areas such as Tokyo and Ōsaka find it very difficult to protect their seats for a decade or longer, whereas candidates from rural constituencies, which are basically stable and conservative, represent the safest seats in Japan. Thus, the LDP Diet members with the best chance to be appointed to the cabinet are those representing rural districts.[36] The list of members in the Kaifu cabinet clearly reflects the strength of the LDP in the rural sectors of Japan.[37] In Table 9.5 the same kind of data is given for Kaifu's second cabinet, which went into effect on February 28, 1990.

TABLE 9.5
The second Kaifu cabinet, formed on February 28, 1990

Ministers and Agencies	*Names*	*Age*	*Factions*	*Number of Times Elected*	*Constituency*
Prime Minister	Kaifu Toshiki	59	Kōmoto	L 11/U 3	Aichi 3
Justice	Hasegawa Shin	72	Takeshita	U 3	Niigata
Foreign Affairs	Nakayama Tarō	66	Abe	L 2/U 3	Ōsaka 5
Finance	Hashimoto Ryūtarō	53	Takeshita	L 10	Okayama 2
Education	Hori Kōsuke	56	Takeshita	L 5	Saga
Health and Welfare	Tsushima Yūji	60	Miyazawa	L 6	Aomori 1
Agriculture and Forestry	Yamamoto Tomio	62	Abe	U 3	Gunma
Trade and Industry	Mutō Kaban	64	Watanabe	L 9	Gifu 1
Transport	Ōno Akira	62	Abe	L 9	Gifu 1
Post and Telecommunications	Fukaya Yakashi	55	Watanabe	L 6	Tokyo 8
Labor	Tsukahara Shunpei	43	Abe	L 6	Ibaragi 2
Construction	Watanuki Tamiyasu	63	Takeshita	L 8	Toyama 2
Home Affairs	Okuda Keiwa	63	Takeshita	L 8	Ishikawa 1
Chief Cabinet Secretary	Sakamoto Misoji	67	Kōmoto	L 9	Ishikawa 2
General Management Agency	Shiozaki Jun	73	Miyazawa	L 8	Ehime 1
Defense Agency	Ishikawa Yōzō	65	Miyazawa	L 6	Tokyo 11
Economic Planning Agency	Aizawa Hideyuki	71	Miyazawa	L 6	Tottori
Science Technology	Ōshiuma Tomoji	74	Watanabe	U 3	Tochigi
Environmental Agency	Kitagawa Ishimatsu	71	Kōmoto	L 6	Ōsaka 7
National Land Management	Satō Moriyoshi	68	Takeshita	L 8	Hiroshima 3
Hokkaidō Okinawa	Sunada Shigetami	73	Watanabe	L 8	Hyōgo 1
Secretary General	Ozawa Ichirō	48	Takeshita	L 8	Iwate 2
Executive Council	Nishioka Takeo	54	Miyazawa	L 9	Nagasaki 1
PARC	Katō Mutsuki	64	Abe	L 9	Okayama

Factional Summary: Takeshita 7, Abe 5, Miyazawa 5, Watanabe 4, Komoto 3

Source: Compiled by Authors.

Appraisals of the LDP's Factional Politics

When scholars and journalists study the LDP's pattern of factional politics, they tend to view it from three major perspectives. First, many in the mass media and academia hold that it is factional politics above all that indicates the backwardness of Japanese politics and constitutes the root cause for the high degree of corruption in conservative politics. As the vital organizations of LDP life, the factions engage in a nearly constant struggle for power in order to control both party and governmental positions. Such a permanent state of conflict requires a great amount of resources, and thus the factions need a constant source of money. In Japan, big business becomes involved in factional politics because it is a primary source of money. The roots of the unprecedented corruption in the Lockheed scandal and the Recruit affair would be found in the institutionalized nature of factional politics. LDP leaders have reputations for collecting money from numerous corporations and then disbursing the funds to Diet members of their respective factions. As the Takeshita faction is the largest in the current conservative political scene, the money needed to support such a group must be enormous. Such a constant demand on the factional leader creates a situation that is ripe for political corruption. For these reasons the Japanese mass media and scholars are nearly unanimous in opposing the factions as obstructions to the health of Japanese politics.[38]

Second, there is the strong belief among many Japanese that the factions prevent the modernization of the party. For all practical purposes, the real organizational strength of the LDP is found in its factions, which gather together under the banner of the LDP only because of political expediency. If a modern party is one that has definite policies and organizations and is also supported by a mass base, then the LDP is clearly not a modern party. It is, however, a party largely found on the national level in the Diet, with only a weak foothold among the people of the nation. Even though its membership base has tripled to 1.5 million members, the level of party identification felt by these alleged party members is not very high.

All of this is related to the nature of the Japanese electoral system. In the electoral system for the House of Representatives, which is based on medium-sized districts, voters cast their ballots for only one candidate, but there are multiple winners in each district. As a result, the LDP often runs several candidates in the same districts, thus leading to a situation in which the intensity of the competition between candidates of the same party exceeds that between the LDP and other parties. This system also works against the strengthening of the LDP's local-level organizations. The candidates find it difficult to rely on the local LDP chapters when more energy is being spent on races against candidates of the same party. Even the party itself finds it very difficult to support all its endorsed candidates equally. For this reason, each candidate generally sets up a support association that is independent of the party and utilized as the main organization for campaigning. These support associations develop extremely personal ties between the candidate and the members of the association. But the loyalty does not automatically transfer to the LDP. When the LDP seeks to expand its membership rolls, these support associations often play a very important part. LDP Diet members take the list of members who are part of the support association and then enroll them as members of the LDP, thus creating the superficial illusion that the party has significantly increased its membership base and, hence, its power. However, the attitudes of those who have become members are unchanged, and their attachments are strong only in their relationship to a particular Diet member. As the various faction members try to increase the number of party members who identify with their faction, they frequently find themselves in conflict with membership recruiters from other factions. This tendency conflicts with the original objective of presidential election reform and modernization of the party. And the sense of failure that has resulted is one reason why many are now calling for another reform of the presidential primary system. A majority of LDP Diet members, however, rejected these reform requests in the spring of 1984. A further criticism of the LDP factions is that all key decisions, including policy and personnel decisions, are made by the factional leaders in secret. Consequently, many feel that the opinions of the general public are not well represented in the LDP, but in fact are seriously distorted.[39]

A third appraisal of the factions is one often voiced by U.S. Japanologists and Japanese scholars who have examined the LDP factions in terms of the functions they perform for the party and the political system. These scholars see the rivalries among the factions as creating a situation similar to that found in countries with multiparty systems. They see the LDP as being made up of five parties, which serve as mutually restraining forces as their constant alliances help to advance Japanese politics. Through this pluralistic process, they argue, the factions give Japanese politics its dynamic quality. Although the factions compete fiercely for power, they do so ostensibly through policy discussions. For this reason, each faction holds repeated research sessions and also tries to secure the services of exceptionally able persons to act as advisers in various policy areas. According to some, the diligence of the LDP Diet members in their studies surpasses even that of the Socialists. One can see the positive outcome of such research in the events that occurred during the "oil shock" of October 1973. Japan's recovery from the effects of the price increases of imported oil was rapid, and the Japanese economy today is relatively stable. Although one might maintain that this stability resulted from the policy adeptness of the Japanese bureaucracy, one could also argue that the intensive debates over energy policy conducted by the factions contributed positively to the restructuring of the Japanese economy into a new economic order.[40]

In the opinion of the aforementioned U.S. and Japanese scholars, the existence of the factions makes the LDP internally pluralistic and stimulates the basic activities of Japanese politics. Moreover, the existence of the factions prevents the LDP from becoming autocratic and thus saves the country from falling into a dictatorial regime. In any case, it is certain that the LDP's factions have both negative and positive aspects.

Although all three perceptions of conservative factions may be legitimate, it may be misleading to view the intraparty rivalries as being fought without any relevance to public sentiment and demands. There appears to be a linkage between the LDP presidential elections and these general public feelings, as evidenced, perhaps, by the types of prime ministers the LDP has given the nation. There is a surprising degree of correlation between the main issue of the day and the person selected by the LDP to lead the nation. When the LDP launched its policy of economic expansion, for instance, such former high-ranking officials as Ikeda and Satō, both having a keen sense for economic affairs, took command of politics. However, as the Japanese public gradually came to have some reservations about politics run by ex-bureaucrats, the LDP was quick to sense the change in the public's mood and elected Tanaka—a man with no previous bureaucratic background. When Tanaka's "money politics" gained notoriety, the conservatives selected Miki, who was viewed as a "clean politician" by the media and the general public. This pattern was later repeated with the selection of Nakasone, whose strong sense of nationalism seemed to fit the mood of the nation in the early 1980s.

These examples make it clear that the selection of LDP president involves more than money and group force. The process often echoes the concerns and problems considered by the public to be important. This fact has often been neglected by both Japanese and U.S. scholars interested in LDP politics. It is a basic rule of politics that politicians must be attentive to the public's mood; if they weren't, their prospects for electoral success would indeed be slim.

Finally, U.S. Japanologists also tend to hold the view that the LDP is made up of parties such as the "Takeshita LDP" and the "Abe LDP," and that these parties, by serving as mutually restraining forces and because of their constantly changing alliances, help to advance Japanese politics. Through this pluralistic process, it has been argued, the factions contribute significantly to the dynamism of Japanese politics. It is certainly true that, in most cases, while the LDP factions compete fiercely for political power, they do so ostensibly around matters of policy. However, the recent political situation—or, more specifically, the rise in influence of money politics—has involved various factors not previously associated with factional politics. Many aspects of LDP politics that seem inseparable from money politics are highly problematic and may necessitate the revision of previously positive evaluations of the usefulness of factions.

THE LDP AND POLICYMAKING IN JAPAN

Because the LDP has been in power for such a long time, major policy decisions have inevitably revolved around the conservative party and its internal political process. In this decisionmaking system, the bureaucrats as well as various interest groups, large and small, play important parts. The labyrinth of relationships among these groups of actors occasionally becomes open to the public's scrutiny; but most of the time, it tends to be covert. Although the Japanese public for the most part assumes that the LDP acts in coordination and cooperation with the bureaucrats and organized interests to shape Japan's public policies, the question of how these actors really help each other formulate governmental decision has in large part been left unanswered.

Only a few studies have tried to uncover the modus operandi of the Japanese policymaking process. In this area of research and writing, Japanologists in the United States have done much of the work. The collection of studies put together by T. J. Pempel in *Policy Making in Contemporary Japan*, for instance, is one of the pioneering works on this topic. There are many reasons for the lack of serious studies in Japan on policymaking. For one thing, Japanese academics seem to have been less than well received by politicians because of the fear of the latter that their comments or remarks about the political process may be used against them at a later time. Nor have the political scientists been welcomed by the bureaucrats or interest groups, both of which are also highly cautious. In all fairness, however, one should note the upsurge in interest in policymaking that has occurred among Japanese scholars during the last several years.[41]

Still, as noted, a serious shortage of empirical studies remains; for this reason, Japanese policymaking is often described in a highly simplified fashion.[42] One of the most popular models for the Japanese policymaking process is the "elitist model." According to this model, various policies in Japan are made exclusively by the LDP, the bureaucrats, and big business. As suggested earlier, there appears to be some degree of truth in this description, which therefore becomes useful to the study of Japanese policymaking. Two political patterns that seem to support this model are the large number of bureaucrats who become LDP candidates for Diet seats and the large amounts of political money going from big business to the LDP and its various factions. Elitist theory sees these three groups as holding compatible interests and values and as acting in concert to produce policies that benefit all three and thus entrench their power position.

The popularity of "elitist theory" notwithstanding, the theory may be too simplistic to explain the subtlety of Japanese politics. As Fukui argues, the elitist perspective totally ignores factionalism and treats the LDP as a cohesive unit. It also fails to account for rivalries among and within the various ministries. As Japanese bureaucracies are characterized by sectionalism and competition, it is difficult for these bureaucracies to achieve harmony and cooperation toward a common objective. The same argument applies to the business community. As a result of the economic slowdown, especially since 1973, a big rift has become evident among major corporations. Those whose businesses are still on the rise, such as the automakers, are often pitted against those who have been seriously hurt by the economic slump, such as the steel industries. As these different groups do not seek the same policy objectives, the chances are good that while one industry may seek the curtailment of governmental spending, another industry may be in favor of the growth of public expenditures.[43]

As the elitist model is too simplistic and fails to describe the fragmented picture of Japan's key policymakers, Fukui has submitted his own version under the label of "limited pluralism." From Fukui's point of view, the major participants in Japanese policymaking are quite limited. They are essentially the same actors as those postulated by the elitist model, but Fukui takes into account their fragmented nature. Thus Fukui sees policymaking to be a result of the interactions among the various factions of the LDP, the various groups of bureaucrats, and diversified business interests.

Although it is somewhat closer to reality than the elitist model, Fukui's concept seems to regard the major actors as being on a rather equal footing. That is, they are treated as being on a par with each other in terms of political resources and influence. However, the common perception is that these power-wielders are not equal in power. Certain groups, owing to their superior position or access to special resources, seem to acquire more political power and thus tend to be more powerful in the political process.

The idea that the bureaucrats predominate in the Japanese policymaking process appears to fit well in this argument and may serve to supplement Fukui's model. The theory of bureaucratic dominance has been argued for some time by Japanese experts and especially by specialists in public administration and local government. Japanese political history tends to support this point. In Japan, high-ranking public officials began to take an active part in national politics in 1918, when a commoner, Hara Takashi, was selected to the prime ministership for the first time in Japanese history. By this time the main architects of the Meiji Restoration had disappeared from the active political scene and had been replaced by graduates from Tokyo University, which had been established in 1877 as a training ground for bureaucrats. The rise of bureaucrats in this century is evidenced by the fact that, of the 21 prime ministers holding office between 1918 and 1945, 20 had former civil or military bureaucratic careers. During the same period, 129 of the 188 cabinet ministers had also served as public officials. Among this latter group, 84 came from such ministries as Home Affairs (23), Finance (14), Foreign Affairs (14), and Justice (11).[44] These data indicate that the bureaucrats had acquired an important position as early as the prewar political period. Up to 1937, the bureaucrats constituted only one group within the power elite, but they were forced to share power with other influential groups including party politicians, the giant conglomerates called *zaibatsu*, and the military establishment. Then, beginning around 1937, the power landscape started to change in the direction of bureaucratic supremacy. It was in this year that Japan entered into a period of war economy and placed the entire economic sector under governmental supervision. The controlled economy, to be successful, required the abilities of expert public officials. The increase in the bureaucrats' power status in national politics was accentuated in 1940, when all political parties were forced to dissolve and the politicians lost their access to the political arena.[45]

The growth of the power of the Japanese bureaucrats became entrenched as a result of the major postwar reforms initiated by the U.S. Occupation. As a consequence of the purges of prewar politicians, the dissolution of the *zaibatsu*, and demilitarization, the bureaucrats found themselves the only major power group untouched by the postwar reforms. In fact, the Occupation forces, in carrying out their mission in Japan, had to depend upon the Japanese civil servants and could not, therefore, make any major changes in the bureaucracy. The bureaucrats were thus eventually able to step onto the center stage of national politics. Their immunity from the sweeping reforms of the Occupation was directly behind the ascendancy of Ikeda and Satō in the early postwar period.[46]

Yet another account often put forward to explain bureaucratic power in Japan is characterized by its focus on the decline of the Diet. In Japan, it is commonly believed that the Diet members leave much to be desired in terms of their policy-planning and oversight functions. But especially in the area of policy formation, the legislators seem to fall far short in their performances, appearing content to follow, instead, the initiatives of the various ministries. Not only is the number of bills sponsored by Diet members substantially lower than that of the bills sponsored by the ministries, but the chances for passage of the legislators' bills are also much less. During the thirty-sixth

Diet Session (July 1980 to November 1983), a total of 446 such bills were presented to the Diet; of that total 269 were cabinet sponsored, whereas 177 were originated by Diet members. Of the cabinet-sponsored bills, 240, or 89.2 percent, were approved by the Diet, whereas only 47, or 26.6 percent, of the Diet members' bills passed.[47] The reason for the lack of success in the case of the Diet members' bills is that they are likely to be products of the opposition parties intended to harass the government. Even so, the generalization that the bills that pass the Japanese Diet are initiated by the bureaucracy appears to be an accurate one.

In Japanese political and administrative milieu, the word *kanryō* (bureaucrats), carries a special meaning. It refers to a limited number of high-level civil servants in the national bureaucracy. There are several good reasons why these elite public officials are regarded as leaders in Japanese politics. For one, Japanese national bureaucrats command a great deal of discretionary powers. When a new law or program is initiated, it is usually the case that a central agency in charge of the problem issues a number of administrative guidelines in the form of cabinet orders, agency circulars, or official notices. One of the rationales for these discretionary policy guidelines lies in the assertion by the *kanryō* that, by these means, the central government has been able to see to it that the original intent of the law or the program is faithfully carried out by both subnational governments and private enterprises.

The frequent and prevalent use of administrative guidelines has not been well received in Japan. In fact, it is labeled as "a *kanryō* practice of making public policy without delegation of power" (*i-nin naki rit'tpou*). Many argue that the discretionary leverage the *kanryō* command is tantamount to making the central bureaucracy "the third house" of the Japanese Diet. This is because in the name of administrative discretion, the bureaucrats are, in effect, legislating various public policies of national significance.

In addition, Japanese central bureaucrats command various licensing and approval powers over more than 10,000 items (Table 9.6), ranging from an approval power of the Ministry of Finance over interest rates charged by private banks to the licensing authority of the Ministry of Health and Welfare on the marketing of a new medicine. These regulations are so extensive in Japan that even to open a small cleaning store, chances are that the Ministry of Health and Welfare will require hundreds of documents and numbers of prolonged interviews before the agency will validate the license.

An increasing number of Japanese have begun to express doubts about the wisdom of bestowing such legal authority upon the central bureaucracy. Whenever these governmental powers are involved, it seems to many Japanese that the market mechanism fails to function and prices of various products begin to rise. Consequently, the Japanese have been forced to pay extremely high prices for beef and rice as well as for airline and movie tickets, among other items. It was not an accident that controversy was raised over the licensing and approval powers of the central bureaucracy when administrative reform became the national issue in the early 1980s. The question was how

TABLE 9.6
Licensing and approval powers by ministry (1987)

Ministry	*Numbers of items*
Prime Minister's Office	27
Fair Trade Commission	26
National Public Safety Commission	95
Management and Coordination Agency	29
Hokkaidō Development Agency	26
National Defense Agency	26
Economic Planning Agency	26
Science and Technology Agency	260
Environmental Protection Agency	149
Okinawa Development Agency	27
National Land Use Agency	81
Justice	146
Foreign Affairs	37
Finance	1,134
Education	308
Health and Welfare	945
Agriculture, Forestry and Fisheries	1,256
International Trade and Industry	1,886
Transportation	1,976
Posts and Telecommunications	273
Labor	559
Construction	770
Home Affairs	107
Total	10,169

Source: Adapted by author from *Kisei Kanwa no Suishin Hosaku ni Kansuru Chosa Hokoku Sho,* 1988, p. 34.

best to eliminate various regulations so as to cut the fat out of central administration. Of the more than 10,000 licensing and approval powers, 258 items were eventually signaled out as unnecessary authority to be deleted at once. Subsequently, more than 476 regulations were also eradicated by the end of 1987. However, despite the attempts to deregulate, a large number of administrative powers still remain in the hands of the *kanryō*, making Japan's central administration the leading branch of national politics.

The third reason bureaucrats are believed to be predominant in public policymaking lies in Japan's unique form of intergovernmental relationships. In these national-local political interactions, the Japanese national government has developed strong centripetal forces with which the *kanryō* have been able to assume a commanding position vis-à-vis contending groups such as big business in the policy process. Although local autonomy is one of the major hallmarks of the postwar constitution, the national government in Japan has kept overwhelming legal and financial power over prefectural and

TABLE 9.7
Economic conditions of Japan before and after the "oil shock" of 1973

Year	*GNP (real) % of Change*	*Percent of Change in Government Expenditures*	*Rate of Growth of Volume of National Bonds Issued*
1969	12.1	16.5	14.7
1970	8.3	18.4	16.5
1971	5.3	16.8	29.6
1972	9.7	24.8	38.4
1973	5.3	23.9	26.8
5-year average	8.1	20.1	25.2
1974	-.2	29.2	26.6
1975	3.6	9.2	50.3
1976	5.1	17.3	45.2
1977	5.3	18.8	43.0
1978	5.1	17.3	33.0
5-year average	3.8	18.4	39.6

Source: Keizai Kikaku Chō [Economic Planning Agency], ed., *Keizai Yoran Gojyū Nananen Ban [Economic conditions at a glance]* (Tokyo: Ōkura Shō Insatsu Kyoku, 1982), pp. 2-3.

municipal policies. To describe the state of affairs regarding Japanese local autonomy, the mass media have coined the expression "30 percent autonomy" to illustrate the lack of a self-government tradition in Japan.[48]

There are some who question the assumed power of the bureaucrats. Muramatsu Michio, for instance, argues against the supremacy of these public officials on the basis of an idea he calls "anticipated reaction." Muramatsu claims that the bureaucrats appear to dominate the policymaking process, but that this appearance is misleading inasmuch as the bureaucrats have designed their bills in such a way as to avoid antagonizing the key members of the Diet. In other words, the civil servants, in anticipation of certain reactions by the Diet members, adjust their bills to ensure their passage. In Muramatsu's opinion, then, the thesis of bureaucratic supremacy must take into account the veto power of the politicians.[49]

Lately, a new perspective on Japan's policy process has gained important recognition. This is the view that places emphasis on the growing role of the LDP in general and on the rise of *zoku* politics in particular. In the daily press, this new phenomenon is described as a shift in the power epicenter from the bureaucrats to the conservative Diet members. A major cause for this change, its supporters argue, was the oil crisis of 1973 and the economic slump that followed. As a result of the oil slump, the prime theme of Japanese politics has been drastically altered. It is no longer "Who gets what, when, and how?" (as it would be in a period of economic growth) but "Who loses what and how?"

As seen in Table 9.7 the economic conditions in Japan underwent a radical transformation in the five-year period prior to the oil slump. The gross national product of the country grew 8.1 percent per year on the average. By contrast, during the five years after the oil crisis, the growth rate was an average of only 3.8 percent. A similar trend can be seen in the general expenditures of the national government. From the five-year average of 20.1 percent in the pre-oil crisis period, the average fell to 18.4 percent during the next five years. Especially noteworthy was the year 1975, when the growth rate of public spending was radically cut by the Diet (it had expanded only 9.2 percent from the preceding year). Owing to the shrinkage in governmental income, the central government began to issue debt bonds after the oil crisis. In 1975, the rate of debt bonds issued increased by 50.3 percent compared to the previous year. Although this rate lessened somewhat since then, the growth rate of the accumulated debt continues to be higher than that of the pre-oil crisis years. As we will note later, this development has had an important political outcome.

This brief economic outline of the pre- and post-oil crisis periods in Japan points to the fact that the Japanese national government no longer had ample resources to continue to fund all existing programs at a constant rate. As it was likely that the national economic pie would grow only slowly or even shrink, the political results were significant. Public spending for agricultural and forestry programs, for instance, was cut by 9.7 percent in 1975. Previously, the LDP had acted as representatives for these sectors; but because agriculture and forestry had given the conservatives so much political support over the years, such cuts were impossible in earlier years. In the yearly negotiations, the LDP Diet members represented farmers and other primary economic sectors in their discussions with the bureaucrats, and the bureaucrats seemed to hold the upper hand in this process because they held final control over the budgets.

As long as fair shares kept coming to the constituencies and clientele groups, the conservatives seemed to be content with the fact that bureaucrats were making the allocational decisions. However, when the economy slowed down, the political bargaining process changed. Because the "pie" is smaller the crucial decisions are not allocational, but the protection of existing subsidies and grants against cuts concerns politicians and bureaucrats alike. Under these new rules, the bureaucrats are not well equipped to deal with the situation. In the politics of "who loses what," any decisions made by the bureaucrats will easily become politicized and expose them to the danger of losing the respect and credibility they had gained over the years. In this new environment, the bureaucrats tend to follow a cautious path by avoiding controversial political decisions. They also appear to feel that it is the responsibility of the LDP to resolve these various tough questions, and thus the weight of policymaking power has shifted from the bureaucrats to the LDP (see Figure 9.3).

With the rise of the LDP in the policymaking process, the various deliberative components of the party have also become more significant. One of the most important is the Policy Research Affairs Council (PARC). The PARC is the place in which the various interest groups and public officials converge to make demands and negotiate with the leaders of the LDP. According to the party bylaws, all matters relevant to policy affairs must first be examined by the PARC. The policies approved by the PARC are then sent to the Executive Council for final approval prior to being brought to the Diet for legislative deliberation. Despite the fact that the PARC is a private part of a private organization, it has become the most critical point of Japanese politics with respect to the negotiation of all types of bargains.

In normal situations, policy matters initiated by the bureaucrats are referred to one of the seventeen divisions (*bukai*) of the PARC (see Figure 9.3). Because these divisions are organized to parallel the standing committees of the Diet, the problem bearing on a construction issue, say, would be assigned to the Construction Division. The various divisions have spun off well over 100 subcommittees in recent years, and they tend to function as mini-pressure groups operating within the organizational structure of the LDP. One such subcommittee functions as the voice of the Japan Medical Association.

The bureaucrats are not legally required to bring the matter to the appropriate division, but they appear to be well aware that it is very unwise to skip a divisional deliberation as a bill would face stiff opposition on the floor of the Diet if it did not have the formal blessing of the PARC. It has become customary for the bureaucrats to participate in such divisional discussions and to make their appeals to the LDP.

In these PARC divisions there are LDP Diet members who are known for their policy expertise. Once a Diet member joins a division, he or she tends to remain with that division as long as he or she has a seat in the Diet. By virtue of their long tenure, some LDP Diet members are able to accumulate impressive knowledge on specific policy topics. It is not uncommon to find a group of former division chairpersons who have decided to maintain their membership in a specific division. In fact, the division members are often involved with an issue for longer periods than their counterparts in the various ministries. In this way, a close personal relationship can be built by a conservative politician with both bureaucrats and interest groups. This pattern has become so familiar in recent years that the media has labeled it "*zoku* politics." *Zoku* literally means tribe—in this context, a tribe of powerful LDP members with years of experience in a particular division, working for the best interests of their clientele groups (including the interest groups and the appropriate groups of bureaucrats). Thus the *zoku* is the spearhead of pressure group politics within the LDP. Several *zoku* politicians can be easily identified (see Table 9.8).

The LDP has ruled Japan since 1955, and, as the above discussion indicates, its influence appears to be increasing as the power of the bureaucrats has declined in the current period of relatively slow economic growth. In the final section of this chapter, the formal organization of the LDP beyond the party presidency and PARC will be briefly discussed.

The Formal Organization of the LDP

As Haruhiro Fukui has written so extensively on the organizational structure of the LDP, the need to elaborate on the various committees and offices of the conservative party is much less than for the relatively unknown

FIGURE 9.3
Overview of the decisionmaking process of the Liberal Democratic party (1990)

I.	Policy Initiation	Diet members
		↓
II.	Policy Formulation	Ministries/Agencies
		Adjustments at Section Level
		↓
	Vertical/ Horizontal Coordination	Adjustments at Bureau Level
		↓
		Inter-Ministerial Adjustments
		↓
III.	Policy Deliberation	Divisional Deliberation in the PARC
	A. Division in the PARC	Cabinet (Division)
	(In the policy deliberation at one of the Divisions, all members attend meetings and receive briefing and explanations from senior public officials.)	Local Government Defense Legal Affairs Foreign Affairs Finance Education Social Welfare Labor Agriculture Fisheries Commerce and Industry Transportation Postal and Telecommunication Construction Science and Technology Environment
	B. Research Committees in the PARC (Total = 39)	Constitution Foreign Affairs Public Administration and Finance Economy and Consumer Affairs -- --
	C. Special Committees in the PARC (Total = 46)	Public Safety Foreign Aid Regional Development Narita Airport Development -- --
		↓

IV.	Policy Confirmation (The chairmen of the divisions attend the meetings of the Deliberation Committee of the PARC. They will explain the purpose and intent of various policies examined by the divisions. Senior public officials accompany the chairmen of divisions.)	Deliberation Committee of the Policy Affairs Research Council Chairman Katō Mutsuki Deputy Chairman Ochi Michio Vice Chairmen 7 (HR 5, HC 2) Councillors 20 (HR 15, HC 5) ↓
V.	Policy Approval (The Executive Council is the highest decisionmaking body in the LDP. Without its approval, any program or policy will not move forward to the Diet. Heads of the Divisions of the PARC attend and explain policy intent to the 30 members of the council. Bureau chiefs are also present.)	Executive Council (30 members) Chairman Nishioka Takeo Deputy Chairman Imai Isamu Vice Chairman 5 (HR 4, HC 1) Members 23 (HR 16, HC 7) ↓
VI.	Policy Authentication (Opposition parties become active to participate in policy examination.)	Diet Deliberation

Source: Compiled by authors.

TABLE 9.8
Leading zoku members of the LDP

Policy Areas	*Leading Experts (zoku Diet members)*	*Faction*
Commerce and Industry	Kajiyama Seiroku Noda Takeshi	Takeshita Watanabe
Agriculture	Watanabe Michio Hata Tsutomu	Watanabe Takeshita
Transportation	Okonogi Hikosaburō Mitsuzuka Hiroshi	Watanabe Abe
Construction	Kanemaru Shin Murata Keijirō	Takeshita Abe
Social Welfare	Hashimoto Ryūtarō Ozawa Tatsuo	Takeshita Independent
Education	Nishioka Takeo Mori Yoshirō	Miyazawa Abe
Postal and Telecommunication	Satō Megumu Satō Moriyoshi	Takeshita Takeshita

Source: Compiled by authors.

FIGURE 9.4
Formal organization of the Liberal Democratic party

Executive Bodies	Decisionmakers	Policy Research
-President	-Party Convention	-Deliberation Committee of the PARC
-Vice President	-Joint Meeting of Diet members	-Divisions of the PARC
-Secretariat Secretary-General Deputy Secretary Secretaries	-Executive Council	-Special Committee of the PARC
-General Management		-Research Committee of the PARC
-Party Finance Committee		
-Committee on National Party Organization		
-Conference of Executive Officers		
-National Office of Political Campaigns		
-Diet Committee		
-Public Relations		
Elections	**Party Discipline**	**Audit**
-Committee for Election Campaigns	-Committee on Discipline	-Audit Committee

Source: Compiled by author.

center parties.[50] The organizational structure of the LDP is presented in Figure 9.4. Nearly every major Japanese party has roughly the same organizational structure. They are all headed by a party president or chairman, who, in the case of the LDP, is always one of the major factional leaders in the party. In this regard, incumbent Prime Minister Kaifu is an interesting case. He is neither a leader nor a member of a major faction. The LDP has provisions for a party vice-president, but the post was vacant in recent years until Nakasone appointed Nikaidō Susumu, a senior-level aide of Tanaka, in 1984. Vice-presidents are usually senior-level LDP Diet members with independent power.

The secretary-general *kanjichō*) is the second most important party post. The secretary-general and the chairmen of the two major party committees, Executive Council and PARC, are considered to be the three top-level party appointments beyond that of the party president. These posts are usually announced at the time a cabinet is formed and are considered in the factional balancing that occurs then. The secretary-general runs the everyday administration of the party and is in control of such activities as fund-raising and candidate selection. Because of these significant activities, the post is considered a stepping stone to the party presidency.

The chairman of the Executive Council, who is on roughly the same level as the secretary-general, not only guides the Council in formulating the party's basic policies but also guides the party program through the Diet. Of the last nine prime ministers, all but Kishi served as chairman of either the PARC or Executive Council.[51]

Among the other major divisions of the national-level LDP are the National Organizing Committee, which is in charge of youth, women's and local politics development activities; the Central Institute of Politics, which operates the LDP's internal education program; and the LDP Convention, which approves decisions made by the party leadership and focuses media attention on the speeches of the party leaders. The party also has the usual array of finance, discipline, Diet policy, and audit committees.

The LDP is structured much like the modern mass parties found in some Western European nations. On the local level it has branch offices in approximately 80 percent of the urban centers of the nation. But almost all meaningful political activities are conducted by the personal support or campaign organizations of the major LDP politicians in each area. As the *kōenkai* (supporters' association) is the real subunit of the LDP, there is little incentive for the party to develop meaningful party organizations separate from their candidates' personal organizations.

The LDP has ruled the national level of Japanese politics single-handedly from the party's establishment in 1955 for more than thirty-five years. During this time period, the opposition parties tried to replace the conservative government by some combination of different forces out of power and on several occasions appeared very close to accomplishing this objective. The election for the House of Councillors in 1989 was a prime example of this. For the first time in the party history, the LDP lost its majority in the upper chamber. However, as already noted, in the subsequent election for the House of Representatives in 1990, the LDP once again showed its strength and succeeded in keeping itself in power. In the meantime, disappointingly for the large number of Socialist supporters, the Japan Socialist party has been unable to take full advantage of the "golden" opportunity. Indeed, the party does not know how to avail itself of unprecedented momentum and instead tends to miss one chance after another to demonstrate its ability to govern. In the case of the Tokyo gubernatorial election in April 1991, for instance, the JSP found it hard to pick a candidate to vie against two candidates backed by the conservatives. Consequently, it appeared the opposition parties in general and the JSP in particular would be unable to take the government away from the Liberal Democrats for the foreseeable future. For all intents and purposes, they may have to wait for special circumstances such as another scandal over money politics or a severe lapse of political ethics on the part of the LDP. If this happens, the conservative party would receive a severe public reprimand in the form of a sharp electoral defeat, and it might self-destruct.

NOTES

1. Michael W. Donnelly and Akira Nakamura, "LDP Bashing: The Day Japan's Ruling Party Was Defeated," *Pacific Review* 3, no. 2 (1990), pp. 163–170.
2. *Asahi Shimbun* (July 4, 1989), p. 1.
3. *Asahi Shimbun* (December 1, 1989), p. 3.
4. *Asahi Shimbun* (December 14, 1989), p. 1.
5. Michael W. Donnelly, "No Great Reversal in Japan: Elections for the House of Representatives in 1990," *Pacific Affairs* 63, no. 3 (Fall 1990), pp. 303–320.

6. A highly interesting work consisting of the record of discussions by leading journalists on the question of postwar politics has recently become available. In fact, it serves as a concise summary of the history of the postwar conservative party. Chapter 9 has depended heavily on this material. See Gotō Moto, Uchida Kenzō, and Ishikawa Masumi, *Sengo Hoshu Seiji no Kiseki* [The development of postwar conservative politics] (Tokyo: Iwanami Shoten, 1982), hereafter referred to as *Sengo*.

7. *Asahi Shimbun* (September 14, 1990), pp. 1–3 and 10–11. Also see *Nihon Keizai Shimbun* (September 14, 1990), p. 9; Iwai Tomoaki, *Seiji Shikin no Kenkyū* [A study of political finance] (Tokyo: Nihon Keizai Shimbun, 1990); Tomita Nobuo, "Kokkai Giin to Okane" [Diet members and monies], *Hōgaku Semina*, no. 419 (November 1989), pp. 50–51.

8. Strangely enough, there are not many secondary sources dealing with the postwar development of the major Japanese parties. A reliable source that does exist is Tominomori Yoji's *Sengo Hoshutō Shi* [The history of the conservative parties in postwar Japan], hereafter referred to as *Hoshutō*.

9. Haruhiro Fukui, *Party in Power: The Japanese Liberal-Democrats and Policy-making* (Berkeley and Los Angeles: University of California Press, 1970), p. 146.

10. Tomita Nobuo et al., *Nihon Seiji no Hensen* [Transitions in Japanese politics] (Tokyo: Hokuju Shupan, 1983), pp. 202–203.

11. See Jichi-shō Senkyo-bu, *Kakkai Shūgiin Giin Sōsenkyo Kekka Shirabe oyobi Kakkai Sangiin Tsujyō Senkyo Kekka Shirabe* [The official records of past elections for the House of Representatives and the House of Councillors] (Tokyo: Jichi-ō, 1983).

12. Tominomori, *Hoshutō*, pp. 67–72. With respect to the role of Miki Bukichi in the formation of the LDP, see Uchida Kenzō, "Miki Bukichi," in *Nihon Seiji no Jitsuryokusha Tachi III* (Tokyo: Yōhikaku, 1981).

13. Robert E. Ward's *Japan's Political System*, 2d ed. (Englewood Cliffs, N.J.: Prentice-Hall, 1978), pp. 87–112, includes a brief summary of the rise of the DSP and the Kōmeitō. See also Nishijima Hisashi, *Kōmeitō* (Tokyo: Sekkasha, 1968).

14. Nobuo Tomita, Hans Baerwald, and Akira Nakamura, "Japanese Politics at the Crossroads: The 11th House of Councillors Election," *Bulletin of the Institute of Social Sciences* (Meiji University) 2, no. 3 (1978).

15. Ishida Hirohide, "Hoshu Seitō no Bijon" [The future visions of the conservative party], *Chūō Kōron*, no. 903 (January 1963), pp. 88–97.

16. Nakamura Akio, "Teisū Fukinkō" [Malapportionment], in Nobuo Tomita and Horie Fukashi, eds., *Senkyō to Demokurashī* (Tokyo: Gakuyō Shobo, 1982), pp. 79–96.

17. By the beginning of 1986, the Diet was deliberating the so-called "6-6" reform proposal to subtract one seat from 6 rural districts and to add one seat to 6 urban districts. It was stalled in late 1985, however, due to opposition from some LDP factions and the opposition parties. After the census of 1985, it became apparent that a "10-10" reform was needed, and that became the issue for discussion as 1986 began.

18. Much of what follows in this section with regard to the factional alignments within the LDP is drawn from Uchida Kenzō, *Habatsu* [Factions] (Tokyo: Chuko Shinsho, 1983).

19. Regarding these transformations of politics, see Uchida, *Habatsu*, pp. 108–132, and Gotō, Uchida, and Ishikawa, *Sengo*, pp. 140–156.

20. Akira Nakamura, "Factions and Fragmentation: Party Politics in Japan," *Brookings Review* 6, no. 2 (Spring 1988), pp. 30–34.

21. Gotō, Uchida, and Ishikawa, *Sengo*, pp. 138–160; Uchida, *Habatsu*, pp. 26–60; Tominomori, *Hoshutō*, pp. 45–56.

22. Nobuo Tomita, Hans Baerwald, and Akira Nakamura, "Prerequisites to Ministerial Careers in Japan: 1885–1980," *International Political Science Review* 2 (April 1981), pp. 235–256.

23. Gotō, Uchida, and Ishikawa, *Sengo*, pp. 68–101; Tominomori, *Hoshutō*, pp. 45–56.

24. Gotō, Uchida, and Ishikawa, *Sengo*, pp. 104–136.

25. Tominomori, *Hoshutō*, p. 81.

26. Robert A. Scalapino and Junnosuke Masumi, in *Parties and Politics in Contemporary Japan* (Berkeley: University of California Press, 1962), delineate Japanese politics at that time with special reference to the revision of the security treaty with the United States.

27. Horie Fukashi, "Ikeda Hayato Naikaku" [The Ikeda Hayato cabinet], in Shiratori Rei, ed., *Nihon no Naikaku III* (Tokyo: Shin Hyoron, 1981), pp. 11–50. See also Gotō, Uchida, and Ishikawa, *Sengo*, pp. 198–227; Tominomori, *Hoshutō*, pp. 109–135; and Itoh Taichi's article on the Ikeda administration, in Tsuji Seimei, ed., *Nihon Naikaku Shiroku* (Tokyo: Daiichi Hoki, 1981).

28. Tomita Nobuo, "Satō Eisaku Naikaku" [The Satō Eisaku cabinet], in Shiratori, *Nihon no Naikaku III*, pp. 96–128.

29. Iizuka Shigetaro, "Tanaka Kakuei Naikaku" [The Tanaka Kakuei cabinet], in Shiratori, *Nihon no Naikaku III*, pp. 96–128.

30. See Iwami Takeo, "Ōhira Masayoshi Naikaku" [The Ōhira Masayoshi cabinet], in Shiratori, *Nihon no Naikaku III*, pp. 211-236. See also Itoh's *Jitsuroku* for more about the Ōhira administration.

31. *Asahi Shimbun* (September 14, 1990), p. 11.

32. Nakano Minoru, "Senkyō no Keizaigaku" [The Economics of Elections], in Shiratori Rei, ed., *Senkyō no Keizaigaku* (Tokyo: Daiamondosha, 1982), pp. 16–66. See also Jichi Shō, "Showa Goju Gonen Do Seiji Shikin Shūshi Hokokusho no Yoshi no Kohhy ni tomonau Setsumei Shiryo" [Explanatary materials on the announcement of the record of political contributions during fiscal year 1980], mimeo (Tokyo: Ministry of Home Affairs, 1980).

33. *Asahi Shimbun* (August 24, 1983).

34. For information regarding the party nomination process, see Gerald L. Curtis, *Election Campaigning Japanese Style* (New York and London: Columbia University Press, 1971), pp. 1–32.

35. *Yomiuri Shimbun* (June 4, 1983), p. 9.

36. Tomita, Baerwald, and Nakamura, "Prerequisites to Ministerial Careers," pp. 235–256.

37. *Asahi Shimbun* (December 27, 1983).

38. Gotō, Uchida, and Ishikawa, *Sengo*, pp. 294–320.

39. Uchida, *Habatsu*, pp. 174–181.

40. For example, see Hans H. Baerwald, *Japan's Parliament: An Introduction* (London: Cambridge University Press, 1974); and George Totten and Tamio Kawakami, "The Functions of Factionalism in Japanese Politics," *Pacific Affairs* 38 (Summer 1965), pp. 109–122.

41. An excellent summary of studies on Japanese policymaking has recently become available. See Igarashi Hitoshi, "Gendai Nihon no Seisaku Katei to Jimintō" [The Policymaking process and the LDP), in *Kenkyū Shiryō Geppo*, no. 319 (June 1985); Doi Mitsuo et al., "Gendai Nihon ni okeru Seiji Katei eno Apurōchi" [An approach to the study of the political process in contemporary Japan], in *Handai Hogaku*, no. 136 (September 1985); T. J. Pempel, *Policy Making in Contemporary Japan*

(Ithaca and London: Cornell University Press, 1977); and Pempel, *Policy and Politics in Japan* (Philadelphia: Temple University Press, 1982).

42. Haruhiro Fukui, "Studies in Policy Making: A Review of the Literature," in Pempel, *Policy Making*, pp. 22–59.

43. Gerald Curtis made a similar argument in "Big Business and Political Influence," in Ezra F. Vogel, ed., *Modern Japanese Organization and Decision Making* (Berkeley: University of California, 1975), pp. 33–70. See also Akira Nakamura, "The Transformation of the Japanese Policy-Making Process: The LDP Governance at the Crossroads," *Governance* 3, no. 2 (April 1990), pp. 219–233. In Japanese, See Nakamura Akira and Takeishita Yuzuru, eds., *Nihon no Seisaku Katei* [Policymaking process in Japan] (Chiba: Azusa Shuppan, 1984).

44. Tomita, Baerwald, and Nakamura, "Prerequisites to Ministerial Careers," pp. 235–256.

45. Chalmers Johnson, "Japan: Who Governs? An Essay on Official Bureaucracy," *Journal of Japanese Studies* 2 (1975), pp. 13–15.

46. Tsuji Kiyoaki, "Kanryō Kikō no Onzon to Kyōka" [The Sustenance of the bureaucracy and its consolidation), in Oka Yoshitake, ed., *Gendai Nihon no Seiji Katei* (Tokyo: Iwanami Shoten, 1968), pp. 109–125.

47. Tajima Nobuitsu, "Giin Rippō no Jittai to Kinō" [The problems and significance of bills sponsored by legislators], *Jurisuto*, no. 805 (January 1984), p. 149.

48. For details, see Akira Nakamura, "Different Faces with a Familiar Style: From Bureaucratic Dominance to Conservative Party Governance in Japanese Public Policymaking," *Journal of Management Science and Policy Analysis* 7, no. 3 (Spring 1990), pp. 191–210.

49. Muramatsu Michio, *Sengo Nihon no Kanryōsei* [The bureaucracy in postwar Japan] (Tokyo: Toyō Keizai Shimpō Sha, 1981).

50. We strongly urge all readers to consult the excellent article written by Haruhiro Fukui, "The Liberal Democratic Party Revisited: Continuity and Change in the Party's Structure and Performance," *Journal of Japanese Studies* 10, no. 2 (Summer 1984), pp. 385–435. Of course, Fukui's book on the LDP is one of the two basic books on the party: Haruhiro Fukui, *Party in Power: The Liberal Democrats and Policy-Making* (Canberra: Australian National University Press; and Berkeley and Los Angeles: University of California Press, 1970). One can also consult Fukui's entry on the LDP in the *Kōdansha Encyclopedia of Japan* (Tokyo: Kōdansha; and New York: Kōdansha International, 1983), vol. 4, pp. 384–386. The other basic book written in English on the LDP organization is that by Nathaniel B. Thayer, *How the Conservatives Rule Japan* (Princeton, N.J.: Princeton University Press, 1969).

51. Keio University Law School Seminar on the New LDP Leaders; *Bungei Shunjū* (January 1984).

10

The Changing Japanese Party System in the 1990s

RONALD J. HREBENAR

As the preceding chapters have suggested, the Japanese party system has undergone fundamental changes in the postwar era. It has evolved from what was essentially a two-party system in 1955 to one characterized by fragmentation with six parties on the national level. This situation has been called the *tatōka* (proliferation in minor parties) era by the Japanese. In addition, the authors in this book have identified several other current themes that characterize the current state of the Japanese party system. These themes are as follows:

1. The LDP's long-term decline during the 1960s and 1970s was reversed in the 1980s. Spectacular victories in lower house elections in 1980, 1986, and 1990 have confirmed the LDP as Japan's ruling party.
2. House of Representatives election results during the last fifteen years have followed a roller-coaster pattern of near parity (1976, 1979, and 1983) followed by huge LDP victories (1980, 1986, and 1990). This pattern reflects the Japanese electorate's simultaneous desires to continue the LDP in power as the steward of Japan's postwar economic success and to remind the party that it must behave in a responsible manner in its everyday political activities.
3. Despite the JSP's increase in seats in the House of Representatives in 1990 and victory in the 1989 House of Councillors elections, the JSP still fails to win the confidence of the Japanese electorate. There continues to be no clear alternative to the LDP as the governing party on the national level.
4. The other parties (CGP, DSP, JCP, and SDF) have proved extremely vulnerable to changes in public opinion and electoral events. The continued survival during the 1990s of any or all four of these parties

cannot be predicted with any certainty. It seems clear at this time that these parties will not be the core of a new fundamental challenge to the LDP.

5. Despite the appearance of several new mini-parties in the upper house, the fragmentation of the party system in the lower house seems to have ended, and the House of Representatives perhaps is moving toward a pattern of consolidation of parties similar to the pattern found in the "system of 1955" when the LDP and the JSP completely dominated the chamber.
6. The opposition parties continue to move toward the LDP as they attempt to position themselves as possible future coalition government partners.
7. The Japanese electorate appears to have accepted the idea of a coalition government consisting of the LDP and some of the opposition parties.
8. The long-term pattern of increased moderation in the behavior of the parties in the Diet continues, with a simultaneous increase in the stability of the governmental and party systems.

THE RESURGENCE OF THE LDP

At the beginning of the 1980s, it was unclear whether the LDP would be forced to share power with the opposition parties or whether it would return to the one-party domination of the House of Representatives it enjoyed in the 1960s. It was also unclear at that time as to whether the JSP could restructure itself sufficiently to make itself a real alternative to the LDP.

As the 1990s began, we had partial answers to these questions. The LDP has been forced to share power with the opposition parties in a variety of ways. First, the NLC joined three of the LDP Nakasone cabinets in the early 1980s. Then, the JSP and other opposition parties defeated the LDP in the 1989 upper house elections and took control of half—admittedly the much weaker half—of the Diet. Finally, on dozens of other issues in the Diet during the 1980s, the LDP sought the support and votes of opposition parties to pass important pieces of legislation.

The second question is much more difficult to answer, but despite the victories of the JSP in both the 1989 and 1990 elections, the JSP has not been able to convince Japanese voters that it could replace the LDP as Japan's ruling party. Later in this chapter, we will further address the continuing problems of the JSP.

But perhaps the most interesting question of all about the Japanese party system is this: How has the LDP managed to dominate the system since 1955? This is a feat that no other democratic party can claim in an advanced Western democracy. The reasons behind the LDP domination are several. First, it has been unbelievably successful in the development of policies that have made Japan the success story of the postwar era. As those policies (some with significant modifications) continue to bring Japan great security and prosperity, the Japanese electorate is understandably reluctant to retire the governing party in question. This reluctance is the greater for the fact that the alternative governing party is the JSP—a party widely viewed as inept, partly as a result of its one-time failure to run Japan in 1947 and partly as a consequence of its seemingly constant internal debate on Marxist concepts, which have little appeal to most Japanese voters. To an essentially conservative electorate, the LDP has managed to use effectively the symbols of authority dating back to the prewar era and to project itself as the only legitimate safe ruler in Japan. It has also played the political game with extraordinary skill by distributing resources and establishing policies in such a way as to create clienteles ranging from the rural agricultural sector to corporate giants to the average urban dweller.[1] In fact, one would be hard-pressed to name any group within the Japanese electorate that has not been well served by the LDP. In a 1985 Prime Minister's poll, a record 70.6 percent of the Japanese people said they were satisfied with their present standard of living.[2] Even organized labor, the foundation of the two Socialist parties, recognizes its debts to the LDP. A 1985 poll of the 38,700 members of the Steelworkers Union revealed the LDP as the most supported party (16.1 percent) and the Socialist parties as trailing badly (DSP 11.2 percent, and JSP 10.2 percent).[3] Compared to a similar poll of the union taken two years earlier, the LDP had gained 2 percent whereas both Socialist parties had lost ground.

The LDP has made a dramatic comeback following its decline throughout the 1960s and into the mid-1970s. The pattern of decline was so clear that it prompted many observers to predict that the JSP would replace the LDP in power during the 1980s. That prediction, of course, did not come true, as the LDP reversed its decline in the late 1970s and the JSP continued to lose votes and seats to the other parties in the opposition. By the 1983 elections, support for the LDP had returned to levels close to those attained by the party at its beginning in 1955. Although the LDP can no longer expect to run Japanese government in the single-handed manner it used in the 1960s, it clearly remains the most popular and powerful party in the system with little or no chance of losing these advantages to its archrival, the JSP.

Unless the LDP self-destructs or the Japanese economy falls apart, it is almost impossible to construct a reasonable scenario for a national-level government that is not dominated by the LDP. The concept of an all-opposition party coalition government is now, for all practical purposes, dead in Japan. The inability of the moderate centrist parties to cooperate with the JCP and a major part of the JSP appears to preclude this long-cherished goal of the Japanese Left.

THE PATTERN OF PARITY IN THE DIET

From its founding in 1955 through the 1972 elections, the LDP always had comfortable margins in the House of Representatives. Twice the conservatives had seat totals in the 290s; three times in the 280s; and twice in the 270s. Never during this period did the LDP drop below 271 seats in a lower house election. Most political observers consider 270 seats the minimum needed to comfortably manage the Diet. However, beginning in 1976, the pattern changed sharply. The LDP won only 249 seats in 1976, and then only 248 seats in October 1979. In both cases, after the conservatives elected as independents were added to the party rolls following the elections the LDP was able to secure a meager majority in the Diet. In 1980 the "double elections," the death of the incumbent, Prime Minister Ōhira, and the talk of opposition party coalitions combined to give the LDP a big victory (284 seats). In 1983, of course, the LDP won only 250 seats, and only 259 of the 511 total seats after enrolling independents. The LDP consolidated its hold on the House of Representatives with continued victories in 1986 (300 seats) and 1990 (275). When conservative candidates and the NLC joined the LDP after the 1986 elections, it held 307 seats and 285 after the 1990 elections. However, spaced between these two clear victories in the lower house elections was the significant defeat in the 1989 House of Councillors elections.

A "yo-yo" pattern in the results seems to have emerged since the 1979 elections. If the LDP wins a big victory, the next election will bring it back to earth, as it were. And it will win big if it hangs on to a bare majority despite the opposition's talk of organizing the next government. Takashi Inoguchi suggests that a "buffer factor" may be operating.[4] That is, the smaller the buffer of seats the LDP has over its opponents, the more likely marginal voters are to vote for the LDP. In this respect, the most significant factor in recent Japanese elections has been the turnout. Quite simply, when the voter turnout is low, the LDP has great difficulty winning over 250 seats; but when the turnout skyrockets, so does the number of LDP seats.

In a related vein, Horie Fukashi suggests that one-third of the electorate in large cities are active supporters of a party; one-third are passive supporters, and one-third are indifferent.[5] Large numbers of these passive supporters tend to be LDP supporters, but they vote only when they have some special reason to make the special effort required to get them to the polls. One motivating factor appears to be the prospect that the opposition parties might win control of the government. Prior to the 1980 elections, the situation in the Diet was one of near parity between the conservative and opposition parties; moreover, there was a great deal of coalition talk among the leaders of the JSP, CGP, and DSP. After the vote was counted, the LDP had their safest Diet majorities in years. However, when the public was asked if they were happy with the size of the LDP victory, only one-third indicated that they were pleased that the LDP had won so many seats. When the Japan Broadcasting Corporation (NHK) asked the voters just before the 1983 elections if they thought the LDP majorities in the Diet were detrimental, half the sample agreed. Other surveys indicated that 43 percent of the electorate hoped for a near balance in the Diet between the LDP and the opposition parties.[6] In their next opportunity to vote for the House of Representatives, the public reduced the LDP seat totals by 34 seats to only 250 seats. Sixty-one LDP candidates finished as runners-up in their districts. As Yasusuke Murakami concluded, "Recent elections have been decided not so much by the choice of parties as by the choice of whether or not to vote.

When the [LDP] majority is threatened, those of the interest-oriented New Middle Mass return to vote for their immediate choice, the LDP."[7]

All polling data indicate that the Japanese voters desire continued LDP rule combined with near parity in seat totals with the opposition—in other words, LDP rule tempered with political checks, or a variation on the checks-and-balance concept. Following the LDP victory in 1990, a *Mainichi Shimbun* poll indicated that the Japanese public was almost evenly divided in terms of whether they were satisfied with the election results. However, two-thirds of the public concluded that "bipolarized" politics (the opposition parties in control of the House of Councillors and the LDP in control of the House of Representatives) was good for Japanese politics.[8] The Japanese party system has entered a new era of parity, and such a pattern has greatly changed the behavior of both the parties and the electorate in their respective decision-making processes. The LDP is more popular now in terms of polls and voting percentages than it was in the early 1970s, and it is performing well in a variety of electoral arenas; on the other hand, it is no longer able to dominate the Diet the way it did in less complicated times.

The Continuation of the JSP's Decline

In retrospect, the JSP peaked with respect to HR Diet seats in the 1955 to 1967 electoral period, when it ranged from a low of 140 seats to a high of 166 seats in 1958. The HR elections of 1969 were a disaster for the JSP, which won only 90 seats. With that election began a period in which the JSP has managed to win more than 120 seats only twice. The average number of seats the JSP has won since the 1969 elections has been 109, compared to an average of 150 during the period from 1955 to 1967.

Another indication of the declining fortunes of the Left in Japan has been the end of the era of progressive governments on the prefectural level. In the late 1960s and early 1970s, the leaders of many of the largest cities and/or prefectures in Japan were leftists such as Governor Minobe Ryōkichi of Tokyo. Some perceived this situation as an intermediary step in the inevitable march toward leftist control of the national-level politics as well. However, the period of leftist domination was short-lived. In city after city, in prefecture after prefecture, the conservatives forged coalitions with the moderate centrist parties to replace the leftists in power. Two additional factors facilitated this shift in power at the local level. First, the LDP moved to co-opt many of the progressive policies by deliberately appealing to dissatisfied urban voters, thereby cutting the political ground from under the leftist parties. Second, after the oil crisis of 1973, the amount of revenue available to local government was sharply reduced, and the leftists were hard-pressed to maintain existing programs much less to try to establish new social programs. As measured by the *Asahi Shimbun* public opinion polls, LDP support in the major cities between November 1966 and December 1982 rose from 42 percent to 49 percent—a total only 8 points behind its support rate in rural Japan. As Satō Seizaburō has suggested, the loss of power in the nation's big cities was as severe a blow to the JSP and the JCP as the failure of the Katayama government in 1947 had been. He also noted that according to the 1980 poll results for Kyōto, where leftist governments had ruled for a very long period, only 4 percent of the respondents gave a positive response to the JSP's ability to govern whereas a full 53 percent gave this response to the LDP.[9]

In 1985 the JSP, under the leadership of party Chairman Ishibashi, tried to reform itself in such a way as to make itself more attractive to the Japanese electorate. It began by attempting to reduce the influence of the Socialist Association, the group of Marxists within the JSP who demanded that the party keep faith with traditional Marxist ideology. It followed with attempts to rewrite the JSP party platform in more moderate language and to develop more popular policies on subjects such as the peaceful use of nuclear power. However, the JSP delegates at its Fiftieth Convention held in Tokyo in December 1985 refused to approve the New Party Declaration, which would have officially made the JSP a social democratic party of "all the people" rather than a "Marxist-Leninist party of the working class." A second attempt to pass the new platform over the objections of the Marxists was successful in early 1986. However, the JSP has an enormous distance to go in significantly altering its image. As a *Yomiuri Shimbun* poll released in September 1985 indicated, four times as many Japanese believed the JSP would continue to decline than believed it would increase its political power in the future. According to the same poll, only 1.8 percent felt that the JSP had made a big change in 1985.[10]

The JSP tried to change its image in the late 1980s with the selection of a female party leader, Doi Takako, and the elimination of some Socialist planks in its party platform. It attempted at its February 1991 convention to move closer to a new image by changing its name (at least in its official English translation) to the Social Democratic party of Japan. Despite the name change, the party decided to maintain its principle of "unarmed neutrality." As some political observers noted, the JSP continued its old policy lines despite its moderate party leadership.[11]

Another indication that the JSP's victory in 1989 was an isolated event is the party's decline in the public opinion polls in terms of party support. In late January 1991, the JSP had the support of 16.9 percent of the public compared to 49.0 percent support for the LDP. The other four parties combined for 7.1 percent support.[12]

The next major set of elections after the JSP's 1990 HR success was the 1991 unified prefectural assembly and local government elections. The JSP failed miserably to capitalize on its two previous national-level victories. It won the fewest subnational-level seats in the JSP's history. Subsequently, the JSP fell into internal disarray. Observers expected the party's chairwoman, Doi Takako, to resign in July 1991 to take responsibility for the disaster and to ease the political pressures on party leadership generated by younger JSP Diet members demanding a sweeping overhaul of the party's organization and policies.

THE STAGNATION OF THE OTHER PARTIES IN THE SYSTEM

While noting the great change in Japan from a two-party system to a multiparty system, we can also appreciate the stability of the party system. In election after election since the Katayama JSP coalition in 1947, the conservative forces have been able to patch together at least a pure majority in the House of Representatives. Since the establishment of the main portion of the current system by the 1967 elections, the parties have maintained roughly their relative positions in the system, and their seat totals have fluctuated within a predictable range from election to election. The LDP, for example, has won between 248 and 300 seats in the last seven elections, whereas the range for the JSP has been between 85 and 140 seats. For the third- , fourth- , and fifth-ranking parties, the ranges have been as follows: CGP, 25 to 58; DSP, 14 to 38; and JCP, 5 to 39. The 58 seats won by the CGP in the 1983 elections represented its all-time high (although seat totals in the low 60s are possible, it is difficult to project totals for the CGP much beyond this level). In 1983, meanwhile, the DSP also secured its highest number of seats (38) since its formation in 1960. Both the DSP and JCP seem to fluctuate in seat totals within the 15-to-40-seat range in election after election. Finally, the SDF's four seats appear to approximate its maximum seat-winning potential.

Japan's party system can accurately be portrayed as having one giant ruling party (LDP), one large permanent opposition party (JSP), three parties of respectable size (CGP, DSP, and JCP), and one mini-party (SDF). When the seat results in the Diet from one election to another are compared with those of other democratic industrial nations, the Japanese scores are found to be among the most stable in the world.[13] And for the reader who wishes to be guided in the prospects for future Japanese elections, the following questions represent the major issues to watch for: (1) How large will the LDP majorities be—Commanding (280)? Or just able to govern (250 plus conservative independents)? (2) Do the 1989 and 1990 victories represent a new trend for the JSP, or are they just a short-term surge in response to the special political conditions of the late 1980s? (3) Will the CGP be able to build on its apparently solid base of 50-plus HR seats to become a more powerful force in Japanese politics, perhaps as a coalition partner of the LDP? (4) Will the DSP, JCP, and SDF be able to hold on to their few remaining seats and continue to be significant actors on the national level?

RESISTANCE TO FURTHER FRAGMENTATION

The Japanese party system could hardly be described as dynamic and full of major surprises. It does seem clear that the pattern of increasing fragmentation of the system since 1960 has also probably reached an end.[14] For one thing, the last two parties formed were splinters from the LDP and JSP, and their relative lack of subsequent political success would not likely encourage other politicians to follow their examples. Second, the societal trend of urbanization that facilitated the rise of the new parties in the 1960s and 1970s has largely run its course. Third, the LDP has moved to broaden its appeal to urban voters. As Satō Seizaburō and Matsuzaki Tetsuhisa have argued, the LDP has maintained its control over government in Japan because it has been sensitive both to the public's demands and to opportunities created in the political world. It has also been able to co-opt new interest groups into becoming LDP supporters while the LDP factional struggles have forced the party to seek out allies among these interests.[15] The JSP, for its part, has attempted to moderate its policy positions, thus placating its less radical members and reducing the incentives for moderate JSP Diet members to leave the party. Thus, it seems unlikely that new parties will appear on the horizon in future House of Representatives elections.

The other trend in recent years has been the movement of the so-called center parties toward the LDP in the process of positioning themselves for an invitation to join the LDP in a coalition government. The NLC, as the first such "lucky party" in 1983, participated in three straight cabinets between 1983 and 1986. A poll of LDP Diet members taken in July 1985 revealed general LDP happiness with the LDP-NLC coalition, with increased stability of the government as the major reason given. The poll also indicated that a majority of Diet members overall felt that the "age of coalition government" was inevitable and imminent; in fact, many believed that it had already arrived.[16] By 1986 it had become clear that the DSP and CGP were both very serious rivals in their desires to be the second party to join the LDP in coalition. The LDP and these moderate parties have joined together in dozens of coalition governments on the prefectural and city levels throughout Japan, and they know that they can work together in such situations. Almost no policy differences exist between the LDP and these parties on the domestic level, and most of the foreign and security policy differences have been eliminated or significantly reduced in the last decade.

Consequently, even if coalition governments become the norm of the 1990s, they may not mark the beginning of a new period of instability. Given the growing congruence in policies mentioned earlier, there is no reason why an LDP-DSP government could not be as stable as the LDP-NLC governments of the mid-1980s.[17]

Another consequence of the above-mentioned trends is the growing moderation of all the parties in the Diet. As Ellis Krauss has noted, behavior patterns and the course of legislation in the Diet have indeed become more moderate in recent years.[18] Especially in an era of parity, the parties have had to learn how to cooperate and work together.

THE FUTURE OF THE JAPANESE PARTY SYSTEM

The future of the Japanese party system is difficult to predict. The near future could be a continuation of the patterns of the late 1980s, or it could be a complete restructuring of Japanese politics with a return to the "1955 (two-party) system." More likely, a series of coalition governments between

TABLE 10.1
Ideological groupings within the Japanese Diet, 1990

Faction	*Lower House*	*Upper House*	*Total*
Right-Moderate			
Takeshita	71	35	106
Kōmeitō	46	21	67
Miyazawa	63	21	84
Abe	63	24	87
Watanabe	50	16	66
DSP	14	10	24
Kōmoto	26	7	33
Independent	12	7	19
Rengō	0	12	12
Left			
JSP	139	73	212
JCP	14	14	28
SDF	5	0	5
Others	7	13	20

Source: Compiled by authors.

the LDP and various centrist parties is possible in the 1990s. If formal coalitions do not occur, then one would expect the existing pattern of issue-specific informal agreements to continue.

Whatever the exact forms of the governmental and ruling party or parties, it seems unlikely that a radical departure from past political patterns will occur. Even if the LDP drops below a pure majority of 256 seats in some future election, it is extremely unlikely that the general nature of the Japanese government will be seriously altered. Perhaps the best way to view the future for stable government in Japan is to look at the Diet as a broad collection of factions among which the five factions of the LDP along with the DSP constitute the conservative wing (see Table 10.1 for a list of the major factions in the Diet). Even if the LDP splits into two or more parts, it would not be a very difficult task to patch together the 256 seats necessary to have a pure majority and thereby form a government. A hypothetical combination of the various LDP factions plus the DSP and the CGP would produce not only a pure majority but a healthy working majority of 271 seats. Such a government would, in all probability, continue the existing policies of the current government and conservative rule would be maintained.

The initial paragraph of Chapter 1 described the Japanese party system as a multiparty system operating within the framework of a working democratic parliamentary system characterized by continuous rule by the conservative Liberal Democratic party and supported by a well-educated, loyal, but basically disinterested electorate. It seems probable that this description will continue to hold true for the Japanese party system of the foreseeable future.

NOTES

1. Michisada Hirose, "The Ingredients of LDP Success," *Japan Echo* 10, no. 2 (1983), pp. 54–61. Reprinted from *Sekai* (March 1983), pp. 105–113.

2. Poll from the Prime Minister's Office, *Japan Times* (August 12, 1985).

3. Poll of Japanese Federation of Iron and Steel Workers Union members, *Japan Times* (September 20, 1985).

4. Takashi Inoguchi, "Explaining and Predicting Japanese General Elections, 1960–1980," *Journal of Japanese Studies* 8, no. 1 (1982), pp. 285–318.

5. Horie Fukashi, "Interpreting the Voice of the People," *Japan Echo* 11, no. 2 (1984), pp. 17–22.

6. Quoted in Kunio Arai, "Why the Liberal Democrats Barely Survived," *Japan Echo* 11, no. 2 (1984), pp. 11–16. From the original, in Japanese: "Jimintō haiboku no haikei," in *Hōsō Kenkyū to Chōsa* (February 1984), pp. 35–41.

7. Yasusuke Murakami, "The Age of New Middle Mass Politics: The Case of Japan," *Journal of Japanese Studies* 8, no. 1 (1982), pp. 29–72.

8. *Mainichi Shimbun* (April 23, 1990).

9. Satō Seizaburō, "The Sifting Political Spectrum," *Japan Echo* 11, no. 2 (1984), pp. 27–35. Reprinted from *Chūō Kōron* (March 1984), pp. 62–72.

10. *Yomiuri Shimbun* (September 21, 1985).

11. *Yomiuri Shimbun* (February 2, 1991).

12. *Yomiuri Shimbun* (January 31, 1991).

13. Assuming 1.0 as a perfect fit, the indexes for recent Japanese House of Representatives elections when compared with the 1983 elections have been as follows: 1976, .945; 1979, .973; and 1980, .969. In Kenneth Janda's calculation of the similarity indexes for selected elections in the United States, Canada, France, Netherlands, India, Burma, and Portugal, all of the Japanese index figures were above the highest scores from the above-named nations. See Kenneth Janda, "A Note on Measures of Party System Change," *Comparative Political Studies* 10, no. 4 (January 1980), pp. 412–423. See also Shankar Bose, "An Index for Measuring Similarity over Time," *Comparative Political Studies* 10, no. 4 (January 1980), pp. 404–411; Janda, "A Note on Measures of Party System Change," pp. 412–423; and Mogen S. Pedersen, "On Measuring Party System Change: A Methodological Critique and a Suggestion," *Comparative Political Studies* 10, no. 4 (January 1980), pp. 387–403.

14. Bradley M. Richardson and Scott C. Flanagan, *Politics in Japan* (Boston: Little, Brown, 1984), p. 246.

15. Satō Seizaburō and Matsuzaka Tetsuhisa, "Jimintō chō chōki seiken no kaibō" [Examining the long period of Liberal Democratic party rule," *Chuō Kōron* (November 1984).

16. Kyōdo news poll, *Japan Times* (July 1, 1985).

17. See Horie, "Interpreting the Voice," and Inoguchi, "Explaining and Predicting Japanese Elections."

18. See Ellis Krause et al., eds., *Conflict in Japan* (Honolulu: University of Hawaii Press, 1984), ch. 10; see also Richardson and Flanagan, *Politics in Japan*, ch. 6.

Appendix

TABLE A.1
House of Representatives election results, seats and votes percentages, 1955-1990

Election	*Liberal Party*	*Democratic Party*	*Right-wing Socialist Party*	*Left-wing Socialist Party*	*Labor Peasant Party*	*Kōmeitō*	*JCP*	*Other*	*Independent*	*Total*
Feb 27, 1955	112	18.5	67	89	4		2	2	6	467
	(26.6)	(36.5)	(13.8)	(15.3)	(0.9)		(1.9)	(1.3)	(3.3)	(100)
	LDP		JSP							
May 22, 1958	287		166				1	1	12	467
	(57.8)		(32.9)				(2.5)	(0.7)	(5.9)	(100)
					DSP					
Nov 20, 1960	296		145		17		3	1	5	467
	(57.5)		(27.5)		(8.7)		(2.9)	(0.3)	(2.8)	(100)
Nov 21, 1963	283		144		23		5	0	12	467
	(54.6)		(29.0)		(7.3)		(4.0)	(0.1)	(4.7)	(100)
Jan 29, 1967	277		140		30	25	5	0	9	486
	(48.8)		(27.8)		(7.4)	(5.3)	(4.7)	(0.2)	(5.5)	(100)
Dec 27, 1969	288		90		31	47	14	0	16	486
	(47.6)		(21.4)		(7.7)	(10.9)	(6.8)	(0.1)	(5.3)	(100)
Dec 10, 1972	271		118		19	29	38	2	14	491
	(46.8)		(21.9)		(6.9)	(8.4)	(10.4)	(0.2)	(5.0)	(100)
		NLC								
Dec 5, 1976	249	17	123		29	55	17	0	21	511
	(41.7)	(4.1)	(20.6)		(6.2)	(10.9)	(10.3)	(0.0)	(5.7)	(100)
				SDF						
Oct 7, 1979	248	4	107	2	35	57	39	0	19	511
	(44.5)	(3.0)	(19.7)	(0.6)	(6.7)	(9.7)	(10.4)	(0.1)	(4.8)	(100)
June 22, 1980	284	12	107	3	32	33	29	0	11	511
	(47.9)	(3.0)	(19.3)	(0.7)	(6.6)	(9.0)	(9.8)	(0.2)	(3.5)	(100)
Dec 12, 1983	250	8	112	3	38	58	26	0	16	511
	(45.7)	(2.3)	(19.5)	(.6)	(7.2)	10.1)	(9.3)	(.1)	(4.8)	(100)
July 6, 1986	300	6	85	4	26	56	26	0	9	512
	(49.4)	(1.8)	(17.2)	(.8)	(8.8)	(9.4)	(6.4)	(0.2)	(5.8)	(100)
Feb 18, 1990	275		136	4	14	45	16	1	21	512
	(46.1)		(24.4)	(0.8)	(4.8)	(8.0)	(8.0)	(0.4)	(7.3)	(100)

Note: Figures in parentheses represent the percentages of votes.

Source: Ministry of Home Affairs.

TABLE A.2
1990 House of Representatives election results (February 18, 1990)

Party	*Seats*	*Inc.*	*Former*	*New*	*Seat Totals Prior To Election*	*Seat Totals After Independents Absorbed*
LDP	275	228	4	43	295	285
JSP	136	64	16	56	83	139
CGP	45	34	0	11	54	46
DSP	14	8	3	3	25	16
JCP	16	10	2	4	26	14
SDF	4	4	0	0	4	4
Minor	1	1	0	0	1	1
Independents	21	4	1	16	7	7
(Conservatives)	15	2	1	12	--	--
(Leftist)	5	1	0	4	--	--
(Other)	1	1	0	0	--	--

Note: Inc. = incumbent candidates

Source: Adapted from *Yomiuri Shimbun* (February 19, 1990).

TABLE A.3
Political party joint struggles in HR elections, 1980-1990

Joint Efforts	*1980*	*1983*	*1986*	*1990*
JSP-CGP-DSP	1-0	--	--	0-1
JSP-CGP	3-0	5-1	4-1	--
JSP-DSP	--	--	--	1-2
CGP-DSP-SDF	7-9	7-1	1-0	--
CGP-DSP	9-11	20-2	23-5	10-9
CGP-SDF	--	1-0	--	--
DSP-SDF	1-1	3-3	0-1	--
Totals	42	43	35	23
Wins/Losses	21-21	36-7	28-7	11-12
Percent Wins	50.0	83.7	80.0	47.8

Note: Joint struggles between a major party and an independent candidate are not included. Joint struggles with the NLC are not included in table.

Source: Calculated by author from election results.

TABLE A.4
Seats won by party (local constituency) in House of Councillors, 1956-1989

	1956	*1959*	*1962*	*1965*	*1968*	*1971*	*1974*	*1977*	*1980*	*1983*	*1986*	*1989*
LDP	42	49	48	46	48	42	43	45	48	49	50	21
JSP	28	21	22	24	16	28	18	17	13	13	11	26
CGP	---	---	2	2	4	2	5	5	3	6	3	4
DSP	---	---	1	1	3	2	1	2	2	2	2	1
JCP	1	0	1	1	1	1	5	2	4	2	4	1
Ind/Other	4	5	2	1	1	3	4	5*	6	4**	6	23***

Notes: *NLC 2; other parties 1; Independents 2. **SDF 1; Independents 3. ***Rengo 11; Independents 11; other parties 1.

Source: Ministry of Home Affairs.

TABLE A.5
Voting percentages by party (local constituency) in House of Councillors, 1956-1990

	1956	*1959*	*1962*	*1965*	*1968*	*1971*	*1974*	*1977*	*1980*	*1983*	*1986*	*1990*
LDP	48.8	52.0	47.1	44.2	44.9	43.9	39.5	39.4	43.2	43.2	45.0	30.7
JSP	37.6	34.1	32.8	32.8	29.2	31.2	26.0	25.8	22.4	24.2	21.5	26.4
CGP	--	--	2.6	5.1	6.1	3.5	12.6	6.2	1.9	7.8	4.4	5.1
DSP	--	--	7.3	6.1	6.9	4.8	4.4	4.5	5.1	5.7	4.6	3.6
JCP	3.9	3.3	4.8	6.9	8.3	12.1	12.0	10.0	11.7	10.5	11.4	8.8
	--	--	--	--	--	--	--	5.7	.6	2.6*	--	--
Ind/Other	10.1	10.6	5.4	4.9	4.6	4.4	5.5	8.3	11.8	7.3	13.0	25.4

Notes: *Alliance with SDF.

Source: Ministry of Home Affairs.

TABLE A.6
Seats won by party (national constituency) in House of Councillors, 1956-1990

	1956	*1959*	*1962*	*1965*	*1968*	*1971*	*1974*	*1977*	*1980*	*1983*	*1986*	*1990*
LDP	19	22	21	25	21	21	19	18	21	19	22	15
JSP	21	17	15	12	12	11	10	10	9	9	9	20
CGP	--	1	7	9	9	8	9	9	9	8	7	6
DSP	--	--	3	2	4	4	4	4	4	4	3	2
JCP	1	--	2	2	3	5	8	3	3	5	5	4
NLC	--	--	--	--	--	--	--	1	--	1	1	--
SDF	--	--	--	--	--	--	--	--	--	--	--	--
Ind/Other	11	12	3	2	2	1	4	5	4	4	3	3
Totals	52	52	51	52	51	50	54	50	50	50	50	50

Source: Ministry of Home Affairs.

TABLE A.7
Vote percentages by party (national constituency) in House of Councillors, 1956-1990

	1956	*1959*	*1962*	*1965*	*1968*	*1971*	*1974*	*1977*	*1980*	*1983*	*1986*	*1990*
LDP	39.7	41.2	46.4	47.2	46.7	44.4	44.3	35.8	42.5	35.3	38.6	27.3
JSP	29.9	26.5	24.3	24.3	19.8	21.2	15.1	17.3	13.1	16.3	17.2	35.1
CGP	---	---	11.5	13.7	15.4	14.0	12.0	14.1	11.9	15.7	13.0	10.9
DSP	---	---	5.3	5.9	6.0	6.1	5.9	6.6	6.0	8.3	6.9	4.8
JCP	2.1	1.9	3.1	4.4	5.0	8.0	9.3	8.4	7.2	8.9	9.5	7.0
NLC	---	---	---	--	---	---	---	3.8	.6	2.6	2.3	---
SDF	---	---	---	---	---	---	---	---	1.1	*	---	---
Ind/Other	28.3	30.4	9.4	5.4	7.1	6.0	13.1	13.6	18.5	12.3	12.5	14.9

Note: *SDF in alliance with NLC.

Source: Ministry of Home Affairs.

TABLE A.8
Political party support by the Japanese public, in percents

		Gender		Age Group					
Party	National	Men	Women	20's	30's	40's	50's	60's	70's
LDP	49.1	48.9	49.3	37.9	39.3	48.5	55.4	56.7	67.9
JSP	21.2	20.6	21.7	22.0	22.3	22.6	23.4	18.7	10.7
CGP	3.4	2.3	4.2	1.6	4.2	4.2	2.8	2.8	4.8
JCP	1.6	2.0	1.3	1.9	2.1	1.7	1.6	1.4	--
DSP	1.6	1.8	1.5	.6	1.9	2.5	1.8	1.0	.6
SDF	.3	.6	.1	--	.2	.6	.2	.7	--
Other	.3	.5	.1	.3	.2	.4	--	.7	--
No Party	20.3	21.5	19.4	33.1	27.4	17.4	13.6	15.2	14.3
No Answer	2.1	1.7	2.5	2.5	2.3	2.3	1.1	2.8	1.8

Source: Adapted from the *Yomiuri Shimbun* (March 15, 1990).

TABLE A.9
Degrees of public support for parties, in percents

	Very Active in Political Organization	*Always Votes for Party*	*No Strong Feelings But Votes For*	*No Answer*	*Political Party Supported*
LDP	8.4	53.1	36.1	2.4	53.4
JSP	5.1	61.2	32.9	0.8	10.2
CGP	34.1	51.6	14.7	0.0	3.9
DSP	11.1	47.6	39.7	1.6	2.7
JCP	12.9	53.2	33.9	0.0	2.7
Total	9.6	53.7	34.7	2.0	

Note: NLC voter support, .6%; SDF, 0%; no party supported or no answer, 26.4%.

Source: Adapted from the *Yomiuri Shimbun* (September 2, 1985).

FIGURE A.1
Evolution of the Japanese party system: Conservatives, 1945-1990

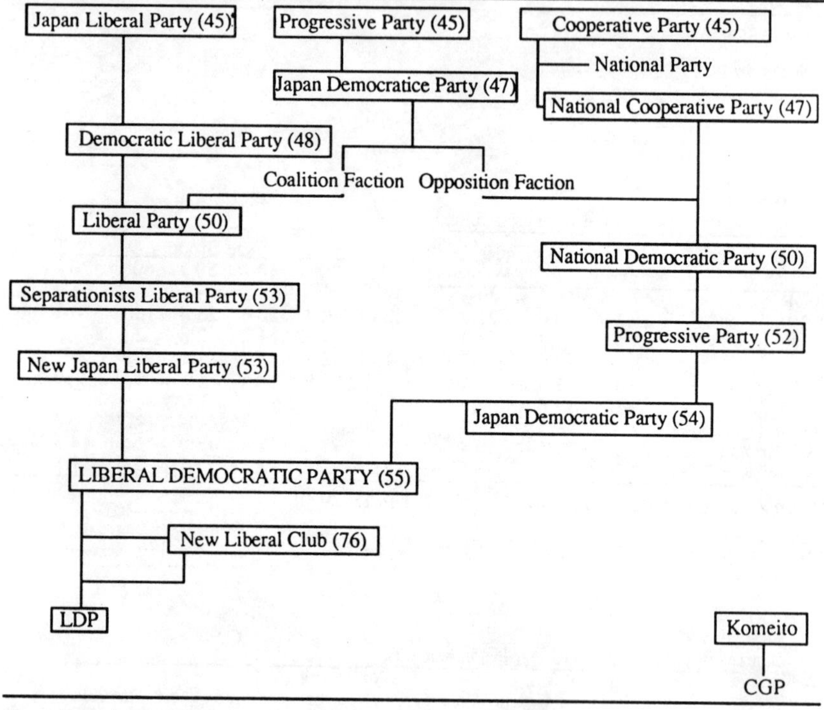

Note: Parentheses indicate year formed

Source: Compiled by authors.

FIGURE A.2
Evolution of the Japanese party system: Leftists, 1945-1990

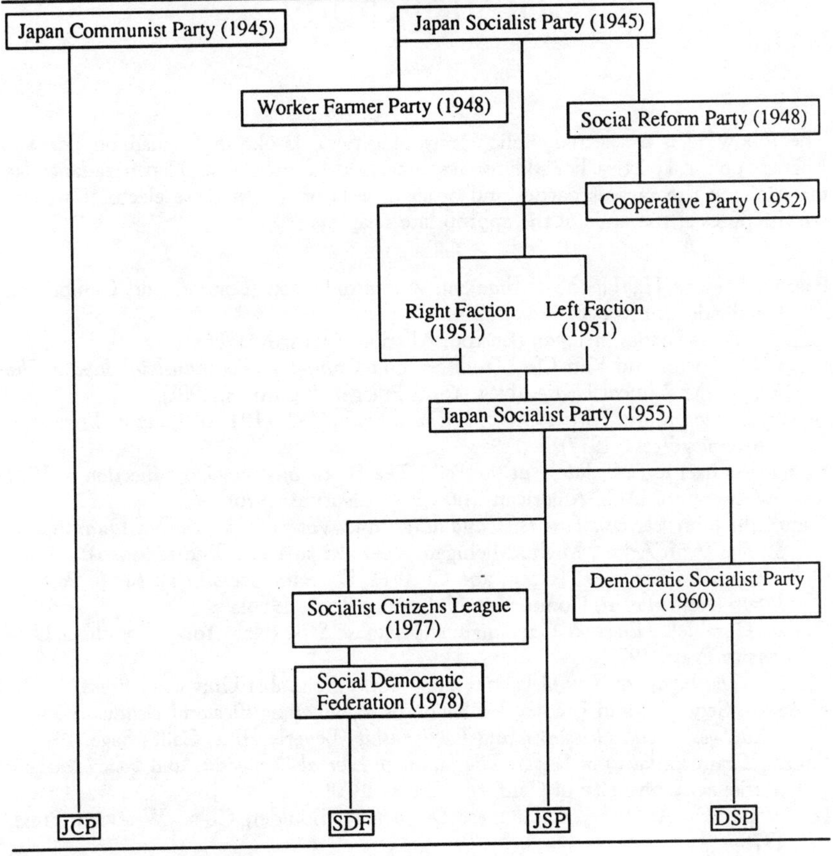

Source: Compiled by authors.

Bibliography

The following is a selected bibliography of general books in English on postwar Japanese political parties. For additional sources, journal articles, and Japanese-language materials on the various parties and other aspects of the Japanese electoral system, see the notes at the ends of the appropriate chapters.

Baerwald, Hans H., *Japan's Parliament: An Introduction* (London and Cambridge: Cambridge University Press, 1974).

———, *Party Politics in Japan* (Boston: Allen and Unwin, 1986).

Benjamin, Roger, and Kan Ori, *Tradition and Change in Postindustrial Japan: The Role of the Political Parties* (New York: Praeger Publishers, 1981).

Berger, Gordon Mark, *Parties Out of Power in Japan: 1931–1941* (Princeton: Princeton University Press, 1977).

Blaker, Michael K., ed., *Japan at the Polls: The House of Councillors Election of 1974* (Washington, D.C.: American Enterprise Institute, 1976).

Campbell, John C., ed., *Parties, Candidates, and Voters in Japan: Six Quantitative Studies* (Ann Arbor, Mich.: Michigan Papers in Japanese Studies, no. 1).

Cole, Allan B, George O. Totten, and Cecil H. Uyehara, *Socialist Parties in Postwar Japan* (New Haven, Conn.: Yale University Press, 1966).

Curtis, Gerald L., *Election Campaigning Japanese Style* (New York: Columbia University Press, 1971).

———, *The Japanese Way of Politics* (New York: Columbia University Press, 1988).

Flanagan, Scott C., and Bradley M. Richardson, *Japanese Electoral Behavior: Social Cleavages, Social Networks, and Partisanship* (Beverly Hills, Calif.: Sage, 1977).

Fukui, Haruhiro, *Party in Power: The Japanese Liberal Democrats and Policy Making* (Berkeley: University of California Press, 1970).

Ike, Nobutaka, *A Theory of Japanese Democracy* (Boulder, Colo.: Westview Press, 1978).

———, *Japanese Politics: Patron-Client Democracy* (New York: Alfred Knopf, 1972).

Ishida, Takeshi, and Ellis S. Krauss, eds., *Democracy in Japan* (Pittsburgh: University of Pittsburgh Press, 1989).

MacDougall, Terry E., *Political Leadership in Contemporary Japan* (Ann Arbor, Mich.: Michigan Papers in Japanese Studies, no. 1).

Murakami, Hyoe, and Johannes Hirschmeier, eds., *Politics and Economics in Contemporary Japan* (Tokyo: Japan Culture Institute, 1979).

Pempel, T. J., ed., *Uncommon Democracies: The One-Party-Dominant Regimes* (Ithaca, N.Y.: Cornell University Press, 1990).

Richardson, Bradley M., and Scott C. Flanagan, *Politics in Japan* (Boston: Little Brown, 1984).
______, *The Political Culture of Japan* (Berkeley: University of California Press, 1974).
Scalapino, Robert A., *The Japanese Communist Movement, 1920–1966* (Berkeley: University of California Press, 1967).
Scalapino, Robert A., and Junnosuke Masumi, *Parties and Politics in Contemporary Japan* (Berkeley: University of California Press, 1962).
Steiner, Kurt, Ellis Krauss, and Scott Flanagan, eds., *Political Opposition and Local Politics in Japan* (Princeton, N.J.: Princeton University Press, 1980).
Stockwin, J.A.A., *The Japanese Socialist Party and Neutralism* (London: Cambridge University Press, 1968).
______, ed., *Dynamic and Immobilist Politics in Japan* (London: Macmillan, 1988).
Thayer, Nathaniel B., *How the Conservatives Rule Japan* (Princeton, N.J.: Princeton University Press, 1969).
Tsurutani, Taketsugu, *Political Change in Japan: Response to Postindustrial Change* (New York: David McKay, 1977).
van Wolfren, Karel, *The Enigma of Japanese Power* (New York: Alfred Knopf, 1989).
Ward, Robert E., *Political Development in Modern Japan* (Princeton, N.J.: Princeton University Press, 1968).
Watanuki, Joji, *Politics in Postwar Japanese Society* (Tokyo: University of Tokyo Press, 1977).

About the Book

"This is a nuts and bolts textbook in the best sense of the term. . . . It is bound to be a great boon both to teachers and students of contemporary Japanese politics."

—from the Foreword
by Haruhiro Fukui

This thoroughly updated edition of *The Japanese Party System* provides a detailed review of the significant political events in Japan through the 1990 elections. The country's six-party system and the election and political finance laws that govern it constitute the core of this timely book, which continues to serve as the standard treatment of Japan's major and minor national-level parties.

The book opens with thematic analyses of the laws and political forces affecting the parties. The authors describe the basic characteristics of the Japanese party system since 1945, providing an overview of Japanese voting behavior and political values. They assess the "rules of the game," electoral laws, the ongoing political problem of malapportionment, and current proposals for electoral reform.

The second half of the book examines each of the five major parties in turn, providing the reader with a detailed understanding of party histories, leadership, financing, internal organizations, interest-group ties, and prospects for the future. A separate chapter recounts the fate of the now-defunct New Liberal Club and other minor parties that proliferated during the 1970s and 1980s.

Along with a firm foundation of information and interpretation intrinsic to the Japanese system, the authors offer insight into the common patterns Japan shares with democracies around the world.

About the Author and Contributors

Peter Berton is professor of international relations and coordinator of the East Asian Regional Studies Program at the School of International Relations at the University of Southern California. He received his Ph.D. in international relations from Columbia University and was editor of the journal *Studies of Comparative Communism* from 1970 to 1983. Dr. Berton has written numerous books and articles on Japanese, Chinese, and Soviet affairs and is one of the most respected experts on the Japanese Communist party. Among his recent publications are *The Fateful Choice: Japan's Advance into Southeast Asia, 1939-1941; Eurocommunism Between East and West,* and *The Russian Impact on Japan;* he has also published articles in *Asian Survey* and *Studies in Comparative Communism* on the relationship between the Japanese and Soviet Communist parties.

Ronald J. Hrebenar is professor of political science at the University of Utah in Salt Lake City. He received his Ph.D. from the University of Washington. He is coauthor of *Parties in Crisis: Party Politics in America* and *Interest Group Politics in America,* and editor of the book *Interest Group Politics in the American West.* He has also contributed articles to social science and political science journals in the United States and Japan. Among his writings on Japanese politics have been articles about the rise of the New Liberal Club, the impact of Japanese electoral laws on the Japanese party system, and the problems of political finance in Japan. During 1982-1983, he was visiting Fulbright professor at the Faculty of Law in Tohoku University in Sendai, Japan.

Akira Nakamura is professor of political science at Meiji University in Tokyo, Japan. He received his undergraduate education at Kwansei Gakuin University and the University of California, Berkeley. His graduate training was at the University of Southern California, where he attained a Ph.D. He was visiting professor at the University of Utah and guest scholar at the Brookings Institution from 1986 to 1987. He has published frequently on the topics of Japanese public administration, both in English and in Japanese. Among his recent publications in English are *Factions and Fragmentation: Party Politics in Japan, The Transformations of the Japanese Policy-Making Process: The LDP Governance at the Crossroads,* and *Myth and Reality in Local Social Policy Implementation in Japan.*

J.A.A. Stockwin is Nissan Professor of Modern Japanese Studies and the director of the Nissan Institute of Japanese Studies at Oxford University in Great Britain. He performed his graduate work at Australian National University, where he wrote his Ph.D. thesis on the Japan Socialist party. Between 1964 and 1981 he was successively lecturer, senior lecturer, and reader in the Department of Political Science at the Australian National University. His publications include *The Japanese Socialist Party and Neutralism; Japan: Divided Politics in a Growth Economy;* and *Dynamic and Immobilist Politics in Japan.* He is considered to be one of the world's most knowledgeable scholars of the Socialist party of Japan.

Nobuo Tomita is professor of political science at Meiji University in Tokyo, Japan. He is a former chairman of his department and dean of Academic Affairs at Meiji University. He performed his undergraduate training at the University of Tokyo and his graduate work at Meiji University. He was a founding member and the first president of the Japanese Association of Election Studies. He has also held visiting research positions at UCLA and the Johns Hopkins University. He is the author of over two dozen books and is a frequent contributor to such leading newspapers as *Yomiuri Shimbun* and *Tokyo Shimbun.*

Index